Theorizing Women and Leadership

D1572003

A volume in
Women and Leadership: Research, Theory, and Practice
Susan R. Madsen, Karen A. Longman, and Faith Wambura Ngunjiri, *Series Editors*

Theorizing Women and Leadership

New Insights and Contributions From Multiple Perspectives

edited by

Julia Storberg-Walker
George Washington University

Paige Haber-Curran
Texas State University

INFORMATION AGE PUBLISHING, INC.
Charlotte, NC • www.infoagepub.com

Library of Congress Cataloging-in-Publication Data

A CIP record for this book is available from the Library of Congress
http://www.loc.gov

ISBN: 978-1-68123-682-7 (Paperback)
      978-1-68123-683-4 (Hardcover)
      978-1-68123-684-1 (ebook)

Printed in the United States of America

CONTENTS

v

FOREWORD

Laura L. Bierema
University of Georgia

Abby Wambach, retired U.S. soccer player, coach, two-time Olympic gold medalist, FIFA Women's World Cup champion, and six-time winner of the U.S. Soccer Athlete of the Year award, observed, "It's a heavy burden to look up at the mountain and want to start the climb" (Fagan, para. 60). Being an elite woman athlete in the sports industry is not unlike women leaders in any setting. They are novel, few, scrutinized—and the climb can be brutal. Women leaders face *implicit bias* at every turn: the unspoken, perhaps even unconscious, preference for a leader (or soccer player) meeting the "ideal" image. The ideal image of a leader is typically a White, able-bodied, hetero-sexual male who is solely committed to his work at the expense of family, personal needs, and health (Acker, 2006).

We all carry implicit biases with us in everyday life, but I believe few understand the many ways these biases matter. I facilitate an exercise in a graduate course in which I list social roles and ask learners to note what image immediately comes to mind as they hear each role (e.g., a nurse, a teacher, a drug dealer, a master burglar, a welfare recipient, a renowned surgeon, an elite athlete, etc.). Gender, race, and class stereotypes are usually pronounced, and students are often surprised and disappointed at how stereotypical they are when they analyze the instant images that pop into their minds during the activity.

Theorizing Women and Leadership, pages ix–xii
Copyright © 2017 by Information Age Publishing

The exercise serves as a simple, potent reminder of the implicit biases we hold. This is particularly true when students are asked to "visualize a great leader," as many, regardless of gender, will imagine male leaders, usually White male leaders, unless they have personal experience with a leader who does not fit that profile. The exercise is a way to help learners face their theories about race, class, and gender—mindsets they have tacitly adapted from the male-normed social expectations about how women or other underrepresented groups should behave. Sadly, this exercise gives a hint of how quickly society judges women leaders as being not quite right, unprepared for the job, too soft, too hard, or not competent. As this volume makes clear, part of this problem lies in society's unchallenged, tacit theories of women's leadership.

Although leadership has been theorized as a gender-neutral activity (e.g., leadership theories such as transactional, transformational, authentic, and servant leadership do not include gender as a meaningful concept), the gender-neutrality, in reality, hides gendered power relations (Acker, 1990; 2006). Leadership theories and the implicit ideal worker image subtly function to marginalize women, as Acker (1990) explained:

> The closest the disembodied worker doing the abstract job comes to a real worker is the male worker whose life centers on his full-time, life-long job, while his wife or another woman takes care of his personal needs and his children. (p. 149)

Correspondingly, leadership literature has long been dominated by representations of the ideal leader as an individual who operates within a culture- and value-free space, demonstrates agentic masculine traits, and is, ideally, male. When the literature focuses on women leaders, it is riddled with theories that blame women for lacking confidence, not leaning in, opting out, or being deficient in some other way (e.g., Kay & Shipman, 2014; Sandberg, 2013). The problem with these individually-focused, male-normed, fix-the-woman views of leadership is that they distract from the changes needed at theoretical and practical levels to alter the system of ubiquitous, asymmetrical gendered power relations that thwart women's career-building intentions and experience.

Talk with any scholar of women's learning, leadership, or development, and you will hear laments that we are too reliant on decades-old theories created by White men and that we need more nimble, contemporary theories to understand and discuss women's leadership. This volume takes an important step in that direction by offering a range of perspectives on women leaders. While affirming the value of traditional research, the volume editors are unafraid to challenge dominant, male-normed theorizing processes in order to generate new theories of leadership created by women for women.

The goal of the volume is not small; the goal is radical in that a new vision of theory, theorizing, and knowledge creation is presented. The volume editors intend to change how we think about theorizing women's leadership in three important ways: first, theorizing will create social transformation; second, theorizing will shift how we prepare and develop women leaders; and third, theorizing will enable us to restructure organizations to be more equitable and sustainable. The editors advocate shifting our "theorizing what was to theorizing what could be" (Storberg-Walker & Haber-Curran, this volume, p. 5). "What could be" represents dislodging male-normed assumptions about theorizing leadership to allow the space and support for women-normed theories and practices that honor their multiple roles and identities in both life and work.

Through theorizing, the book creates new knowledge about women's leadership and affirms multiple ways of knowing. Knowledge is a contested entity, and those in power usually have the privilege of deciding what counts as legitimate knowledge, hence the dominance of male-centric leadership theory and practice. Patriarchal understandings of leaders and leadership delegitimize the interpretations of women and other underrepresented leaders. The editors of this volume observe that theory itself can be a self-fulfilling prophecy that protects the ruling elite's interpretations of our theories of leadership. Thus, leadership theory and practice reifies the experience of White males in Western culture and is designed to keep them in power with patriarchy as the predominant organizing principle.

Although this book represents an important departure from the male-normed rhetoric about leadership theory and practice, we should also heed the important women leadership theorists who have come before us, such as Mary Parker Follett, whose ideas were summarized by Hamel and Breen (2007): "Leadership is not defined by the exercise of power but by the capacity to increase the sense of power among the led. The most essential work of the leader is to create more leaders" (p. 186). Her commitment was to develop leaders who benefited the organization, its stakeholders, and the broader community. Follett critiqued the dominant male-leadership archetype as *power over* noting that *power with* was more desirable, although most organizations were not patient enough for the education and time needed to permit the shift. Orthodoxou (n.d.) offered the idea of "improvisational expertise" to create new knowledge about leadership advocating that it required experimenting with untried relationships, communication methods, and interactions in ways that transcend current wisdom. With this book, Julia Storberg-Walker, Paige Haber-Curran, and its inventive chapter authors strive to do just that.

REFERENCES

Acker, J. (1990). Hierarchies, jobs, bodies: A theory of gendered organizations. *Gender & Society, 4*(2), 139–158.

Acker, J. (2006). Inequality regimes: Gender, class and race in organizations. *Gender & Society, 20*(4), 441–464.

Fagan, K. (n.d.). After the storm. Retrieved from http://espn.go.com/espn/feature/story/_/id/11655083/us-women-soccer-star-abby-wambach-lives-extreme

Hamel, G., & Breen, B. (2007). *The future of management.* Boston, MA: Harvard Business Review.

Kay, K., & Shipman, C. (2014). *The confidence code: The science and art of self-assurance—What women should know.* New York, NY: Harper Collins.

Orthodoxou, C. (n.d.) Leadership for equity and excellence: Crossing the divide in Cyprus's diverse schools. http://eprints.ioe.ac.uk/6492/1/534790.pdf

Sandberg, S. (2013). *Lean in: Women, work, and the will to lead.* New York, NY: Random House.

Storberg-Walker, J., & Haber-Curran, P. (2017). Theorizing women's leadership as praxis: Creating new knowledge for social change. In J. Storberg-Walker, & P. Haber-Curran (Eds.), *Theorizing women and leadership: New insights and contributions from multiple perspectives* (pp. 1–16). Charlotte, NC: Information Age.

CHAPTER 1

THEORIZING WOMEN'S LEADERSHIP AS PRAXIS

Creating New Knowledge for Social Change

Julia Storberg-Walker
George Washington University

Paige Haber-Curran
Texas State University

Social theories, like women and leadership theory, have had a complicated history. Academics debate the merits of theories, classify and define theories, and provide a wide range of processes for developing theories (see, for example, 1989 and 1999 *Academy of Management Review* special issues on theory building). It has been suggested that practitioners often do not take theories into account when making decisions about practice (Christensen & Raynor, 2003), possibly, in part, because theories are not always seen to produce practical knowledge (Kennelly, 2009). Theories have been called artificial creations (Weick, 1989) and ideological (Hannah, Sumanth,

Theorizing Women and Leadership, pages 1–16
Copyright © 2017 by Information Age Publishing
All rights of reproduction in any form reserved.

Lester, & Cavarretta, 2014), so it is easy to understand why many individuals, both practitioners and academics, tend to discount the value of theory in their work.

We believe passionately that new theories generated by women for women are needed for two reasons. First, women theorists are needed because theory has been recognized as a gendered activity: "[T]heory tends to be culturally marked as a male domain of intellectual labor and is a vocation that occupies more men than women" (Gross, 2012, p. 214). Second, the experiences of the theorist (in our case, as a woman leader) are a needed element of the theorizing process (Swedberg, 2012). Theories generated from women's experience would be called "women-normed" and take women's multiple roles and identities into account. The theories would also represent multiple paradigms, reflect different ways of knowing, and be context dependent.

Theorizing is becoming at once more transparent (e.g., Richard Swedberg's *Theorizing in Social Science: The Context of Discovery*) and more complex (Alvesson & Spicer, 2012; Corley & Gioia, 2011). Consequently, without the active and intentional involvement of women—both theorists and practitioners—collaborating together to generate women-normed theory, we believe that equality for women and girls will remain elusive. In other words, we believe woman-normed leadership theories are the lynchpin needed to catalyze change.

The chapters in this book represent theoretical and/or conceptual contributions to a new generation of woman-normed leadership theories. As will be described in more detail below, these chapters add diverse ideas and strategies for catalyzing social change. In this view, theories use language that forms and perpetuates social norms and expectations as well as in- and out-group beliefs. The chapters also represent a diverse spectrum of epistemological perspectives and ways of knowing. This plurality, we argue, is needed to ensure that all voices continue to be heard, valued, and legitimated during the theorizing process.

The 15 chapters in this volume are organized into three sections: (a) new concepts and theories, (b) new models and methods, and (c) new insights and ideas. This organization signifies the key contributions of the chapters in each section, and at the same time some chapters clearly offer contributions that cross all sections. It may be helpful to consider the different chapters as 15 different, valuable, partial, tentative, and temporary ways to understand the complexity of women's leadership. Each chapter attempts to use language to explore, explain, and/or understand, and each chapter paints a picture of one of the multiple facets of women's leadership.

The language used in each chapter is based on the different beliefs and assumptions of the chapter authors. This is important to recognize, and we believe that the affirmation of different beliefs and assumptions is critical for the advancement of women and leadership theory. On a related note, we also believe the standards for evaluating theory and theoretical contributions (e.g., Dubin, 1976; Patterson, 1983) do not apply to all forms of knowledge, theory, or theorizing practices. These standards apply to functionalist (Burrell & Morgan, 1979) beliefs and assumptions but not to the beliefs undergirding critique, radical interpretation, precarity, postcolonialism, feminism, critical race theory, queer theory, and other foundations for women and leadership theorizing. Instead, we suggest that readers evaluate the chapters based on resonance—Do the chapters resonate with you? If so, why? If not, why not? As Carolyn Ellis and Art Bochner (2006) so eloquently describe:

> The fact is that when I read Leon's [analytical] article, I become a detached spectator. I become only a head, cut off from my body and emotions. There's no personal story to engage me. Knowledge and theory become disembodied words on the page and I lose connection. I want to linger in the world of experience, you know, feel it, taste it, sense it, live in it; but Leon wants to use the world of experience primarily as a vehicle for exercising his head.... We think of [research] as a journey; they think of it as a destination. They want to master, explain, grasp.... But we don't think they're necessarily important. Caring and empathizing is for us what abstracting and controlling is for them.... They want to appropriate lived experience for the purpose of abstracting something they call knowledge or theory. (p. 431)

We do not expect all readers to resonate with all chapters, just as we do not expect all readers to be the same type of leader. What we do hope for is that readers will be conscious of their evaluative judgments of the chapters and reflect on how and why the judgments—whether positive or not positive—emerge. This type of reflection is a key component of theorizing because it has the potential to illuminate hidden assumptions, biases, preferences, and beliefs. As will be described later in this chapter, these hidden foundations directly relate to the theorizing process in social science.

In this first chapter we lay the foundation for understanding the chapters as various examples of contributions to women and leadership theory. The purpose of the chapter is to give readers a framework for how to understand the way theory influences beliefs and behaviors and how knowing relates to theorizing. We hope that perhaps a new appreciation for theory and theorizing will result. We do this by addressing two related issues that we see facing women theorists[1] as they work together to generate new leadership theories for women. First, we urge women theorists to view theorizing as a catalyst for social change and to consider the act of theorizing as a form of praxis. Second, we believe the typical formulas for generating theories have delegitimized non-rational and non-logical influences on knowing and knowledge. Combined, we believe these two issues—theorizing as social change and knowing differently—have the potential to radically contribute to advancing women and leadership theory.

We present the remainder of the chapter in three sections. In the first section we describe the various elements of theorizing as social change and make the case that theories can and do generate human actions and beliefs. In the second section we focus on alternative ways of knowing and generating knowledge relevant to women and leadership theorizing. In the final section we discuss the implications of combining social change and theorizing focused on women's ways of knowing and engaging in leadership.

THEORIZING AS SOCIAL CHANGE

The influence of words and language on thoughts, actions, and beliefs has been well documented in both the scholarly (e.g., Fairclough, 1992, 2010; Foucault, 1977, 1980; Iedema & Scheeres, 2003) and popular (e.g., Dweck, 2007; Kahneman, 2011) literature. However, there is limited exploration of how theories, theorists, and theorizing can intentionally and strategically influence the future. Indeed, a review of the history of theorizing suggests that, until very recently, theories were created based on the past (Gioia, Corley, & Fabbri, 2002). Traditional theory building methods were presented as linear processes based on data collected from quantitative research (Storberg-Walker & Chermak, 2007). These methods emphasized the neutrality of the theorist and the objective nature of theorizing.

A more recent article in the *Academy of Management Review* (*AMR*) by Kevin Corley and Dennis Gioia (2011) argued that theorists should be prescient. The dictionary definition of prescience, to "know what will or might happen in the future" (Prescience, n.d.), suggests a fundamental re-visioning of theory and the values, goals, and interests of the theorist. In essence, Corley and Gioia (2011) flipped theorizing on its head. In this view, rather than theories representing how things worked in the past, theories should be created in order to influence, mold, or shape the future to accomplish some desired outcome. After an extensive review of theory building research, Corley and Gioia (2011) stated, "We believe that theoretical contributions in management and organization studies have not done an adequate job of anticipating the important conceptual, as well as practical, needs of society's now most prominent members—business and social organizations" (p. 20).

That this idea was published in the *AMR* is path-breaking, and it illustrates a profound de-centering of the neutrality and objectivity so deeply embedded in the theorizing process. *AMR*, one of the top journals in the management field, typically publishes scholarship representing the views of a more conservative knowledge community. Consequently, it is notable that the article was published because it sends a signal that the canons of theorizing—neutrality and objectivity—may not be sufficient for the future needs of "society's now most prominent members—business and social organizations" (Corley & Gioia, 2011, p. 20).

The role of theorists, in this view, move from *theorizing what was* to *theorizing what can be*. Looking forward means that the values, goals, and interests of the theorist matter to theorizing, and that the theorist is no longer an invisible element behind a theory. We extend this view to women and leadership; we believe that equality for women and girls is sorely needed in today's world, and we believe that theorizing in this domain has the power to positively impact the future. We now describe how theories have altered human behavior and thinking in the past, and we illustrate how the beliefs generated by theories impact the practical world.

What Are Theories?

Theories deeply influence the way we understand and make sense of the world, and, as is described in more detail in this section, theories can influence the future. We rely on Corley and Gioia's (2011) definition of theory, which is: "[T]heory is a statement of concepts and their interrelationships that shows how and/or why a phenomenon occurs" (p. 12). Theories name things, and in the process of naming and communicating, a reality is constructed. We humans absorb the language and words used in the theory and are consciously and unconsciously guided by our interpretation of those words. In other words, humans make meaning of theories and then, consciously or unconsciously, make judgments about the worth or value or appropriateness of a situation.

Theories Are Self-Fulfilling Prophesies

In 1948, and reprinted again in 2010, Robert Merton, one of the recognized fathers of sociology who was noted for his contributions to the sociology of science, highlighted the role of interpretation and the self-fulfilling nature of social theories. He described many instances in the real world that illustrate how humans make judgments and/or take action based on how we understand a situation. Merton argued that "men respond not only to the objective features of a situation, but also, and at times primarily, to the meaning this situation has for them" (p. 194). Merton then extended this line of reasoning to social theories to suggest that human actions, guided by a social theory, can actually generate the "facts" that support or confirm the theory. A relatively clear example of this influence can be seen in Marxist theory, which predicted that capitalism would concentrate wealth into fewer and fewer hands and leave the vast majority of people in poverty. Merton suggested that this theory was the catalyst for the growth of the socialist movement; we could also argue that this theory granted legitimacy to wealth accumulation and income disparity.

Theories Generate Social Norms

Most importantly for our purposes, however, is Merton's (1948/2010) discussion of the role of in-groups and out-groups in creating (through meaning making and/or action) the "facts" that confirm theories. Through multiple examples, ranging from Trobriand chiefs to White gentiles, Merton illuminates how social structures and social norms are created and perpetuated by the "facts" generated by the in-group (e.g., the group in power), and the "facts" themselves were generated by some implicit or explicit theory. To Merton, theories can generate facts that become social norms and expectations. Consequently, theories can be self-fulfilling prophecies that perpetuate the ruling elite's (in-group) interpretation of the theory and at the same time de-legitimize "the other" (out-group) interpretations.

This history is at least as relevant today as it was in 1948. The discussion of theories as self-fulfilling prophecies continues to generate spirited debate (Felin & Foss, 2009), and Merton's ideas have been imported into management theory (Ferraro, Pfeffer, & Sutton, 2005). Because social theories influence human actions, they matter, as Ferarro et al. (2005) noted:

> Social science theories can become self-fulfilling by shaping institutional designs and management practices, as well as social norms and expectations about behavior, thereby creating the behavior they predict. They also perpetuate themselves by promulgating language and assumptions that become widely used and accepted. (p. 8)

Ferraro et al. (2005) suggest that not all theories equally impact practice. The theories that "'win' in the marketplace for ideas ... to the extent that their assumptions and language become taken for granted and normatively valued" (p. 8), influence human behavior. The authors suggest that three mutually reinforcing mechanisms work together to enable theories to create reality: institutional design, societal norms, and language.[2] Institutional structures can be formed based on the "best" theory enabling goal accomplishment; societal norms are generated by theory and set standards for and govern behavior; and the language in a theory "affects what people see, how they see it, and the social categories and descriptors they use to interpret their reality" (Ferraro et al., 2005, p. 9).

Connections to Women and Leadership Theory

Taken as a whole, the ideas described above, namely the tendency for theories to become self-fulfilling prophecies, the tendency for in-group and out-group divergence in understanding/meaning making, and the tendency for theories valued by the in-group to generate societal norms, have numerous implications for women and leadership theorists. Three implications we believe are most relevant for theorists generating new leadership theories for women are the following:

1. By developing new leadership theories for women, theorists can influence understanding, social norms and expectations, and institutional designs favoring gender equality.
2. Theorists can intentionally use theory to reshape the definitions of leadership; the expectations about leaders; and the structures and practices in organizations, communities, and other social structures.
3. Through their work, theorists are, in reality, acting as change agents for social justice in general, and for gender equality specifically.[3]

It may be possible for theorists to accomplish these goals through collective action and sustained efforts. Merton (1948) presented different scenarios of successful change interventions and suggested that "a deliberate and planned halt can be put to the workings of the self-fulfilling prophecy" (p. 208). Merton, a functionalist, suggested, "*The self-fulfilling prophecy, whereby fears are translated into reality, operates only in the absence of deliberate institutional controls*" (p. 210, emphasis in original). His functionalist solution focused on a linear form of cause and effect—change the institution(s), and the effect will be a change in how people understand theories.

Today, we have multiple and non-linear ways to understand large-scale social and organizational change that could support the agenda of women and leadership change agent theorists. For example, Barton (2014) noted that complex adaptive "systems approaches offer the potential for new insights into processes of social change, linkages between the actions of individual human agents and societal-level characteristics, (and) interactions between societies and their environment" (p. 306). The role of technology in social change is significant; possibilities include funding, reaching across distance and difference, crowdsourcing, informing, and empowering (Grindle, 2015). Although exploring the breadth of relevant change literature is beyond the scope of this chapter, readers are encouraged to reflect on the change strategies, practices, and ideas that can be applied to their work as change-agent theorists.

Combining the role of theorist-as-change-agent with the belief that humans socially construct the meaning of theories suggests new roles for theories and theorists. As Corley and Gioia (2011) argue, prescience is needed for more effective and impactful theory. And as Fairclough (2010) and others contend, humans construct meaning from discourse and language; this is directly relevant to theory because theories are narrative linguistic constructions. In essence, these ideas move theory from a past-focused process to a future-generating process and open the door for reflecting on how women and leadership theories can contribute toward a future of equality. This book is one contribution toward this end, and readers are encouraged to frame their theoretical and conceptual work as social change strategies and their resulting theories as guides for the future.

The next section moves to a fundamental component of theorizing: the type of evidence needed to construct or generate a theory. As is illustrated below, the type of evidence routinely used in leadership studies is quantitative, and the acceptance of quantitative evidence mirrors the practice in the larger social science community. We believe, however—and many of the chapters in this book illustrate—that other forms of evidence can and should be relied on while theorizing for women leaders. We suggest that women's ways of knowing (WWK) is particularly relevant for understanding and theorizing about how women experience and learn leadership. This way of knowing requires different forms of evidence, as will be described below. WWK emerged from the groundbreaking work of Belenky, Clinchy, Goldberger, and Tarule (1986/1997); their book, titled *Women's Ways of Knowing*, is "one of the most highly cited books on women's intellectual development" (Walsh, 1997, p. 249). We are grateful for the contributions of Belenky et al.'s (1986) work and believe there are many untapped opportunities to extend WWK into the leadership domain, as described in the next section.

ALTERNATIVE WAYS OF KNOWING

One of the canons of traditional theorizing is the belief that scientific knowledge is objective and neutral. Objectivity and neutrality are fundamental assumptions of a particular paradigm or worldview, but other paradigms and worldviews exist. These alternative paradigms represent a broad spectrum of values, goals, and assumptions about the world. They also represent different forms of evidence used to "know" something. Functionalism, one of the four paradigms found within Burrell and Morgan's (1979) framework, represents the assumptions and goals connected to objective and neutral research. Functionalist research has contributed a lot to leadership in general (Avolio, Walumbwa, & Weber, 2009) and to women and leadership in particular (e.g., Eagly & Johannesen-Schmidt, 2001; Eagly, Johannesen-Schmidt, & van Engen, 2003; Eagly & Johnson, 1990; Eagly & Karau, 1991; Eagly & Karau, 2002; Eagly, Makhijani, & Klonsky, 1992).

It is clear that functionalist research has dominated leadership research (Alvesson & Spicer, 2012) and theory building (Gioia & Pitre, 1990) and the methods used to generate new knowledge have influenced the type of data or evidence that "counts" as legitimate: "We have tended to operate by using a deductive approach to theory building, specifying hypotheses deemed appropriate for the organizational world and testing them against hypothesis-driven data via statistical analyses" (Gioia & Pitre, 1990, p. 584).

"Theory building" and "theory construction" continue to be the terms used to describe the process of developing new knowledge, and the type of knowledge being developed is uniformly based on hypothesis testing. For example, Meuser et al. (2016) present a comprehensive analysis of 864 scholarly leadership articles in order to understand what they call "leadership theory integration" (p. 1374). Integration, to these scholars, seems to be similar to qualitative themes. Their analysis suggests there are six types of leadership approaches or theoretical families of leadership theory: transformational, charismatic, strategic, participative/shared, diversity, and trait. Of most importance to us is the fact that the authors implicitly rely on functionalist assumptions, as represented by the citations (e.g., Bacharach, 1989; Dubin, 1976; Kaplan, 1964; Reichers & Schneider, 1990) and analytical categories (e.g., theoretical units, laws of interactions, boundaries, and propositions). What is left unsaid in the article is any acknowledgement that other forms of knowing exist.

A more recent article in the *Academy of Management Learning and Education* journal offers a step away from functionalist beliefs and values and opens the door to alternative ways of knowing. Feldman and Worline (2016) suggest that *practical rationality* is needed to develop relevant and actionable (*practical*) theories: "practical rationality is different from the scientific rationality that stands outside of practice and creates generalizable knowledge, which is accurate only when many cases are aggregated" (p. 320). Theories of practice and theorizing practice are not new (e.g., Lave, 1996; Orr, 1996), and it will be interesting to see how or if leadership scholars in general and women and leadership scholars in particular adopt these ideas, which we believe can further the development of women and leadership theories.

At this time, however, the field of leadership seems to lag behind, and more theorizing processes, practices, and methods are needed. Although functionalist types of knowledge are valuable and can contribute to equality for women and girls and to the development of impactful women and leadership theories, we are aligned with a very large academic community in the belief that non-functionalist ways of knowing exist, are important, and need to be valued in social science efforts. Functionalist knowledge is only one type of the multiple knowledges relevant to women; focusing heavily on functionalist knowledge can leave out knowledge gained from embodied and contextual experience. To capture the diversity of women's experiences, alternative ways of knowing must be the legitimate source of and goal for women-centered leadership theories.

Note how we use the term "alternative" ways of knowing to describe the type of knowledge that is not often considered legitimate in normal science. While we recognize the binary nature of this opposition, we use the term as an umbrella concept to signify the broad spectrum of different ways of knowing. Alternative forms of knowing include indigenous ways of knowing, WWK, intuiting, and imagining. Abduction, a mental process closely related to theorizing, can also be seen as generating a different type of knowledge. What these have in common is that, unlike normal science knowledge, the knowledge in these other forms represents a more holistic and comprehensive knowledge that expands beyond rational thought.

Knowledge in this view can include physical sensations, bodily or mystical experiences, connections to lands or tribes, emotions, and intuitions, among others. This type of knowing can be generated by empathy, the "sixth sense," relationships, beliefs, physical movement, religion, and feelings. Knowing is contextual and in the moment, and knowledge is the store of experiences that interact with body, mind, and spirit (Damasio, 1994). The next section describes one of the many forms of knowledge and ways of knowing that is important for theorizing women and leadership theory. We acknowledge that multiple forms exist and urge readers to follow their internal guide(s) to identify the form that most resonates to them.

Women's Ways of Knowing

As described earlier, one particularly relevant form of knowledge for women leaders, which also is women-centered, is called *Women's Ways of Knowing* or WWK (Belenky et al., 1986). Because the focus of this volume is on women and leadership, we will focus on this form of knowledge in this chapter. However, readers are urged to reflect on and then research the "best" form(s) of knowledge for their particular context. More is written about WWK in Chapter 15, in which we (as co-authors with four others) describe our struggle with the type of knowledge favored by normal science. WWK is relevant to women and leadership theorizing because it impacts both the process of generating theory and the implementation or application of theory. In the following paragraphs, we describe WWK, illustrate how it informs theorizing, and suggest that WWK can be the basis for the implementation phase of theorizing, which we have labeled social change.

WWK was generated from a woman-centered study that initially used, as one of its guiding theories, a male-normed development model (Perry, 1970) to craft interview questions. Perry's model was based on Harvard male student experiences, and, like many beliefs found in normal science, it was thought that the model was applicable to all humans. However, early in the WWK data analysis process, disconnects between Perry's model and the data began to emerge that carried through the WWK study. For example, "[W]e [Belenky et al., 1986/97] found that the women's thinking did not fit so neatly into his categories" (Belenky et al., 1986/1997, p. 14). Perry's work assumed a growth or developmental/teleological process, and for the WWK study "the developmental pathways were far less obvious" (p. 15). WWK consequently is not understood as a sequence of phases building on each other; rather, the researchers included different "epistemological perspectives from which women know and view the world" (p. 15).

Readers are encouraged to read the full WWK book to more deeply understand the methods used in the study, the influence of researcher feminist values, and the resulting findings. Of primary importance for women and leadership theorists, we believe, is that the women in the study said that "deflation of authority [was] a powerful learning experience" (Belenky et al., 1986/97, p. 216) because "women have been taught by generations of men that males have greater powers of rationality" (p. 217). The researchers found that women need "models of thinking as a human, imperfect, and attainable activity" (p. 217) that look like them.

WWK and Theorizing

WWK has been widely accepted as a breakthrough study and has earned legitimacy across many domains. Consequently, extending these ideas into theorizing leadership *for* women and learning leadership *by* women is a realistic strategy. Theorizing for women leaders based on WWK means that the theorists themselves draw from their own woman's way of knowing as part of the theorizing process. In other words, the personal experience of the theorist matters in the theorizing process, and these personal experiences can draw from multiple—and, at times conflicting—events and episodes.

Working in collaboration based on WWK, women theorists would share their leadership experiences and would learn from the diverse experiences in the group (remember, a combination of scholars and practitioners would be the "theorists" developing theory together). A number of chapters in this book illustrate this type of collaborative process based on personal experience and WWK. To some degree, the women theorists, like those in this book, would also draw from relevant research literature as they move forward to put names to the ideas and/or concepts of the emerging theory. Much like Swedberg's (2012) theory creation phase of theory building, this phase of generating theory through WWK is non-linear, recursive, and, at times, messy. Ultimately through the process, a tentative theory emerges.

Implementing or Applying WWK

At this point, the tentative theory may be put through mini- or micro-tests to ascertain its ability to resonate with the leadership experiences of women. The theory could be a guide for action or suggestions for reflection. The theory could focus on leadership identity, stereotype threat, relationships—essentially anything relevant to helping women move forward in their leadership abilities. Using WWK as a guide to implementation would mean that the epistemological perspectives of women would be taken into account, and appropriate pedagogical and communicative tactics would be used for teaching and learning.

An interesting example is included in Chapter 3 of this book. The group of women theorists who authored the chapter found that, during the theorizing process, they in essence developed their own leadership abilities. These women found that WWK itself could contribute to leadership development for women. Other chapters, including Chapters 7 and 15, also highlight the connections between theorizing, WWK, and leadership development. We suggest that more research on these connections may further legitimize WWK as relevant to women and leadership theory.

SOCIAL CHANGE AND PRAXIS

As we described at the beginning of this chapter, theory and theoretical contributions are best viewed as different, valuable, partial, tentative, and temporary. The explicit acknowledgment of transitory theory is a radical departure of the codification of theory found in Dubin (1976), Patterson (1983), and others. At the same time, however, we suggested that through theorizing, women theorists (e.g., the collaboration between scholars and practitioners) can influence the future and catalyze social change. In this final section of the chapter we highlight the key ideas in social change and praxis, and we describe the foundational need for diverse spaces in the women and leadership theory domain. The former (social change and praxis) will not happen without the latter (diverse spaces). To clarify our ideas, we offer working definitions for social change and praxis: Social change requires collaboration and relationship building in a community context and seeks to address root causes of issues and problems through sustained efforts (Wagner, 2009); and "put simply, praxis is the synthesis of theory and practice and the reciprocal relationship between them" (Cowley, n.d., para. 4).

The "synthesis of theory and practice" is much more than adding theory and practice together. To us, and to scholars like Cowley (n.d.), the reciprocal relationship between theory and practice can ensure the following: that the embodied experiences of women leaders are not subsumed by theory, that cognitive thinking is not more highly valued than these experiences, and that theory is elevated to a higher "status" than women's practice of leadership. In this view, theory should be generated from practice and serve the needs of average, everyday women leaders across multiple cultures, contexts, and conditions.

Praxis, then, is the keystone for accomplishing social change. Only through praxis can the diverse experiences of women leaders be fully integrated into the theorizing process. Praxis requires an acknowledgement of difference; legitimation of different ways of knowing; and space for different leadership goals, objectives, and intentions. Praxis will not result in a harmonious or parsimonious theory of women's leadership, and praxis requires a pluralist acceptance of different belief systems (e.g., paradigms). Women scholars choosing praxis will be challenged to move beyond their comfort zones in terms of research methods and paradigms—and possibly beyond their own identities as women and leadership scholars. Women leaders choosing praxis will be challenged also but in a different way. To these women, praxis may require them to understand their leadership experiences in new ways—in ways that break free of male-normed models and frameworks. These women may need to develop a new language to communicate their experiences, for example, the use of indigenous concepts (e.g., *kapwa*) or the use of images (e.g., photovoice). Both scholars and practitioners will need to critically reflect on how they evaluate research, scholarship, and theoretical contributions.

These changes will not be easy, but this book contributes to the ongoing re-structuring and re-thinking of women and leadership theory. This chapter suggests that through praxis, theorizing for women leaders can catalyze social change and create conditions for equality for women and girls. Like all theories, women-centered leadership theories should be connected to evidence and crafted with rigor. Unlike previous generations of scholarly theorists, however, women-centered leadership theorists must look forward and accept the great responsibility of influencing the future of humankind. The future will not be one of consensus or homogeneity, but it can be one where women and girls are safe, where their voices have social, economic, political, religious, and environmental influence, and where people of all genders stand as equals. This future can be imagined through rigorous scholarly research, and it is not out of our reach. Our challenge today is to do the hard work of developing these theories and continuing to create scholarly legitimacy for this form of research.

NOTES

1. Women theorists mean the women collaborating together to generate new theory. These women should represent both scholarly and practical frames/

sources of knowledge. Consequently, "women theorists" represent academics and practitioners engaged together in a process of theorizing.

2. Interestingly, Alvesson and Spicer's (2012) advocacy for a performative view of leadership relies on using discourse (language) "in such a way that has an impact, both in terms of emancipatory effect and practical organizational work" (p. 376).

3. Because the focus of this volume is on women and leadership theory, we specify here that the goal of theorizing is equality for women. Note, however, that we believe a focus on women exclusively will not generate the contextualized theories needed. Other markers of identity, especially race, are necessary in order to generate theories that resonate with women of all differences.

REFERENCES

Alvesson, M., & Spicer, A. (2012). Critical leadership studies: The case for critical performativity. *Human Relations, 65*(3), 367–390.

Avolio, B. J., Walumbwa, F. O., & Weber, T. J. (2009). Leadership: Current theories, research, and future directions. *Annual Review of Psychology, 60,* 421–449.

Bacharach, S. B. (1989). Organizational theories: Some criteria for evaluation. *Academy of Management Review, 14*(4), 496–515.

Barton, C. M. (2014). Complexity, social complexity, and modeling. *Journal of Archaeological Method and Theory, 21*(2), 306–324. doi: 10.1007/s10816-013-9187-2

Belenky, M. F., Clinchy, B. M., Goldberger, N. R., & Tarule, J. M. (1986/1997). *Women's ways of knowing: The development of self, voice, and mind.* New York, NY: Basic Books.

Burrell, G., & Morgan, G., (1979). *Sociological paradigms and organisational analysis: Elements of the sociology of corporate life.* London, England: Heinemann.

Christensen, C. M., & Raynor, M. E. (2003). Why hard-nosed executives should care about management theory. *Harvard Business Review, 81*(9), 66–75.

Corley, K. G., & Gioia, D. A. (2011). Building theory about theory building: What constitutes a theoretical contribution? *Academy of Management Review, 36*(1), 12–32.

Cowley, N. (n.d.). What is praxis? Discussed in relation to Hegel, Marx, Nietzsche and Sartre. *Te Kura Kete Aronui E-journal.* Retrieved from http://www.waikato.ac.nz/__data/assets/pdf_file/0005/149261/NatalieCowley.pdf

Damasio, A. R. (1994). Descartes' error and the future of human life. *Scientific American, 27*(4), 2–3.

Dubin, R. (1976). Theory building in applied areas. In M. C. Dunnette (Ed.), *Handbook of industrial and organizational psychology* (pp. 17–39). Chicago, IL: Rand McNally.

Dweck, C. (2007). *Mindset: The new psychology of success.* New York, NY: Ballantine Books.

Eagly, A. H., & Johannesen-Schmidt, M. C. (2001). The leadership styles of women and men. *Journal of Social Issues, 57*(4), 781–797. doi:10.1111/0022-4537.00241

Eagly, A. H., Johannesen-Schmidt, M. C., & van Engen, M. L. (2003). Transformational, transactional, and laissez-faire leadership styles: A meta-analysis comparing women and men. *Psychological Bulletin, 129*(4), 569–591. http://doi.org/10.1037/0033-2909.129.4.569

Eagly, A. H., & Johnson, B. T. (1990). Gender and leadership style: A meta-analysis. *Psychological Bulletin, 108*(2), 233–256. doi: 10.1037/0033-2909.108.2.233

Eagly, A. H., & Karau, S. J. (1991). Gender and the emergence of leaders: A meta-analysis. *Journal of Personality and Social Psychology, 60*(5), 685–710. http://doi.org/10.1037/0022-3514.60.5.685

Eagly, A. H., & Karau, S. J. (2002). Role congruity theory of prejudice toward female leaders. *Psychological Review, 109*(3), 573–598. http://doi.org/10.1037/0033-295X.109.3.573

Eagly, A. H., Makhijani, M. G., & Klonsky, B. G. (1992). Gender and the effectiveness of leaders: A meta-analysis. *Psychological Bulletin, 111*(1), 3–22. doi: 10.1037/0033-2909.117.1.125

Ellis, C. S., & Bochner, A. P. (2006). Analyzing analytic autoethnography: An autopsy. *Journal of Contemporary Ethnography, 35*(4), 429–449.

Fairclough, N. (1992). *Discourse and social change.* Cambridge, England: Polity Press.

Fairclough, N. (2010). *Critical discourse analysis: The critical study of language.* London, England: Routledge.

Feldman, M., & Worline, M. (2016). The practicality of practical theory. *Academy of Management Learning & Education, 15*(2), 304–324.

Felin, T., & Foss, N. J. (2009). Social reality, the boundaries of self-fulfilling prophecy, and economics. *Organization Science, 20*(3), 654–669.

Ferraro, F., Pfeffer, J., & Sutton, R. I. (2005). Economics language and assumptions: How theories can become self-fulfilling. *Academy of Management Review, 30*(1), 8–24.

Foucault, M. (1977). *Discipline and punish: The birth of the prison.* New York, NY: Pantheon Books.

Foucault, M. (1980). *Power/knowledge: Selected interviews and other writings 1972–1977.* New York, NY: Pantheon Books.

Gioia, D. A., Corley, K. G., & Fabbri, T. (2002). Revising the past (while thinking in the future perfect tense). *Journal of Change Management, 15*(6), 622–634. doi: 10.5465/AMR.1990.4310758

Gioia, D. A., & Pitre, E. (1990). Multiparadigm perspective on theory building. *Academy of Management Review, 15*(4), 584–602.

Grindle, A. (2015). *6 ways technology is breaking barriers to social change.* Retrieved from http://www.fastcoexist.com/3043761/techsocial/6-ways-technology-is-breaking-barriers-to-social-change.

Gross, N. (2012). Afterword. In R. Swedberg (Ed.), *Theorizing in social science: The context of discovery* (pp. 205–215). Palo Alto, CA: Stanford University Press.

Hannah, S. T., Sumanth, J. J., Lester, P., & Cavarretta, F. (2014). Debunking the false dichotomy of leadership idealism and pragmatism: Critical evaluation and support of newer genre leadership theories. *Journal of Organizational Behavior, 35*(5), 598–621.

Iedema, R., & Scheeres, H. (2003). From doing work to talking work: Renegotiating knowing, doing, and identity. *Applied Linguistics, 24*(3), 316–337.

Kahneman, D. (2011). *Thinking, fast and slow.* New York, NY: Farrar, Straus and Giroux.

Kaplan, A. (1964). *The conduct of inquiry: Methodology for the behavioral sciences.* New York, NY: Chandler.

Kennelly, J. J. (2009). Youth cultures, activism and agency: Revisiting feminist debates. *Gender and Education, 21*(3), 259–272. doi: 10.1080/09540250802392281

Lave, J. (1996). *Cognition in practice: Mind, mathematics and culture in everyday life.* Cambridge, England: Cambridge University Press.

Merton, R. K. (1948). The self-fulfilling prophecy. *The Antioch Review, 8*(2), 193–210.

Meuser, J. D., Gardner, W. L., Dihn, J. E., Hu, J., Liden, R. C., & Lord, R. G. (2016). A network analysis of leadership theory: The infancy of integration. *Journal of Management, 42*(5), 1374–1403.

Orr, J. (1996). *Talking about machines: An ethnography of a modern job.* Ithaca: NY: Cornell University Press.

Patterson, C. H. (1983). *Theories of counseling and psychotherapy.* Philadelphia, PA: Harper & Row.

Perry, W. G. (1970). *Forms of intellectual and ethical development in the college years.* New York, NY: Holt, Rinehart & Winston.

Prescience. (n.d.). In *Merriam-Webster Online.* Retrieved from http://www.merriam-webster.com/dictionary/prescience

Reichers, A. E., & Schneider, B. (1990). Climate and culture: An evolution of constructs? In B. Schneider (Ed.), *Organizational climate and culture* (pp. 5–39). San Francisco, CA: Jossey-Bass.

Storberg-Walker, J., & Chermack, T. (2007). Four methods for completing the conceptual development phase of applied theory building research in HRD. *Human Resource Development Quarterly, 18*(4), 499–524.

Swedberg, R. (2012). Theorizing in sociology and social science: Turning to the context of discovery. *Theory and Society, 41*(1), 1–40. doi: 10.1007/s11186-011-9161-5

Wagner, W. (2009). What is social change? In S. R. Komives & W. Wagner (Eds.), *Leadership for a better world* (pp. 7–41). San Francisco, CA: Jossey-Bass.

Walsh, M. R. (1997). *Women, men, and gender: Ongoing debates.* New Haven, CT: Yale University Press.

Weick, K. (1989). Theory construction as disciplined imagination. *Academy of Management Review, 14*(4), 516–531.

PART I

NEW CONCEPTS AND THEORIES

CHAPTER 2

IMPOSSIBLE SELVES

Image Strategies and Identity Threat in Professional Women's Career Transitions

Herminia Ibarra and Jennifer L. Petriglieri
INSEAD

This chapter extends our understanding of the paucity of women in senior leadership positions by identifying specific identity mechanisms that can hinder junior women's transitions to more senior roles. We introduce the term *impossible selves* to describe these cultural prescriptions for leadership identity and behavior that many junior women find unattainable. In the two male- dominated firms we studied, the cultural prescriptions for a leader's identity were associated with a traditionally masculine demeanor. We argue that second-generation gender bias—cultural beliefs about gender, as well as workplace structures, practices, and patterns of interaction that inadvertently favor men—inhibited women from engaging in image and identity work that would align them with these cultural prescriptions. This bias transformed organizational models of success into impossible selves for the women in these demographically skewed contexts. Instead of working toward the organizational model of success, we found that women engaged

Theorizing Women and Leadership, pages 19–36
Copyright © 2017 by Information Age Publishing

in image and identity work to craft a leader identity that allowed them to feel authentic and avoid disapproval from clients and colleagues. Women's efforts to remain authentic, however, undermined their ability to craft identities that were congruent with the kind of professionals they aspired to become.

An important part of assuming a work role is acting and looking the part (Becker & Carper, 1956; Becker & Strauss, 1956; Hochschild, 1983). Role-related expectations, or "display rules" (Rafaeli & Sutton, 1989), confer legitimacy upon the role-holder (Goffman, 1956). As people advance to new and unfamiliar work roles, they engage in image work (Roberts, 2005) to convey public images that conform to role expectations, signal competence, and win the deference of members of their role-set (Goffman, 1956; Ibarra, 1999). They also engage in identity work (Snow & Anderson, 1987) to craft an identity congruent with the image they present. When an individual's claims to an identity are granted by significant others, the person is more likely to internalize the new role identity and thus successfully make the role transition (DeRue & Ashford, 2010).

Which display-rules become prototypic depends on the demographics of a firm or industry, and, in particular, the people in senior leadership positions who serve as role models for what it takes to succeed (Baron & Pfeffer, 1994; Creed, Scully, & Austin, 2002; Ely, 1995; Kanter, 1977). Women currently constitute only 4.6% of S&P 500 CEOs (Catalyst, 2015) and about 19% of these companies' board seats (Catalyst, 2014). Organizational hierarchies in which men predominate not only provide few role models for women but also tend to perpetuate implicit beliefs that equate leadership with behaviors believed to be more common or appropriate in men (Eagly & Carli, 2007; Ely, Ibarra, & Kolb, 2011). The way that women respond to the image requirements of prototypically male roles, however, has been underinvestigated empirically.

This chapter analyzes the way gender affects what image and identity strategies people use to adapt to the demands of more senior leadership roles, in this case, the transition from project and expert work to client advisory, a context in which image is paramount. Both men and women in our study experienced a gap between what they were doing and what was expected of them; consequently, both also experienced threats to their previously successful professional identities. However, the image strategies they used to bridge the gap differed by gender, as did their consequences.

We explain their divergent strategies in terms of second-generation bias defined as the powerful yet often invisible barriers to women's advancement that arise from cultural beliefs about gender, as well as workplace structures, practices, and patterns of interaction that inadvertently favor men (Calás & Smircich, 1991; Eagly & Carli, 2007; Ely & Meyerson, 2000; Kolb & McGinn, 2009; Sturm, 2001) and accumulate to interfere with a woman's ability to see herself and be seen by others as a leader (Ely et al., 2011).

We advance four conceptual arguments that link second-generation bias to image and identity processes. First, we propose that in addition to the generic identity threat caused by the image and identity gap during the role transition, second-generation bias results in a further identity threat to women in the form of a devaluation or disconfirmation of their gender identities (i.e., stereotype threat; Branscombe & Ellemers, 1998; Petriglieri, 2011). Second, we argue that second-generation bias reduces the likelihood that women will respond to the perceived identity threat by acquiring a demeanor that conforms to display rules for professional success. Third, we suggest that the combination of second-generation bias and stereotype threat can transform organizational models of success into impossible selves for women working in demographically skewed professional contexts. Last, we identify social experiences that mitigate threat by providing resources for alternative image and identity strategies, and suggest ways in which they create virtuous developmental cycles.

The chapter is organized into three major sections. Given the theory-generating nature of our work, we begin with the research setting and data collection methods: a pair of qualitative and inductive studies of junior-level management consultants and investment bankers in the midst of career transitions to more senior roles that require them to interact with clients as representatives of their firms. The second section reports the contrast in how men and women used image and identity strategies to gain credibility and elicit deference from their clients. In this section we develop a conceptual framework in which second-generation bias moderates the relationship between identity threat and image strategies, which, in turn, reduce or augment the perceived threat. The final section develops the idea of impossible selves, speculating beyond the current findings and suggesting avenues for future research.

CONTEXT AND METHODS

This chapter builds on a prior study (Ibarra, 1999) that was conducted in two professional services firms—an investment bank and a management consulting firm. The investment bank was part of a large securities firm, which employed approximately 1,000 professionals. The management consulting firm was a rapidly growing, but relatively small, elite firm that employed approximately 350 professionals. Both investment bankers and management consultants begin their careers performing analytic work and providing support to their team. They progress to a conceptual and managerial role, in which they coordinate projects or "deals" and manage junior colleagues. Over time, they move into client advisory roles in which they are expected to generate "follow-on" or new business and to actively cultivate relationships with clients.

Both firms were male dominated, making them ideal case studies for the theory we develop in this chapter. In the consulting firm, women made up 35% of Junior Analysts entering the firm; their numbers fell to 20% at the team leader level; only 7% of Client Account Managers and Partners were women. In the investment bank, women made up less than 10% of Junior Associates entering the bank, at the Vice President level there were 18% women, and at the Director and Managing Director levels there were between 6–9% women, depending on the department.

We investigated the two critical junctures below the Partner or Director level to capture the transition from analytical to client management roles. The transition to client management roles is particularly suited for exploring identity construction processes because image displays are of such central importance in the new role. Generating revenues hinges on the professional's ability to convey an image of competence and credibility to prospective clients since the value of the services rendered is relatively intangible and difficult to evaluate objectively (Ashforth & Humphrey, 1993). Uncertainty places a premium on the outward appearance of being "the right sort of person" (Kanter, 1977), and image becomes a proxy for quality. Style and substance are thus intertwined such that career success depends importantly on self-presentation (Ibarra, 1999).

To ensure adequate familiarization with the firms, the research began with five open-ended interviews with three senior professionals and two human resource (HR) professionals in the investment bank; and three interviews with two senior professionals and one HR professional in the consulting firm. These "informants" also facilitated the selection of participants for the full study. In both firms, we sampled people just before the identified career transitions. The participant group oversampled women to ensure that the transition experiences of men and women could be compared. Thus, the full population of women at the transition points were identified at both firms. We randomly selected an equivalent number of men at the same transition points. The final group included eight women and eleven men from the consulting firm and seven women and eight men from the investment bank.[1]

The first author conducted semi-structured interviews with all 34 participants; the conversations typically lasted 90 minutes, ranging from 60 minutes to more than 2 hours. Data analysis followed an inductive theory development process. Following the methods described by Eisenhardt (1989) and Rafaeli and Sutton (1991), and with the help of two Research Associates, we searched for major themes in the data and compared these themes with concepts from the literature on impression management, identity work, and career socialization. We used an iterative process—moving back and forth between the data and relevant literature (Strauss & Corbin, 1998)—to develop our emerging conceptualization of second-generation bias influencing image and identity processes and our concept of impossible selves.

IDENTITY THREAT, IMAGE WORK, AND SECOND-GENERATION BIAS

In this section we combine emergent themes from the qualitative data analysis with concepts and findings from social identity theory to develop our conceptual framework. We begin by showing how the transition to a client-facing role reveals a gap between junior professionals' previously successful professional identities and the identities they need to claim to be successful in their new roles. We move on to explore how men and women differ in the image strategies they adopt to respond to this threat and draw on second-generation gender bias literature to offer an account for this variance. Finally, we develop the construct of impossible selves, which signifies successful identities that could neither be claimed by nor granted to the majority of the women.

Role Transitions as Identity Threatening

The senior informants stressed that moving into a client contact role requires the junior professional to supplement a tangible skill base with a much more elusive set of success factors. The success factors include the ability to represent the firm, to generate novel ideas, to sell new business, and to develop peer relationships with clients who would come to rely on the professional for counsel on a broad array of business issues. The following comment illustrates a senior informant's view on the range and importance of these factors and the hurdle that managing them can present for the junior professional in transition to greater responsibility in managing client relationships:

> Many people reach a plateau as they struggle to become a client account manager. The challenge is to develop productive relationships with clients who are generally older than you. It requires different skills, and it comes as a big shock. You are selling yourself. You are saying, "For $X million, the project will have my guarantee, my judgment, and my credibility." (Senior Consultant)

All study participants were highly cognizant of these challenges and experienced anxiety about their credibility with clients and struggled to hide their feelings of inexperience and immaturity. As one female consultant noted, "There's a huge hurdle of transitioning from thinking I have to know all the facts to being a general advisor to the client. It's like my whole basis for existence is cut away if I can't rely on my particular expertise." Following Petriglieri (2011), we interpret this anxiety as symptomatic of identity threat, which is defined as "experiences appraised as indicating potential harm to the value, meanings, or enactment of an identity" (p. 644). Both men and women struggled in this transition.[2] One male consultant explained, "I had a feeling of being in over my head; sometimes it was really overwhelming; I didn't know how to ask for the right level of support. I knew I was struggling." This recognized image and identity gap constituted a threat to previously successful professional identities.

In addition to generic worries about bridging the gap between actual and desired identities as senior professionals, women participants expressed concerns about having their identity claims challenged simply by virtue of being women. As one consultant noted:

> Clients are surprised by a woman turning up to advise them. If you say something stupid, it will be remembered. You are more exposed. You are more of a risk to bring on in a marketing situation. I have seen people talk about "too many women look weird." (Female consultant)

Our data suggest that, for women, the professional identity threat generated by the transition to a client management role was accompanied and possibly augmented by a gender-based stereotype threat. Of the 15 women participating in the study, 11 reported experiences that challenged their identity as a professional that they attributed to gender. An investment banker explained with some frustration her inability to measure up to her male peers, "I can't be 6'3", handsome, with a firm handshake. But that's the image people have when they think of power and influence. When people meet me, they don't immediately think, 'This person's a star.' I think gender has a lot to do with it." The stereotype threat experienced by most women seemed to stem from cultural beliefs that are associated with the image of a good client manager to a traditionally masculine demeanor. A form of second-generation bias, these cultural beliefs devalued women's gender identity and created an additional identity threat to which they had to respond alongside the universally experienced threat stemming from the role transition.

Responses to Identity Threat: Gender Differences in Image Strategies

From day one, provoked by the identity threat they experienced, junior professionals were required to adopt a self-presentation strategy in an attempt to portray an image that befitted their new role. Though both men and women reported similar concerns about conveying a credible image to clients, mirroring our informant's comments, they differed significantly in their responses to these performance pressures. A striking pattern in our data was that men's and women's image strategies divided rather neatly into the acquisitive and protective styles described by Arkin, (1981). Arkin proposed two types of image strategies. "Acquisitive" self-presentation entails soliciting approval by ascertaining and signaling those traits that are most likely to result in deference from the pertinent audience. In client interactions, acquisitive strategies consist of active, aggressive attempts to signal credibility. "Protective" self-presentation, by contrast, involves attempts to avoid disapproval and is visible in behaviors such as modesty; reluctance to interact with others freely and actively; and a propensity toward neutral, uncertain, and qualified expressions of judgment such that the impression conveyed is "unassailable." With clients, protective strategies entailed "lying low" so as to avoid making a negative first impression on a client.

Only three of the women used an acquisitive image strategy, while thirteen of the men did. In doing so, they responded to image threats by displaying confidence and focusing their energies on increasing the likelihood of attaining the approval of clients. They also made an effort to establish personal relationships with their clients that were consistent with their roles as professional client advisors. The following quotation illustrates acquisitive strategies:

> You need to develop a sense of maturity so that you can win over clients as a peer. This is signaled through the way you act, the way you dress, the subject matter you talk about—more discussion of client's personal interests, less on analysis. . . . I have learned to go into a client meeting, not talk at all about the analysis, and have it be a VERY successful meeting. (Male Consultant)

In contrast, most of the women who participated in the study showed evidence of protective image strategies. The most common themes among the women in the sample were their discomfort in client interactions and their reluctance to assert themselves. While the men defined the requirements of client interaction as political and stylistic, the women tended to base their credibility claims on technical competence. Instead of using their image to make a positive first impression, the women participants were more likely to try to reduce the requirement of their image as a necessary signal for their underlying competence. The most commonly reported tactics were over-preparing and seeking assignments with long time horizons, in which technical mastery would become apparent—as it might not be in a brief meeting. The quotation below illustrates the contrast:

I tend not to step out on a limb when I'm not fairly confident about an assertion. If I have an idea, I think to myself, "Oh, that's stupid," and I won't say it.
I end up not being as active in meetings with clients. I think to myself, "How
can I tell this 55-year-old guy who's been in the industry his whole life that his
last investment was really stupid?" (Female Consultant)

In the present research context, the choice between acquisitive and protective self-presentation is consequential and problematic for women. The
ability to win client confidence facilitates career advancement, while the use
of protective self-presentation confirms gender stereotypes that may lead to
career stagnation. Failure to convey the expected image not only reduced
women's credibility with clients but also lowered expectations that they had
the potential to excel if promoted to higher positions, which required even
more client contact. All informants stressed that self-presentation was a significant hurdle for women even though the men and women were comparable in their analytic skills. The following comment by a senior investment
banker is exemplary: "A good job is expected. To be on the superstar track
you have to be outspoken, brash, self-promoting. The self-promotion factor
does women in."

Explaining the Gender Difference Between Image Strategies

Although our data did not allow us to explore the way that image processes unfold over time, our emerging theory suggests that preventive self-
presentation styles are the consequences of repeated exposure to second-
generation gender bias and dual professional and gender identity threat.
Accordingly, the section below explores the mechanisms and dynamics
that may lead women to become stuck in a highly gendered self-protective
stance.

Client Interactions

The large majority of the participants' senior clients were male. We argue that this relational demography (Tsui & O'Reilly, 1989) affects the image strategies by its effect on two factors: (a) expectation of clients' gender
bias, and (b) expectations of success with acquisitive and protective strategies. Both of these factors stem from second-generation bias and their
effects demonstrate how this bias can interfere with women's ability to see
themselves and be seen by others as credible leaders.

Junior women perceived that their clients held gender stereotypes that
would place them at a disadvantage. When clients bring to the situation gender-typed expectations and biases, they are more likely to elicit gender-linked
behavior from women professionals (Deaux & Major, 1987). Expectations

states theory (Berger, Fisech, Norman, & Selditch, 1977; Meeker & Weitzel-O'Neill, 1985) suggests that gender is a status characteristic that leads both men and women in mixed-gender groups to assume greater task competence from men until proven otherwise. The following quotation shows that the women tended to believe that being female signaled a lack of authority and competence:

> Being female affects my ability to be impactful. When a man speaks, the message hits home clearer. He will be more persuasive, both internally and with the client. The words are more hard-hitting. I'm more soft-spoken. I think I'm more likely to get challenged on something. (Female Consultant)

When professional women expect their male clients to hold gender biases, they will look for those biases to reveal themselves in their interactions. Influenced by these beliefs, professionals and clients may negotiate a stereotypic male-female professional exchange.

Faced with the expectation that the client may hold gender biases, a competent junior woman has two strategic alternatives, which correspond to Arkin's (1981) acquisitive and protective categories. Using an acquisitive strategy, she can make a direct bid for the client's respect in the immediate encounter. Alternatively, using a protective strategy, she can attempt to not *lose* credibility so that, over time, she can demonstrate competence. As Arkin noted, when people believe that the typical "approval seeking" form of self-presentation will not be successful for them, or that the potential costs of the behavior are greater than its potential benefit, they are more likely to behave protectively.

The second factor that affected the choice of image strategy, therefore, was the women participants' beliefs that they would not succeed if they adopted the acquisitive style displayed by the men. These beliefs are supported by a large body of research indicating that women using masculine leadership styles tend to be judged more negatively by both men and women than male professionals using the same leadership style (Eagly & Wood, 1991; Falbo, Hazen, & Linimon, 1982; Nieva & Gutek 1981; Wiley & Eskilson, 1982). As Schein (1973) demonstrated, the characteristics of a "good manager" are similar to those of a "typical man" and incongruous with those of a "typical woman." The following quotation illustrates participants' expectations of success with acquisitive and protective strategies:

> This is a hard business for a woman to be accepted in. Clients and people who make decisions are more accepting of a man walking in. They get away with bullying and off-the-cuff reactions. It leads to women over-preparing. You have to know more and appear more responsive. (Female Investment Banker)

Because women are evaluated on their qualities as professionals *and* as women, they may be sanctioned for either "acting like men," or conforming too closely to norms for female behavior—being "too timid" or "lacking presence with clients." As a result, women in this study gave a great deal of thought to what demeanor would work for them in client interactions. Because they perceived that either "acting like a man" or "acting like a woman" would likely backfire or reduce their credibility, many chose to adopt a neutral or protective stance.

Organizational Context

The relational demography of client interactions was mirrored in the demographics of the employer firms—particularly in terms of few women being at the senior level; this resulted in a paucity of role models for the women professionals. Ibarra (1999) found that, compared to those who did not seek role models, junior professionals who actively role modeled senior professionals more rapidly adopted their new professional identity, which, in turn, reduced the amount of time they needed to lean on the crutch of an image strategy. Moreover, role modeling was an organizationally legitimate type of identity work likely to elicit social validation, which resulted in a relatively swift reduction in perceived identity threat.

Role modeling involves both cognitive and affective processes (Bandura, 1986; Gibson, 1996). People must not only develop a sophisticated, cognitive understanding of what specific self-presentation behaviors are effective and why they are effective; they must also determine whether those behaviors will likely produce positive consequences for them and whether they are personally appealing (Bandura, 1986). The women who participated in this study were more likely than the men to report that available role models' styles were either not feasible for them or were incongruent with their self-concepts. Women were also more likely than the men to believe that they could not develop a style based on modeling someone else and to expect that modeling the behavior they observed to be successful in men would not produce the same positive outcomes for them. The following comment illustrates this point:

> Men are seen as aggressive or thoughtful while women, for the same behavior, are seen as whiny. I have to watch my words. I'm afraid to seem too whiny and aggressive, whereas a man would be seen as fighting the battle. Will I be viewed as too aggressive if I ask for additional resources or kill myself on deals? (Female Investment Banker)

People may understand tacit behavioral expectations and believe that they will gain approval for conforming to those expectations, yet they may still be unwilling to do so because of the role's incongruence with central and valued aspects of their identity. Because people use their self-presentations to create, maintain, or modify a public self that is congruent with their ideal self (Baumeister, 1982), the attractiveness of the person's role model's behavior and the person's degree of identification with role models significantly affects whether they will adopt the behavior (Foote, 1951). Since most of their colleagues were men, the women in this study tended to experience identification and self-congruence as significant hurdles. In contrast to their male peers, they tended to note how they differed from their associates and to state that they found it difficult to envision adopting styles that they felt to be dramatically at odds with their self-concepts.

The lack of female role models combined with women's beliefs about the efficacy of role modeling led to few women using role modeling identity work strategies favored by their male colleagues. Instead women worked toward their new professional identities by attempting to maintain strong congruence between who they felt they were and who they portrayed themselves to be in public. This "personal crafting" (Ibarra, 1999) identity work strategy was at odds with the organizational model of success for role transitions, and it was accompanied by a slower progress toward a new professional identity that befitted the organization. The use of illegitimate identity work and the slower progress in making the necessary identity transition exacerbated and prolonged women's perceived identity threat.

Transforming Organizational Models of Success Into Impossible Selves

The organizational model of success for managing the required image and identity transition in both firms was one that coupled "acquisitive" image strategies with "role modeling" identity work. This model constitutes one of organizational success, not because it "works" but rather because it is institutionally acceptable to both the firm and its clients. Therefore, it involves a lower image and identity threat, a reduced necessity for protection strategies, and a faster accomplishment of the transition. The problem for women is that this model provides the outline of a self that is impossible to attain. Possible selves are future images of one's self, either desirable or undesirable, that serve as filters through which people adjust their behavior within their current environment, and as motivations for the future (Markus & Nurius, 1986). For the men in the two firms we studied, the organizational model of success provided outlines of possible selves toward which they could strive. On the contrary, for many of the women in the study, the same organizational model represented an "impossible self" that could neither be attained, nor granted if claimed.

First-hand experiences of second-generation biases led the women to expect their clients to hold gender biases. These expectations, in turn, led women to believe that they would not successfully bridge the gap between their image and identity by using the "acquisitive" image strategies of their male peers. Further, the stereotype threat stemming from the incongruence between a demeanor that confirms a professional role and a female gender role may make the choice of a protective image strategy appear less costly than an acquisitive image strategy (Wiley & Eskilson, 1982). Adopting a protective image strategy might occur for women for two reasons: It reduces the risk of disapproval for "acting like men" and failing, and it reduces the potential threat to their self-concept as women. Over time, these processes may lead women to become entrenched in a gender-typed professional identity. Repeated success with "protective" strategies (i.e., not incurring disapproval), therefore, may solidify for women the identity implied by the protective demeanor (e.g., "competent but not bold," "smart but quiet"), thus reinforcing gender stereotypes about interaction styles. Further, this perpetuates and fuels the categorization between genders. It is also a self-reinforcing dynamic. The hidden and often unconscious second-generation gender biases provoke behaviors among female professionals that inadvertently reinforce the very gender stereotypes they are working to escape. Thus, we suggest that for women working in demographically skewed professional contexts, the combination of second-generation bias and stereotype threat can transform organizational models of success into impossible selves.

Creating Virtuous Developmental Cycles for Women

The model we have presented so far is static; it does not address the question of what are the conditions under which people change their image and negotiate new identities, or, alternatively, become entrenched in those they have negotiated previously (Swann, 1987). Just as people can get locked into a particular demeanor, they can also have experiences that free them to experiment with other possibilities. A positive experience with a different interaction style, when it is visible, can provide a window for negotiating not only a new demeanor but also a different professional identity. As illustrated in the quotation below, the positive cycle that ensues from visible success with a client is self-reinforcing because resources and approval garnered in one context serve as currency for approval and resources in subsequent contexts:

> You hear that women aren't "bold." What turned my career around was that I got two accounts where the CFO was a woman. They demanded that I be there at the meetings. When they called, I was the one they wanted to talk to. That's critical—having a client who loves you, when you're the one who gets the phone calls. If you've got the client relationships, the internal relations are easy. If you're on good terms with the person at your level, they can feed you with information, you can run ideas by them. Often people run an idea by the client first—"I'm thinking of proposing this to my boss, what do you

think?" Then you can be bold in the meeting with the MDs (Managing Directors). (Female Investment Banker)

Two themes emerged from our data with regard to women's transitions from a protective to a more acquisitive image strategy. The first, as suggested by the quotation above, is that women experience the dynamics of interacting with female clients very differently from the dynamics with male clients. Their accounts suggest that the different cues and expectations that are exchanged in same-gender interactions may provide an opportunity for the junior professional to experiment with a more acquisitive image strategy. Second, a change of organization or department, independent of its demographic composition, may facilitate a move from protective to acquisitive strategies with clients: Two of the women in our sample whom we coded as "acquisitive" were "lateral hires," brought into their firms after several years with other investment banks. Both reported more protective behavior while with their previous employer. Their accounts are consistent with the argument that professional identities solidify, locking people into behavior they might prefer to change. A move to a different group or organization, therefore, may free the person of an earlier protective reputation, allowing for experimentation with more acquisitive approaches. Theoretically, it is also possible that a significant change in a mentoring or role-modeling relationship may lead to similar changes in demeanor. We did not, however, have any data on such a pattern.

DISCUSSION

At the point of role transition, men and women alike experienced a gap between their current professional image and identity and the one required for the new role, which generated threat to their previously successful professional selves and provoked feelings of anxiety. This threat created an impetus for the junior professionals to engage in the processes of image and identity work. Women additionally experienced stereotype threat that highlighted incongruence between their professional role and female gender role. The image strategies and accompanying identity work strategies employed by men and women in response to these threats were very different, as were their consequences: The strategies most used by women were more likely to exacerbate identity threat while those used most by men tended to attenuate it.

Men more aggressively sought to signal credibility by displaying behaviors that conformed to their firm's norms, even when these behaviors felt unnatural. They engaged in self-promotional image strategies, presenting themselves as competent and confident even when this was incongruent with their true feelings. In contrast, through self-protective image strategies, women modestly asserted more neutral, uncertain, or qualified images, in order to avoid disapproval. For example, women sought to prove their competence by demonstrating technical mastery over the long term; in contrast, men were intent on making a positive first impression. Second-generation gender bias decreased the likelihood that women believed they could successfully use self-promotional image strategies; it also shaped their identity work strategies. Men relied on role modeling identity work, which involved experimenting with traits and behaviors selected from a broad array of mostly male role models, whereas women tended to rely on personal crafting identity work, transferring behaviors from their previous successful professional identity to the new role. Women took pride in their reliance on substance rather than form as a more authentic strategy than their male counterparts, yet they were also frustrated with their inability to win superiors' and clients' recognition. Ironically, women's attempts to remain authentic ultimately undermined their ability to find and internalize identities that were congruent with the kind of professional they aspired to become. The combination of stereotype threat and second-generation bias transformed the possible self outlined by the organizational model of success into an impossible self for the women.

The current study contributes to our understanding of the paucity of women in senior leadership positions by identifying specific identity mechanisms that complicate junior women's transitions to more senior roles. While the notion of developing a leader identity as a critical element of leadership development has gained popularity (Avolio & Gardner, 2005; DeRue & Ashford, 2010; Lord & Hall, 2005; van Knippenberg, van Knippenberg, De Cremer, and Hogg 2004), it has not been linked to theory and research on the gender dynamics associated with leader identity development. Becoming a leader, as our data illustrate, involves a set of relational and social processes through which one comes to see oneself, and is seen by others, as a leader (DeRue & Ashford, 2010). Receiving validation for one's self-view as a leader bolsters self-confidence, which increases one's motivation to lead (Chan & Drasgow, 2001; Kark & van Dijk, 2007) and to seek new opportunities to practice leadership (Day & Harrison, 2007; Day, Harrison, and Halpin, 2009). In many contexts, validation depends on comformity to cultural prescriptions for leadership behaviors, which remain prototypically male and are sustained implicitly by the leadership styles of a firm's most senior and most successful members. Failing to receive validation for one's leadership attempts diminishes self-confidence as well as the motivation to seek developmental opportunities, experiment, and take on new leadership roles (Day et al., 2009). This also weakens one's self-identity as a leader (DeRue & Ashford, 2010) at the individual level and the firm's pipeline in the aggreagate. By calling attention to the impact of gender on the processes of claiming and granting a leader identity, we extend current theorizing about leadership development as an identity transition (Day et al., 2009; DeRue & Ashford, 2010; Ibarra, Carter, and Silva, 2010).

Because increasing diversity at the top of organizations depends on breaking the image and identity cycle described here, one potentially fruitful yet underinvestigated area for further research concerns moderators of the relationship between a firm's current representation of women in the upper echelons and junior members' identity work. For example, we expect that a firm's socialization and career development practices, which are the mechanisms by which they inculcate display rules, may be expected to exacerbate or attenuate the dynamics described here. While some firms strongly socialize new employees to internalize and enact their display rules in a standard way, others explicitly encourage newcomers to express their personal identities and incorporate them into their professional identities (Cable, Gino, & Staats, 2013). By pushing a uniform view of a successful professional, the former are likely to exacerbate the effects of second-generation bias, while the latter, by endorsing multiple possible models successful professionals, may serve to attenuate it.

Similarly, task moderators relate to the nature of the job or role because these vary in the extent to which self-presentation serves as an important signal or proxy for competence. We hypothesize that gender is more likely to serve as a proxy for status and competence in the absence of information based on direct prolonged experience. Thus, the effects we describe here are likely magnified in roles such as those we studied because professional-client relations involve delivery of an intangible service and consist of brief, episodic encounters. Likewise, the importance of demeanor as a signal of competence may be attenuated in jobs that are more specialized, involve longer-term relationships, or have more "objective" performance indicators. Obviously, research in a broader variety of firms, encompassing a greater range of practices and job types, is needed to clarify the boundaries of the perspective developed here.

Exploration of situational factors that affect which strategies are most prevalently used should also prove fertile. Tajfel (1981) argued that strategy choice is contingent upon the extent to which group members view the intergroup power relationship as stable—unchanging over time—and legitimate, based on principles accepted by both groups. This is consistent with Ely's (1995) finding that women lawyers in skewed demographic contexts were more likely to assume stereotypic gender identities (by either "attempting to pass" or by overvaluing "female" traits), while women in more demographically balanced firms were more likely to resist being pigeonholed into either category.

The notion that displaying role-appropriate images is an important hurdle for women working in male-dominated occupations is consistent with previous studies. The results of this study support this claim but also suggest some important new directions for theory and research. Our work extends recent thinking on the notion of identity threat as both the cause and consequence of image work, and we shed additional light on the social processes that motivate distinctiveness or social creativity strategies and, as such, transform organizational models of success into "impossible selves" for professional women.

NOTES

1. After participants were selected, three women dropped out of the consulting firm sample; two transitioned to part-time work, and one decided to leave the firm. As a result, there were three more men than women in the sample.
2. Evidence of threat was manifest in the comments of 13 of the 15 women and 13 of the 19 men.

REFERENCES

Arkin, R. M. (1981). Self-presentation styles. In J. T. Tedeschi (Ed.), *Impression management theory and social psychological research* (pp. 311–333). New York, NY: Academic Press.

Ashforth, B. E., & Humphrey, R. H. (1993). Emotional labor in service roles: The influence of identity. *Academy of Management Review, 18*(1), 88–115.

Avolio, B. J., & Gardner, W. L. (2005). Authentic leadership development: Getting to the root of positive forms of leadership. *Leadership Quarterly, 16*, 315–338.

Bandura, A. (1986). *Social foundations of thought and action: A social cognitive theory.* Englewood Cliffs, NJ: Prentice-Hall.

Baron, J. N., & Pfeffer, J. (1994). The social psychology of organizations and inequality. *Social Psychology Quarterly, 57*(3), 190–209.

Baumeister, R. F. (1982). A self-presentation view of social phenomena. *Psychological Bulletin, 91*(1), 3–26.

Becker, H. S., & Carper, J. (1956). The elements of identification with an occupation. *American Sociological Review, 21*(3), 341–348.

Becker, H. S., & Strauss, A. L. (1956). Careers, personality, and adult socialization. *American Journal of Sociology, 62*(3), 253–263.

Berger, J., Fisech, M. H., Norman, R. Z., & Selditch, M. (1977). *Status characteristics and social interaction: An expectation states approach.* New York, NY: Elsevier.

Branscombe, N. R., & Ellemers, N. (1998). Coping with group-based discrimination: Individualistic versus group-level strategies. In J. Swim & C. Stangor (Eds.), *Prejudice: The target's perspective* (pp. 243–266). San Diego, CA: Academic Press.

Cable, D. M., Gino, F., & Staats, B. R. (2013). Breaking them in or eliciting their best? Reframing socialization around newcomers' authentic self-expression. *Administrative Science Quarterly, 58*(1), 1–36.

Calás, M. B., & Smircich, L. (1991). Voicing seduction to silence leadership. *Organization Studies, 12*(4), 567–601.

Catalyst. (2014). Catalyst census: Women board directors. New York, NY: Catalyst.

Catalyst. (2015). Women CEOs of the S&P 500. New York, NY: Catalyst.

Chan, K. Y., & Drasgow, F. (2001). Toward a theory of individual differences and leadership: Understanding the motivation to lead. *Journal of Applied Psychology, 86*(3), 481–498.

Creed, W. D., Scully, M. A., & Austin, J. R. (2002). Clothes make the person? The tailoring of legitimating accounts and the social construction of identity. *Organization Science, 13*(5), 475–496.

Day, D. V., & Harrison, M. M. (2007). A multilevel, identity-based approach to leadership development. *Human Resource Management Review, 17*(4), 360–373.

Day, D. V., Harrison, M. M., & Halpin, S. M. (2009). *An integrative approach to leader development: Connecting adult development, identity, and expertise.* New York, NY: Psychology Press.

Deaux, K., & Major, B. (1987). Putting gender into context: An interactive model of gender-related behavior. *Psychological Review, 95,* 369–389. doi: 10.1037/0033-295X.94.3.369

DeRue, D. S., & Ashford, S. J. (2010). Who will lead and who will follow? A social process of leadership identity construction in organizations. *Academy of Management Review, 35*(4), 627–647.

Eagly, A. H., & Carli, L. C. (2007). *Through the labyrinth: The truth about how women become leaders.* Boston, MA: Harvard Business School Press.

Eagly, A. H., & Wood, W. (1991). Explaining sex differences in social behavior: A meta-analytic perspective. *Personality and Social Psychology Bulletin, 17*(3), 306–315.

Eisenhardt, K. (1989). Building theories from case study research. *Academy of Management Review, 14*(4), 532–550.

Ely, R. J. (1995). The power in demography: Women's social constructions of gender identity at work. *Academy of Management Journal, 38*(3), 589–634.

Ely, R. J., Ibarra, H., & Kolb, D. M. (2011). Taking gender into account: Theory and design for women's leadership development programs. *Academy of Management Learning & Education, 10*(3), 474–493.

Ely, R. J., & Meyerson, D. E. (2000). Theories of gender in organizations: A new approach to organizational analysis and change. *Research in Organizational Behavior, 22,* 103–151.

Falbo, T., Hazen, M., & Linimon, D. (1982). Costs of selecting power bases associated with the opposite sex. *Sex Roles, 8,* 147–157.

Foote, N. N. (1951). Identification as the basis for a theory of motivation. *American Sociological Review, 16*(1), 14–21.

Gibson, D. (1996, August). *Idols and ideals: A multi-level view of role modeling in organizations.* Paper presented at the Academy of Management annual meeting, Dallas, TX.

Goffman, E. (1956). *The presentation of self in everyday life.* New York, NY: Doubleday.

Hochschild, A. R. (1983). *The managed heart.* Los Angeles, CA: University of California Press.

Ibarra, H. (1999). Provisional selves: Experimenting with image and identity in professional adaptation. *Administrative Science Quarterly, 44*(4), 764–791.

Ibarra, H., Carter, N. M., & Silva, C. (2010). Why men still get more promotions than women. *Harvard Business Review, 88*(9), 80–126.

Kanter, R. M. (1977). *Men and women of the corporation.* New York, NY: Basic Books.

Kark, R., & van Dijk, D. (2007). Motivation to lead, motivation to follow: The role of the self-regulatory focus in leadership processes. *Academy of Management Review, 32*(2), 500–528.

Kolb, D. M., & McGinn, K. (2009). From gender and negotiation to gendered negotiation. *Negotiation and Conflict Management Research, 2*(1), 1–16.

Lord, R. G., & Hall, R. J. (2005). Identity, deep structure and the development of leadership skill. *Leadership Quarterly, 16*(4), 591–615.

Markus, H., & Nurius, P. (1986). Possible selves. *American Psychologist, 41*(9), 954–969.

Meeker, B., & Weitzel-O'Neill, P. (1985). Sex roles and interpersonal behavior in task-oriented groups. In J. Berger, & M. Zelditch (Eds.), *Status, rewards, and influence* (pp. 379–405). San Francisco, CA: Jossey-Bass.

Nieva, V. F., & Gutek, B. A. (1981). *Women and work.* New York, NY: Praeger.

Petriglieri, J. L. (2011). Under threat: Responses to and the consequences of threats to individuals' identities. *Academy of Management Review, 36*(4), 641–662.

Rafaeli, A., & Sutton, R. I. (1989). The expression of emotion in organizational life. *Research in Organizational Behavior, 11,* 1–42.

Rafaeli, A., & Sutton, R. I. (1991). Emotional contrast strategies as means of social influence: Lessons from criminal interrogators and bill collectors. *Academy of Management Journal, 34*(4), 749–775.

Roberts, L. M. (2005). Changing faces: Professional image construction in diverse organizational settings. *Academy of Management Review, 30*(4), 685–711.

Schein, V. (1973). The relationship between sex role stereotypes and requisite management characteristics. *Journal of Applied Psychology, 57,* 95–100.

Snow, D. A., & Anderson, L. (1987). Identity work among the homeless: The verbal construction and avowal of personal identities. *American Journal of Sociology, 92*(6), 1336–1371.

Strauss, A., & Corbin, J. (1998). *Basics of qualitative research: Procedures and techniques for developing grounded theory.* Thousand Oaks, CA: Sage.

Sturm, S. (2001). Second generation employment discrimination: A structural approach. *Columbia Law Review, 101*(3), 458–568.

Swann, W. B. (1987). Identity negotiation: Where two roads meet. *Journal of Personality and Social Psychology, 53*(6), 1038–1051.

Tajfel, H. C. (1981). *Human groups and social categories: Studies in social psychology.* Cambridge, England: Cambridge University Press.

Tsui, A. S., & O'Reilly, C. A. III. (1989). Beyond simple demographic effects: The importance of relational demography in superior–subordinate dyads. *Academy of Management Journal, 32*(2), 402–423.

van Knippenberg, D., van Knippenberg, B., De Cremer, D., & Hogg, M. A. (2004). Leadership, self, and identity: A review and research agenda. *Leadership Quarterly, 15*(6), 825–856.

Wiley, M. G., & Eskilson, A. (1982). The interaction of sex and power base on perceptions of managerial effectiveness. *Academy of Management Journal, 25*(3), 671–677.

CHAPTER 3

COLLABORATIVE THEORY BUILDING ON WOMEN'S LEADERSHIP

An Exercise Toward Responsible Leadership

Valerie Stead
Lancaster University Management School

Carole Elliott
University of Roehampton Business School

Belinda Blevins-Knabe
University of Arkansas at Little Rock

Emily Chan
Claremont Graduate University

Kathleen S. Grove
Indiana University-Purdue University, Indianapolis

Maylon Hanold
Seattle University

Amy E. Smith
University of Massachusetts Boston

Theorizing Women and Leadership, pages 37–49
Copyright © 2017 by Information Age Publishing
All rights of reproduction in any form reserved.

This chapter discusses a collaborative process designed to stimulate theory building about women's leadership that we propose as a model for responsible leadership practice. Ideas of responsible leadership practice address how social responsibility and leadership interrelate (Waldman, 2011). Interest in this interrelationship has risen in the wake of the recent economic crisis, raising concerns for gender equality in leadership roles as well as perceptions that business leaders' decision making and behavior are often unethical and irresponsible (Voegtlin, Patzer, & Scherer, 2012). Responsible leadership is also attracting attention in response to and as a means of calling into question "deficient" leadership theories (Waldman & Galvin, 2008). These theories include capitalist models of leadership that do not take wider stakeholder needs and claims into account (Maak & Pless, 2006) and focus largely on the internal organization, failing to address the economic and moral implications of globalization (Voegtlin et al., 2012). The growing body of literature on responsible leadership emphasizes theorizing and gives relatively limited attention to models of responsible leadership practice.

In this chapter we draw on the experience of a collaborative theory building exercise regarding women's leadership experiences as a foundation upon which we propose a model that facilitates and enables dialogue. The model, which emerges from experience and practice in a higher education context, allows for inclusive processes to attend to competing and diverse stakeholder claims. The strength of this setting is that group members, in collaboration, share a common set of values and commitment to issues of social justice and ethical practice. In addition, in our day-to-day working lives we engage with students and colleagues from diverse backgrounds and are exposed to similar organizational structures and models of leadership. We recognize that other settings may not offer such advantages and that the development of collaborative processes may, therefore, involve additional labor.

We constructed the proposed model by reflecting on the experience of engaging in a process-led event and exploring the ways that it stimulates critique of dominant leadership approaches that assume a top-down hierarchy and limited engagement with stakeholders. We examined how the women's leadership theory building process design, based on principles of inclusivity and enquiry, offers potential for a model of leadership practice that is more distributed and less hierarchical. This proposed model, we argue, enables a responsible and more relevant approach to the complexity of contemporary leadership. Our contribution is threefold. First, we illustrate how we can draw on a design for emergent theory building about women's leadership to inform processes of responsible leadership practice. We provide detailed steps that future researchers could follow when theorizing around key challenges in relation to women's leadership. Second, we propose a model of leadership development that attends to the facilitation and enabling of dialogue toward ethical decision-making, which recognizes the need to balance a diversity of claims. Third, we propose that this model may have value as a framework for addressing a range of social problems and issues encountered by leaders, including issues of fairness and equity, sustainability, and development.

THEORETICAL CONTEXT

Maak's (2007) exploration of responsible leadership in a global stakeholder society as a relational and inherently moral practice provides the foundation for our reflexive exploration. Responsible leadership differs from traditional leader–follower understandings of leadership by recognizing how leaders must acknowledge and manage the moral complexity resulting from multiple relationships with relevant stakeholders (Maak, 2007). As a relational practice, leadership "occurs in social processes of interaction with those who affect or are affected by leadership and have a stake in the purpose and vision of the leadership relationship" (Maak, 2007, p. 334). Responsible leadership not only involves interaction with and between different stakeholders, but it is also concerned with balancing the needs and concerns of various stakeholder groups (Waldman, 2011). Responsible leadership is, therefore, dynamic and requires pro-active engagement with, and consideration of, stakeholders. Inevitably, this process will involve dealing with complex moral dilemmas that emerge from different sociocultural contexts and value bases (Maak, 2007).

Responsible leadership, thus, has ethics at its core (Ciulla, 2006), and it follows that we view leadership as a social-relational and ethical phenomenon that takes places in sites of social interaction (Maak & Pless, 2006). In spite of significant interest in leadership and its practice in a global society, only limited research has examined ways in which responsible leadership might be developed and sustained (Maak, 2007). Our goal is to address this gap by describing responsible leadership as it occurred in the context of a group of women scholars working on a collaborative theory building exercise intended to move the needle forward for women's leadership theory.

COLLABORATIVE THEORY BUILDING

This collaborative exercise, which we call the colloquium model, formed part of a larger initiative to generate and advance theories of women and leadership. The design, developed by women's leadership scholar Susan R. Madsen and research theorist Julia Storberg-Walker, and drawing on theory building research by Gioia and Pitre (1989) and Lynham (2002), was developed in recognition of a dearth of critical research on women's experiences of leadership. The dominance of leadership theory based on the male experience has resulted in a lack of work that attends to the theorizing of women's leadership, thus sustaining a dominant male leadership discourse (Calas & Smircich, 1996; Lamsa & Sintonen, 2001; Stead & Elliott, 2009).

The collaborative theory-building model, intended as a means to address a gap in women's leadership theorizing, aimed to bring together multiple perspectives from researchers working in diverse areas connected to women's leadership. Core to the model is a focus on leadership as process, illuminating its dynamic and shifting nature (Cunliffe & Eriksen, 2011). Also implicit in the model's design is the notion of leadership as responsible—as accounting for and accountable to multiple stakeholders. The colloquium model was thus designed as a collaborative theorizing activity, with the intentional inclusion of the practitioner perspective. Within this collaborative frame, the theory building development process within the group was facilitated rather than directed. Collaboration necessitated an attention to inclusivity across disciplines and views that challenged normative approaches to thinking about and developing leadership that are typically leader centric (Jackson & Parry, 2008). A key feature of the model design is to broaden the hitherto limited experiences and perspectives that tend to (re)produce dominant ways of thinking about and practicing leadership (Stead & Elliott, 2009).

REFLECTIONS ON THE COLLABORATIVE EXERCISE

The empirical foundation for our exploration was our participation in this exercise as members of one of nine collaboratories in the colloquium model formed to focus on the phenomenon of second generation gender bias (SGGB). When we refer to SGGB, we draw on research by Ely, Ibarra, and Kolb (2011), who define SGGB broadly as "the powerful yet often invisible barriers to women's advancement that arise from cultural beliefs about gender, as well as workplace structures, practices, and patterns of interaction that inadvertently favor men" (p. 475). In this context, groups were labeled "collaboratories" to convey a desired way of working that had collaboration at its core, including cooperation, building social capital, trust, informal and formal communication, and avoidance of hierarchy. We follow Cogburn (2003), who defines a collaboratory as a "new networked organizational form that also includes social processes; collaboration techniques; formal and informal communication; and agreement on norms, principles, values, and rules" (p. 86).

Significant to the model of responsible leadership practice that we developed below was the physical co-location of members of the collaboratories. First, this had the benefit of participants, united in a common purpose, meeting and getting to know each other, enabling the development of a climate of trust (Dietz & Hartog, 2006). Second, this provided a basis for the development of higher communication behaviors that enhance learning, including surfacing and questioning assumptions, as a means to challenge and generate possibilities for change (Argyris, 2004). Bringing the collaboratories together facilitated the process of developing understanding about a subject area through a series of exercises. The leaders of each collaboratory were tasked with facilitating the process with clear instructions that there was no specific agenda or desired outcome. For instance, one of the earliest small group activities at the colloquium deepened our understanding of each other's purpose and aims. In round-table fashion, each participant answered two questions: (a) What do you want to contribute to this colloquium?; and (b) What do you want to learn? This exercise led to an exchange during which individuals described their academic backgrounds (e.g., psychology, law, women in sport leadership, sociology, leadership learning, higher education, and public management) and various identities (e.g., administrator, PhD student, assistant professor). At the level of process, this exchange constituted a first step in the emergence of a shared system of meaning that sought to balance a diversity of multiple and conflicting values, which Maak and Pless (2006) claim to be vital to responsible leadership practice.

A subsequent task was an exercise in which each collaboratory explored the construction of theory based on a theory building diagram, a continuation of lessons from the theory building videos, and readings provided on the Moodle site prior to the colloquium. After a large group session to discuss theory building, our collaboratory began working with Lynham's (2002) model on theorizing to practice. The diagram sought to link the phenomenon of SGGB with theorizing. This process provided a meta-framework for viewing our focus. Simultaneously, we individually wrote on sticky pads terms, concepts, theories, and popular names related to second-generation gender bias. The sticky notes were placed on the relevant parts of the theory-building diagram; these included theories relevant to women in leadership (role congruity, social capital, social identity, representative bureaucracy, etc.) and popular terms (lean in, ban bossy, etc.).

Throughout this process, the underlying assumptions of our collaboratory work evolved to include these ideas: everyone has something to offer and holds a perspective, experience, and/or training that brings something new; everyone joins in the process; and we are non-hierarchical in our organization of the activity. Notably, although we did not know each other prior to our first round table, our conversations were open, lively, and full of participation. Over the next two days, through dialogue, sharing and "brainstorming," our collaboratory began to identify the phenomenon of SGGB, based on our reading of the literature as well as our own experiences. The process was a collaborative one, during which everyone added her knowledge to each step. The group facilitators kept the process moving, but there was no formal hierarchy in the group. Everyone had a marker and access to large sheets of presentation paper. Discussion ebbed and flowed as a new idea was posted. There were moments of silence and thoughtful reflection, and there was inquiry and dialogue when a concept was introduced that others did not know. A collegial respect for all contributions and knowledge existed, and each idea was examined thoughtfully and carefully, with no competition to produce the "best" idea as all ideas were welcome.

IDENTIFYING RESPONSIBLE LEADERSHIP PROCESSES

Analysis of our reflections on being involved in our collaboratory led us to identify processes used to explore the phenomenon of SGGB. Here we detail a series of four iterative and mutually reinforcing processes that combine with the use of epistemic objects to illustrate a model of responsible leadership practice (see Figure 3.1). These processes include: scoping, dialogue as an ethical process, affective and cognitive balancing, and building social capital.

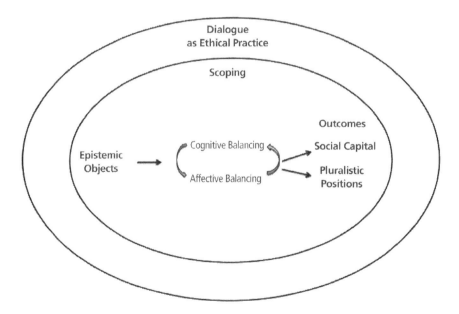

Figure 3.1 Toward a model of responsible leadership practice.

Scoping

Scoping describes the process of sharing ideas and knowledge without evaluation or judgment. In relation to our task (i.e., to advance theory on women's leadership by exploring issues of SGGB), the sharing from each stakeholder's perspective was important to build a multi-dimensional and detailed picture of the issue over time. The scoping process included sharing articles we read and identifying different theories and ideas. Relinquishing the need to set either an agenda or a well-defined goal was effective in enabling a shared sense of power.

Dialogue as an Ethical Process

Dialogue has been explored as a way to have deeper conversations (Gerzon, 2006; Palus & Drath, 2001) in which one of the key aims of responsible leadership, namely a sound process in which shared meanings emerge, can be met. Palus and Drath (2001) noted ways in which the practice of dialogue can be difficult. In the course of exploring theories and ideas related to SGGB, dialogue was used as a means to move the group forward from scoping and the exchange of ideas, toward development of a shared system of meaning. Dialogue involves active engagement with others, and a key aspect of dialogue is suspension of assumptions. In this exercise, dialogue was used not only as a means to share and describe experiences through stories, but also to hold disparate ontological perspectives "in the middle" (Palus & Drath, 2001, p. 29). Here the key shared elements consisted less of language, culture, and education due to the diversity of these aspects among us, but rather a recognition of the experiences of each of us that resulted in an intellectual awareness and feeling that SGGB is a veritable phenomenon. The sharing of power within the process of dialogue, the engagement of everyone in relating experiences and perspectives, and the suspension of goal setting helped to constitute an ethical process. The co-creation of power through the ebb and flow of where our discussions centered meant that no participant felt that she had to keep owning or directing ways of knowing, nor did the participants feel obliged to act as simply followers of directions set by others. The process gave equal power to diverse ontological and epistemological perspectives and allowed the group to use discourse effectively as a tool of discovery.

Cognitive and Affective Balancing

One useful aspect of dialogue that we identified was the balancing of multiple and conflicting values as both an affective and cognitive process. The facilitation role is instrumental in holding space that enables values to emerge and be aired. From a cognitive perspective this involved two types of knowing, what we know and how we know. What we know was grounded in our professional backgrounds, and how we know was based on our experiential knowledge. As various passions, frustrations, hopes, and experiences emerged, holding space for the affective was critical to allowing the dialogue to continue. As women, talking about SGGB is far more than a cognitive experience. Despite our abilities to discuss SGGB from intellectual viewpoints, we had an emotional investment as well. Our passion and emotional investment as women who have experienced SGGB and our empathic selves told stories of women we knew, either through research or personal connections, and kept us moving forward, connected by the sense that we were doing significant and meaningful work. Dialogue as a process was sustained not only by balancing multiple ideas, perspective, and understandings, but also by balancing feelings and felt senses of SGGB. In this way, cognitive and affective balancing held the space for dialogue.

Building Social Capital

One outcome of our dialogue held by both cognitive and affective balancing was increased social capital of individual members of the group. Social capital is the collection of resources gained through social relationships (Burt, 2002; Coleman, 1988). In our collaborative theory building process, social capital took the form of shared values, trust, and relationships. Social capital was gained by contributing a wide array of thoughts and feelings about which we simultaneously recognized moments of synergy and plurality. Through dialogue emerged shared values, trust, networks, and relationships. Deepened insights, both cognitive and affective, continued to be voiced. An inclusive atmosphere was established because we were able to keep talking and contributing without the constraint of wondering "How does this fit in?" or "Will they judge me?" As the level of awareness of social capital of each member grew, we had a richer conceptualization of SGGB, an increased understanding of how SGGB worked in the "real" world, and a stronger network of colleagues to whom we could turn for future collaboration and advice. The inherently inclusive process drew out the strengths of each group member and provided the scaffolding for building social capital.

The Use of Epistemic Objects

The iterative processes described above were enabled through the use of epistemic objects such as frameworks or theories that helped to position us and our values in relation to the task and enabled dialogue as a means to facilitate construction of a coherent meaning from ideas that were constantly changing and often messy. The use of epistemic objects also brought into relief multiple agendas and illuminated multiple—and, at times, competing—values and agendas. Exploring the phenomenon of SGGB through different frames brought into sharp relief both synergy and divergence of ideas and views. In our collaborative exercise, epistemic objects were not subject related, but rather were concerned with the process of knowledge and theory building; for example, we explored different ways in which we might talk about knowledge either from our experience (inductive) or from known evidence (deductive). Also, epistemic objects might take different forms in different settings; for instance, the use of different lenses such as a functionalist versus a distributed perspective. In this exercise, abstract and conceptual questions from theory building helped ground the process, encouraging us to consider, for example, how we might think about or evidence SGGB as a phenomenon by adopting a particular lens. Doing so was important because we recognized that we could not assume a shared view or understanding of the topic (i.e., SGGB) and provided a means of co-constructing our understanding. Exploring different theoretical explanations of SGGB (e.g., by examining our inductive or deductive knowledge of the topic) allowed our diverse theoretical viewpoints to unfold before us. For example, understanding SGGB as a socially constructed phenomenon stimulated discussions of the different ways in which SGGB is (re)produced, including in the media through written text and visual imagery, and in organizations through daily interactions and work-based practices. Alternatively, we also discussed SGGB as a measureable phenomenon and how it is manifest through statistics and trends, including a focus on the disparity between numbers of women in senior leadership roles and women entering managerial roles. These different ways of thinking about SGGB spanned both positivist and non-positivist traditions, adding to individuals' breadth and depth of knowledge and also providing a broad mapping of the topic.

Writing these discussions on large sheets of paper to demonstrate our thinking enabled us to see where manifestations of SGGB and theoretical explanations connected or were demarcated. In other words, the use of theory building ideas invited difference and dissimilarity that drew upon our diverse theoretical standpoints—psychology, sociology, positivist, social constructionist, educational, and practical perspectives about women's leadership. Some ideas built upon other ideas, but certain ideas with less obvious connection to the subject also became part of the norm. For example, discussions moved from defining SGGB to considering the values inherent in definitions and including our own values. We also juxtaposed ideas from the literature with our own observations of SGGB in practice, including our personal experience and as understood and elaborated upon in non-scholarly reports, surveys, and statistics.

TOWARD A MODEL
OF RESPONSIBLE LEADERSHIP PRACTICE

Reflecting the neglect in the literature of alternate views and their effect on the leadership process, our collaborative exercise can be an exemplar for an inclusive process that allows for contributions from people with disparate backgrounds, knowledge, and experience. As such, the exercise acts as a stimulus for exploring fresh ways to think about and practice leadership.

The model (Figure 3.1), based on the iterative processes of dialogue, challenges the assumption of synergistic positioning (Ridder, Hoon, & McCandless Balch, 2014) and the effectiveness of a well-defined goal. Rather, it suggests how an abstract goal may open up more space for dialogue to occur and encourage a pluralistic positioning (Ridder et al., 2014). Ridder and colleagues (2014) employ the terms synergistic and pluralistic positioning in relation to how different phenomena affect theory building. Here, we borrow and adapt the terms to illustrate the way that incorporating processes that stimulate the articulation and exploration of multiple values and beliefs enables theory building that is inclusive rather than theory building that seeks to unify.

The purpose of theory building at this point in the process is to bring difference to the fore and to make explicit multiple views, ideas, and agendas. The iterative processes outlined above promote divergence rather than convergence. They further demonstrate an embracing of not just ideas and concepts that are dissimilar, but also an openness to the various ways that a phenomenon comes into being through different experiences. Pluralistic grounding in this exercise allowed us to resist sense making and meaning making as a first step. Articulating and enabling pluralistic dialogue and cognitive and affective balancing, stimulated by the use of epistemic objects to complicate thinking, can offer a means to unsettle dominant ways of operating and problematizing what counts as knowledge.

CONCLUSION AND FUTURE DIRECTIONS

In this chapter we proposed a model of responsible leadership practice based on the interpretation of our experience of engaging in a collaborative theory building colloquium. We identified that at the core of the model lies an understanding of leadership as a process, alert to leadership's shifting and dynamic nature (Cunliffe & Eriksen, 2011). This understanding requires an approach to leadership practice that is facilitative and is conscious of its responsibility to be accountable to and for multiple stakeholders.

Deeper analysis of our collaborative reflections led to the identification of four iterative and mutually reinforcing processes, which, combined with the use of selected epistemic objects, has led to a model of responsible leadership practice. The model (Figure 3.1), based on the iterative processes of dialogue, challenges the assumption of synergistic positioning (Ridder et al., 2014) and the effectiveness of a well-defined goal. Rather, it suggests ways that an abstract goal may open more spaces for dialogue to occur, thereby encouraging a pluralistic positioning (Ridder et al., 2014) that seeks to reflect the complexities of leadership and the needs and concerns of multiple stakeholders. As noted earlier, this proposed model emerges from experience and practice in a higher education context. Potential (empirical) work could consider exploring how this model might work in workplace contexts with different scales of projects, thereby opening opportunities for further theoretical development. For example, further research could investigate the utility of this model in different cultural contexts and with projects that span diverse social and cultural boundaries. Our reflections pointed to the diversity of cultural and geographical backgrounds among the group of women involved in this exercise. Respect for diversity was helpful in working toward pluralism, including resisting assumptions of participants' knowledge and avoiding setting an agenda. Future research could consider how this proposed model might be operationalized within a multicultural context.

Our model emphasizes the combination of iterative processes with the use of epistemic objects to stimulate and direct dialogue. Future research could examine these processes in more depth, in particular the ways they are operationalized and how and when epistemic objects might be used to best effect. The concept of responsible leadership draws our attention to how it was possible to work as a collective group, to be part of a collaboratory. Although we discuss how this example of responsible leadership in practice involved the group's participation and what emerged from our joint participation, the exercise was established, orchestrated, and facilitated by another group of stakeholders: the women's leadership scholars who designed the theory building process. This chapter contributes to leadership theory by developing a model that illustrates the mutually reinforcing nature of responsible and relational understandings of leadership. That is, responsible leadership is necessarily relational, and the relational cycles go beyond co-located relationships. This development encourages further empirical research to explore the dynamics of these relational cycles, including their facilitation and co-ordination, in order to gain greater insight into how responsible leadership is enacted. Finally, empirical studies could further explore the practical setup of responsible leadership, including the skills and organizational value base required to enable this theory.

REFERENCES

Argyris, C. (2004). Double-loop learning and organizational change. In J. J. Boonstra (Ed.), *Dynamics of organizational change and learning* (pp. 389–402). Chichester, England: John Wiley & Sons Ltd.

Burt, R. S. (2002). The social capital of structural holes. In M. F. Guillen, R. Collins, P. England, & M. Meyer (Eds.), *The new economic sociology: Developments in an emerging field* (pp. 148–190). New York, NY: Russell Sage Foundation.

Calas, M. B., & Smircich, L. (1996). The woman's point of view: Feminist approaches to organization studies. In S. R. Clegg, C. Hardy, & W. R. Nord (Eds.), *Handbook of organization studies* (pp. 218–257). London, England: Sage.

Ciulla, J. B. (2006). Ethics: The heart of leadership. In T. Maak & N. M. Pless (Eds.). *Responsible leadership* (pp. 17–32). Oxon, England: Routledge.

Cogburn, D. L. (2003). HCI in the so-called developing world: What's in it for everyone, *Interactions, 10*(2), 80–87.

Coleman, J. S. (1988). Social capital in the creation of human capital. *American Journal of Sociology, 94,* S95-S120.

Cunliffe, A. L., & Eriksen, M. (2011). Relational leadership. *Human Relations, 64*(11), 1425–1449.

Dietz, G., & Hartog, D. N. D. (2006). Measuring trust inside organisations. *Personnel Review, 35*(5), 557–588.

Ely, R. J., Ibarra, H., & Kolb, D. M. (2011). Taking gender into account: Theory and design for women's leadership development programs. *Academy of Management Learning & Education, 10*(3), 474–493.

Gerzon, M. (2006). *Leading through conflict: How successful leaders transform differences into opportunities.* Cambridge, MA: Harvard Business Press.

Gioia, D. A., & Pitre, E. (1989). Multiple perspectives on theory building. *Academy of Management Review, 15*(4), 584–602.

Jackson, B., & Parry, K. (2008). *A very short, fairly interesting and reasonably cheap book about studying leadership.* London, England: Sage.

Lamsa, A. M., & Sintonen, T. (2001). A discursive approach to understanding women leaders in working life. *Journal of Business Ethics, 34*(3/4), 255–267.

Lynham, S. A. (2002). The general method of theory building research in applied disciplines. *Advances in Developing Human Resources, 4*(3), 221–241.

Maak, T. (2007). Responsible leadership, stakeholder engagement, and the emergence of social capital. *Journal of Business Ethics, 74*(4), 329–343.

Maak, T., & Pless, N. M. (2006). Responsible leadership in a stakeholder society: A relational perspective. *Journal of Business Ethics, 66*(1), 99–115.

Palus, C. J., & Drath, W. H. (2001). Putting something in the middle: An approach to dialogue. *Reflections, 3*(2), 28–39. doi:10.1162/15241730152695216

Ridder, H. G., Hoon, C., & McCandless Baluch, A. (2014). Entering a dialogue: Positioning case study findings towards theory. *British Journal of Management, 25*(2), 373–387.

Stead, V., & Elliott, C. (2009). *Women's leadership.* Basingstoke, England: Palgrave Macmillan.

Voegtlin, C., Patzer, M., & Scherer, A. G. (2012). Responsible leadership in global business: A new approach to leadership and its multi-level outcomes. *Journal of Business Ethics, 105*(1), 1–16.

Waldman, D. A. (2011). Moving forward with the concept of responsible leadership: Three caveats to guide theory and research. *Journal of Business Ethics, 98*, 75–83.

Waldman, D. A., & Galvin, B. M. (2008). Alternative perspectives of responsible leadership. *Organizational Dynamics, 37*(4), 327–341.

CHAPTER 4

CONSTRUCTING
THE DOUBLE BIND

The Discursive Framing
of Gendered Images of Leadership
in *The Chronicle of Higher Education*

Susan V. Iverson
Manhattanville College

Elizabeth J. Allan
University of Maine

Suzanne P. Gordon
Husson University

For decades, it has been argued that women are underrepresented in leadership positions because they are "crowded in dead-end jobs at the bottom and exposed as tokens at the top" (Acker, 1990, p. 143; see also Kanter, 1977; and Schull, Shaw, & Kihl, 2013). To understand this phenomenon, many scholars have shifted away from the premise that women's gendered

Theorizing Women and Leadership, pages 51–68
Copyright © 2017 by Information Age Publishing
All rights of reproduction in any form reserved.

perceptions may be the source of their own leadership limitations, to argue instead that the organization is gendered, and the resulting patterns constrain women's aspirations and possibilities for leadership (Acker, 2006; Eddy & Cox, 2008; Iverson, 2011). Acker (1990) defined a gendered organization as a place where "advantage and disadvantage, exploitation and control, action and emotion, meaning and identity, are patterned through and in terms of a distinction between male and female, masculine and feminine" (p. 146). We argue that the ways in which leadership is commonly understood, and the lenses through which leaders are perceived, may shape understanding and performance of leadership, and could produce differential effects for leaders of all genders. In this paper, we illuminate the potential of discourse theory as an analytic lens to reveal the constitutive effects of dominant gender discourses. We assert that knowledge of leadership discourses and how they operate within higher education will not only provide educational leaders with understandings of how dominant discourses shape, and may constrain, possibilities for their performance of leadership, but additionally that our use of critical/feminist discourse analysis will provide scholars with an analytic tool for advancing theory on women and leadership.

In order to better understand the gendered constructions of leadership in U.S. higher education, we sought to identify and analyze discourses taken up to construct images of leadership. Higher education, like any complex social system, encounters problems that need solutions, and leaders within these academic institutions have "some commonalities with leadership in general" but also face "special challenges" (Sathye, 2004, para. 2) in this unique context. Unlike other contexts (e.g., private businesses or government agencies), leaders in higher education have more diverse stakeholders (e.g., students, employees, community, and funding agencies), which raises questions about what it means to lead in this context (Sathye, 2004).

We focused our analysis on images of leadership conveyed in *The Chronicle of Higher Education* because it is one of the most widely read periodicals focused on higher education in North America. Published weekly, *The Chronicle* has a readership of more than 315,000 college and university administrators and faculty members, and as such, it provides an important window through which to analyze the predominant discourses related to leadership in U.S. higher education. In analyzing gendered images of leadership that emerge from writings in *The Chronicle of Higher Education*, we are not accepting language as simply a reflection of journalists' perspectives or the views of those quoted. *The Chronicle* is a mediating site that carries and circulates discourses that contribute to constructing perceptions of leadership. These discourses are seldom questioned and thus tend to eclipse alternative possibilities for constructing images of female leaders, thereby influencing and shaping perspectives of women in positions of leadership in higher education. We employ a critical/feminist discourse analysis to explore the text as part of institutional and discursive practices in which they are embedded (Gavey, 1989; Smith, 2013). Like others who examine text to uncover how discourses both reflect and shape identities (Allan, Gordon, & Iverson, 2006; Echner & Prasad, 2003; Rhee & Sagaria, 2004), we draw upon *The Chronicle* to reveal insights about discourses of leadership as they relate to higher education.

This examination of gendered constructions of leadership depicted in *The Chronicle of Higher Education* provides a valuable opportunity to consider ways in which dominant discourses may contribute to shaping gendered constructions in leadership. Understanding the discursive constitution of these images is important because discourses "as systematic sets of meanings, regulate how we understand who we are [and] . . . constrain and shape possibilities for action" (Blackmore, 1999, pp. 16–17). Theorizing may also be constrained as scholars draw from available discourses to make sense of data and build theories about leadership. Identifying dominant discourses that reflect and shape contemporary images of leadership in higher education has potential to help leaders be more strategic about how they re/position themselves in dynamic and complex college and university environments.

THEORETICAL FRAMING: DISCOURSE AND GENDER

For this analysis of leadership images, we draw upon understandings of discourse largely influenced by the work of French philosopher Michel Foucault (Allan, Iverson, & Ropers-Huilman, 2010; Baxter, 2003; Mills, 1997; Weedon, 1997). Informed by this body of work, we understand discourses in the plural sense to be dynamic constellations of words and images that legitimate and produce a given reality (Allan, 2008). Thus, it is through discourse that we come to interpret the physical and social aspects of the world in which we live and also our sense of self in relation to these realities (Mills, 1997). Since discourses serve as lenses for making sense of the world and ourselves in relation to it, they shape both thought and practice. Thus *discursive practice* is a term that refers to practices produced by/through discourse (Baxter, 2003). In this investigation we frame leadership as a form of discursive practice.

People construct meaning on the basis of their "available stock of discursive resources" (Luke, 1995, p. 15). However, in any society, some discourses are taken up and supported more readily than others. For this reason, these discourses can be labeled dominant, while others are considered to provide alternatives to the normative ways of making sense of everyday life in a particular society (Blackmore, 1999; Mills, 1997; Thomas & Davies,

2005). Discourses taken up more readily tend to be reaffirmed through their institutionalization, and, as a result, other discourses may not appear as obvious or familiar.

Dominant discourses can be identified most easily by the way in which they appear to be "natural." For instance, the dominant discourses of femininity and masculinity provide parameters for acceptable behavior on the part of women and men in a particular context. The discursive production of the "good mother," by example, would involve self-sacrifice, "always smiling and understanding" (Powell, 2010, p. 38) and exhibiting "boundless, unflagging, and total love" (Douglas & Michaels, 2004, p. 15). Discourses, thus, produce subjectivities; that is, ways of being, identities, and ways of behaving (Gavey, 1989; Weedon, 1997). Discourses also have a (self)regulatory effect; as with mothering, "everyone watches us, we watch ourselves, and other mothers and we watch ourselves watching ourselves" (Douglas & Michaels, 2004, p. 6). As a result, it comes to be seen as normal or natural for women and men to perform in ways that fall within these discursive boundaries (Allan, 2008).

REVIEW OF LITERATURE: GENDER AND LEADERSHIP

Early notions of leadership focused on the individual, typically represented as "the great man," who successfully leads, regardless of environmental influences, through the skilled use of personal attributes, interpersonal abilities, and technical management skills (Bensimon & Neumann, 1993; Kezar, Carducci, & Contreras-McGavin, 2006). More recently, scholars have expanded the conceptualization of leadership to include the role of followers, the constantly changing environment, and variable power, carried by campus culture, gender, and race (Amey, 2005; Eddy & VanDerLinden, 2006; Kezar et al., 2006).

Some studies examining the influences of gender on leadership suggest a distinction between the preferred leadership processes of men (with a tendency toward autonomous authoritative processes) and those of women (with a preference for collaborative and relational processes) (Holmes & Marra, 2004; Kezar et al., 2006; Paris, Howell, Dorman, & Hanges, 2009), labeling women's ways of leading as "caring and sharing" (Acker, 2012, p. 412). However, several scholars have argued that non-cognitive skills— stereotypically feminine traits that were viewed as "women's ways of leading"—can matter in workplace success, thus elevating compassion, care, and relational behavior in importance for effective leadership (Goleman, Boyatzis, & McKee, 2002; Roffey, 2007).

In a review of studies describing women and leadership, female leaders tend to be "rated more highly on measures of transformational leadership, have less hierarchical and more collective views of leadership, are oriented toward care, and are oriented toward empowerment" (Kezar et al., 2006, p. 128). Women's leadership processes are described as being generative in encouraging participation, creativity, empowerment, and open communication (Acker, 2012; Astin & Leland, 1991; Lipman-Blumen, 1992; Pasque & Nicholson, 2011; Tonnsen, Alexander, Topolka-Jorissen, & Jacobs, 2011). Yet, gendered organizations continue to be unsupportive to women and advantageous to men; thus, women's success in leadership positions is hampered by an organization that is male centered (Banihani, Lewis, & Syed, 2013; Eddy, 2003; Kezar et al., 2006; Servon & Visser, 2011). As a result, female leaders may face the constraints imposed by the male-centered leadership norms either through resistance or through reconciliation, adapting their preferred process to better fit with male-normed expectations (Holmes & Marra, 2004; Kezar et al., 2006). Theoretical approaches that foreground gender and illuminate how (dominant) constructions of femininity and masculinity shape conceptions of leadership are needed. Further, studies on "discursive leadership" are limited (Bendl, 2008; Blackmore & Sachs, 2007; Fairhurst, 2009). For instance, Ford's (2006) discourse analysis of leadership in a United Kingdom public sector organization revealed gendered performances, discursive tensions, and contradictory subjectivities for male and female leaders. In this chapter, we employ a critical/feminist discourse analysis as one such approach that holds theoretical power for thinking differently about leadership and gender.

METHODS

This study is the third phase of a multi-phase inquiry that investigated how discourses of leadership reflect and re/produce particular gendered images about leaders in higher education. The initial phase (Allan et al., 2006) did not explore, yet revealed, gendered constructions of leadership, and led us to new questions and the next phase of inquiry, in which we focused explicitly on women and leadership (Gordon, Iverson, & Allan, 2010). Our analysis illuminated tensions between the discourses of femininity and masculinity and gendered norms and expectations for leaders. These findings (Gordon et al., 2010) led us back to our original research question, "What are the predominant images of leadership found in *The Chronicle of Higher Education*?" (Allan et al., 2006), with a focus on the discourses shaping gendered images of leadership—the focus of the current, third phase of this inquiry. The following research questions guided this third phase of the study: (a) What are the gendered images of leadership in *The Chronicle of Higher Education*?; and (b) What discourses are employed to shape these images?

The data for this project included 302 items (articles and opinion pieces) published in *The Chronicle of Higher Education* between February 10, 2009, and February 8, 2010, (retrieved February 20, 2010, from http://chronicle.com). These items were selected from a larger pool generated by searching *The Chronicle* using the keyword "leadership." We eliminated articles with only a superficial reference to leadership. For example, in some articles the word "leadership" appeared only in the title of a program. The sample was further refined by focusing on leadership in U.S. postsecondary education, meaning that any items in the "international" section were eliminated.

There are various ways to analyze text, and it should be noted that the purpose of this paper is *not* to provide a systemic content analysis of one periodical. Rather, we focused on identifying the discourses that make it possible for particular characterizations to be understood. Informed by methods of critical/feminist discourse analysis (Allan, 2008; Marshall, 1999; Smith, 1990; Smith, 2013), three researchers read and analyzed the data set to discern "discursive patterns of meaning, contradictions, and inconsistencies" (Gavey, 1989, p. 467). We initially worked independently to read and analyze the data, employing an inductive level of analysis to identify broad themes and predominant images of leadership and conducting a deductive level of analysis informed by our previous findings (Allan et al., 2006; Gordon et al., 2010). Codes were then compared and determinations were made about emergent categories and themes relative to the central question: "What are the gendered images of leadership in *The Chronicle of Higher Education?*" We then re-read the data with an agreed-upon set of codes to identify the predominant images of leadership in *The Chronicle*. From there, we identified the discourses shaping leadership images. These images and the discourses supporting them are the focus of our findings.

FINDINGS AND INTERPRETATIONS

In this analysis, we identified dominant discourses of masculinity and femininity that give rise to images of leaders as *autonomous* and *relational*, respectively. At the intersection of these gender discourses is the construction of the leader-as-negotiator. Yet, the performance of these gendered identities appears to have differential consequences for men and women leaders, benefiting men and situating women leaders in a "double bind." In what follows, we elaborate on these findings.

Discourse of Masculinity: *The Autonomous Leader*

The presence of a dominant masculinity discourse is evidenced by ways in which masculine traits are taken for granted as desired leader behaviors in a given social context. Traits that characterize masculinity tend to include rationality, invulnerability, and independence. In our analysis, this dominant discourse of masculinity foregrounds the importance of leaders as strong and athletic, in control, analytical, decisive, and forceful. For instance, this data excerpt illustrates stereotypical physical attributes associated with a male leader: "Tall, scholarly, and bespectacled, . . . fit [with] an athletic build," who was direct and powerful. "From his bully pulpit, he pushed for tougher academic policies" (Sander, 2009, para. 5). The leader, discursively constituted through masculinity, is typically described as "decisive" and "swift and strong," individualistic, asocial, independent from close interpersonal relationships with others, a "remarkable force," and someone who will "not back down" (e.g., Fain, 2009; Monaghan, 2010). A description of poor leadership also tacitly illustrates these expectations: "At too many colleges, administrators cannot foster agreement among constituents on important issues, do not have the will to make tough decisions, and are not setting out a vision" (Carlson, 2010, para. 8).

This image of a solo leader is consistent with the Western view of the autonomous individual who holds the right to self-determination, self-regulation, and self-government (Barclay, 2000; Christman, 2003); an individual who is competent, uniquely qualified, and morally principled. This view of leadership as independent, individualistic, and autonomous is "often described as a masculine prototype" (Paris et al., 2009, p. 1397). Autonomy, in this traditional sense, includes the ability to freely discover the self and make decisions unencumbered by societal constraints—social pressure, external coercion, and cultural patterns (Barclay, 2000; Christman, 2003). Pronounced in the data are examples of the autonomous leader as principled, inspiring, visionary, and able to do the right thing (e.g., Foley, 2010; Masterson, 2009; Selingo, 2010; Wilson, 2010). These images of the autonomous, and principled, leader are supported by a dominant discourse of masculinity.

Discourse of Femininity: *Relational Leader*

A dominant discourse of femininity gives rise to images of leaders as caring, nurturing, relational, collaborative, and supportive (Allan, 2008; Holmes & Marra, 2004; Uhl-Bien, 2006). Femininity is also characterized by compassion and belonging, vulnerability and dependence, and cooperation and communication. In general, hegemonic femininity is more passive than active, valuing relationships over directive hierarchy and collaboration over solo authority (Ridgeway & Correll, 2004; Tarule, Applegate, Earley, & Blackwell, 2009).

Findings reveal that leadership images shaped by a dominant discourse of femininity foreground different traits, such as mutuality, collaboration, cooperative interchange, and relationship building. We refer to this predominant leadership image as the *relational leader* because the emergent image emphasizes attentiveness to relationships and being "caring and compassionate" (Jun, 1999, p. 224). Sometimes referred to as "the care perspective" (Burnier, 2003), this leader accepts emotions, rejects a privileging of reason over affect, and starts first with "the compelling moral salience of attending to and meeting the needs of the particular others for whom we take responsibility" (Held, 2006, p. 2). This data quote is illustrative:

> Timothy P. White, chancellor of the University of California at Riverside, believes in the *high-touch* approach, *making people feel noticed and heard*. In one of his first letters last year, he acknowledged the angst people were feeling over the economy. "Please *be supportive of each other* and yourselves as we navigate through these times," he wrote. (Masterson, 2009, para. 36, emphasis added)

Later, in this article about presidential communication (Masterson, 2009), presidents asserted that their campus communities "must work together" (para. 2) and "be supportive" (para. 36); that they are being candid with constituents, "giving up control" (para. 22), building consensus and ensuring campus agreement, conveying "care...no matter what" (para. 31). Other illustrative data describes leaders as able to build community support, work with people, generate bottom-up ideas, share responsibility, and build consensus (e.g., Glaser, 2009; Hebel, 2009; Hendry, 2009). The relational leader, then, facilitates collective decision-making and shared responsibility.

DISCURSIVE TENSIONS

The dominant gender discourses—masculinity and femininity—are dichotomized but do not exist as isolated poles; rather, tensions were evident between these gender discourses of femininity and masculinity, producing gendered norms and expectations for leaders that may benefit male-identified leaders and construct a double bind for female-identified leaders. The tensions and the realities produced for leaders are discussed in this section.

Leader as Negotiator

The leadership identities—autonomous and relational—that were constructed by gender discourses (masculinity and femininity, respectively) can be embodied by the same individual, regardless of gender. Lazar (2005) refers to the phenomenon as the ways in which discourses "work in tandem" (p. 373). Lipman-Blumen (1992) provides another example, noting that in the U.S. "devotion to individualism" is tempered "with a schizoid love affair with teamwork" (p. 190). The autonomy of self as an independent, rational, and knowing agent competes with the notion of the self in the context of interdependent, dynamic, and often unpredictable social relationships (Barclay, 2000; Christman, 2003; Lipman-Blumen, 1992).

From this tension emerges a broader view of leadership, one that acknowledges the leader in relation to others. According to Maak and Pless (2006), "winning the mandate to lead requires a relational leadership approach based on inclusion, collaboration and co-operation with different stakeholder groups" (p. 100). The embodiment of this leader, in today's politicized and corporatized educational environments, is evident in the image of the leader as a *negotiator*. The following data excerpts serve to illustrate: (a) "I'm definitely a consensus builder, but I'm decisive" (Hebel, 2009, para. 10); and (b) one university president "saw a chance to *push through big changes* [yet] he wanted to *encourage cooperation*" (Masterson, 2009, para. 11, emphasis added). Another excerpt asserts, "The best leaders need to be *authentic partners* with faculty and staff members *while at the same time decisive and assertive* in their decisions" (Mead-Fox, 2009, para. 13, emphasis added).

As these data excerpts illustrate, through the discursive construction of the negotiator, leadership success is understood as a result of alliances formed in relationships. Yet this tension between autonomous and relational that constructs the negotiator does not give rise to leadership as a collective act. The "traditional desire for a 'hero' leader, who is always male and who lives on in these times of tight fiscal constraints" (Dean, Bracken, & Allen, 2009, p. 24) dominates. Alternative conceptualizations of leadership as a collective act are available in the literature (Acker, 2012; Astin & Leland, 1991; Bensimon & Neumann, 1993; Kezar & Lester, 2011; Meyerson, 2001; Meyerson & Tompkins, 2007); however, they are nearly invisible in the data. The following data excerpt illustrates the concealed image of leadership as collective act:

> "As a coalition, we've been working on documenting the issues related to contingent faculty and bringing awareness to them," says Rosemary G. Feal, executive director of the Modern Language Association, which is a member of the [Coalition on the Academic Workforce]. "Contingent faculty members

in all of our associations should feel that *we've all collectively taken a step in support* of them." (June, 2010, para. 3, emphasis added)

This possibility of leadership as a collective act stands in stark contrast with dominant notions of leadership as a solo, autonomous effort. Dominant conceptualizations of leadership are so inextricably linked with positional authority or solo action that—even when enacted with others—the possibility of the relational leader acting in concert with others remains marginalized or concealed in the data (Kezar & Lester, 2011).

The Double Bind

Although both male and female leaders take up the autonomous and relational subject positions, Eddy (2009) observes that men "used relationships to foster and build on their hero image" (p. 24); in contrast, according to Gordon et al. (2010), women leaders faced a double bind; they were unable to benefit from the masculine autonomous image of leadership, being perceived as weak or ineffective as relational leaders. Acker (2012) notes that this reinforces expectations that "men will be powerful and women subordinate" (p. 417). For women-identified leaders, adopting any of these leader identities can be risky—being the autonomous leader, or even the leader as negotiator, can be viewed as incongruent with stereotypical feminine roles (Gordon et al., 2010; Kezar & Lester, 2011), but adopting the relational status may result in being perceived as a weak leader. Jamieson (1995) identifies this as the femininity/competence bind, positing that women who are considered feminine will be judged to be incompetent, given that competence is associated with masculinity; thus, competent women are perceived as unfeminine.

Applied to this analysis of leadership, dominant constructions of gender—masculinity and femininity—contribute to the assumption that men are generally more competent than women and give rise to what is often referred to as *the double bind*, a situation in which a woman cannot win no matter what she does (Appelbaum, Audet, & Miller, 2003). These data excerpts illuminate the double bind for women leaders:

> I applaud the *strong women* who have reached the top positions in their colleges and universities, sometimes at great personal sacrifice. I know that they *face many challenges breaking into the male leadership culture*, including *walking the tightrope of being assertive while not being perceived as aggressive.* . . . Often subtle discrimination is rooted in gender stereotypes—especially when it comes to the "leadership issue." Female candidates are purportedly passed up for promotions based on a conscious or unconscious *belief that women do not have what it takes to lead* men. The English reputedly have a test for that kind of

leadership—"Who among you would kill the tiger if attacked?" But *if a woman displays the qualities of a tiger killer, she may be dismissed as too masculine.* (Mason, 2009, para. 4, emphasis added)

Schmidt (2009) elaborates on other aspects of the double bind, highlighting the reluctance of women to aspire to leadership positions and work-life balance issues that can alter the trajectory of women's career paths:

> Women present a distinct set of challenges to those seeking to increase their representation in top posts....Compared with male CAO's [sic], they are about a fourth *less likely to express ambitions* for the presidency and, when asked about their career paths so far, are *more than three times as likely to report having altered their careers to care* for dependents, parents, or a spouse or partner. (para. 6, emphasis added)

This double bind leaves women leaders with limited, conflicting, and, at times, unfavorable options. It also yields advice for women to "work twice as hard, don't complain, demonstrate the ability to get things done, find a mentor, and assert yourself at an appropriate time" (Wood, 2009, p. 81). Solutions risk making "women *the problem* in educational leadership rather than problematizing the concept of leadership itself relative to wider dominant power/gender relations" (Blackmore, 1999, pp. 5–6, emphasis in original). Against the backdrop of "the stereotypical male model of leadership" (Bornstein, 2009, p. 214), gender appears to be "an impediment for some women...[and] a handicap in their quest for legitimacy" as leaders (p. 215). Further reifying the ideal worker as male-identified, Bornstein noted that women leaders "who do not fit" are more likely to be "rejected" or "viewed as outsiders, as alien tissues," and they "must work harder to achieve a good fit and the legitimacy that depends upon it" (p. 215).

DISCUSSION AND IMPLICATIONS

The findings of this study offer a theoretical perspective that invites an opportunity for thinking differently about leadership. In particular, our use of discourse theory as an analytic lens revealed ways in which dominant gender discourses contribute to shaping perceptions about leadership. By positioning gender at the center of the question of what leadership means and who can be effective leaders, we revealed how images of leaders—as autonomous or relational—are not neutral. On the contrary, the discursive construction of leaders as decisive, forceful, and rational benefits male-identified leaders, while leaders who are discursively constructed as caring, collaborative, and supportive can disadvantage female-identified leaders who may be perceived as less capable and vulnerable. Thus, female-identified leaders are at risk when taking up either discursive construction—at risk for appearing weak if they are caring and collaborative, but being seen as performing a role incongruent with their femininity if they are too autonomous or powerful (Jamieson, 1995). Finally, we contend that the constitutive effects of these gendered discourses can become "institutionalized cultural barriers...that are compounded by the structural barriers of centralized bureaucracies that privilege transitional male-oriented conceptions of leadership" (Gordon et al., 2010, p. 98).

Our hope is that discursive analyses such as this will spur practitioners to interrogate the construction of deeply gendered structures that prescribe gendered norms for defining and evaluating good leadership rather than designing (more) developmental and compensatory programs to help female-identified leaders "heed the assimilation imperative in order to attain career advancement, success, and legitimacy" (Dean et al., 2009, p. 240). Further, this theoretical approach may yield recognition of "male dominance in social arrangements and [assert] a desire for change from this form of dominance" (Calas & Smircich, 1996, p. 219). Change may be achieved by destabilizing and interrupting normative gendered leadership performances—what Foucault (1978) refers to as "tactical polyvalence" (p. 100). Discourse is comprised of "discontinuous segments" with various meanings; thus, at any point there is a "multiplicity of discursive elements that can come into play" (Foucault, 1978, p. 110). Leaders, then, can purposefully and strategically disrupt dominant discourses by, for instance, taking power rather than waiting to be given it and sharing power, and, in turn, troubling the solo authority of leadership, to instead lead as part of a collective (Allan et al., 2006; Gordon et al., 2010; Pomerantz, Raby, & Stefanik, 2013). When discourse is viewed as something that can be actively chosen by subjects, then leaders have "at their disposal an opportunity to subvert and resist prevailing and dominant understandings" of leadership (Osgood, 2006, p. 12).

Our findings add to the limited body of work on leadership discourses and illuminate how "leadership actors can be passive receptors of meaning;" but also how, "as agents of change, [leaders] are...constructed in and through discourse" (Fairhurst, 2009, p. 1608; see also Bendl, 2008; and Blackmore & Sachs, 2007). Further, we argue that more inquiry is needed regarding leadership discourses, and, in particular, how texts (e.g., *The Chronicle*) may serve as "identity resources" for "naturalizing masculinity and males as the leadership norm and 'othering' the female leader" (Fairhurst, 2009, p. 1621). This theoretical and practical un/thinking about leadership can enable new possibilities for reconceptualizing and theory building about leadership.

Scholars are encouraged to draw upon these findings, to deploy this theoretical approach (of critical/feminist discourse analysis), and to think more strategically about the discourses taken up when describing and theorizing about leadership. Further exploration of the "double bind" for women leaders is also needed to deconstruct the (falsely) ungendered notions of the ideal leader. As Acker (2006) noted, the gendered organization and gendered notions of work remain resistant to change in spite of efforts to erase inequalities. Instead of simply allowing women to work on the same terms traditionally available to men, we need to restructure the work conditions under which both men and women work and eliminate the masculinist norm of the ideal worker (Acker, 2012; Williams, 2000). Additionally, inquiry is needed to explore how discourses can support the advancement of alternative conceptualizations of leadership including collective and grassroots leadership, leaders as "organizational catalysts" (Sturm, 2007) and "institutional change agents" (Meyerson & Tompkins, 2007), and the ways in which discourses shaping other dimensions of identity (e.g., race) may operate in constructing images of leadership (Bell, Meyerson, Nkomo, & Scully, 2003). Continued research is warranted to extend the study of leadership discourses and the gendered images they produce, as well as their contribution to gender equity in higher education.

REFERENCES

Acker, S. (2012). Chairing and caring: Gendered dimensions of leadership in academe. *Gender and Education, 24*(4), 411-428.

Acker, J. (2006). Inequality regimes: Gender, class, and race in organizations. *Gender & Society, 20*(4), 441–464.

Acker, J. (1990). Hierarchies, jobs, and bodies: A theory of gendered organizations. *Gender & Society, 4*(2), 139–158.

Allan, E. (2008). *Policy discourses, gender and education: Constructing women's status.* New York, NY: Routledge.

Allan, E. J., Gordon, S. P., & Iverson, S. V. (2006). Re/thinking practices of power: The discursive framing of leadership in *The Chronicle of Higher Education. Review of Higher Education, 30*(1), 41–68.

Allan, E. J., Iverson, S. V., & Ropers-Huilman, R. (Eds.) (2010). *Reconstructing policy in higher education: Feminist poststructural perspectives.* New York, NY: Routledge.

Amey, M. J. (2005). Leadership as learning: Conceptualizing the process. *Community College Journal of Research and Practice, 29*(9/10), 689–704.

Appelbaum, S., Audet, L., & Miller, J. (2003). Gender and leadership? Leadership and gender? A journey through the landscape of theories. *Leadership & Organization Development Journal, 24*(1), 43–51.

Astin, H., & Leland, C. (1991). *Women of influence, women of vision: A cross-generational study of leaders and change.* San Francisco, CA: Jossey-Bass.

Banihani, M., Lewis, P., & Syed, J. (2013). Is work engagement gendered? *Gender in Management: An International Journal, 28*(7), 400–423.

Barclay, L. (2000). Autonomy and the social self. In C. Mackenzie & N. Stoljar (Eds.), *Relational autonomy: Feminist perspectives on autonomy, agency, and the social self* (pp. 52–71). New York, NY: Oxford University.

Baxter, J. (2003). *Positioning gender in discourse: A feminist methodology*. New York, NY: Palgrave Macmillan.

Bell, E. L., Meyerson, D., Nkomo, S., & Scully, M. (2003). Interpreting silence and voice in the workplace: A conversation about tempered radicalism among Black and White women researchers. *The Journal of Applied Behavioral Science, 39*(4), 381–414.

Bendl, R. (2008). Gender subtexts—Reproduction of exclusion in organizational discourse. *British Journal of Management, 19,* S50–S64.

Bensimon, E., & Neumann, A. (1993). *Redesigning collegiate leadership: Teams and teamwork in higher education*. Baltimore, MD: Johns Hopkins University.

Blackmore, J. (1999). *Troubling women: Feminism, leadership, and educational change*. Philadelphia, PA: Open University.

Blackmore, J., & Sachs, J. (2007). *Performing and reforming leaders: Gender, educational restricting, and organizational change*. Albany, NY: State University of New York Press.

Bornstein, R. (2009). Women and the quest for presidential legitimacy. In D. Dean, S. J. Bracken, & J. Allen, (Eds.), *Women in academic leadership: Professional strategies, personal choices* (pp. 208–237). Sterling, VA: Stylus.

Burnier, D. (2003). Other voices/other rooms: Toward a care-centered public administration. *Administrative Theory & Praxis, 25*(4), 529–544.

Calas, M., & Smircich, L. (1996). From "The Woman's" point of view: Feminist approaches to organization studies. In S. R., Clegg, C. Hardy, and W. R. Nord (Eds.), *Handbook of Organization Studies* (pp. 218–257). Thousand Oaks, CA: Sage.

Carlson, S. (2010, February 2). More remedies for colleges in trouble: Distinct visions and strong leaders. *The Chronicle of Higher Education* [online]. Retrieved from http://chronicle.com/article/More-Remedies-for-Colleges-/63877/

Christman, J. (2003). Autonomy in moral and political philosophy. In E. N. Zalta (Ed.), The Stanford encyclopedia of philosophy (Fall 2003 edition). Retrieved from http://plato.stanford.edu/entries/autonomy-moral/

Dean, D., Bracken, S. J., & Allen, J. (Eds.). (2009). *Women in academic leadership: Professional strategies, personal choices*. Sterling, VA: Stylus.

Douglas, S., & Michaels, M. (2004). *The mommy myth: The idealization of motherhood and how it has undermined women*. New York, NY: Simon and Schuster.

Echner, C., & Prasad, P. (2003). The context of third world tourism marketing. *Annals of Tourism Research, 30*(3), 660–682.

Eddy, P. L. (2003). Sensemaking on campus: How community college presidents frame change. *Community College Journal of Research and Practice, 27*(6), 453–471.

Eddy, P. L., & Cox, E. (2008). Gendered leadership: An organizational perspective. In J. Lester (Ed.), Gendered perspectives on community colleges. *New Directions in Community Colleges,* no. 142 (pp. 69–80). San Francisco, CA: Jossey-Bass.

Eddy, P. L. & VanDerLinden, K. E. (2006). Emerging definitions of leadership in higher education: New visions of leadership or the same old "hero" leader? *Community College Review, 34*(1), 5–26.

Fain, P. (2009, February 11). Nancy Zimpher tackles a big challenge as SUNY's new chancellor. *The Chronicle of Higher Education* [online]. Retrieved from http://chronicle.com/article/Nancy-Zimpher-Tackles-a-Big/1521/

Fairhurst, G. T. (2009). Considering context in discursive leadership research. *Human Relations, 62*(11), 1607–1633.

Foley, T. (2010, February 3). College presidents' salaries. *The Chronicle of Higher Education* [online]. Retrieved from http://chronicle.com/article/College-Presidents-Salaries/63874/

Ford, J. (2006). Discourses of leadership: Gender, identity and contradiction in a UK public sector organization. *Leadership 2*(1), 77–99.

Foucault, M. (1978). *The history of sexuality: An introduction.* New York, NY: Vintage Books.

Gavey, N. (1989). Feminist poststructuralism and discourse analysis: Contributions to feminist psychology. *Psychology of Women Quarterly, 13*(4), 459–475.

Glaser, J. M. (2009, November 29). Do and don'ts of task forces. *The Chronicle of Higher Education* [online]. Retrieved from http://chronicle.com/article/DosDonts-of-Task-Forces/49267/

Goleman, D., Boyatzis, R., & McKee, A. (2002). *Primal leadership: Realizing the power of emotional intelligence.* Boston, MA: Harvard Business School.

Gordon, S. P., Iverson, S. V., & Allan, E. J. (2010). The discursive framing of women leaders in higher education. In E. J. Allan, S. V. Iverson, & R. Ropers-Huilman (Eds.), *Reconstructing policy in higher education: Feminist poststructural perspectives* (pp. 81–105). New York, NY: Routledge.

Hebel, S. (2009, April 1). New leader aims to keep public colleges high on nation's priorities. *The Chronicle of Higher Education* [online]. Retrieved from http://chronicle.com/article/New-Leader-Aims-to-Keep-Pub/47154/

Held, V. (2006). The ethics of care. In D. Copp (Ed.), *Oxford handbook of ethical theory* (pp. 1–44). New York, NY: Oxford University.

Hendry, E. R. (2009, August 10). New dean wants engineering students to look at the big picture. *The Chronicle of Higher Education* [online]. Retrieved from http://chronicle.com/article/New-Dean-Wants-Engineering-/47953/

Holmes, J., & Marra, M. (2004). Relational practice in the workplace: Women's talk or gendered discourse? *Language in Society, 33*(3), 377–398.

Iverson, S. V. (2011). Glass ceilings and sticky floors: Women and advancement in higher education. In J. Martin (Ed.), *Women as leaders in education: Succeeding despite inequity, discrimination, and other challenges, volume I: Women's leadership in higher education* (pp. 79–105). Santa Barbara, CA: Praeger.

Jamieson. K. H. (1995). *Beyond the double bind: Women and leadership.* New York, NY: Oxford University.

Jun, J. S. (1999). The need for autonomy and virtues: Civic-minded administrators in a civil society. *Administrative Theory & Praxis, 21*(2), 218–226.

June, A. W. (2010, February 8). Coalition seeks better conditions for those off the tenure track. *The Chronicle of Higher Education* [online]. Retrieved from http://chronicle.com/article/Coalition-Seeks-Better-Cond/64054/

Kanter, R. M. (1977). *Men and women of the corporation.* New York, NY: Basic Books.

Kezar, A., Carducci, R., & Contraras-McGavin, M. (2006). Rethinking the "L" word in higher education: The revolution of research on leadership. *ASHE Higher Education Report, 31*(6). San Francisco, CA: Jossey-Bass.

Kezar, A. J., & Lester, J. (2011). *Enhancing campus capacity for leadership: An examination of grassroots leaders in higher education.* Palo Alto, CA: Stanford University.

Lazar, M. (Ed.). (2005). *Feminist critical discourse analysis: Gender, power and ideology in discourse.* New York, NY: Palgrave Macmillan.

Lipman-Blumen, J. (1992). Connective leadership: Female leadership styles in the 21st-century workplace. *Sociological Perspectives, 35*(1), 183–203.

Luke, A. (1995). Text and discourse in education: An introduction to critical discourse analysis. *Review of Research in Education, 21,* 3–47.

Maak, T., & Pless, N. M. (2006). Responsible leadership in a stakeholder society: A relational perspective. *Journal of Business Ethics, 66*(1), 99–115.

Marshall, C. (1999). Researching the margins: Feminist critical policy analysis. *Educational Policy, 13*(1), 59–77.

Mason, M. A. (2009, September 16). How the 'Snow-Woman Effect' slows women's progress. *The Chronicle of Higher Education* [online]. Retrieved from http://chronicle.com/article/How-the-Snow-Woman-Effect/48377/

Masterson, K. (2009, November 29). Economic crisis creates a new brand of communication from the top. *The Chronicle of Higher Education* [online]. Retrieved from http://chronicle.com/article/Economic-Crisis-Creates-a-N/49286/

Mead-Fox, D. (2009, April 24). Tackling the leadership scarcity. *The Chronicle of Higher Education* [online]. Retrieved from http://chronicle.com/article/Tackling-the-Leadership-Sca/44809/

Meyerson, D. (2001). *Tempered radicals: How people use difference to inspire change at work.* Cambridge, MA: Harvard Business.

Meyerson, D., & Tompkins, M. (2007). Tempered radicals as institutional change agents: The case of advancing gender equity at the University of Michigan. *Harvard Journal of Law & Gender, 30*(2), 303–322.

Mills, S. (1997). *Discourse.* New York, NY: Routledge.

Monaghan, P. (2010, January 17). MIT president who weathered Vietnam war-era protests dies at 87. *The Chronicle of Higher Education* [online]. Retrieved from http://chronicle.com/article/MIT-President-Who-Weathered/63538/

Osgood, J. (2006). Deconstructing professionalism in early childhood education: Resisting the regulatory gaze. *Contemporary Issues in Early Childhood, 7*(1), 5–14.

Paris, L. D., Howell, J. P., Dorfman, P. W., & Hanges, P. J. (2009). Preferred leadership prototypes of male and female leaders in 27 countries. *Journal of International Business Studies, 40*(8), 1396–1405.

Pasque, P. A., & Nicholson, S. E. (2011). (Eds.). *Empowering women in higher education and student affairs: Theory, research, narratives, and practice from feminist perspectives.* Sterling, VA: Stylus Publishing.

Pomerantz, S., Raby, R., & Stefanik, A. (2013). Girls run the world? Caught between sexism and postfeminism in school. *Gender & Society, 27*(2), 185–207.

Powell, R. (2010). Good mothers, bad mothers and mommy bloggers: Rhetorical resistance and fluid subjectivities. *MP: An Online Feminist Journal, 2*(5), 37–50.

Rhee, J., & Sagaria, M. A. D. (2004). International students: Constructions of imperialism in *The Chronicle of Higher Education*. *The Review of Higher Education, 28*(1), 77–96.

Ridgeway, C. L., & Correll, S. J. (2004). Unpacking the gender system: A theoretical perspective on gender beliefs and social relations. *Gender & Society, 18*(4), 510–531.

Roffey, S. (2007). Transformation and emotional literacy: The role of school leaders in developing a caring community. *Leading & Managing, 13*(1), 16–30.

Sander, L. (2009, September 16). Myles Brand, first college president to lead NCAA, dies at 67. *The Chronicle of Higher Education* [online]. Retrieved from http://chronicle.com/article/Myles-Brand-First-College-/48457/

Sathye, M. (2004). Leadership in higher education: A qualitative study [35 paragraphs]. *Forum Qualitative Sozialforschung/Forum: Qualitative Social Research, 5*(3), Art. 26, Retrieved from http://nbn-resolving.de/urn:nbn:de:0114-fqs0403266

Schmidt, P. (2009, February 10). Survey of chief academic officers raises concerns about diversity and longevity. *The Chronicle of Higher Education* [online]. Retrieved from http://chronicle.com/article/Survey-of-Chief-Academic-Of/1518/

Schull, V., Shaw, S., & Kihl, L. A. (2013). "If a woman came in . . . she would have been eaten up alive": Analyzing gendered political processes in the search for an athletic director. *Gender & Society, 27*(1), 56–81.

Selingo, J. J. (2010, February 8). Tufts U.'s president will step down to return to teaching. *The Chronicle of Higher Education* [online]. Retrieved from http://chronicle.com/article/Tufts-Us-President-Will-S/64051/

Servon, L. J., & Visser, M. A. (2011). Progress hindered: The retention and advancement of women in science, engineering and technology careers. *Human Resource Management Journal, 21*(3), 272–284.

Smith, D. E. (1990). *Texts, facts, and femininity: Exploring the relations of ruling.* London, England: Routledge.

Smith, K. (2013). Critical discourse analysis and higher education research. In J. Huisman, & M. Tight (Eds.), *Theory and method in higher education research* (International Perspectives on Higher Education Research, Vol. 9, pp. 61–79). Cambridge, MA: Emerald Group.

Sturm, S. (2007). Gender equity as institutional transformation: The pivotal role of organizational catalysts. In A. J. Stewart, J. E. Malley, D. LaVaque-Manty (Eds.), *Transforming science and engineering: Advancing academic women* (pp. 262–280). Ann Arbor: University of Michigan Press.

Tarule, J. M., Applegate, J. H., Earley, P. M., & Blackwell, P. J. (2009). Narrating gendered leadership. In D. Dean, S. J. Bracken, & J. Allen, (Eds.), *Women in academic leadership: Professional strategies, personal choices* (pp. 31–49). Sterling, VA: Stylus.

Thomas, R., & Davies, A. (2005). Theorizing the micro-politics of resistance: New public management and managerial identities in the UK public services. *Organization Studies, 26*(5), 683–706.

Tonnsen, S., Alexander, A., Topolka-Jorissen, K., & Jacobs, J. (2011). Influences of early life experiences on the generative leadership roles of four female professors of educational leadership. *Advancing Women in Leadership, 31*(1), 34–39. Retrieved from http://advancingwomen.com/awl/awl_wordpress/

Uhl-Bien, M. (2006). Relational leadership theory: Exploring the social processes of leadership and organizing. *The Leadership Quarterly, 17*(6), 654–676.

Weedon, C. (1997). *Feminist practice and poststructuralist theory* (3rd ed.). Cambridge, MA: Blackwell.

Williams, J. (2000). *Unbending gender: Why family and work conflict and what to do about it.* New York, NY: Oxford University.

Wilson, R. (2010, January 5). Small-college presidents hear tips on building a leadership team. *The Chronicle of Higher Education* [online]. Retrieved from http://chronicle.com/article/Small-College-Presidents-Hear/63429/

Wood, D. F. (2009). Barriers to women's leadership in faith-based colleges and universities: Strategies for change. In D. Dean, S. J. Bracken, & J. Allen (Eds.), *Women in academic leadership: Professional strategies, personal choices* (pp. 74–94). Sterling, VA: Stylus.

CHAPTER 5

REVOLUTION FROM WITHIN

A Theory of Embodied Transformation of Roles for Girls and Women Through Leadership Blockbusters

Carol Burbank
Independent Scholar, Coach, and Educator

In a world rocked by crisis, transformation, and double-edged innovation, contemporary leaders struggle with identities and obligations. Leadership scholars often ask, "What is leadership?" or "What makes a great leader?" Leaders often ask themselves: "Who am I?" "How must I shift?" Vibrating at the intersections of self, social roles, and cultural/organizational situations, the leadership process is an intimate dance, balancing and negotiating change and stability. Successful leaders leverage intersecting challenges by integrating the stories they activate, from internalized fictional selves to well-rehearsed personal narratives, with the collective myths that guide professional relationships or organizational identities. These leadership identities can and must transform as the culture transforms. Visionary leaders from marginalized populations are key in shifting leadership norms and roles that create a foundation for sustainable and inclusive transformation.

Theorizing Women and Leadership, pages 69–87

New roles and expectations for girls and women are one of the most important markers of transformation in the contemporary leadership landscape, and the field of leadership studies needs to utilize every tool available to understand that shift.

In this chapter, I theorize that creative fictional experience is one of the most important sites of resistance to dominant cultural leadership norms in the 21st century, offering a space to develop authentic, embodied, and empowered female/feminist resistance, especially for girls and women. The interactive multimedia context of contemporary entertainment presents pockets of revolution, leadership blockbusters that create embodied experiences of alternative, imaginary realities that can inspire expanded leadership roles and expectations, particularly as they reflect the unresolved crises that shape our planet now. These imaginal roles are a precursor for challenges to conservative leadership paradigms in mainstream culture, reflecting potential or latent shifts before they are evident in contemporary organizations, political structures, and global networks. Using a turning point in the television popularization of a new kind of female hero and two leadership blockbusters of Young Adult (YA) fiction, I model strategic analysis to track an important trend reflected in the influential new female warrior leader who is, as yet, largely fictional. This female leader models a radical generational and pop cultural retreat from binary gender roles as conditions of authentic leadership identity, a difference that will manifest in new and unexpected negotiations as millennials develop into the leaders they now only imagine they might become.

I examine *The Hunger Games* and *Divergent* trilogies, two leadership blockbusters in YA fiction and film, as examples of the ways feminist pop culture experiences articulate changing leadership norms and cultural challenges for women and girls, while simultaneously providing an opportunity for leadership development as a result of the embodied, neuropsychological, and socially intermediated opportunities for authentic identity formation and transformation. I ground this analysis with a summary of the power of story, already acknowledged in the leadership field; new research in human neurology, physiology, and psychology; and a thorough consideration of the influence and function of YA fiction. I conclude by illuminating how YA leadership blockbusters offer a dynamic and foundational aesthetic experience, as powerful as the "real world," because of the transformative power of the imaginary in the cultural negotiations of daily performances of leadership.

The dialogue between imaginary and external narratives is a meaningful part of cultural change, personal leadership development, and organizational change, whether explicitly or implicitly. The position adopted in this chapter is that art and popular culture are key parts of the intimate conscientization of girls and young women as future leaders. Specific artifacts are created with specific purposes, on a spectrum of cultural resistance to propaganda persuasion to mainstream entertainment. But once these narratives enter the marketplace, readers and audiences establish their own relationships with the embodied experience of consuming and responding to art. Because of contemporary social media networks, this relationship with fictionalized artifacts can become a central site of resistance and transformation once lessons have been internalized and integrated.

It is necessary to expand our theoretical understanding of popular culture in the evolving interdisciplinary field of leadership studies in order to map these points of resistance and transformation. The individual and social power of our relationship with popular culture has become an increasingly potent source of identity formation and transformation in the 21st century, particularly for populations underrepresented in mainstream leadership circles. Once evolving leadership paradigms are identified, it will be possible to harness the alchemy of aesthetic experience and pop culture community to support embodied, authentic, and transformative leadership practices.

Three key assertions form the foundation of this chapter:

1. Cultural shifts, transgressions, and evolution are mirrored and negotiated in popular culture's multimedia, layered representations of leadership narratives and are an important access to developing leadership models for marginalized groups.
2. The transformation of normative cultural roles is a gradual process, marked by resistance on both sides of the change, and fraught with complex cultural negotiations alternately interpreted as transgression, revolution, and justice. Fiction, film, and other creative arts are an ideal Petri dish in which to observe the narratives resulting from these cultural clashes. In the case of changes in the leadership roles of women, it is particularly useful to examine new models in pop culture artifacts produced by and for young girls and women.
3. Vital leadership skills and identities are formed and kindled by a dynamic and negotiated authenticity, a relational process embedded in multiple cultural experiences, including the alternative space of popular culture. The imaginary realm of art, books, and film has significant influence and power on individual development and expectations and, therefore, on the negotiations of authentic and transformative leadership in a changing world.

These assertions combine to generate the two key contributions of this chapter. First, the chapter suggests that theorizing the role of literary and cinematic fiction in women's leadership development highlights how the leadership blockbuster creates imaginaries (e.g., new embodied leadership identities) for the authentic leadership development of young adults. The leadership blockbuster, as theorized in this chapter, influences the mindset and behavioral development of young women toward an alternatively gendered heroism, beyond sexist stereotypes. Second, the chapter suggests that the leadership blockbuster can and should be more integrated into leadership development sessions as a teaching/learning tool. The transformative role of literary and cinematic fiction in leadership development goes beyond the most common current applications of classroom discussion or training case study. In the interactive multimedia context of contemporary entertainment, the leadership blockbuster is a development tool that offers embodied experiences of alternative, imaginary realities. The purpose of this chapter is to catalyze new directions in leadership development and continued empirical research to understand the mechanisms of and outcomes for leadership development for young adult women and girls.

NEW LEADERSHIP SEEDS FOR THE 21ST CENTURY: *BUFFY THE VAMPIRE SLAYER* AND FEMINIST PARADIGMS FOR TRANSFORMATIVE MEDIA NARRATIVES

The appearance of transgressive and transformative feminist narratives in popular culture offers a revealing trace of the emergence of a new breed of female leaders and leadership expectations. For fans of dystopian, supernatural, alternative universes, one visionary moment in 2003 epitomized the embodied power of leadership storytelling and the rise of a new kind of female leader. During the last episode of *Buffy the Vampire Slayer*, Joss Whedon's cult television show, a new kind of pop cultural leadership became visible. The final moment in the "Buffyverse," with its powerful feminist message about sisterhood, offered transformational leadership as well as entertainment. In the process, this episode cemented the place of a new kind of feminist leader in the heart of Hollywood: a physically strong, fierce warrior with a complex internal life; and a role model "the girls could look up to, and relate to, showing not only a hero but how difficult it is to be a hero" (Pascale & Fillion, 2014, p. 83).

In the series' final episode, "The Chosen" (Whedon, *The Chosen*, Season 7, Episode 2, 2003), Buffy and her team of famously ironic misfits face (and finally defeat) the ultimate evil. Buffy is the only Slayer; that is, she is the one chosen, the sole superhero leading the fight for good, in a world peppered with devils, vampires, and other demonic destroyers. In the last episode, realizing that her strength alone is not enough to save humanity, she makes a radical invitation to potential Slayers in her world and among her millions of fans. In the process, she creates an invincible human army of girls and young women, calling for a mass awakening of female power:

So here's the part where you make a choice. What if you could have that power, now? In every generation, one Slayer is born, because a bunch of men who
died thousands of years ago made up that rule. . . . I say my power, should be
our power. . . . Every girl who could have the power, will have the power. Can
stand up, will stand up. Slayers, every one of us. Make your choice. Are you
ready to be strong? (Whedon, *The Chosen*, Season 7, Episode 2, 2003)

A moving feminist montage parallels Buffy's speech, with girls of all ages
rising to their strength, defending themselves against bullying and domes-
tic abuse, excelling as athletes, standing to their full height, smiling as they
sense their new strength. The onscreen demonic enemy transforms into a
more realistic oppressor as the new slayers are born—strong, clever, and
adaptable—able to defend themselves and the world against oppression of
all kinds. The main difference between Buffy's mythos and previous female
warrior leaders is that Buffy not only claimed her power, but literally gave
it away to other young women by breaking the spell that created her. Other
warrior super leaders like Wonder Woman (1941, 1960, 2015) and Xena,
Warrior Princess (1995–2001) remain locked into their unique and inspiring isolation, never ordinary or longing for normal lives, but celebrated as
individuals with a gift and a mythic calling (Nel, 2011).

Buffy's collective heroism is part of a trend Kociemba (2011) calls the "rejection of traditional epic heroism" (p. 95), celebrating community over individualism. After seven successful seasons, the final episode "drew the biggest
audience for the show since October 2002 and finished well above *Buffy's*
season average of 3.8 million viewers" (Zap2it, 2003, p. 1). In addition, *Buffy*
fans in online communities paid particularly close attention to this somewhat
controversial and surprising ending, which broke the central rule of Buffy's
creation and transformed her into one-among-many, somehow more ordinary, certainly less lonely, and definitely, no longer unique. Whedon and his
team created Buffy's story in active dialogue with the demanding fan communities of what some cultural critics call the digital generation, which "seems to
be no longer content to remain receivers of messages but instead demands to
be part of their creation" (Urbanski, 2011, p. 3).

The dialogic, internalized engagement with a female warrior leader is
therefore far more than entertainment or educational material although it
is commonly viewed as both. Immersion in this imaginary experience has
the potential to spark a moment of personal transformation for girls and
women, as viewers identify first with Buffy, then with their own liberated
Slayer nature. The projection of self into a compelling narrative awakens
an inner process that rehearses a leadership role that is, for most females,
unavailable in the outside world. As a result, these cultural artifacts offer a
window not only into resistances and transformations in cultural roles of
women and girls but also into the intimate, internal process of creating a

potentially transformational leadership identity to negotiate future leadership challenges.

Since Whedon's groundbreaking feminist series, there have been many Buffys in many dark, dystopian worlds. This pop culture trend reflects the leadership shifts of third wave feminism, a new socially centered movement with girls and young women feeling "entitled to interact with men as equals, claim sexual pleasure as they desire it (heterosexual or otherwise), and actively play with femininity" (Snyder, 2008, p. 178) and masculinity as a fluid performance. Emphasizing engagement with community values rather than with individualistic ones, the invitation to stand as a leader is compelling in the dialogic 21st-century media world. The internally activated invitation also qualifies as a kind of cognitive leadership transformation, demonstrating a new application of the value of narrative in leadership strength as a way of "activating possible selves, [representing] the ideal model an individual may be striving for and something that could be leveraged by the leader to motivate and develop followers [and fans] into...leaders themselves" (Avolio, Wolumba, & Weber, 2009, p. 427).

FOUNDATIONAL LITERATURE: THE POWER OF STORY IN LEADERSHIP DEVELOPMENT AND THE NEUROPSYCHOLOGY OF IDENTITY

Although it may seem radical to claim that inner experiences generated by media narratives can inspire leadership development and motivation, the power of story has been long acknowledged in leadership research, and theorizing the impact of fictional "sheros" builds on that foundation. In fact, with the rising influence of media blockbusters and the virtual and face-to-face fan networks that rise in tandem, the influence of internalized role play has become increasingly clear as a tool for personal transformation. It is shortsighted to limit our leadership research by considering these influential shapers of 21st-century identity as adjunct to "the real world." In fact, as described above, recognizing the neurological power of the imaginary in the transformative negotiations of leadership authenticity, identity, and influence deepens established leadership development theories and practices.

The most influential foundational exploration of narrative and leadership largely focuses on the importance of an authentic and meaningful life story to affect consistency, persuasion, and influence through constant application of values and purpose (Gardner, Cogliser, Davis, & Dickens, 2011; George, 2003, 2007; Shamir & Eilam, 2005). Another thread of literature supporting the power of story is in leadership development and education, exploring the ways popular culture, particularly film, can be used to stimulate integration of key leadership concepts (Asbjornson, 2007; Badaracco, 2006; Callahan,

Whitener, & Sandlin, 2007; Huczynski & Buchanan, 2004; Nelson, 2008; Nicholson, 2015; Rosser, 2007; Sucher, 2007). A final area, relatively new, is the application of storytelling techniques from art, performance, and writing, either as metaphors or practices for leadership learning, not just as case studies (Cronin, 2008; Denhardt & Vinzant, 2005; Harrison & Akinc, 2000; Wong-Ming Ji, Kessler, Khilji, & Gopalakrishnan, 2014).

Storytelling and the reception of imaginary narrative are already seen as key languages of leadership development and learning, as well as a force in establishing effective relationships between leaders and followers. It is not much of a stretch to extend that understanding through new research in neurology and social psychology, detailed below, which demonstrates the deep influence of stories in human development, social change, and identity formation. These influences include the following potentials relevant to leadership development:

- to generate emotional and psychological outcomes in relationships and real-world success,
- to stimulate physiological and biochemical responses that create an inner reality, and
- to manifest in society as transformative or resistant trends.

Literature and film are transformative through three processes: simulation of other selves and other minds, fluctuations of personality, and persuasive indirect communication (Djikik & Oatley, 2014). This research demonstrates that reading fiction and watching films train social behavior, which can, in the short term, increase empathy and prosocial behavior. Training and enjoyment of the arts have also been shown to expand what Djikik & Oatley (2014) describe as *theory of mind*—an adaptive quality that supports the prosocial interpretation of beliefs, intents, desire, imagination, knowledge, and values for oneself and others, decreasing prejudice and increasing confidence and other avenues for personal connection. This change is both physiological and psychological. Studies using magnetic resonance imaging (MRI) indicate that poetic and aesthetic narratives activate the brain in areas associated with the story, including visual, aural, and emotional regions; narratives simulate outside-world experiences in interior space (Djikik & Oatley, 2014). Fictional narratives can temporarily destabilize the normally stable structures of personality and identity in ways that permit positive developmentally active learning and growth. These changes, while short-lived, "prompt emotions that are the reader's own" (Djikik & Oatley, 2014, p. 502), mirroring the characters' emotional journey. In sum, according to Djikik and Oatley (2014):

Art involves the non-directive property of inviting those who engage with it to experience their own emotions and thoughts [through another world]. Literature can help us navigate our self-development by transcending our current self while at the same time making available to us a multitude of potential future selves. (p. 503)

The power of literary exploration is magnified as literature is adapted to interconnected spaces of film and web communities. As fan groups form, consumers embrace the paradoxical experience of the suspension of disbelief in which the audience agrees to experience a fiction as real, a process that opens neural pathways and stimulates physiological experiences associated with "aesthetic delight" (Mukhopadhyay, 2014, p. 237). This critical engagement with playful identification is created by complex biochemical oscillations between the feeling of the real and the feeling of introspective detached contemplation, in which the audience is aware of the artistic product and appreciates it as an event (Mukhopadhyay, 2014). Mukhopadhyay's highly technical research seems to suggest that the paradox of aesthetic delight engages both cognitive and emotional parts of the brain, both task-based and self-referential, in a dynamic of appraisal and aversion that engages the imagination and the intellect in tandem, challenging habitual awareness and stimulating an active experience.

As part of cultural socialization, literature and film therefore offer a grounded psychophysical social process through the experience of story, part of a cultural ecology that reflects the ongoing transformation of norms and expectations as well as resistance to those changes. At their best, when literature and film challenge the status quo, they become part of experiential "conscientization" (Burton & Kagan, 2009, p. 56) in which an individual changes her perception of reality "by means of an active process of dialogue in which there is a gradual decoding of the world, [leading] to new self-understanding about the roots of what people are at present and what they could become" (Burton & Kagan, 2009, p. 56).

Leaders who ask "Who am I?" or "What can I contribute?" refer to formative narrative experiences that have shaped their perceptions of self and society to find the answers. For marginalized leaders, many of these experiences come from a lived imaginary that has been experienced internally as real, as a part of their self-selected and sometimes obsessive consumption of narratives through literature and media, where alternative and sometimes revolutionary roles are compellingly presented. Because girls' daily experiences generally model more stereotypical roles for female leaders, fiction becomes a place where young women can expand their identities and leadership expectations. YA dystopian fiction, film, and television offer a particularly fruitful source to track the power of that lived imaginary realm. The internal "rehearsal" of leadership narratives is part of establishing a new critical mindset, applicable to leadership studies through interdisciplinary analysis of popular YA dystopian trilogies/film adaptations, or transformational leadership blockbusters.

THE DYSTOPIAN YOUNG ADULT LEADERSHIP BLOCKBUSTER: MARKING CULTURAL CRISIS, TRANSFORMING LEADERSHIP MINDSET

The powerful imaginary space of leadership evolution is articulated, and can be studied, through new and evolving narratives of popular culture. Fiction and art are key in transforming individual and group mindsets in the bridges between the world and the individual human psyche. According to Donald (2014), "Art and popular culture artifacts... provide public, political information that expresses or constructs a political self in aesthetic form... [through] a metonymic... field in which cultural objects are interrelated and mutually reinforcing" (p. 658). The aesthetic language created by a genre can also generate a context for constructing a dynamic authenticity, depending on the audience and its engagement with the dialogue created with the art experience. In terms of YA dystopian fiction and film, the activity of fans, celebrities, and critics creates a rich cultural community in which non-traditional gender roles and embedded social criticism inform and transform participants.

Arguing in the interdisciplinary field of religious studies, Erb (2014) uses the term "spiritual blockbusters" (p. 6) to describe Hollywood films that reflect and create new spiritual cultures in contemporary Western society. She argues, "since the eighteenth century, there has been a turn away from external institutional authority and consensus values and toward an inner-directed quest for freedom and self-fulfillment" (p. 4). The influence of the inner quest in new leadership paradigms in YA fiction and film is most visibly expressed through leadership blockbusters, popular experiences that reflect changing cultural norms and the search for freedom and self-fulfillment by arguing for authenticity through revolutionary leadership. Girls and women, frequently the liberators in these narratives, use the vicarious experience to turn radically away from what Erb describes as external institutional authority to find their own authenticity, creating alternative roles outside of gender convention as part of the process.

The leadership blockbuster creates an opportunity for rehearsing roles and experiences in the unique biochemistry of the human psyche, physically and emotionally. Such rehearsals are not limited to gender, but can affect the ways identity and the capacity to influence others develop in a leader, and, even temporarily, alter core personality traits and beliefs. YA dystopian fiction bridges the possible and the daily, opening reception to social responses such as critique, desire, irony, or resistance. While subverting dominant cultural expectations, the most influential YA fiction tends to mirror the transformation of gender and other social expectations in the generational shift of millennials, born between 1980 and 2000. Brendler (2014) has observed: "Many of today's teenagers... reject the idea of gender as a determinant of societal roles.... There is as much diversity within gender as across genders" (p. 222). Further, the millennial generation has seen violent intercultural social and environmental upheavals that have transformed the way Western government regulates and monitors citizens. Dystopian distortions feel quite realistic in this context, as described vividly below:

> These texts force readers to examine themselves and question their potential responses to circumstances that seem very possible given our current global trajectory, yet they can ask those "what if" questions within the safety of their own [internal] world. The protagonists are dealing with very real ethical issues, such as whether it is ever moral to kill another human being or steal from others to survive, when civil disobedience is necessary, and will they be able to stand alone against an immoral society rather than acquiesce to corruption. (Brendler, 2014, p. 222)

In the increasingly "panopticon" lens (Foucault's all-seeing authoritarian eye) of post-9/11 culture, teens grow up in a world characterized by increasing regulation of civil liberties through surveillance and corporate power, paradoxically paired with increasing social freedoms like the fluid identity-play of the internet and the widespread legalization of gay marriage. Millennials are, therefore, faced with conflicting ideals about citizenship, leadership, and personal identity. The dystopian novel provides a realm of psychosocial exploration, an experiential space where consumers can try on alternative roles and know themselves as the protagonist in a revolutionary context. YA dystopian novels also provide a space to look back at the panopticon, claiming an imaginary leadership role, which may or may not be mirrored in their daily lives.

YA novelist Scott Westerfeld has noted: "Teen readers... question the way the world works and they question their place in it.... Being a teenager is a fundamentally alien experience" (as cited in Stone, 2006, para. 4). Dystopian fiction marks "the return of the repressed, all of [our] anxieties reappearing" (Hickey, 2013, p. 1) in an extreme, super-real/surreal context. These narratively-framed, imaginatively-lived questions of morality, history, and identity potentially impact future actions. The films and fiction are influential beyond their themes because of the indirect social influence of these internal, physiologically powerful, and chemically stimulating simulations of narrative. The films moderate and mirror social stresses and alternative authenticities and work as tools for conscientization in contemporary society (Burton & Kagan, 2009; Grant, Finkelstein, & Lyons, 2003).

As a case studies of alternative and authentic models for young girls and women, I briefly analyze two current leadership blockbusters: *The Hunger Games* (2008–2016) and *Divergent* (2011–2016). Both began as novels and have been made into blockbuster films (the former series completed this year; the latter, with promised sequels, is still in production), supported by a broad and active fan base celebrating the blockbusters' transformative leadership models for millennials.

Warrior Authenticity and Cultural Resistance in *The Hunger Games*

In terms of challenging conventional leadership gender roles, one of the most powerful and popular recent examples of a YA dystopia is Suzanne Collins' trilogy, *The Hunger Games*. Collins tells the story of Katniss Everdeen, a slave laborer from District 12 in a post-apocalyptic world controlled by the fascist President Snow from a city known only as the Capitol. When her little sister Prim is chosen in the annual lottery to stock the annual Hunger Games with child gladiators from each district, Katniss volunteers to replace her as a tribute. She fights to be the sole victor in the compulsory reality-TV-style spectacle designed to discourage rebellion. Katniss's brave and almost instinctive decision to volunteer is only the first step in her rise to becoming the Mockingjay, the hero of the revolution that ultimately overthrows the Capitol. Along the way, she fights twice in the Capitol's gladiatorial arena, struggles with PTSD, resists the possibility of love in her bleak and unforgiving world, and gradually moves from reluctant hero to consciously authentic leader, as both symbol and embodiment of freedom and resistance against the Capitol.

The series, which includes *The Hunger Games* (Collins, 2008), *Catching Fire* (Collins, 2009), and *Mockingjay* (Collins, 2010), is, by any standard, an unqualified hit, a multimedia blockbuster with international scope and an active, loyal, and diverse fan base (Lammers, Curwood, & Magnifico, 2012, p. 46). Pollitt (2012) calls *The Hunger Games* franchise "feral feminism," a useful catchphrase for this fierce revision of warrior leadership that moves beyond traditional gender roles. She describes Katniss as:

> A rare thing in pop fiction: a complex female character with courage, brains and a quest of her own. . . . We're worlds away from the vicious-little-rich-girls of *Gossip Girl* and its many knockoffs, where everything revolves around looks, clothes, consumerism, social status and sexual competition. (Pollitt, 2012)

By transcending their personal biographies through this fictional feral feminist world, audiences experiment with their own leadership development, a kind of armchair heroism that teaches through nondirective influence. The story offers a relentless and fierce lesson in the challenges of transformational leadership, with an adrenaline rush of betrayals, illusions, and leadership puzzles. Until the final 10 pages of the last book, Katniss never truly exercises control over her body, her sexuality, or her expected role in the dramas playing out in the culture around her. She must fight for her life, first in District 12's starvation conditions, then in a televised prison, and finally in an actual war zone. Along the way, she must submit to repeated hyper-feminine and propagandistic makeovers in the public eye, first as a tribute in the Capitol, then as a victor, and finally as the Mockingjay, symbol of the rebellion.

Being herself, whatever that might mean, is subsumed by the struggle for survival and the manipulations of those in power. As a result, it is only in flashes of resistance that Katniss can be authentic. Compellingly, these moments of authenticity make her the Mockingjay, as she is unpredictable, volatile, and honest. The most compelling leadership lesson of the story is woven into this vision of instinctive authenticity, a primal refusal to submit to a makeover that overwrites her true self. Drawn to this deeply felt refusal, audiences lose themselves in Katniss, in the possibility of standing up as leaders in their own lives, experiencing authenticity as a kind of post-feminine androgyny. In this world, gender and sexuality are not innate qualities that make good leaders successful. Rather, the concepts of masculine and feminine are so commodified that they become nearly meaningless. They are presented as a performance of privilege, stylized and disengaged from authentic identity. Good leadership, therefore, is independent of conformity to social gender norms or success in sexually defined roles because rules for gender conformity are explicitly arbitrary and political, a performance of privilege, cultural context, and the oppressions that shaped the rules in the first place.

Katniss's success has nothing to do with her beauty and more to do with her scars, her bluntness, her heart, and her warrior strength. To the extent any of the trilogy characters exercise gendered charisma or conformity, they become more suspect and corrupt, buying into norms of privilege that are both inauthentic and oppressive. Internal identity and values are far more important than social role play, which brings audiences emotionally and persuasively to consider two powerful leadership questions: What are my values as a leader? Who am I really, when everything superficial, including cultural gender roles, is stripped away, and I am revealed in my wounded, wise authenticity?

Leadership Through Self-Determination and Revolutionary Integration in *Divergent*

In 2013, Veronica Roth's *Divergent* series pushed *The Hunger Games* off the top of the YA books charts, selling 6.7 million copies (Roback, 2014).

Within two months of its release in 2014, the first film adapted from the series earned more than $250 million worldwide in 55 markets, and the film's release pushed book sales to 21 million copies worldwide (McNary, 2014). As with *The Hunger Games*, a Google search reveals that Internet fan sites bloomed internationally, with activities to bolster identification with its androgynous female hero and her society, and seemingly infinite opportunities to debate plot points and create fan fiction. Roth's trilogy is an equally influential leadership blockbuster, in terms of capital-generation, community-building, popularity, and thematic power.

Roth's trilogy, consisting of *Divergent* (2011), *Insurgent* (2012), and *Allegiant* (2013), tells the story of Beatrice Prior, born into a society that divides its citizens into factions according to certain qualities. Beatrice is born into Abnegation (selfless administrators), the group assigned to govern an isolated post-war cluster of survivors in bombed-out Chicago. The other factions include Dauntless (brave warriors), Amity (peaceful farmers), Erudite (intelligent researchers/scientists), Candor (honest protectors of law), and the Factionless (outliers who failed initiation or were exiled from a faction).

When Beatrice comes of age, she takes a virtual reality aptitude test that reveals she is (as the title of the first book declares) "divergent"—that is, combining qualities from many factions. In the annual ritual for all 16-year-olds, she claims Dauntless and changes her name to Tris and learns to fight, master pain, and find courage. She also learns she must hide her divergence or be killed as a perceived threat to society. Soon after she is initiated into her new faction, civil war between Erudite and Abnegation breaks out, and the Dauntless soldiers are chemically brainwashed into fighting the war. Tris and her Dauntless boyfriend Four organize an intervention in the civil war, barely survive, and go on to lead a revolution against the real oppressors behind the scenes. Throughout the series, Tris emerges as a clear leader above all others and, in each of the factions she encounters, she gains greater influence and respect as she embraces her divergent authenticity. Responding to revelations of genetic experiments, socially motivated manipulations, and sinister plans to use drugs to keep people in rigid factions, she leads a rebellion against the experimenters and ultimately sacrifices herself in order to free the city.

Like Katniss, Tris is a feral feminist who has chosen an androgynous role and gaining strength from inner authenticity rather than from femininity. However, she masters the complex, less overtly fascist structure of her society strategically, with each choice claiming and achieving control over her destiny. Like Katniss, though, her difference becomes the problem she must solve, the quality she must honor in order to lead. Tris's divergence is powerful and dangerous, the paradox that helps her become a great leader, engaging reader/viewer feelings of exclusion and exile to activate their own inner divergence. Her strength is a difficult one, growing out of her ability

to find ways to conform on the surface without compromising her true nature, revealing herself more and more only as society changes through her
leadership. In the end, even her martyrdom grows out of her divergence,
which makes her both stubbornly idealistic and resistant to being controlled
through drugs and brainwashing:

> Every faction conditions its members to think and act a certain way.... But
> our minds move in a dozen different directions. We can't be confined to one
> way of thinking, and that terrifies our leaders. It means we can't be controlled.
> (Roth, 2011, pp. 441–442)

Gender performance in the *Divergent* world is less visible and less oppressive than it is in Katniss's universe. Within factions, men and women rise
based on their abilities, not their gender conformity. The performance of
gender is subsumed in different faction personality structures because the
function of mating is to purify faction genetics, with the faction values creating a person's most important identity. This plot rule creates a world where,
intriguingly, gender is unimportant to leadership. Tris ultimately expresses
her gender as an androgynous warrior, true to the Dauntless ideal, offering
a powerful experience for girls and young women for whom gender performance is a defining characteristic. Her tattoos, muscles, and physical prowess
are universally attractive in the Dauntless culture reflecting the transformation into a disciplined warrior, the foundation of her divergent authenticity.

Readers/viewers have the opportunity to experience her strength and
fierceness as desirable but not gender-based. She is more than a sexy, battle-
ready virago. As divergent, she has qualities of all the factions, including
modesty, honesty, and intelligence; by the end of the trilogy, she embodies
each in her performance as a leader. She also finds a partner in another
strong leader and divergent Dauntless, Four, an emotionally sensitive and
equally strategic mate who recognizes and honors her many strengths. Their
equal relationship eroticizes divergence to celebrate Tris's budding sexuality while modeling co-leadership and a meeting of equals.

What makes Tris's warrior leadership most radical is that it comes from
a calculated and strategic insistence on subversive and/or explicit rebellion and from using the gifts of all five factions. She is much more than a
warrior; she is a shapeshifting leader with the integrity to make her vision
effective and transformative (Burbank, 2012). She is powerful because she
can't be controlled, which means that the shifting identity and perspectives she
embodies invite readers/viewers to explore multiple leadership styles and
solutions, compellingly framed by a just war in the face of dystopian betray-
al. In this context, leadership is what she makes of it, not what her society
dictates. Audiences internalizing this narrative emotionally and persuasively
consider two powerful leadership questions: What leadership qualities am I

masking in order to survive? Who might I be, when these masks, including the cultural limitations of dominant stereotypes, are stripped away, and I am revealed in my full power?

THE ROLE OF LEADERSHIP BLOCKBUSTERS IN TRACKING GENDER SHIFTS AND SUPPORTING TRANSFORMATIONAL LEADERSHIP DEVELOPMENT AND LEADERSHIP RESEARCH

These blockbusters are more than carefully constructed entertainment reflecting powerful contemporary issues and anxieties. For millions of fans, they create internalized, biochemically, and psychologically powerful experiences that offer a felt-as-real rehearsal of radical female leadership. When leadership blockbusters offer crucibles that transform conventional cultural leadership roles, they have the ability to transform personal identity on the deepest levels of neuropsychological development, particularly for girls and women searching for an empowering and transformational leadership mindset. These lived imaginary selves have a reality that reflects changing values and struggles in the real world, often signaling changes that we have yet to see in mainstream leadership circles. As a result, they offer a window not only into resistances and transformations in cultural roles of women and girls, but also into the intimate and mediated development of new leadership paradigms, a revolution from within. The internal process of creating a potentially transformational leadership identity supports future negotiations of leadership challenges and creates new roles by establishing a persuasive and critical inner reality as a foundation for action.

Therefore, the transformative role for literary and cinematic fiction in leadership development goes beyond the most common current applications of classroom discussion or training case study. In the interactive multimedia context of contemporary entertainment, the leadership blockbuster is a development tool that offers embodied experiences of alternative, imaginary realities. If we acknowledge the influence of this tool on mindset and behavioral development, we can then apply and study what they reveal in several ways:

1. When choosing case studies from popular culture, teachers/trainers can be attentive to holistic and transformational learning, not just intellectual exploration, which is the tip of the iceberg in terms of the power of the imagined life. Since learners internalize lessons as part of their own process of negotiating leadership authenticity, their responses could be used to challenge and problematize dominant leadership paradigms through the choice of leadership blockbusters that challenge gendered leadership assumptions. Further data and case studies can be drawn from students' favorite pop

culture leadership narratives, with opportunities to reflect, analyze, and share foundational stories as part of ongoing leadership
development, or as a way to track and challenge the generational
evolution of gendered leadership roles. Since conscientization and
authenticity are, or should be, goals in leadership development,
making these inner experiences more conscious and accessing
their power by encouraging learners to take practical steps based
on these internal realities can encourage more effective and authentic negotiations with mainstream leadership roles. This active
application is particularly important for girls and women, but it can
be effective for other marginalized populations and even for leaders born into privileged roles who may be able to better embody
their transformational vision in the process of conscientization.

2. These popular cultural documents offer a space to track leadership values and identities that so far exist largely in the imaginary
processes of pop culture consumers, in particular girls and women
exploring and developing. Interdisciplinary methodologies are
needed to effectively study this space, since it covers such complicated narrative negotiations and artifacts that reflect an interior
shift as well as mediated cultural blockbusters. Critical analysis of
leadership narratives and character development must be supple-
mented with ethnographic, statistical, and nuanced theoretical
analysis of the online fan spaces, which offer layered evidence of
influence and mindset.

3. Biographical studies of leaders should highlight fictional and
imaginary leaders who shaped a living leader's life, practices, and
expectations. These memories of popular culture are more than
reminders of youthful entertainments; they serve as spaces for
personal and social development. It may well be that in the globalized realm of leadership, the intersectionality of a leader's identity
and roles will be illuminated by identifying which narratives from
national and international culture influenced their personal and
professional development. With particular focus on gendered imaginaries, both transgressive and traditional, we can better understand the ways visionary and transformational leaders have mined
cultural experiences to create the tools they use to persist despite
resistance and other obstacles. An interesting by-product of this
understanding will be to track the identities that are foregrounded
or hidden in leaders' strategic performance of their authenticity as
they build influence. For female leaders, this strategic negotiation
is of special interest. The leadership blockbusters, specifically the
two series highlighted in this chapter, are valuable tools to examine

the self-shaping leadership narratives that create the identity tools that fuel efficacy and vision for marginalized, influential leaders.

4. Finally, acknowledging the internalized process of gendered leadership development formation and/or radicalization through the dystopian leadership blockbuster opens a valuable resource for examining the complex gender assumptions in leadership roles for girls and women. Since transformational leadership is, at its heart, about creating a world that does not yet exist, new gendered cultural imaginaries serve as a space of self-invention, cultural change, and strategic problem solving that must not be ignored. Considering the intersectionality of multiple economic, racial, and national identities, these blockbusters and others like them can open up multiple discourses with layered coding that tracks the negotiations of identity, gender roles, and the stories (public and private) that shape those negotiations.

YA dystopian leadership blockbusters, tracking and animating the multiple crises that face the world, create an authentic inner experience of revolution that has captured a generation's creative imagination and shaped a new kind of female leadership narrative, popular both because of and despite its resistance to conventional leadership roles for women. Individuals and organizations are potentially shaped by these neuropsychological developmental experiences. Given the popularity of these gender-bending leadership blockbusters, transformative imaginary experience is key in framing new potentials for leadership and change. As we explore the dynamic and foundational role of aesthetic experience, we should no longer treat fiction as adjunct to "the real world," but rather we must acknowledge the power of internalized story in the transformative negotiations of leadership authenticity, identity, and influence.

REFERENCES

Asbjornson, K. (2007). Issues & observations: Making the connection between art and leadership. *Leadership in Action, 27*(4), 22–24.

Avolio, B. J., Walumba, F. O., & Weber, T. J. (2009). Leadership: Current theories, research, and future directions. *Annual Review of Psychology, 60,* 421–449.

Badaracco, J. L. (2006). *Questions of character: Illuminating the heart of leadership through literature.* Boston, MA: Harvard Business School Press.

Brendler, B. M. (2014). Blurring gender lines in reader's advisory for young adults. *Reference and User Services Quarterly, 53*(3), 221–224.

Burbank, C. (2012). Shapeshifter leadership: Responding creatively to the challenges of a complex world. In C. S. Pearson (Ed.), *The transforming leader: New approaches to leadership for the twenty-first century* (pp. 140–149). San Francisco, CA: Berrett-Kochler.

Burton, M., & Kagan, C. (2009). Towards a really social psychology: Liberation psychology beyond Latin America. In M. Montero & C. C. Sonn, (Eds.), *Psychology of liberation: Theory and applications* (pp. 51–72). New York, NY: Springer.

Callahan, J. L., Whitener, J., & Sandlin, J. A. (2007). The art of creating leaders: Popular culture artifacts as pathways for development. *Advances in Developing Human Resources, 9*(2), 146–165.

Collins, S. (2008). *The hunger games.* New York, NY: Scholastic Press. Kindle Edition.

Collins, S. (2009). *Catching fire.* New York, NY: Scholastic Press. Kindle Edition.

Collins, S. (2010). *Mockingjay.* New York, NY: Scholastic Press. Kindle Edition.

Cronin, T. E. (2008). "All the world's a stage . . . " Acting and the art of political leadership. *The Leadership Quarterly, 19*(4), 459–468.

Denhardt, R. B., & Denhardt, J. V. (2005). *The dance of leadership: The art of leading in business, government, and society.* Armonk, NY: M. E. Sharpe.

Djikic, M., & Oatley, K. (2014). The art in fiction: From indirect communication to changes of the self. *Psychology of Aesthetics, Creativity, & the Arts, 8*(4), 498–505.

Donald, S. H. (2014). Red aesthetics, intermediality and the use of posters in Chinese cinema after 1949. *Asian Studies Review, 38*(4), 658–675.

Erb, C. M. (2014). A spiritual blockbuster: *Avatar,* environmentalism and the new religions. *Journal of Film and Video, 66*(3), 3–17.

Gardner, W. L., Cogliser, C. C., Davis, K. M. & Dickens, M. P. (2011). Authentic leadership: A review of the literature and research agenda. *The Leadership Quarterly, 22*(6), 1120–1145.

George, B. (2003). *Authentic leadership: Rediscovering the secrets to creating lasting value.* San Francisco, CA: Jossey-Bass.

George, B. (2007). *True north: Discover your authentic leadership.* San Francisco, CA: Jossey-Bass.

Grant, K. E., Finkelstein, J. S., & Lyons, A. L. (2003). Integrating psychological research on girls with feminist activism: A model for building a liberation psychology in the United States. *American Journal of Community Psychology, 31*(1–2), 143–155.

Hickey, K. (2013, November 20). M. T. Anderson reflects on where we are, years after his iconic book, Feed. *The Yalsa Hub.* Retrieved from http://www.yalsa.ala.org/thehub/2013/11/20/m-t-anderson-reflects-on-where-we-are-years-after-his-iconic-book-feed/

Huczynski, A., & Buchanan, D. (2004). Theory from fiction: A narrative process perspective on the pedagogical use of feature film. *Journal of Management Education, 28*(6), 707–726.

Harrison, J. K., & Akinc, H. (2000). Lessons in leadership from the arts and literature: A liberal arts approach to management education through fifth discipline learning. *Journal of Management Education, 24*(3), 391–413.

Kociemba, D. (2011). Why Xander matters: The extraordinary ordinary in *Buffy the Vampire Slayer.* In J. Battis (Ed.), *Supernatural youth: The rise of the teen hero in literature and popular culture* (pp. 80–101). Lanham, MD: Lexington Books.

Lammers, J. C., Curwood, J. S., & Magnifico, A. M. (2012). Toward an affinity space methodology: Considerations for literacy research. *English Teaching, Practice and Critique, 11*(2), 44–58.

McNary, D. (2014, May 5). Divergent hits $250 million worldwide. *Variety*. Retrieved from http://variety.com/2014/film/news/divergent-box-office-1201172446/

Mukhopadhyay, D. (2014). Understanding the neuropsychology of aesthetic paradox: The dual phase oscillation. *Review of General Psychology, 18*(3), 237–248.

Nel, D. (2011). "Does the phrase 'vampire slayer' mean anything to you?": The discursive construction of the just woman warrior trope in Joss Whedon's *Buffy the Vampire Slayer* TV xseries. In J. Battis (Ed.), *Supernatural youth: The rise of the teen hero in literature and popular culture* (pp. 65–79). Lanham, MD: Lexington Books.

Nelson, M. (2008). Odysseus and Aeneas: A classical perspective on leadership. *The Leadership Quarterly, 19*(4), 469–477.

Nicholson, M. A. (2015). What films reveal about women as global leaders. In F. W. Ngunjuri & S. R. Madsen (Eds.), *Women as global leaders* (pp. 233–249). Charlotte, NC: Information Age.

Pascale, A. & Fillion, N. (2014). *Joss Whedon: The biography*. Chicago, IL: Chicago Review.

Pollitt, K. (2012, April 23). The Hunger Games: Feral feminism. *Nation*. Retrieved from http://www.thenation.com/article/167182/hunger-games-feral-feminism#

Roback, D. (2014, March 14). Facts & figures 2013: For children's books, Divergent led the pack. *Publisher's Weekly*. Retrieved from http://www.publishersweekly.com/pw/by-topic/childrens/childrens-industry-news/article/61447-for-children-s-books-in-2013-divergent-led-the-pack-facts-figures-2013.html

Rosser, M. H. (2007). The magic of leadership: An exploration of *Harry Potter and the Goblet of Fire*. *Advances in Developing Human Resources, 9*(2), 236–250.

Roth, V. (2011). *Divergent*. New York, NY: HarperCollins.

Roth, V. (2012). *Insurgent*. New York, NY: HarperCollins.

Roth, V. (2013). *Allegiant*. New York, NY: HarperCollins.

Shamir, B., & Eilam, G. (2005). "What's your story?" A life-stories approach to authentic leadership development. *The Leadership Quarterly, 16*(3), 395–417.

Snyder, R. C. (2008). What is third-wave feminism? A new directions essay. *Signs, 34*(1), 175–196.

Stone, K. (2006, December). A conversation with Scott Westerfeld. *SF Site*. Retrieved from https://www.sfsite.com/12b/sc238.htm

Sucher, S. J. (2007). *Teaching the moral leader: A literature-based leadership course: A guide for instructors*. New York, NY: Routledge.

Urbanski, H. (Ed.). (2011). *Writing and the digital generation: Essays on new media rhetoric*. Jefferson, NC: McFarland.

Whedon. J. (Writer, Director). (2003, May 20). The chosen [Television series episode]. In *Buffy the Vampire Slayer*. Los Angeles, CA: Warner Brothers Studio.

Wong-MingJi, D. J., Kessler, E. H., Khilji, S. E., & Gopalakrishnan, S. (2014). Cross-cultural comparison of cultural mythologies and leadership patterns. *South Asian Journal of Global Business Research, 3*(1), 79–101.

Zap2it.com. (2003, May 21). *'Buffy' finale stakes strong ratings for UPN*. Retrieved from http://web.archive.org/web/20030524173301/http://tv.zap2it.com/news/tvnewsdaily.html?31651

CHAPTER 6

EMBRACING CONTEXT IN LEADERSHIP THEORY

Lessons From Negotiation Research

Mary M. Keegin
DePaul University

Alice F. Stuhlmacher
DePaul University

Amber S. Cotton
DePaul University

Many prominent leadership theories discuss leader behavior or style but pay less attention to how context may influence the effectiveness of different leadership approaches (Dinh et al., 2014). While it is useful for theories to consider universal themes, it seems that the "devil is in the details" as far as understanding women's advancement in leadership. This chapter encourages researchers to attend to the specific role of context for theory building. For us, context refers to the interrelated conditions or circumstances in the environment that vary across organizations, settings, people,

Theorizing Women and Leadership, pages 89–100
Copyright © 2017 by Information Age Publishing
All rights of reproduction in any form reserved.

and time. We call for increased theorizing that integrates contextual variables in the design and testing of interventions that advance women leaders. To do this, we use examples from research in workplace negotiation to illustrate that contextual variables are crucial to understanding the role of gender in the workplace. Increased attention to context in leadership theory can lead to testing strategies for equalizing workplace outcomes between men and women.

LEADERSHIP AND CONTEXT

Examining context in leadership theory is not new. Contingency theories of leadership assert that there is no single best way to lead; rather, the features of an organization's environment or situation are important (e.g., choosing a task-motivated or relationship-motivated style; Fiedler, 1964). A recent review of leadership theories found that interest in the classic contingency theories has dwindled, while theories that take a systems approach (e.g., contextual, complexity, and social network) are growing (Dinh et al., 2014). An example is the theorizing of Hogue and Lord (2007) relative to complexity and connectivity, who examine how bias against women leaders is generated and reinforced at various levels of analysis within organizations. We also see a healthy line of research using role congruity theory (Eagly & Karau, 2002), which discusses the gender context as a set of socially constructed norms and expectations.

In addition to context being found in some leadership theories, the impact of context is evident in research findings. A meta-analysis comparing men and women in the same leadership situations and using the same behaviors found that ratings of effectiveness varied by the masculinity or femininity of leader style, the distribution of men and women in leadership, the sex of subordinates, and the organization type (Eagly, Makhijani, & Klonsky, 1992). A recent meta-analysis suggests that women leaders are perceived differently from men depending on the level of management and whether the industry is male or female dominated (Paustian-Underdahl, Walker, & Woehr, 2014). Important context dimensions include the type of job (Heilman, Wallen, Fuchs, & Tamkins, 2004) and the gender composition of the workgroup in relation to the leader (McDonald, Toussaint, & Schweiger, 2004; Yoder, Schleicher, & McDonald, 1998). For example, Heilman and colleagues (2004) found that women who excelled in masculine-typed tasks were liked less than men were, which drove negative evaluations of women's performance and led to fewer opportunities for organizational rewards. In such situations, the context was not aligned with the expectations for women's behavior and resulted in more negative evaluations relative to men. Yoder and colleagues (1998) also found that women's likability, an important factor in establishing power as a leader, depended on the gender composition of their work groups. They found that women who were appointed as leader of an entirely male work group received the highest likability ratings when they were formally trained and legitimated by a credible male. Comparatively, token women leaders who were not endorsed by a male colleague (or were endorsed by a colleague whose credibility has yet to be established) received lower likeability ratings.

Given the importance of context, this chapter urges leadership theorists to clearly articulate the nuances of context in explaining women leaders' struggle with advancement. To illustrate, we offer some intriguing examples of context in workplace negotiations.

NEGOTIATION AND CONTEXT

Negotiation is an appropriate literature base to consider in relation to research on women in leadership. Like leadership, negotiation is a masculine-stereotyped role (Stuhlmacher & Linnabery, 2013). The assertiveness expected of negotiators creates a double bind for women as they face a tradeoff between being seen as a successful negotiator (tough and aggressive) or a likeable woman (friendly and helpful). Negotiation is more than exchanging offers when buying a house or agreeing on a labor contract; it is the "deliberate interactions of two or more complex social units which are attempting to define or redefine the terms of their interdependence" (Walton & McKersie, 1965, p. 3). Beyond the formal negotiations required to reach agreements, negotiation infuses everyday interactions, particularly in the actions and decisions that are part of being a leader. Through negotiation, individuals acquire the tangible and intangible resources related to achieving goals and influencing others.

Forty years ago, negotiation researchers discounted the existence of gender differences in negotiation (Rubin & Brown, 1975). Later research took a closer look at the negotiation context and found subtle but pervasive effects for gender on negotiation processes and outcomes (for a review see Stuhlmacher & Linnabery, 2013). Substantial evidence in the negotiation literature now shows that women are more reluctant negotiators and face challenges that male negotiators do not in achieving positive outcomes for themselves. However, there are also contexts we discuss later in which women tend to outperform men (e.g., feminine-stereotyped topics and advocacy situations). The understanding of gender in negotiation has been aided by theorizing that moves away from models that consider gender as a stable individual difference to gender-in-context models that recognize situational influences on gender differences (cf. Bowles & McGinn, 2008). To highlight this concept, we discuss how negotiation research examines context as it relates to the strength or salience of the situation as examined in structural ambiguity, task framing, the presence and type of constituents, experience, and status.

Situation Strength as Context

In both negotiation and leadership, the role of ambiguous contexts operates similarly. That is, the clarity of norms and expectations for behavior in a particular situation (i.e., the situation strength) determines the salience of the gender norms and the strength of the gender differences that are found (Eagly & Karau, 2002; Mischel, 1977). In this way, there is a parallel with personality and other individual difference variables. In strong situations (e.g., situations with clear norms and expectations for appropriate behavior), individual difference variables have small effects (Bowles, Babcock, & McGinn, 2005; Mischel, 1977). Strong situations, which involve firm norms and scripts for actions, decrease the variability in people's behaviors compared to weaker situations. In weak situations, with few prescriptions about behavior, there is more opportunity to see the effect of individual differences in behaviors. The negotiation literature has delineated the role of ambiguous situations on gender differences in several important ways that can contribute to theory building on women in leadership.

Structural Ambiguity

One aspect of the situational strength is structural ambiguity, or, in the case of negotiation, the clarity of information about options, issues, and outcomes available in the negotiation space (Bowles et al., 2005). In industries characterized by structural ambiguity in pay ranges (e.g., advertising/marketing, retail, entertainment/media), Bowles and colleagues (2005) found a difference of $10,000 between the starting salaries of male and female MBAs even after controlling for salary-related factors such as job function, pre-MBA work experience, job market activity, the geographic location of the position, and job preferences. No such difference was found in industries with low structural ambiguity (e.g., investment banking, consulting, and consumer products).

In a lab-based experiment, Bowles and colleagues (2005) tested the effects of structural ambiguity in a stereotypically masculine, competitive, single-issue negotiation. Structural ambiguity was manipulated such that the buyers in a negotiation were either given a target price for purchasing halogen headlights for motorcycles (i.e., low ambiguity) or no target price (i.e., high ambiguity). Under high ambiguity, men (compared to women) expected to achieve a price that was 10% better, made initial price offers 19% lower, and agreed on final price values that were 27% lower.

Under conditions of low structural ambiguity in which there was a target price, there were no significant gender differences. These findings indicate that industries with high structural ambiguity (characterized by fewer cues about outcomes) may increase reliance on the stereotypes, therefore placing women in a less effective position.

The effects of structural ambiguity were confirmed in a 2015 meta-analysis that found that the gender difference in negotiation outcomes favoring men was significantly reduced when negotiators were provided with information about the bargaining range (Mazei et al., 2015). A reduction in structural ambiguity may make it easier for women to justify the use of a broader range of negotiation tactics, including those that are stereotypically masculine. Therefore, the negotiation literature builds on the contributions from leadership theory about the boundary conditions of gender effects by incorporating theory on situation strength as a feature of negotiation contexts. It is important to note, however, that the impact of ambiguity can be different for men and women and by situation, which we will return to later in considering implications for women's advancement in leadership.

Framing

Structural ambiguity is one form of situation strength; another aspect is how the situation is framed. Here, *framing* refers to the concept of attribute framing, "in which some characteristic of an object or event serves as the focus" of attention (Levin, Schneider, & Gaeth, 1998, p. 150). The framing of the situation imposes certain expectations, which may change when the context is framed differently. The negotiation literature provides evidence for the influence of framing on gender differences and serves as a useful area of research that can also be applied to leadership.

In a gender-related framing context, Small, Gelfand, Babcock, and Gettman (2007) found that women were more likely to initiate a negotiation if they were encouraged to "ask" rather than "negotiate," given that asking is more in line with politeness stereotypes for women. Surprisingly, small differences in how the context is framed can have a large impact on women's success, reiterating that theory should be attentive to subtleties of the situation.

Negotiation research has also demonstrated that women are more successful in tasks that are framed as congruent with the female gender role (Bear, 2011; Bear & Babcock, 2012). This theory has been tested by comparing identically structured tasks but with gendered negotiation topics. Men had better negotiation outcomes with masculine stereotyped issues (e.g., motorcycle halogen headlights) but not feminine stereotyped issues (e.g., buying/selling jewelry beads, workplace lactation rooms; Bear, 2011). Bear (2011) found that women were more likely than men to avoid negotiations that were masculine-typed (e.g, compensation), whereas men were more likely than women to avoid negotiations that were feminine-typed (e.g., access to a lactation room). In these studies, the requirements of the task were exactly the same, but the context was varied. Women may receive discouraging feedback about their negotiation skills when, in actuality, it may be the gender-related framing of the task that is an initial barrier. Bear and Babcock (2012) make a compelling point that the business world may be evaluating negotiation success only on masculine topics and standards, which would lead men to overestimate their negotiation skills and women to underestimate their skills. The effects would be compounded if, as Sax (2008) suggests, women tend to underestimate their ability to perform compared to men (i.e., lower self-efficacy), even when they possess similar skill sets and performance.

Findings relating to framing and structural ambiguity suggest that situation strength can be an important contextual feature to incorporate into leadership theorizing relating to gender differences.

Constituents as Context

Negotiation research suggests that another important aspect of context consists of the presence and type of constituents. Given that leaders are often advocating for others (e.g., on behalf of subordinates or customers), findings from the negotiation literature can provide additional justification for a focus on constituents as a feature of context that impacts men and women leaders differently. As one example, women perform better in negotiation when the task is advocacy or negotiating on another's behalf rather than solely for themselves (Amanatullah & Morris, 2010; Bowles et al., 2005; Mazei et al., 2015). This tendency to perform better was especially strong under conditions without target goals for outcomes in the negotiation (Bowles et al., 2005). Women's reluctance to initiate negotiations on their own behalf may stem from the real concern that they will be perceived negatively and face backlash (Amanatullah & Morris, 2010; Bowles, Babcock, & Lai, 2007). Notably, when working on behalf of another person, women received fewer negative evaluations and fewer social sanctions than when they were negotiating for themselves (Amanatullah & Morris, 2010). Women's performance advantage for advocacy is robust; meta-analytic results find that the gender difference favoring men in negotiation was significantly reduced when negotiators acted on behalf of a single individual as compared to negotiating for themselves or on behalf of a larger entity (Mazei et al., 2015). Based on these findings, gender-related norms and scripts for behavior (e.g., women's advocacy on behalf of others) serve as elements for manipulation in certain contexts to reduce gender differences.

To aid the research on women in leadership, the inclusion of constituent-related factors can improve our understanding of when and why women leaders may face challenges that are not present for men.

Experience and Status as Context

Women's experience and authority represent another way context has been examined in negotiation theory on gender differences. Past experiences and legitimate power provide a context to situations and expectations. For example, negotiation outcomes differ for those with and without experience. Negotiation experience allows practice in various approaches and skills that reduces ambiguity for appropriate behavior; even a single negotiation opportunity can increase future performance (Zerres, Hüffmeier, Freund, Backhaus, & Hertel, 2013). A recent meta-analysis found that women who have experience in management and negotiation do better in gaining resources in a negotiation than those without experience (Mazei et al., 2015). In another example, when negotiators were asked to recall a past incident in which they felt powerful (a power prime), women reported that they were less intimidated by the prospect of negotiating; the same variable had no effect on men's performance (Small et al., 2007).

Similarly, the status of individuals involved in negotiation can create a strong situation that reduces ambiguity. Amanatullah and Tinsley (2013) found that negotiation requests made by women with externally conferred status (e.g., overt respect from colleagues) and legitimate power (e.g., high rank) were as successful as those made by men, which was not the case for low-status women. Higher organizational rank was associated with more perceived legitimacy and led to less social and financial backlash for women. These context variables warrant more study in relation to leadership.

Context in Aggregate

Gender can have small effect sizes in relation to overall behavior, but the effects can be large in weak situations and when they are aggregated across time and contexts. For example, women who fail to negotiate successfully for their starting salary see a compounding effect over time that widens the discrepancy between themselves and their male counterparts, especially when raises are based on percent increases of current pay.

Small changes in the context (e.g., re-framing tasks, having experience) can have a noticeable impact on gender outcomes in negotiation, often through a reduction in ambiguity about what behaviors are appropriate or expected. This underscores the idea that integrating context into theories is helpful. For example, in 1999, Stuhlmacher and Walters published a meta-analysis showing a small but significant effect for a negotiation advantage for men. The study findings ran counter to the prevailing notion of nonexistent gender differences in negotiation. An update and expansion of that meta-analysis by Mazei et al. (2015) found even larger and more variable effect sizes (ranging from Hedges g of -2.07 to g of 2.14) than the 1999 study. This variability can be attributed to an increased focus in negotiation research testing and manipulating contextual variables related to gender differences. This aggregated effect of context can be seen in Mazei et al.'s (2015) analysis that combined sets of moderators: Situations that were predicted to advantage men were compared to situations that were predicted to advantage women. The combined effect sized moved from a g of 0.49 to a g of -0.17—a difference of 0.66—when comparing conditions with varying amounts of congruence for women. The effect sizes indicate that when women negotiators were in situations that are favorable to them (e.g., low structural ambiguity, experience, and negotiating on behalf of another), their outcomes exceed those of male negotiators.

By integrating context and gender in negotiation, leadership scholars might expect that the leadership disadvantage for women may be canceled out depending on the ability of women to manipulate the context (e.g., shift the frame of the situation). Alternatively, other variables women bring to a situation (e.g., previous experience) can reduce the ambiguity in the leader role.

CONTEXT IN EVIDENCE-BASED INTERVENTIONS

Theory that thoroughly incorporates context to explain influences on leader success could guide evidence-based interventions to attenuate backlash and increase women's leadership effectiveness. The gender and negotiation literature is moving from describing the situation to testing theory-driven interventions and applications in the workplace. For example, Bowles and Babcock (2013) tested how women legitimated their requests for higher pay and the social and economic outcomes that resulted. The negotiation research of Bowles and Babcock is widely distributed in MBA negotiation courses, as it has been translated by scholars and picked up by organizations and news outlets. Reducing ambiguity regarding salary negotiations was applied recently at Reddit, where salary negotiation was "banned" as part of the employment process (O'Brien, 2015). The key aspects of a no-negotiation policy are that it should help organizations reevaluate what determines pay, and some of the ambiguity of the hiring process is therefore removed. Determining pay level by the job and the needed qualifications, rather than whether a person negotiates, could equalize economic resources among men and women beginning their careers.

Leadership theorists can address the steps needed to reduce ambiguity and help women navigate situations where their work roles are not congruent with traditional female gender roles. How do theories adjust for men's and women's experiences with leadership? What is the impact of interventions aimed at early educational opportunities for developing leadership skills or reframing previous experiences as congruent with leader and female gender roles? Research on leaders and leadership development could further address these questions by layering in an understanding of context. The short-term interventions that are traditionally studied (e.g., training) could be expanded to consider how that skill development may be enhanced or inhibited as a byproduct of previous work and life experiences.

Theorists could pay attention to situational factors that build the legitimacy granted to women leaders or the ways that recognizing women for their contributions and their formal role behavior may aid in reducing backlash effects. A promising area of existing leadership research is based on leader identity development (Ely, Ibarra, & Kolb, 2011). Ely and colleagues outline the theory of identity work as it pertains to women's cultivation of their identities as leaders and explain that a number of factors (e.g., masculine stereotypes) inhibit this process. Leadership research can expand these ideas through considering how ambiguity and framing relate to the complexities women face in tackling novel environments and tasks that are important experience markers for their potential as leaders.

Theory-based applications could test how the structure of an organization's selection, training, and rewards for leadership could reframe policies and procedures in gender-neutral terms about how to be effective, rather than perpetuating stereotypes about leadership. This could involve studying organizational cultures and systems, then reevaluating the leader role and normative role behavior. For example, women who occupy work roles that are not congruent for leadership (e.g., assistant or support roles aligned with "organizational housekeeping") may not be perceived as leader candidates or as possessing succession potential. Women's competence in these roles does not highlight their potential in other roles, requiring something in the situation to change.

CONCLUSION

Like leadership, negotiation is a masculine-stereotyped work activity. Negotiation researchers have proposed and tested areas that are relevant to gender and leadership theory and can be used to design theory-based interventions to mitigate gender differences. This paper discussed how context can impact the negotiation process and outcome for gender differences in negotiating on behalf of others rather than one's self (Amanatullah & Morris, 2010; Mazei et al., 2015), negotiating for female-stereotyped issues (Bear & Babcock, 2012), stressing the value of female-congruent negotiation behaviors (Kray, Galinsky, & Thompson, 2002), and creating situations with low ambiguity (Bowles et al., 2005) that can improve outcomes for women negotiators. These findings are leading to the testing of interventions in organizations and training of negotiators.

Leadership theorists have an emerging opportunity to incorporate theory into prescriptive advice to organizations and women leaders in various contexts. Contextual theories of leadership are a growing area (Dinh et al., 2014) but have more work to do mapping how context relates to gender effects. Complexity theories of leadership (Hogue & Lord, 2007), identity work theory (Ely et al., 2011), and social role theory (Eagly, 1987; Eagly & Karau, 2002) offer many possibilities to build upon.

Exciting possibilities exist for gender and leadership research to integrate context into theoretical frameworks and to offer prescriptive recommendations and interventions that increase women's leadership opportunities and success. We hope this chapter stimulates new efforts in the next wave of theories to advance women in the workplace.

REFERENCES

Amanatullah, E. T., & Morris, M. W. (2010). Negotiating gender roles: Gender differences in assertive negotiating are mediated by women's fear of backlash and attenuated when negotiating on behalf of others. *Journal of Personality and Social Psychology, 98*(2), 256–267.

Amanatullah, E. T., & Tinsley, C. H. (2013). Punishing female negotiators for asserting too much . . . or not enough: Exploring why advocacy moderates backlash against assertive female negotiators. *Organizational Behavior and Human Decision Processes, 120*(1), 110–122.

Bear, J. (2011). "Passing the buck": Incongruence between gender role and topic leads to avoidance of negotiation. *Negotiation and Conflict Management Research, 4*(1), 47–72.

Bear, J. B., & Babcock, L. (2012). Negotiation topic as a moderator of gender differences in negotiation. *Psychological Science, 23*(7), 743–744.

Bowles, H. R., & Babcock, L. (2013). How can women escape the compensation negotiation dilemma? Relational accounts are one answer. *Psychology of Women Quarterly, 37*, 80–96.

Bowles, H. R., Babcock, L., & Lai, L. (2007). Social incentives for gender differences in the propensity to initiate negotiations: Sometimes it does hurt to ask. *Organizational Behavior and Human Decision Processes, 103*(1), 84–103.

Bowles, H. R., Babcock, L., & McGinn, K. L. (2005). Constraints and triggers: Situational mechanics of gender in negotiation. *Journal of Personality and Social Psychology, 89*(6), 951–965.

Bowles, H. R., & McGinn, K. L. (2008). Untapped potential in the study of negotiation and gender inequality in organizations. *The Academy of Management Annals, 2*(1), 99–132.

Dinh, J. E., Lord, R. G., Gardner, W. L., Meuser, J. D., Liden, R. C., & Hu, J. (2014). Leadership theory and research in the new millennium: Current theoretical trends and changing perspectives. *The Leadership Quarterly, 25*(1), 36–62.

Eagly, A. H. (1987). *Sex differences in social behavior: A social-role interpretation.* Hillsdale, NJ: Lawrence Erlbaum.

Eagly, A, H., & Karau, S. J. (2002). Role congruity theory of prejudice toward female leaders. *Psychological Review, 109*(3), 573–598.

Eagly, A. H., Makhijani, M. G., & Klonsky, B. G. (1992). Gender and the evaluation of leaders: A meta-analysis. *Psychological Bulletin, 111*, 3–22.

Ely, R., Ibarra, H., & Kolb, D. M. (2011). Taking gender into account: Theory and design for women's leadership development program. *Academy of Management Learning & Education, 10*(3), 474–493.

Fiedler, F. E. (1964). A contingency model of leadership effectiveness. *Advances in Experimental Social Psychology, 1*, 149–190.

Heilman, M. E., Wallen, A. S., Fuchs, D., & Tamkins, M. M. (2004). Penalties for success: Reactions to women who succeed at male gender-typed tasks. *Journal of Applied Psychology, 89*(3), 416–427.

Hogue, M., & Lord, R. G. (2007). A multilevel, complexity theory approach to understanding gender bias in leadership. *The Leadership Quarterly, 18*(4), 370–390.

Kray, L. J., Galinsky, A. D., & Thompson, L. (2002). Reversing the gender gap in negotiations: An exploration of stereotype regeneration. *Organizational Behavior and Human Decision Processes, 87*(2), 386–409.

Levin, I. P., Schneider, S. L., & Gaeth, G. J. (1998). All frames are not created equal: A typology and critical analysis of framing effects. *Organizational Behavior and Human Decision Processes, 76*(2), 149–188.

Mazei, J., Hüffmeier, J., Freund, P. A., Stuhlmacher, A. F., Bilke, L., & Hertel, G. (2015). A meta-analysis on gender differences in negotiation outcomes and their moderators. *Psychological Bulletin, 141*(1), 85–104.

McDonald, T. W., Toussaint, L. L., & Schweiger, J. A. (2004). The influence of social status on token women leaders' expectations about leading male-dominated groups. *Sex Roles, 50*(5–6), 401–409.

Mischel, W. (1977). The interaction of person and situation. In D. S. Magnusson, & N. S. Endler (Eds.), *Personality at the crossroads: Current issues in interactional psychology* (pp. 333–352). Hillsdale, NJ: Lawrence Erlbaum.

O'Brien, S. A. (2015, April 7). Reddit: You can't negotiate your salary. *CNNMoney.* Retrieved from http://money.cnn.com/2015/04/07/technology/reddit-pao-negotiations/

Paustian-Underdahl, S. C., Walker, L. S., & Woehr, D. J. (2014). Gender and perceptions of leadership effectiveness: A meta-analysis of contextual moderators. *Journal of Applied Psychology, 99*(6), 1129–1145.

Rubin, J. Z., & Brown, B. R. (1975). *The social psychology of bargaining and negotiation.* New York, NY: Academic Press.

Sax, L. J. (2008). *The gender gap in college: Maximizing the developmental potential of women and men.* San Francisco, CA: Jossey-Bass.

Small, D. A., Gelfand, M., Babcock, L., & Gettman, H. (2007). Who goes to the bargaining table? The influence of gender and framing on the initiation of negotiation. *Journal of Personality and Social Psychology, 93*(4), 600–613.

Stuhlmacher, A. F., & Linnabery, E. (2013). Gender and negotiation: A social role analysis. In M. Olekalns, & W. L. Adair (Eds.), *Handbook of negotiation research* (pp. 221–248). London, England: Edward Elgar.

Stuhlmacher, A. F., & Walters, A. E. (1999). Gender differences in negotiation outcome: A meta-analysis. *Personnel Psychology, 52*(3), 653–677.

Walton, R. E., & McKersie, R. B. (1965). *A behavioral theory of labor relations.* New York, NY: McGraw-Hill.

Yoder, J. D., Schleicher, T. L., & McDonald, T. W. (1998). Empowering token women leaders: The importance of organizationally legitimated credibility. *Psychology of Women Quarterly, 22*(2), 209–222.

Zerres, A., Hüffmeier, J., Freund, P. A., Backhaus, K., & Hertel, G. (2013). Does it take two to tango? Longitudinal effects of unilateral and bilateral integrative negotiation training. *Journal of Applied Psychology, 98*(3), 478–491.

PART II

NEW MODELS AND METHODS

CHAPTER 7

MULTIVOCAL MEANING MAKING

Using Collaborative Autoethnography to Advance Theory on Women and Leadership

Faith Wambura Ngunjiri
Concordia College

Heewon Chang
Eastern University

Kathy-Ann C. Hernandez
Eastern University

After wrapping up a presentation at the International Leadership Conference in San Diego in 2014, we, (Faith and Kathy-Ann) along with another co-presenter, prepared to field questions from the audience. We had just presented the findings of a collaborative autoethnographic study on the experiences of Black women in academe, exploring the intersections of

Theorizing Women and Leadership, pages 103–119
Copyright © 2017 by Information Age Publishing
All rights of reproduction in any form reserved.

race, gender, class, religion, and leadership (Ngunjiri, Hernandez, & El-bert, 2014). One of the first questions raised by a member of the audience was: "So what? These stories are all great and moving accounts of your experiences, but do they amount to anything other than mere story telling?" We have grown accustomed to hearing and answering this question.

As a nascent research method, collaborative autoethnography (CAE) is particularly vulnerable to criticism and skepticism about its utility in advancing work that has both practical and scholarly significance. For those who do not understand the approach, it is easy to brush off CAE studies as mere narcissism by a few self-obsessed scholars. In fact, a recent submission of a CAE study by Kathy-Ann and another colleague, which was presented at the American Educational Research Association, was rejected by reviewers with the terse statement: "A sample of two subjects is too limited and does not warrant publication."

In spite of such rejections, the literature is replete with published CAE studies on a wide variety of subjects, most of those appearing in the last 10 years (see particularly *Qualitative Inquiry, Journal of Contemporary Ethnography, Cultural Studies ≠ Critical Methodologies*, and *Journal of Research Practice* for a plethora of autoethnographic works). Our experience with using CAE together began in 2008, when we recognized our similarities as immigrant women and leaders in the university who were also learning to articulate a racial identity that we had not articulated (or needed) prior to coming to the United States as graduate students. Thus began the project that culminated in our recent article titled *Exploiting the Margins in Higher Education: A Collaborative Autoethnography of Three Foreign-Born Female Faculty of Color*, in which we interrogated our experiences as immigrant faculty of color in predominantly White institutions. Three themes emerged from that study—exploiting multifocal lenses, reconfiguring identities, and engaging tempered radicalism, which are now part of the theory-building conversation related to how immigrants navigate tenure, promotion, and leadership in U.S. institutions (Hernandez, Ngunjiri, & Chang, 2015). That partnership also resulted in the book that we cite liberally in this chapter, *Collaborative Autoethnography* (Chang, Ngunjiri, & Hernandez, 2013), as well as many workshops and presentations at various academic conferences.

Autoethnography (AE) has developed as a robust qualitative research method within the past three decades, infusing its focus on self into investigating society (Adams, 2012; Adams, Holman Jones, & Ellis, 2015; Chang, 2008). AE allows researchers to use their own life stories to articulate and problematize social and cultural arrangements (Chang, 2008). Adams, Holman Jones, and Ellis (2015) highlight that AE not only uses "personal experience to describe and critique cultural beliefs, practices...and experiences" but also "acknowledges and values a researcher's relationships with others" and engenders reflexivity to "interrogate the intersections between self and society" (pp. 1–2). CAE is a collective approach to AE in which multiple autoethnographers create a rich pool of autobiographic experiences and look for emerging themes from their combined data. AE and CAE have been used by a wide variety of scholars from many disciplines to narrate and interrogate topics such as illness, grief, life in academia, cross-cultural experiences, and various identities and socializations, to name a few, always with a focus on unpacking individuals' experiences in particular contexts (Brogden, 2010; Geist-Martin et al., 2010; Lapadat et al., 2009). What remains relatively unexplored, however, is how CAE can be used to narrate the experiences of women as leaders and to develop theories from such studies.

We see CAE as having great potential for using people's experiences—in this case, women's experiences, to inform, enhance, critique, and build leadership theories. We propose that with a judicious application of analytical tools (Anderson, 2006a, 2006b; Hughes, Pennington, & Makris, 2012; Vryan, 2006), CAE can provide an appropriate avenue for building theories grounded in real women's experiences of being or becoming leaders. In this chapter, we elaborate on the use of CAE and its suitability in pursuit of advancing women and leadership theory. We argue that, through the autoethnographic research process, women leaders who may have had marginalized voices can add their perspectives to enhance and/or critique the canon of traditional leadership literature. Further, the stories and analyses of women's voices provide the foundation for further theorization in leadership scholarship. First, we begin with an exploration of the ways that CAE works as a grounded approach to theory building in women and leadership scholarship.

CAE FOR THEORY BUILDING
ABOUT WOMEN AND LEADERSHIP

Thornberg and Charmaz (2012) explain that "a theory states relationships between abstract concepts and may aim for explanation or understanding" (p. 41). In this instance, theories can be advanced to explain and understand women and leadership—women as leaders, or how women become leaders. The utility of such theory building is grounded in how accessible it is to end-users. As such, theory-building methods addressing leadership concerns of women must be amenable to women's ways of knowing and feminist sensitivities—that is, foregrounding women's experience as a valid standpoint from which to theorize (Hartsock, 2004). Smith articulates a perspective shared by many feminist researchers and women's leadership scholars:

> Women were largely excluded from the work of producing forms of thought and the images and symbols in which thought is expressed and ordered.... The circle of men whose writing and talk was significant to each other extends backwards in time as far as our records reach. What men were doing was relevant to men, was written by men about men for men. Men listened to what one another said. (as cited in Hesse-Biber, 2007, p. 2)

In leadership scholarship, the experiences of minority women and women from non-Western contexts remain under-theorized, necessitating non-hegemonizing and postcolonial approaches (Pathak, 2010). Most of the canon of leadership theory is based on a White, male, middle class, heterosexual experience; most of the available literature on women and leadership development is from a Western perspective and framework, eliciting criticism from non-Western scholars who argue that such theories are not necessarily generalizable to all women everywhere. Should, for example, *Lean In* (Sandberg, 2013), based primarily on the autobiographical leadership experiences of one White/Jewish, ivy-educated millionaire woman from the United States, be the frame of reference for a relevant "theory" or praxis for women in Uganda? The *Lean In* approach is touted as being relevant for women without contextualizing class systems, racial power dynamics, and political contexts. Using CAE with women from diverse contexts and positionalities would enable the crafting of theories relevant to them. As Grant (2010) has observed:

> Autoethnography appeals to the marginalized. Autoethnographic storytellers draw people into evocative texts rather than making them feel distanced from what they read.... The deeply personal narratives constituting autoethnography expose people to stories that had otherwise been historically shrouded in secrecy or eclipsed by the distanced writing of dominant ethnographic discourse. (p. 112)

CAE can provide opportunities for diverse teams of women to narrate their stories and interrogate the themes relevant to the larger metanarrative that has theoretical and practical implications for women and leadership development. Through our various collaborative work as women of color leading within predominantly White institutions, we have found CAE to be a valuable tool that has allowed us to "create community, advance scholarship, and be empowered to effect changes" (Hernandez et al., 2015, p. 547) at our various institutions. In sum, it has helped us grow as leaders and has allowed us to study marginalized topics such as *minoritized* women's experiences as leaders within predominantly White institutional contexts.

CAE helps in building community and researching marginalized topics, which is empowering for a diverse range of women researchers engaged in producing knowledge about leaders and the leadership process. Such scholars are then able to contribute, critique, and interrogate accepted canons and produce knowledge that is inclusive of diverse standpoints (e.g., May & Pattillo-McCoy, 2000; Mayuzumi, 2009; Murakami-Ramalho, Piert, & Militello, 2008). As Hesse-Biber (2007) argues, "feminist perspectives also carry messages of empowerment that challenge the encircling of knowledge claims by those who occupy privileged positions" (p. 3). Building community among scholars, between scholars and practitioners, and among minority women has the impact of contributing to more democratically produced knowledge (as further discussed later in the chapter).

CAE is powerful as a tool for narrating our counter-stories, interrogating the intersections of our identities in the matrix of domination (Collins, 2009), critically deconstructing the role of context in our leadership experiences, and decolonizing the knowledge-production process not only by speaking for ourselves as women, but also by extending that process to those in the margins of the knowledge-building enterprise. Before discussing the four characteristics of CAE that make it particularly amenable to women and leadership theory building research, we start by digging deeper into the suitability of CAE for theory-building scholarship with examples from leadership studies.

Suitability of Collaborative Autoethnography

In CAE, two or more researchers use their personal stories as data to problematize social phenomena, to illuminate and critique existing theory (Chang et al., 2013; Geist-Martin et al., 2010; Kempster & Stewart, 2010; Murakami-Ramalho et al., 2008; Ngunjiri, Hernandez, & Chang, 2010), and, as we propose here, to provide a basis for novel theoretical formulations (Hernandez et al., 2015; Hughes et al., 2012). In Hernandez et al. (2015), we used CAE and intersectionality as an interpretative framework to articulate the leadership experiences of three differentially placed Black women—two immigrant and one native-born—as leaders within higher education. We challenged the articulations of "Black" as a unitary identity, demonstrating how being immigrants impacted our racial identity development in ways not present in the leadership literature. In fact, as Ospina and Foldy (2009) argue, it is imperative to come up with new ways to conceptualize how race-ethnicity is implicated in leadership experiences. Our study further enhanced their argument, adding gender and national origins to further complicate leadership experience and identity development. Similarly, Chang, Longman, and Franco (2014) engaged 14 autoethnographers in CAE effort to construct a grounded theory for minority leadership mentoring in higher education. They challenged the leadership mentoring theory grounded on formalized, long-term, and hierarchical mentor-protégé relationships; they discovered through their CAE that emerging women leaders of minority backgrounds instead relied more on a variety of developmental relationships for their leadership growth, which did not fit the traditional mold of mentor-protégé relationships.

Researchers can adopt an evocative approach to their interrogations (Ellis, 1997) or a more analytic approach that is consistent with traditional ethnographic work (Anderson, 2006a, 2006b; Chang, 2008; Reed-Danahay, 1997). All approaches—evocative, performative, interpretive, or analytical—can contribute to informing and illustrating theory. However, we suggest that using analytical tools (irrespective of approach) increases the likelihood of achieving explicit theory-building goals, especially in collaborative projects (Anderson, 2006a, 2006b; Pace, 2012; Vryan, 2006). Theory development usually requires data from multiple sources, making a qualitative, inductive approach particularly appropriate, where researchers begin with stories culled from their experiences and look for patterns applicable to crafting new theoretical perspectives or augmenting existing ones. CAE brings together people who share both convergent and divergent experiences with the intention to analyze their self-stories for emerging themes that contribute to theory development. As Witz (2007) argues, this process of "articulating what has not been articulated before" (p. 242) is dependent upon researchers' ability to engage in "sympathetic introspection" (p. 242), or reflexivity germane to CAE work. Methodological Characteristics of CAE

We identify four characteristics of CAE as a research approach that adds credence to its suitability for building theory about women and leadership: the fact that it is self-focused and makes the researcher visible; it is context-conscious and, thus grounds research (and emergent theories) in lived experience; it is critically dialogic and incorporates multiple voices; and, finally, it has the potential to democratize the research endeavor, creating the conditions necessary to add unheard voices to the canon of leadership scholarship.

CAE as Self-Focused and Researcher-Visible

The self-focused element of CAE provides opportunities for researchers to situate themselves squarely and unapologetically within their work and answer questions that only they can answer—to make the researcher visible. In spite of the personal nature of our research interest on women and leadership, it was not until we started using CAE that we became the subjects of our own research. For example, in Hernandez et al. (2015) we posed these questions:

1. How do we, three foreign-born females of color, position ourselves and navigate advancement in U.S. higher education?

2. How do our gender and cultural ethnicity intersect as we identify, fulfill, and negotiate our roles in traditionally White-male dominant academia?

Two elements of the project are relevant to illustrate the utility of the self-focused element of CAE. First, we disrupted monolithic constructions of women of color, giving voice to self and, in so doing, to women like us—to create critical counter narratives to the predominant focus on Western, White, middle class articulations. Second, the personal nature of the inquiry provided opportunity for us to engage in intrapersonal self-reflection and uncover strategies that we are using to succeed as leaders in predominantly White institutions. Are these strategies unique to us, or do they also have relevance and resonance to other women like us? Here is the starting point for theory building sparked by this line of inquiry.

Other researchers have done similar works, using autobiographical data that make them visible as both researchers and participants in their own studies. In so doing, they explore ways that experiences can have a wider socio-cultural significance (e.g., Brown & William-White, 2010; Coia & Taylor, 2009). This self-focus and researcher visibility empowers researchers to speak up about marginalization, to articulate voice and identity in ways often missing from other research approaches (Tsalach, 2013), and to take context seriously in this endeavor, especially in constructing new or enhancing existing leadership theories as relevant to the intersecting identities of women's lives.

CAE as Context-Conscious: Grounding Theories in Lived Experience

CAE, as Spry (2001) aptly observes, is "a self narrative that *critiques the situatedness* of self and others in social context" (p. 710, emphasis added). CAE is inextricably context-conscious and begins with the clear understanding that participants' experiences are limited to their individual social contexts. This attends to the criticisms of much of the canon of leadership theory as hinted at previously that, although this canon arose out of the experiences of White, middle class, western men as leaders or managers, it is written as to suggest generalizability to all people everywhere irrespective of context and social location (Alston, 2005; Ngunjiri, 2010). Further, the existing articulations of women and leadership are limited by their lack of diverse perspectives. The radical specificity (Sotirin, 2010) of autoethnographic explorations provides a built-in check against over-generalizing our attendant-emerging theories until such a time as meta-analytic studies (see subsequent section on enhancing rigor) demonstrate that those theories are indeed applicable to a wider audience.

The intent of researchers in CAE is not to provide sweeping statements about what is true for individuals like themselves, but to illuminate an accurate account of personal experiences with phenomena that are unique to their contextual experiences. Hence, as is true with the rest of social science research, if what emerges from the researchers' experiences in one context mirrors what others are experiencing in other contexts, an opportunity then exists to suggest a big-picture theory worthy of further investigations. The use of meta-analyses of these various context-specific studies can provide the foundational elements in advancing theoretical frameworks that harmonize various voices. In order to contribute new theories or enhance existing leadership theories, it is critical to pay attention to the context in which leadership is enacted—the role that gender and other identities play in the experiences of women as leaders in specific social, cultural, and organizational contexts. In the combination of various voices and similar themes is a grand theoretical undercurrent waiting to be articulated.

CAE as Critically Dialogic: Engendering Multivocality

CAE is critically dialogic, inviting multiple voices and perspectives in the meaning-making process and engendering critical reflexivity and collective exploration of subjectivity. This is essential to fully apprehending the lived experiences of women as leaders and how women become leaders, as co-researchers dig deep into their own leadership journeys. Without the individual and collective reflexivity, one could be forgiven for thinking that her experience is totally unique to her. Unlike AE, the collaborative element of a CAE team of co-researchers, working together from different disciplinary and theoretical frames of reference, is a built-in check against uni-dimensional *etic* perspectives that a lone researcher can bring to a research study. The collective exploration of researchers' subjectivities enhances and deepens leadership storytelling and analysis. This adds methodological rigor to the research process and also provides opportunities to examine phenomena from multiple/interdisciplinary frames of reference simultaneously on the way to meaning making.

We have found this capacity of CAE to be particularly useful in our work since each of us comes from a different disciplinary perspective—leadership and organization studies, educational anthropology, and educational psychology, respectively. Our collective meaning making is not only more rigorous, but more theoretically robust as we each bring different theories and lenses from our disciplinary backgrounds. The collective reflexivity (Wyatt, Gale, Gannon, & Davies, 2010) of CAE that emerges from multiple perspectives and ways of looking at phenomena can afford researchers "a deeper level of analysis, connect stories to wider issues within the disciplines, link to existing literature, and overall provide a scholarly balance necessary to keep it from being mere navel-gazing" (Chang et al., 2013, p. 29). The collective effort has the potential to break down silos and build theoretical bridges across disciplines and perspectives, and thus enhance and contribute to building robust theories about women and leadership.

CAE as Democratic Knowledge Production: Engaging Power Sharing

One of the critical characteristics in CAE that makes it suitable for theory building is its capacity for engendering a democratic and non-hegemonic approach to engaging in research, as was hinted at in a prior section. This has particular significance for crafting theories that are relevant to the lived experiences of women as leaders, based on elicited stories and reflections from diverse women who can be at any stage of the leadership journey—emerging or experienced. We describe the power-sharing capacity thus:

> The relationship between researchers and participants in traditional paradigms is unequal. The researcher holds the power to interrogate, analyze, interpret, and represent the perspectives of research participants. This paradigm gets a dramatic makeover in CAE where researchers are participants in their own studies. When researchers pool their personal stories and autobiographical material for collective examination, all become subjects to collective interrogation. This flipping of dynamics among researcher-participants puts all members of a research team on an even playing field. (Chang et al., 2013, p. 26)

The democratic and non-hegemonic approach to knowledge production aligns with women's ways of knowing (Gilligan, 1997; Stead & Elliott, 2012), which we must consider in building theories that are relevant and appropriate to women and leadership. The power sharing engendered in CAE contributes to the democratization and feminization of the entire epistemological project. If we intend to craft theories more representative of women's actual experiences and expertise, then our research methods ought to facilitate the process to reach that end goal. CAE calls women to define themselves, to articulate their own ideas, and to respect and represent their experiences in the knowledge-building project, and to do so together.

COLLABORATIVE AUTOETHNOGRAPHY RESEARCH PROCESS

Both evocative (Ellis & Bochner, 2006) and analytical (Anderson, 2006a; Vryan, 2006) approaches of CAE help contribute to knowledge. However, we proffer that the more analytical end of the continuum is particularly amenable to building theories grounded in people's experiences (Pace, 2012; Sykes, 2014). Using CAE for theory building can be seen as the difference between mere biographical and narrative methods that have the purpose of telling stories, as opposed to a deeper analysis of those narratives for the purpose of theory building. Those on the more evocative end of the CAE continuum are primarily interested in deep exploration of radical specificity (Sotirin, 2010). Those on the more analytical end of the continuum adapt what Anderson (2006b) refers to as "theoretically informed, inductively grounded" (p. 451) autoethnographic praxis in order to contribute toward theory building. That is, we want that radical specificity (Sotirin, 2010) to engage existing theoretical constructs—our stories as illustrations or critiques to existing theories—thus we move from mere story telling (memoir) toward analysis and theory building.

Identification of CAE Topic and Team Formation

There are as many topics that can be studied using CAE methods as there are researchers, as is already evident in the myriad of published studies. In this case, the topics selected should relate to either experiences being leaders or the way women become leaders. Currently, there are very few CAE leadership studies, creating a gap which women scholars and practitioners can fill with their self-focused works.

The first approach to topic and team selection is having a team leader who already has a topic invite others to join her exploration (e.g., Geist-Martin et al., 2010). A second approach, illustrated by our own story, involves researchers discussing their common interest and collaboratively coming up with a research topic (Hernandez et al., 2015). While a sample of two could potentially contribute to building theory, a larger sample is more amenable to creating *grounded* theories, since including more participants adds to the diversity of theoretical backgrounds and lived experiences from which to draw data.

However, the larger the team, the more complicated the collaborative process becomes. Management of the research process, communication among a large number of participants, inclusion of many voices, and coordination among multiple perspectives becomes more challenging with a large-group CAE process (see for example, Geist-Martin et. al., 2010; Hernandez, Sancho, Creus, & Montané, 2010). With careful planning, intergroup communication, and possibly partial collaboration for some research steps such as data analysis, interpretation, or writing, large-group CAE teams can maximize data from multiple sources while effectively managing large-group dynamics. Chang et al. (2014) involved 14 participants: They adopted a partial CAE model in which two lead researchers determined the research topic, recruited volunteer autoethnographers, collected data from all, and finally engaged a self-selected few who chose to engage in the data analysis, interpretation, and writing.

Whichever approach is used in team formation and topic selection, team members must be willing to be vulnerable to one another and utilize appropriate ethical guidelines to protect not only themselves (Catham-Carpenter, 2010) but also those implicated in their self-stories (Ellis, 2007; Hernandez & Ngunjiri, 2013). The team must also determine ownership of the collective data to avoid conflicts later on. Further, the team needs to utilize some estimation of constructivist grounded theory approach toward meaning making in order to contribute to theory building about women and leadership.

Data Collection, Analysis, and Interpretation for Theory Building

CAE employs a variety of data from multiple sources. Each researcher contributes her autobiographical material to the common pool of data (e.g., memory writings, self-reflective and self-analytical material, journals, self-observation logs, artifacts, official documents, and interviews). Researchers can include their present perspectives on issues related to their research topic, their self-observation of current leadership behaviors and thoughts, and interviews with other leaders who are related to the researchers or have similar experiences on the topic. CAE data collection, therefore, can include data sources beyond the CAE research team, cover a wide span of time, and represent a variety of data types. The variety of data types and expansiveness of data sources enable CAE teams to triangulate data, a critical process to increase credibility, accuracy, dependability, and transferability in qualitative research (for more, see Chang et al., 2013, Chapters 4 & 5; Patton, 2002).

When researchers foreground theory-generation, they should employ constructivist or interpretive approaches to grounded theory data analysis and interpretation approach (Charmaz, 2014; Pace, 2012), in which qualitative data—textual, auditory, and visual—are coded (fragmented) by subtopics emerging from the data; codes are grouped into larger topical categories; tentative themes (micro-theories) are uncovered from analyzed codes and organized categories; the theories are tested against the original body of data; and the theories are confirmed and supported with examples from the data. This methodical and systematic approach to data analysis enables autoethnographers to present their grounded theories confidently. Since their data, the origin of their theories, are experientially real to them, theories grounded in their collected autobiographical data give further credence to the researchers' emerging leadership theories. In addition, researchers should engage with existing literature to shed critical, contradictory, or affirming light to theories generated from CAE data. Autoethnographers are responsible for explaining why their theories emerged from CAE data corroborate or contradict existing theories. The iterative process of comparing what emerged from CAE data and what has been discovered from a review of existing leadership literature enables autoethnographers to bridge the gap between the extant and the new.

Credibility and Dependability in CAE

As we alluded to in the introduction, questions regarding credibility and dependability in CAE continue to plague the field. We view such questions as legitimate and useful critiques. They are legitimate as a rite of passage if CAE is to continue to grow and solidify its place alongside other established qualitative research methods. They are also useful because such critiques challenge us to attend to methodological rigor in CAE projects, which can only serve to benefit leadership scholarship and theory development.

Since the approach to CAE with which we are aligned is intentionally analytic (Chang et al., 2013), it is malleable to traditional strategies for building in credibility and dependability into qualitative research and grounding theories in lived experience. However, as a nascent approach to qualitative research, there are numerous creative possibilities for framing and reframing the way we conceptualize CAE projects. We have indicated above that having multiple researchers can enhance the rigor of the CAE project, as doing so assures analysis triangulation and theoretical triangulation; it also enhances the data interpretation process (Patton, 2002) indicative of the multivocality that we are highlighting. We also identified other forms of triangulation above, including the use of multiple data sources and data-gathering tools (see also Chang, 2008; Chang et al., 2013; Tolich, 2010). Word limits do not allow for an exhaustive discussion of the various ways to assure credibility and trustworthiness of a CAE project, so we discuss a few more approaches and recommend further readings.

The discipline within which leadership work is situated will influence the standards for quality and credibility of a CAE project. The authors share one broad discipline in common—education—and the American Educational Research Association provides guidelines on appropriate standards for publishing in their flagship journals. Responding to *The Standards for Reporting on Empirical Social Science Research in AERA Journals* (2006), Hughes et al. (2012) published *Translating Autoethnography Across the AERA Standards: Toward Understanding Autoethnographic Scholarship as Empirical Research,* an influential article that focuses on four main areas that are appropriate for using CAE as a method for building theory:

1. How autoethnography formulates social scientific problems.

2. How autoethnography facilitates critical, careful, and thoughtful discussion of methodological choices and claims.
3. How autoethnography offers multiple levels of critical analysis, including self-critique, naming privilege and penalty, and selecting classification schemes and units of analysis while being critically self-reflexive about the selection criteria.
4. How autoethnography provides opportunities for credible analysis and interpretation of evidence from narrative and connects them to researching the self via triangulation, member checks, and related ethical issues.

Further, the quality and credibility of CAE projects can be enhanced by engaging in 360 models of data collection—that is, inviting followers and subordinates to recollect, write, and offer their own interpretations of the critical incidents in your leadership stories. Finally, we envision larger CAE projects in which a lead researcher organizes multiple sites to conduct research around the leadership topic using the same research questions. Those independent pools of data and preliminary findings can increase the potential for robust theory building grounded in women's lived experiences.

CONCLUSION AND IMPLICATIONS

Adams (2012) notes that autoethnography has excellent potential in several areas, including "illuminating complexities of cultural phenomena...generating insider knowledge...[and] more meaningful, socially relevant...research" (p. 182). In this chapter, we argued that CAE is an appropriate research method in the project of knowledge production regarding women and leadership development. It helps to generate insider knowledge that is relevant to the lived experiences of women across all forms of difference—race, gender, ethnicity, nationality, and scholar-practitioner contexts. CAE has, so far, been under-utilized in leadership studies (Kempster & Iszatt-White, 2013; Kempster & Stewart, 2010; Theoharis, 2008); we see great potential, as is evidenced by some of the work that started at the Advancing Women and Leadership Theory colloquium in May 2014, which served as the genesis of this book project.

We discern a powerful role that CAE can play when women collectivize to build knowledge that contributes to their own and others' development as leaders. CAE is empowering for the women working together to craft contextually relevant theories grounded in their real life experiences in organizations and society. Further, CAE studies can not only contribute to knowledge production, but also do so in ways that are accessible to a wide variety of audiences, as the method allows for the use of different ways to write (e.g., poems, narratives, and dialogues) and present (e.g., in a traditional research presentation or performance format) the research findings. Thus, both the process and the product would contribute to helping women and girls, in any social location, develop as leaders. It is particularly appropriate for use in leadership development within the context of leadership education in our institutions, as is illustrated by studies of teacher education (Coia & Taylor, 2009), executive coaching praxis (Kempster & Iszatt-White, 2013), situated leadership learning (Kempster & Stewart, 2010), and leadership mentoring (Chang et al., 2014). Our own experience as collaborators has helped us to enhance our leadership practice, as it offered us a space for reflexively engaging in praxis and peer feedback.

REFERENCES

Adams, T. E. (2012). The joys of autoethnography: Possibilities for communication research. *Qualitative Communication Research, 1*(2), 181–194.

Adams, T. E., Holman Jones, S. L., & Ellis, C. (2015). *Autoethnography.* New York, NY: Oxford University.

Alston, J. A. (2005). Tempered radicals and servant leaders: Black females persevering in the superintendency. *Educational Administration Quarterly, 41*(4), 675–688.

Anderson, L. (2006a). Analytic autoethnography. *Journal of Contemporary Ethnography, 35*(4), 373–395. doi: 10.1177/0891241605280449

Anderson, L. (2006b). On apples, oranges, and autopsies: A response to commentators. *Journal of Contemporary Ethnography, 35*(4), 450–465. doi:10.1177/08912 41606287395

Brogden, L. M. (2010). Identities (academic + private) = subjectivities(desire): Re:collecting art.I/f/acts. *Qualitative Inquiry, 16*(5), 368–377. doi: 10.1177/ 1077800410364354

Brown, A. F., & William-White, L. (2010). "We are not the same minority": The narratives of two sisters navigating identity and discourse at public and private White institutions. In C. C. Robinson & P. Clardy (Eds.), *Tedious journeys: Autoethnography by women of color in academe* (pp. 149–176). New York, NY: Peter Lang.

Catham-Carpenter, A. (2010). "Do thyself no harm": Protecting ourselves as autoethnographers. *Journal of Research Practice, 6*(1). Retrieved from http://jrp. icaap.org/index.php/jrp/article/view/213/222

Chang, H. (2008). *Autoethnography as method.* Walnut Creek, CA: Left Coast Press.

Chang, H., Longman, K., & Franco, M. (2014). Leadership development through mentoring in higher education: A collaborative autoethnography of leaders of color. *Mentoring & Tutoring: Partnership in Learning, 22*(4), 373–389. doi: 10.1080/13611267.2014.945734

Chang, H., Ngunjiri, F. W., & Hernandez, K.C. (2013). *Collaborative autoethnography.* Walnut Creek, CA: Left Coast.

Charmaz, K. (2014). *Constructing grounded theory.* Thousand Oaks, CA: Sage.

Coia, L., & Taylor, M. (2009). Co/autoethnography: Exploring our teaching selves collaboratively. In L. Fitzgerald, M. Heston, & D. Tidwell (Eds.), *Research methods for the self-study of practice* (Vol. 9, pp. 3–16). Amsterdam, Netherlands: Springer.

Collins, P. H. (2009). *Black feminist thought: Knowledge, consciousness, and the politics of empowerment* (Routledge Classics ed.). New York, NY: Routledge.

Ellis, C. (1997). Evocative autoethnography: Writing emotionally about our lives. In W. Tierney & Y. Lincoln (Eds.), *Representation and the text: Re-framing the narrative voice* (pp. 115–139). Albany, NY: SUNY.

Ellis, C. (2007). Telling secrets, revealing lives: Relational ethics in research with intimate others. *Qualitative Inquiry, 13*(1), 3–29. doi: 10.1177/1077800406294947

Ellis, C., & Bochner, A. (2006). Analyzing analytic autoethnography: An autopsy. *Journal of Contemporary Ethnography, 35*(4), 429–449.

Geist-Martin, P., Gates, L., Wiering, L., Kirby, E., Houston, R., Lilly, A., & Moreno, J. (2010). Exemplifying collaborative autoethnographic practice via shared stories of mothering. *Journal of Research Practice, 6*(1). Article M8. Retrieved from http://jrp.icaap.org/index.php/jrp/article/view/209/187

Gilligan, C. (1997). In a different voice. In S. Kemp & J. Squires (Eds.), *Feminisms* (pp. 146–152). Oxford, UK: Oxford University.

Grant, A. (2010). Autoethnographic ethics and rewriting the fragmented self. *Journal of Psychiatric and Mental Health Nursing, 17*(2), 111–116. doi: 10.1111/j.1365-2850.2009.01478.x

Hartsock, N. C. M. (2004). The feminist standpoint: Developing the ground for a specifically feminist historical materialism. In S. Harding (Ed.), *The feminist standpoint theory reader: Intellectual and political controversies* (pp. 35–54). New York, NY: Routledge.

Hernandez, K. C., & Ngunjiri, F. W. (2013). Relationships and communities in autoethnography. In T. E. Adams, C. Ellis & S. Holman Jones (Eds.), *Handbook of Autoethnography* (pp. 262–280). Walnut Creek, CA: Left Coast.

Hernandez, K. C., Ngunjiri, F. W., & Chang, H. (2015). Exploiting the margins in higher education: A collaborative autoethnography of three foreign-born female faculty of color. *International Journal of Qualitative Studies in Education, 28*(5), 533–551. doi: 10.1080/09518398.2014.933910

Hernandez, F., Sancho, J., Creus, A., & Montanè, A. (2010). Becoming university scholars: Inside professional autoethnographies. *Journal of Research Practice, 6*(1). Retrieved from http://jrp.icaap.org/index.php/jrp/article/view/204

Hesse-Biber, S. N. (2007). *Handbook of feminist research: Theory and praxis.* Thousand Oaks, CA: Sage.

Hughes, S., Pennington, J. L., & Makris, S. (2012). Translating autoethnography across the AERA standards: Toward understanding autoethnographic scholarship as empirical research. *Educational Researcher, 41*(6), 209–219. doi: 10.3102/0013189x12442983

Kempster, S., & Iszatt-White, M. (2013). Towards co-constructed coaching: Exploring the integration of coaching and co-constructed autoethnography in leadership development. *Management Learning, 44*(4), 319–336. doi: 10.1177/1350507612449959

Kempster, S., & Stewart, J. (2010). Becoming a leader: A co-produced autoethnographic exploration of situated learning of leadership practice. *Management Learning, 41*(2), 205–219. doi: 10.1177/1350507609355496

Lapadat, J., Bryant, L., Burrows, M., Greenlees, S., Hill, A., Alexander, J.,... Rendell, D. (2009). An identity montage using collaborative autobiography: Eighteen ways to bend the light. *International Review of Qualitative Research, 1*(4), 515–540.

May, R. A. B., & Pattillo-McCoy, M. (2000). Do you see what I see? Examining a collaborative ethnography. *Qualitative Inquiry, 6*(1), 65–87.

Mayuzumi, K. (2009). Unfolding possibilities through a decolonizing project: Indigenous knowledges and rural Japanese women. *International Journal of Qualitative Studies in Education, 22*(5), 507–526. doi: 10.1080/09518390903048800

Murakami-Ramalho, E., Piert, J., & Militello, M. (2008). The wanderer, the chameleon, and the warrior. *Qualitative Inquiry, 14*(5), 806–834. doi: 10.1177/1077800408318309

Ngunjiri, F. W. (2010). Lessons in spiritual leadership from Kenyan women. *Journal of Educational Administration, 48*(6), 755–768.

Ngunjiri, F. W., Hernandez, K. C., & Chang, H. (2010). Living autoethnography: Connecting life and research [Editorial]. *Journal of Research Practice, 6*(1). Article E1. Retrieved from http://jrp.icaap.org/index.php/jrp/article/view/241/186

Ngunjiri, F. W., Hernandez, K. C., & Elbert, C. (2014, October). *The spiritual strivings of Black women in the academy: Unpacking our collective realities.* Paper presented at the International Leadership Association Annual Conference. San Diego, CA.

Ospina, S., & Foldy, E. (2009). A critical review of race and ethnicity in the leadership literature: Surfacing context, power, and the collective dimensions of leadership. *The Leadership Quarterly, 20*(6), 876–896.

Pace, S. (2012). Writing the self into research using grounded theory analytic strategies in autoethnography. *TEXT Special Issue: Creativity: Cognitive, Social and Cultural Perspectives.* Retrieved from http://www.textjournal.com.au/speciss/issue13/Pace.pdf

Patton, M. Q. (2002). *Qualitative research & evaluation methods* (3rd ed.). Thousand Oaks, CA: Sage.

Pathak, A. A. (2010). Opening my voice, claiming my space: Theorizing the possibilities of postcolonial approaches to autoethnography. *Journal of Research Practice, 6*(1), Article M10. Retrieved from http://jrp.icaap.org/index.php/jrp/article/viewFile/231/221

Reed-Danahay, D. (Ed.). (1997). *Auto/ethnography: Rewriting the self and the social, explorations in anthropology.* Oxford, England: Berg.

Sandberg, S. (2013). *Lean in: Women, work, and the will to lead.* New York, NY: Knopf.

Sotirin, P. (2010). Autoethnographic mother-writing: Advocating radical specificity. *Journal of Research Practice, 6*(1), Article M9 retrieved from http://jrp.icaap.org/index.php/jrp/article/view/220/189

Spry, T. (2001). Performing autoethnography: An embodied methodological praxis. *Qualitative Inquiry, 7*(6), 706–732. doi:10.1177/107780040100700605

Standards for Reporting on Empirical Social Science Research in AERA Publications: American Educational Research Association. (2006). *Educational Researcher, 35*(6), 33–40. doi:10.3102/0013189x035006033

Stead, V., & Elliott, C. (2012). Women's leadership learning: A reflexive review of representations and leadership teaching. *Management Learning, 44*(4), 373–394. doi: 10.1177/1350507612449504

Sykes, B. E. (2014). Transformative autoethnography: An examination of cultural identity and its implications for learners. *Adult Learning, 25*(1), 3–10. doi: 10.1177/1045159513510147

Theoharis, G. (2008). Woven in deeply: Identity and leadership of urban social justice principals. *Education and Urban Society, 41*(1), 3–25. doi: 10.1177/0013124508321372

Thornberg, R., & Charmaz, K. (2012). Grounded theory. In S. D. Lapan, M. T. Quartaroli, and F. J. Riemer, *Qualitative research: An introduction to methods and designs* (pp. 41–67). San Francisco, CA: Wiley.

Tolich, M. (2010). A critique of current practice: Ten foundational guidelines for autoethnographers. *Qualitative Health Research, 20*(12), 1599–1610. doi: 10.1177/1049732310376076

Tsalach, C. (2013). Between silence and speech: Autoethnography as an otherness-resisting practice. *Qualitative Inquiry, 19*(2), 71–80. doi: 10.1177/1077800412462986

Vryan, K. D. (2006). Expanding analytic autoethnography and enhancing its potential. *Journal of Contemporary Ethnography, 35*(4), 405–409. doi: 10.1177/0891241606286977

Witz, K. G. (2007). "Awakening to" an aspect in the other: On developing insights and concepts in qualitative research. *Qualitative Inquiry, 13*(2), 235–258. doi: 10.1177/1077800406295634

Wyatt, J., Gale, K., Gannon, S., & Davies, B. (2010). Deleuzian thought and collaborative writing: A play in four acts. *Qualitative Inquiry, 16*(9), 730–741. doi: 10.1177/1077800410374299

CAPACIOUS MODEL OF LEADERSHIP IDENTITIES CONSTRUCTION

Chrys Egan
Salisbury University

S. Lynn Shollen
Christopher Newport University

Constance Campbell
Georgia Southern University

Karen A. Longman
Azusa Pacific University

Kelly Fisher
West Chester University

Wendy Fox-Kirk
Weber State University

Brionne G. Neilson
Utah State University

Theorizing Women and Leadership, pages 121–140
Copyright © 2017 by Information Age Publishing
All rights of reproduction in any form reserved.

Construction of a leadership identity is integral to an individual's leadership and entails a complex process of identity work (DeRue & Ashford, 2010; Ely, Ibarra, & Kolb, 2011; Karp & Helge, 2009; van Knippenberg, van Knippenberg, Cremer, & Hogg, 2004). The Capacious Model of Leadership Identities Construction described in this chapter (see Figure 8.1) presents an inclusive theoretical representation of the co-construction of leadership identities based on "capaciousness," meaning the spaciousness to move and the capacity to hold much (Capacious, n. d.). Capaciousness is also a prime characteristic of the process of the model's development, as it was formulated by a group of authors with various ontologies and epistemologies. As we applied our different paradigms in the process of articulating a new theoretical perspective on the construction of leadership identities, we unintentionally invoked scientific perspectivism, which argues that objectivity is colored by a person's perspective and that one perspective is never fully accurate or complete (Giere, 2006). We thus examined the phenomenon of leadership identities construction through multiple lenses, resulting in a richer and more complex representation and new insights. Consequently, the Capacious Model offers an innovative theoretical interplay across ontologies and epistemologies, while simultaneously providing practical application as a diagnostic tool for understanding and constructing leadership identities, especially for women.

Gender has been ignored or relegated to a secondary discussion in much of the leadership literature (Fulop, Linstead, & Lilley, 2009), implying that leadership is inherently construed as a masculine gender role—a notion that is supported by research (Eagly & Karau, 2002). This bias portends an identity struggle for anyone who does not fit the norm (Alvesson & Billing, 2009). Indeed, "if a central developmental task for an aspiring leader is to integrate the leader identity into the core self, then this task is fraught at the outset for a woman, who must establish credibility in a culture that is deeply conflicted about her authority" (Ely et al., 2011, p. 477). Further, discourse about leader identities has been described as "fragmented, contradictory, and androcentric" (Ford, 2006, p. 78), within attempts to integrate leader identity approaches (Stets & Burke, 2000). There is a clear need for a more fulsome approach to understanding leadership identities construction that considers gender and other diversity factors as components in the process of seeing oneself, and being seen by others, as a leader. To address this need, our bi-national, all-female research team utilizes multiple bodies of literature represented by the members' domains of expertise, as well as deliberative interaction—an approach to contemporary organizational theory evaluation and construction advocated by Suddaby, Hardy, and Huy (2011)—to synergistically develop and sharpen a new model for understanding the construction of leadership identities, of particular relevance for women.

Capacious Model of Leadership Identities Construction

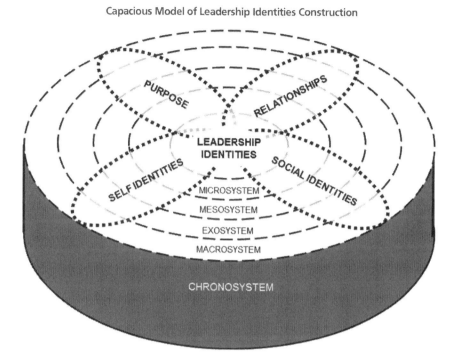

Figure 8.1 Model depicting leadership identities construction within systems and influences.

In drawing on an ecological systems approach (Bronfenbrenner, 2009; Bronfenbrenner & Morris, 1998) in the development of our model, the role of context is explicitly acknowledged as shaping leaders and their actions. Notably, the heroic, masculine, solitary notion of leadership is rejected not only in the Capacious Model that emerged from our collaborative work but also in our group process. An alternative to centering leadership within a lone actor is to recognize leadership as occurring as a practice. This dimension of our model and group process is important given that practice "calls attention to the intersection between the material world and human consciousness" (Vygotsky as cited in Raelin, 2011, pp. 196–197). "Leadership-as-practice" (L-A-P) is a useful perspective that focuses on the moral, emotional, and relational aspects of leadership rather than the rational, objective, technical aspects (Carroll, Levey, & Richmond, 2008). L-A-P looks for leadership in the "doing" rather than the "being"; thus, the paradigm is inherently collaborative and focuses on what people may accomplish together through their daily interactions (Raelin, 2011). Because one of our goals is to explore leadership identity experiences outside mainstream, male-centric leadership theory (see Höpfl & Case, 2007), L-A-P offers an implicitly democratic process that focuses on the *where, how,* and *why* of leadership work, rather than on the *who.*

It was while working within the freedom of such a "leaderful" space at the Advancing Theory on Women and Leadership research colloquium hosted by Utah Valley University in May 2014 that our model emerged from our group's collaborative work. Typically, groups follow a masculinist process, characterized by hierarchical, status-based relations and rational problem solving, and driven by competition; in contrast, our process of theory development was driven by a feminist process (Schniedewind, 1987). For example, no formal leader was designated for the group, instead, leadership shifted among members with the expert on a topic naturally taking the lead. In addition, despite status differences within the group, our discussions and decisions were shaped through cooperative, egalitarian, and democratic procedures. From the seasoned research academics to the novice graduate student researcher, all voices were heard and respected, and constructive feedback was given and accepted by all. Feminist process also shaped the way in which *capacious* space was made for creativity, imagination, and emotions, in addition to intellect, reason, and rationality. Creating a safe space for the perspectives of members from diverse disciplinary and experiential backgrounds provided an element of healthy debate, discomfort, and tension that ensured exploration of key assumptions in our thinking and process. Our work also benefited immensely from our integration of action and reflection, both individually and collaboratively.

In hindsight, we recognize that none of us came to this project with an explicitly feminist approach to group process or scholarship; rather, a feminist ethos was overlaid on us by the lack of a formally assigned leader, the absence of hard rules about our process, and encouragement by those guiding the research colloquium to think outside of the objectivist paradigm. At times we struggled to work in an openly creative, egalitarian way, because we do not often find ourselves in spaces that allow us to legitimately operate with such freedom. Over time, we found that valuing and embracing a deliberatively feminist process allowed us to co-create a more capacious model that more accurately illustrates the process of leadership identity construction than alternative models currently reflected in the literature.

In the following sections, we: (a) define the terms used in the model title and provide an overview of the systems and influences associated with the model; (b) explain the model's use of and departure from systems theories, along with the model's five systems; (c) explain four of the numerous influences that could be included in the model; (d) provide examples of the complex, dynamic nature of the model; and, (e) discuss the model's contributions to leadership theory and practice.

CAPACIOUS MODEL OVERVIEW

The Capacious Model of Leadership Identities Construction (see Figure 8.1) captures how individuals create and recreate their leadership identities over time and context. The figure depicts one possible snapshot of a person's leadership identity at one given moment. Each person's model will change over a lifetime of experiences and in particular environments. Similarly, each individual's leadership identity model will differ from another person's model. The shapes depicted in the model are customizable and permeable because the key concepts will expand or contract in both positive and negative ways to describe a person's leadership identity in the moment. The model situates constructed leadership identities as central to understanding leadership practices (Ely, 1995; Ely et al., 2011; Ibarra 1999); in contrast, other models typically view leader identity as a role, category, or process (Ibarra, Wittman, Petriglieri, & Day, 2014). The Capacious Model also addresses the call for leadership theories that situate the locus of leadership across multiple contexts and the enactment of leadership across multiple mechanisms (Hernandez, Eberly, Avolio, & Johnson, 2011), rather than as leader-centric. Our model approaches leadership as a social and relational process in which the individual and context are interlinked through a dialectic process (Uhl-Bien, Riggio, Lowe, & Carsten, 2014). The leader is not depicted as a lone actor, but rather as a "relational reality" (Hosking as cited in Uhl-Bien & Ospina, 2012, p. 465), inseparable from relationships with others and the leadership context, broadly considered.

Dimensions of the Capacious Model include *capaciousness*—the space and fluidity for individuals to explore and construct their leadership identities with movement, reflection, flexibility, and potential; *systems*—distinct, yet related, contexts that intersect with individual leadership identities construction; and *influences*—concepts of noted significance to leadership identities construction, especially for women and other groups who have been historically marginalized in much of the world. The Capacious Model aligns with Keohane's (2014) call to "build plans and expectations for the future on a more capacious conception of leadership" (pp. 52–53).

Consistent with our perspective on leadership, the Capacious Model considers a leader to be anyone who is engaged in moving the collective in a common direction, irrespective of formal position. Our choice of the term *leadership* rather than *leader* indicates the inclusive appreciation of the leader, leadership, follower, and followership within their co-constructed, relational, holistic practice, action, and roles. Further, this word choice recognizes that leadership identities are constructed and internalized not just intrapersonally, but through a complex process influenced by social interactions and contextual factors (DeRue & Ashford, 2010).

We use the term *identities* in its plural form to indicate that leadership identities are multifaceted and changeable over space/context and time/life, and that an individual may hold more than one conceptualization of leadership identity at a time. We include the term *construction* to recognize that identities are socially constructed phenomena based on individuals' subjective conceptions of themselves and their realities. Further, the model focuses on the dynamic building and re-building of leadership identities, rather than assuming that a singular identity is achieved and remains static.

By combining *capacious leadership identities construction*, the model captures who and where we are in relation to others, envisioning ourselves as leaders, and the perceptions of others about our leadership potential. Joining these key concepts yields the model's conceptualization of leadership identities as the coalescence of multiple contexts and key influences into a co-created, relational understanding of oneself as leader. Notably, the Capacious Model encompasses diverse conceptions of leadership and identities by considering subjective perspectives and experiences. The model is pertinent not *only* to women, but conceptually and empirically applicable to the leadership identity construction of all individuals.

The Capacious Model proposes five interconnected systems that can affect leadership identities construction, as well as four particular influences (acknowledging other possible influences) on leadership identities construction. In contrast to various male-normed, role-centered, logical positivist leadership models, the Capacious Model illustrates the interconnectivity of capacity, systems, and gendered influences. Thus, this model offers a more holistic representation of the complex, interpretive process of the construction of individuals' diverse leadership identities.

CAPACIOUS MODEL SYSTEMS

The Capacious Model of Leadership Identities Construction applies Uri Bronfenbrenner's "mature" model of Ecological Theory of Child Development (ETCD; Bronfenbrenner, 2009; Bronfenbrenner & Morris, 1998) to the process of leadership identities construction (see Figure 8.2 for an abbreviated illustration of ETCD). As with General Systems Theory (Von Bertalanffy, 1968), Bronfenbrenner's theory stresses the role of contextual interrelatedness in a person's development. According to Bronfenbrenner and Morris (1998), "Human development takes place through processes of progressively more complex, reciprocal interaction between an active and evolving biopsychological human organism and the persons, objects and symbols in its immediate external environment" (p. 996). Bronfenbrenner's ETCD identifies person, process, and context as essential to identity development and envisions them in his model's first four layered

Ecological Theory of Childhood Development

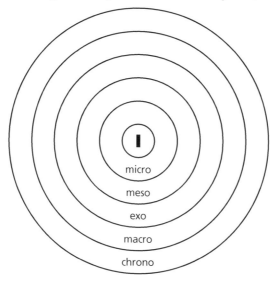

Figure 8.2   Bronfenbrenner's ETCD model depicting systems impacting development.

systems: microsystem, mesosystem, exosystem, and macrosystem. These four systems are interconnected and all immersed within the larger chronosystem: time and experiences over a lifespan within social and historical contexts. Although the systems are represented as separate circles in the figure, it is noteworthy that they are, indeed, nested, interrelated, and dynamic.

While the ETCD model centers the individual as the focus of the process, the Capacious Model anchors leadership identities as central to the understanding of leadership. By placing the individual's leadership identities construction process at the center of a set of nested systems, the individual is seen as situated within relevant contexts. This placement means that an understanding of the way by which leadership identities are shaped cannot be reached by observing the individual alone. The Capacious Model also extends the application of the ETCD model by including adult development, recognizing particular influences relevant to leadership identities construction within and across the systems, and reflecting changes in contemporary life since ETCD model's publication (Tudge, Mokrova, Hatfield, & Karnick, 2009). Further, Bronfenbrenner's model and the Capacious Model both depart from the objectivist paradigm of traditional systems theories by recognizing the equal importance of the subjective in the individual's experience and development (Bronfenbrenner & Morris, 1998).

Microsystem

The ETCD microsystem is the individual's immediate environment where relationships are face-to-face, such as family, school, peer group, and neighborhood. The Capacious Model microsystem encompasses not only relational aspects, but factors internal to the individual, such as self-talk, perspective, and contemplation (e.g., Neck & Millman, 1994). Therefore, the Capacious Model microsystem is both intrapersonal and interpersonal.

Mesosystem

The ETCD mesosystem refers to the interaction between micro-environments, such as the connection between family, school, and work. The Capacious Model emphasizes dynamic interplay between systems that can impact performance, motivation, and leadership identity (e.g., Howell & Avolio, 1993; Tierney, Farmer, & Graen, 1999).

Exosystem

The exosystem indirectly affects the individual, since he or she may not be directly involved with this system. For example, the workplaces of life partners can affect individuals even if those individuals are not directly engaged with their partners' workplaces. Because the exosystem's influence on the individual is incidental, its impact on development and leadership identities construction is likely subtle and less conscious.

Macrosystem

The macrosystem captures the larger cultural context, including issues of social values, attitudes, ideologies, and expectations. The Capacious Model considers the macrosystem to also include larger organizations and institutions with their structures, explicit objectives, and members (e.g., Dansereau, Graen, & Haga, 1975). This addition allows our model to reflect organizational culture as relevant to leadership identities construction; indeed, commonly experienced language and jargon, belief systems, rituals and ceremonies, institutional histories, symbols, and shared organizational values (Bolman & Deal, 2013) may affect the construction of one's leadership identities. At the farthest edges of the macrosystem are media and global culture, capturing the public sphere of globalization, mass media, and diverse traditions and norms (Scharmer, 2009). This outer shell includes the public, mediated, and international cultures (e.g., House, Javidan, Hanges, & Dorfman, 2002; Slater, 2007) that have become increasingly interwoven and prominent in daily life through social media, international mass media, intercultural travel, and interdependent global economic and political systems (Egan, 2015; Karim, 2003; Sheridan, 2005).

Chronosystem

Finally, the ETCD chronosystem represents events occurring in the context of passing time relative to social, cultural, and historical conditions. A person's positive and negative experiences exist in all of the systems, and may best be explored in the chronosystem. The effect of the chronosystem can be seen through cohort effects, such as similarities within a generation of people and through experiences of common historical events. The chronosystem is crucial to the Capacious Model because time is a fundamental element in the construction of leadership identities. For example, an individual's leadership identity is shaped by her development over time, life span, generation, past and present experiences, and potential future influences (e.g., Day, Zaccaro, & Halpin, 2004). The chronosystem also encompasses latent, dormant influences on leadership identities construction that may be hidden until they arise over time or in particular contexts. Further, time is needed to develop key relational values such as trust, loyalty, and commitment (Dinh et al., 2014; Uhl-Bien & Ospina, 2012), which can affect an individual's leadership identity construction.

CAPACIOUS MODEL INFLUENCES

To illustrate how influences can shape an individual's leadership identities construction, the Capacious Model includes four key influences, among many possible, that research has demonstrated as particularly relevant to women's leadership identities construction (see Figure 8.1): (a) Purpose and Calling—why a person is inspired or chosen to lead; (b) Self-Identities—our answers to who we are; (c) Social Identities—how we and others shape our self-concept through group associations; and (d) Relationships—personal and professional connections with others that help define our leadership. These four influences are inherently embedded in Bronfenbrenner's systems, but drawing them into the forefront is justified for many reasons. First, leadership literature suggests that these influences are important in the development and maintenance of leadership identities, in general, and to women's leadership identities in particular (Eagly & Johannesen-Schmidt, 2001; Parker, 2001; Trinidad & Normore, 2005). Second, in their review of leadership theories, Hernandez and colleagues (2011) note that theories typically specify some mechanism of leadership identity connected to traits, behaviors, cognition, or affect. The Capacious Model views leadership identities as potentially emanating from any or all the influences included in the model, depending on the individual. Third, these influences are consistent with and span across the systems of the ETCD model. Finally, these four influences support an interpretive epistemology through the lived experiences of diverse leaders. Consistent with the fluidity of the Capacious Model, any influence(s) could be more or less significant in the construction of an individual's leadership identities at a given time. Further, influences can also act synergistically or discordantly with one another to influence leadership identities construction. In the remainder of this section, we explain each influence selected for our model and provide further rationale for its inclusion.

Purpose and Calling

Having an elevated sense of purpose or reason for leadership, and conveying that purpose to others is central to leadership identities construction (Ely et al., 2011). Specifically for women,

> anchoring in purpose enables women to redirect their attention toward shared goals and to consider who they need to be and what they need to learn in order to achieve those goals. Instead of defining themselves in relation to gender stereotypes... female leaders can focus on behaving in ways that advance the purposes for which they stand. Focusing on purpose can also lead women to take up activities that are critical to their [leadership] success, such as networking. (Ibarra, Ely, & Kolb, 2013, p. 66)

Women also tend to base their career decisions more on what they find meaningful than on money or status (Helgesen & Johnson, 2010), choices which can arguably affect their leadership identities. Similarly, Keohane (2014) found that many women undergraduate students prefer to shape their leadership identities by making a difference in "high-impact" (p. 47) leadership roles related to causes they cared about rather than "high-profile" (p. 47) leadership positions. Discernment of calling, or feeling drawn to one's life work, can inform one's sense of purpose and consequently influence leadership identities (Longman, Dahlvig, Wikkerink, Cunningham, & O'Connor, 2011; Madsen, 2016). Interviews with top women leaders in higher education and the political realm revealed that

> understanding life and vocational calling can inform their choices, career paths, identities, and world lens with a sense of being called to something

greater than themselves. In addition, awareness of calling for women is a critical motivator that can lead to leadership self-efficacy, leadership experience, and finally, leadership competence. (Madsen, 2016)

Youthful Nobel Prize winner Malala Yousafzai (2013) serves as an example of how having a sense of purpose and discernment of calling can influence one's leadership identity and how the influence of purpose and calling can interact with the Capacious Model's systems to affect leadership identity construction. Although Malala held no formal leadership role when she was shot by Islamic fundamentalists for her commitment to girls' education, her sense of purpose and calling to fight for girls' education informed her leadership identity. The influence of purpose and calling was relevant to her leadership identity at the microsystem level of school, peers, family, and neighborhood, as well as at the macrosystem level of cultural attitudes and ideologies.

Self-Identity

Self-identity is an individual's answer to the question: Who am I? (Maddux & Gosselin, 2003). Although core self-identity is relatively stable over time, it is typically revised somewhat throughout one's lifetime (Giddens, 1991). Self-identity is appropriately rooted in the microsystem, but it can also influence and be influenced by other systems, as "the self is not a passive entity, determined by external influences; in forging their self-identities, no matter how local their specific contexts of action, individuals contribute to and directly promote social influences that are global in their consequences and implications" (Giddens, 1991, p. 2). Self-identity is interdependent with leadership identity through the impact of self-identity on shaping leadership identity as a role identity (Ibarra et al., 2014; Klenke, 2007), which informs the answer to the question "Who am I in the role of leader?"

Social Identities

Social identities inform an individual's larger sense of identity based on meaningful, claimed memberships to social groups that are of emotional and value significance to the individual (Brewer, 1991; Tajfel, 1972). Examples could include gender, sexual orientation, race, ethnicity, physical ability, age, religion, socioeconomic level, profession, political affiliation, and other social classifications. Relevant to leadership identities, claimed group memberships "profoundly influence how we view ourselves; they influence the type of people we are, the things we do, the attitudes and values we hold, and the way we perceive and react to people around us" (Hogg, 2003, p. 462). Social identities also affect others' perceptions of the individual due to implicit leadership theories, or people's own mental representations of effective leaders (Lord & Maher, 1993). For example, those who socially identify as women may be more likely to question their ability to identify as leader because leader is typically mentally associated with male (Eagly & Karau, 2002). This example reflects how social identities interact with the macrosystem because the belief that leadership is naturally a masculine concept stems in part from the dominant discourse promulgated by the larger culture. The influence of social identities on constructing leadership identities is also complicated by fluctuations over time because particular identities are more prominent at certain moments and life stages (Brewer, 1991), by the overlap among multiple social identities (Roccas & Brewer, 2002), and by the dynamic nature of social identities as different identities are added or discarded throughout life (Deaux, 2001).

Relationships

Relationships are significant to leadership for women across cultures (Graen & Uhl-Bien, 1995; Killeen, López-Zafra, & Eagly, 2006). The Capacious Model's relationship influence considers interpersonal skills, relational networking, relational support, and work–life enrichment. Interpersonal skills include verbal and nonverbal expression, listening aptitude, and interpretation of feedback. For example, historically marginalized individuals tend to be more skilled at decoding—reading and interpreting—non-verbal cues (Leathers & Eaves, 2008). Relational networks shape an individual's leadership identity, likelihood of success, management of group dynamics, and accomplishment of goals (Eagly & Carli, 2003; Eagly & Karau, 2002). Relational support is the empathy and encouragement from others that allows people to realize and fulfill their potential (Murray, Tremaine, & Fountaine, 2012). Work–life enrichment is the integration of labor, leisure, family, community, culture, and health (Marks, 1977), where work may positively or negatively affect home life, and home can positively or negatively affect work life (Grzywacz & Carlson, 2007; Grzywacz & Marks, 2000). While the ETCD model roots relationships in the microsystem, the evidence on women and leadership demonstrates that women's leadership identities are impacted by relational influences throughout all the systems. For example, women working in higher education are more likely than their male colleagues to apply for and accept promotions if they have encouragement from their colleagues and are persuaded that the organization needs them (Murray et al., 2012). Women showed greater reliance on interpersonal communication, relational support, networking, and work–life enrichment considerations before accepting professional responsibilities that might be less common for them to undertake within their mesosystems, exosystems, and macrosystems.

CAPACIOUS MODEL DYNAMICS

The Capacious Model stems from hierarchical systems grounded in the ETCD model, but it overlays the influences of purpose, self-identity, social identities, and relationships (among others) as a heterarchy—an organizational system in which the elements have the potential to be ordered in a number of different ways (Crumley, 1995). The salience of the systems and influences, as well as their interactions with one another, are fluid in their effect on leadership identities construction in particular contexts and times. In this section, we explain and provide examples of the complex, interactive nature of the Capacious Model—a nature that reflects the inclusivity of the model for understanding the construction of leadership identities for women leaders. To this end, we address: (a) the hierarchical interplay of the five systems with leadership identities, and (b) the heterarchical interplay of the four influences with the systems and leadership identities.

Hierarchical Interplay of Systems

As depicted in Figure 8.1, the Capacious Model anchors leadership identities centrally within the five systems, which are represented as permeable rings indicating that each system dynamically interacts to impact leadership identities. For example, in the United States, there is a movement to reconsider gender roles and stereotypes concerning perceptions of women leaders (e.g., "assertive" is not "bossy"). The movement has utilized the mass media, located in the macrosystem, by promoting commercials, TED talks, and websites devoted to challenging current norms. Exposure to mass media may then inspire a CEO to reshape her organization's culture; such cultural change has implications for the macrosystem in terms of making the culture more supportive of aspiring women leaders. A mid-level leader in that organization may then engage in relationships, located in the microsystem, that involve mentoring aspiring women leaders within the organization. Also at the microsystem level, a coworker may reflect on the choice to be a mentor for women and experience enhanced positive self-talk. The chronosystem comes into play because these dynamics occur over time, and involve the employee's development over time. All of these systems compound upon one another to affect how an individual constructs her leadership identities. Although the dynamics of the systems may not always be linear and unidirectional and are much more complex, this example illustrates the inter-relatedness of the systems in ways that affect the construction of leadership identities.

Heterarchical Interplay of Influences

The four influences included in the Capacious Model span the boundaries of the systems and the core of leadership identities. The capacious and fluid nature of the model allows for flexibility in the arrangement of the influences. The influences are depicted in one possible sequence in the model, but can be examined in any order because, in reality, influences advance and recede in their prominence across time and space in a heterarchical, dynamic manner.

An example considers interplay of purpose and calling with social identities, as shown in Figure 8.3. At age 30, Ahanu had never considered herself as a "real" leader even though she had taken on informal leadership roles in

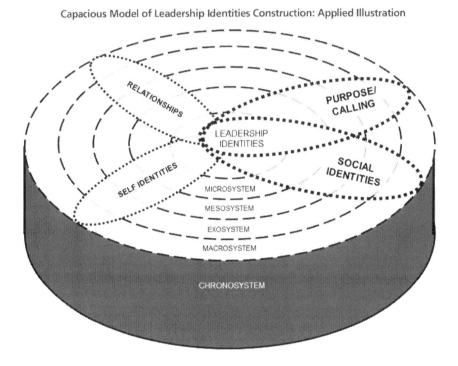

Figure 8.3 Model application for a leader strongly influenced by purpose and social identities.

her family and community for years. She identified her sense of purpose and calling as being a good mother. Now age 47, Ahanu claims a social identity of breast cancer survivor. This new social identity has caused her to rethink her purpose in life and as a leader. In terms of the systems, on the macrosystem level, Ahanu may experience a larger culture that is more openly aware and supportive of those who identify as breast cancer survivors, and she can join a breast cancer support organization that holds particular values and practices certain rituals. At the microsystem level, Ahanu may find herself working to motivate other women who are fighting breast cancer, and she may experience a shift in her self-concept to a woman who is strong and healthy. The impact of the chronosystem is exemplified by the change in Ahanu's social identities, purpose and calling, and leadership identities *over time* based on her experiences. In sum, the social identities and purpose and calling influences interplay with one another, and with the five systems, to affect how Ahanu thinks of herself as a leader. She may now include in her leadership identities the notion that she is a "real" leader.

The examples provided in this section represent only a sliver of the possibilities of how the Capacious Model may work in practice. The dynamic nature of the model allows space for innumerable ways in which the systems and influences can interact, especially over time, to affect the construction of an individual's leadership identities. Figure 8.4 illustrates one possible cross-section of an individual's leadership identity at one point in time. Taking other cross-sections at different times would reveal alternate proportions and strengths of the systems and influences. Indeed, the point of the model is to provide an inclusive space in which leadership identities construction can be examined with respect to the complexity of individualized experiences of diverse individuals.

DISCUSSION AND IMPLICATIONS

The Capacious Model of Leadership Identities Construction is a viable and compelling alternative to traditional male-normed models, and one that moves the needle on leadership identity theories—and women's leadership identity construction—by acknowledging and integrating complex facets of leadership identities. With respect to theory, the Capacious Model spans the boundaries between paradigms by both encompassing and extending existing theoretical depictions of leadership identity. The model makes leadership identity amenable to study through various exploratory approaches and from a variety of epistemological assumptions. The Capacious Model also spans boundaries by being the first to bring Bronfenbrenner's ETCD model from the human development field into the leadership field and specifically into the study of leadership identities. Further, we anticipate that, similar to

Capacious Model of Leadership Identities Construction

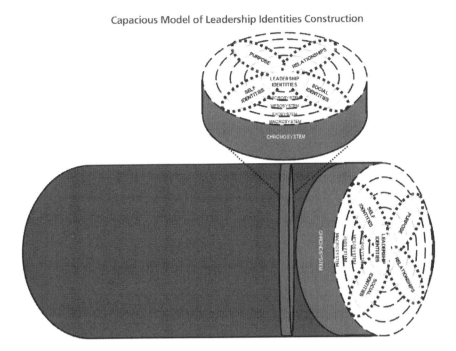

Figure 8.4 Cross-section of the model depicting one possible snapshot of leadership identity at a given moment.

Bronfenbrenner's model undergoing modifications over the decades, the Capacious Model will also likely evolve as it is studied and applied.

With respect to leadership identities construction, the Capacious Model can be used as a diagnostic tool for pinpointing particular areas pertaining to the construction of leadership identities. An important contribution of the model is that it is liberating rather than prescriptive; individual leaders can apply the model from their personal standpoints (Hartsock, 1983). For example, if a goal were to strengthen leadership identity among women in Tanzania, the Capacious Model could be used to ensure that all systems that impact women's leadership identities are examined for their contributions, positive or negative, to the construction of their identities. Programs could then be developed to address the specific issues identified. Further, special consideration could be given to the influences that are especially pertinent to constructing Tanzanian women's leadership identities. A group wishing to build leadership identity among women in Canada could similarly use the Capacious Model as a diagnostic tool, but would likely find different conclusions regarding the areas they need to address. Thus, the Capacious Model guides the identification of areas of strength or need for building leadership identities, while also ensuring that the conclusions are individual and context specific. In sum, the Capacious Model: (a) provides a framework for future research that explores any of the intersections among systems and influences present in the model, and that builds upon the proposed model; (b) serves as a practical, diagnostic tool for helping diverse individuals understand and construct their leadership identities; and (c) invites the examination of the phenomenon of leadership identities construction through a variety of paradigms.

REFERENCES

Alvesson, M., & Billing, Y. D. (2009). *Understanding gender and organizations.* Thousand Oaks, CA: Sage.

Bolman, L. G., & Deal, T. E. (2013). *Reframing organizations: Artistry, choice, and leadership* (5th ed.). San Francisco, CA: Jossey-Bass.

Brewer, M. B. (1991). The social self: On being the same and different at the same time. *Personality and Social Psychology Bulletin, 17*(5), 475–482.

Bronfenbrenner, U. (2009). *The ecology of human development: Experiments by nature and design.* Cambridge, MA: Harvard University.

Bronfenbrenner, U., & Morris, P.A. (1998). The ecology of developmental processes. In W. Damon, & R. Lerner (Eds.), *Handbook of child psychology: Theoretical models of human development* (5th ed., Vol. 1, pp. 993–1028). Hoboken, NJ: Wiley & Sons.

Capacious. (n.d.). In *The Collins English Dictionary online.* Retrieved from http://www.collinsdictionary.com/dictionary/english/capacious

Carroll, B., Levy, L., & Richmond, D. (2008). Leadership as practice: Challenging the competency paradigm. *Leadership, 4*(4), 363–379.

Crumley, C. L. (1995). Heterarchy and the analysis of complex societies. *Archeological Papers of the American Anthropological Association, 6*(1), 1–5.

Dansereau, F., Graen, G., & Haga, W. J. (1975). A vertical dyad linkage approach to leadership within formal organizations: A longitudinal investigation of the role making process. *Organizational Behavior and Human Performance, 13*(1), 46–78.

Day, D. V., Zaccaro, S. J., & Halpin, S. M. (2004). *Leader development for transforming organizations: growing leaders for tomorrow.* New York, NY: Routledge.

Deaux, K. (2001). Social identity. In J. Worrell (Ed.), *Encyclopedia of women and gender* (pp. 1059–1068). New York, NY: Academic.

DeRue, D. S., & Ashford, S. J. (2010). Who will lead and who will follow? A social process of leadership identity construction in organizations. *Academy of Management Review, 35*(4), 627–647.

Dinh, J. E., Lord, R. G., Gardner, W. L., Meuser, J. D., Liden, R. C., & Hu, J. (2014). Leadership theory and research in the new millennium: Current theoretical trends and changing perspectives. *The Leadership Quarterly, 25*(1), 36–62.

Eagly, A. H., & Carli, L. L. (2003). The female leadership advantage: An evaluation of the evidence. *The Leadership Quarterly, 13*(6), 807–834.

Eagly, A. H., & Johannesen-Schmidt, M. C. (2001). The leadership styles of women and men. *Journal of Social Issues, 57*(4), 781–797.

Eagly, A. H., & Karau, S. J. (2002). Role congruity theory of prejudice toward female leaders. *Psychological Review, 109*(3), 573–598.

Egan, C. (2015). Relational leadership across cultural boundaries: Communication, diversity and cultural awareness in the age of globalization. In R. Williams Davis, & A. Patterson-Masuka (Eds.), *Communication and global engagement across cultural boundaries* (pp. 32–43). Dubuque, IA: Kendall Hunt.

Ely, R. J. (1995). The power in demography: Women's social constructions of gender identity at work. *Academy of Management Journal, 38*(3), 589–634.

Ely, R. J., Ibarra, H., & Kolb, D. M. (2011). Taking gender into account: Theory and design for women's leadership development programs. *Academy of Management Learning & Education, 10*(3), 474–493.

Ford, J. (2006). Discourses of leadership: Gender, identity and contradiction in a UK public sector organization. *Leadership, 2*(1), 77–99.

Fulop, L. E., Linstead, S., & Lilley, S. (2009). *Management and organization: A critical text.* Houndsmill, England: Palgrave Macmillan.

Giddens, A. (1991). *Modernity and self-identity: Self and society in the late modern age.* Stanford, CA: Stanford University.

Giere, R. N. (2006). *Scientific perspectivism.* Chicago, IL: University of Chicago.

Graen, G. B., & Uhl-Bien, M. (1995). Relationship-based approach to leadership: Development of leader-member exchange (LMX) theory of leadership over 25 years: Applying a multi-level multi-domain perspective. *The Leadership Quarterly, 6*(2), 219–247.

Grzywacz, J. G., & Carlson, D. S. (2007). Conceptualizing work-family balance: Implications for practice and research. *Advances in Developing Human Resources, 9*(4), 455–471.

Grzywacz, J. G., & Marks, N. F. (2000). Reconceptualising the work-family interface: An ecological perspective on the correlates of positive and negative spillover between work and family. *Journal of Occupational Health Psychology, 5*(1), 111–126.

Hartsock, N. (1983). The feminist stand point: Developing ground for a specifically feminist historical materialism. In S. Harding, & M. Hintikka (Eds.), *Discovering reality: Feminist perspectives on epistemology, methodology, and philosophy of science* (pp. 283–310). Dordrecht, Netherlands: Reidel.

Helgesen, S., & Johnson, H. (2010). *The female vision: Women's real power at work.* San Francisco, CA: Berrett-Kochler.

Hernandez, M., Eberly, M. B., Avolio, B. J., & Johnson, M. D. (2011). The loci and mechanisms of leadership: Exploring a more comprehensive view of leadership theory. *The Leadership Quarterly, 22*(6), 1165–1185.

Hogg, M. A. (2003). Social identity. In M. R. Leary, & J. P. Tangney (Eds.), *Handbook of self and identity* (pp. 462–479). New York, NY: Guilford.

Höpfl, H., & Case, P. (2007). *Women and leadership.* Bingley, England: Emerald.

House, R., Javidan, M., Hanges, P., & Dorfman, P. (2002). Understanding cultures and implicit leadership theories across the globe: An introduction to project GLOBE. *Journal of World Business, 37*(1), 3–10.

Howell, J. M., & Avolio, B. J. (1993). Transformational leadership, transactional leadership, locus of control, and support for innovation: Key predictors of consolidated-business-unit performance. *Journal of Applied Psychology, 78*(6), 891–902.

Ibarra, H. (1999). Provisional selves: Experimenting with image and identity in professional adaptation. *Administrative Science Quarterly, 44*(4), 764–791.

Ibarra, H., Ely, R., & Kolb, D. (2013). Women rising: The unseen barriers. *Harvard Business Review, 91*(9), 60–66.

Ibarra, H., Wittman, S., Petriglieri, G., & Day, D. V. (2014). Leadership and identity: An examination of three theories and new research directions. In D. V. Day (Ed.), *The Oxford handbook of leadership and organizations* (pp. 285–304). Oxford, England: Oxford University.

Karim, A. U. (2003). A developmental progression model for intercultural consciousness: A leadership imperative. *Journal of Education for Business, 79*(1), 34–39.

Karp. T., & Helge, T. (2009). Leadership as identity construction: The act of leading people in organisations: A perspective from the complexity sciences. *Journal of Management Development, 28*(10), 880–896.

Keohane, N. O. (2014). Leadership out front and behind the scenes: Young women's ambitions for leadership today. In K. A. Longman, & S. R. Madsen (Eds.), *Women and leadership in higher education* (pp. 41–55). Charlotte, NC: Information Age.

Killeen, L. A., López-Zafra, E., & Eagly, A. H. (2006). Envisioning oneself as a leader: Comparisons of women and men in Spain and the United States. *Psychology of Women Quarterly, 30*(3), 312–322.

Klenke, K. (2007). Authentic leadership: A self, leader, and spiritual identity perspective. *International Journal of Leadership Studies, 3*(1), 68–97.

Leathers, D., & Eaves, M. H. (2008). *Successful nonverbal communication: Principles and applications* (4th ed.). Old Tappan, NJ: Pearson.

Longman, K., Dahlvig, J., Wikkerink, R., Cunningham, D., & O'Connor, C. M. (2011). Conceptualization of calling: A grounded theory exploration of CCCU women leaders. *Christian Higher Education, 10*(3–4), 254–275.

Lord, R. G., & Maher, K. J. (1993). *Leadership and information processing: Linking perceptions and performance.* New York, NY: Routledge.

Maddux, J. E., & Gosselin, J. T. (2003). Self-efficacy. In M. R. Leary & J. P. Tangney (Eds.), *Handbook of self and identity* (pp. 198–224). New York, NY: Guilford.

Madsen, S. R. (2016). Leadership responsibility and calling: The role of calling in a woman's choice to lead. In M. Iszatt-White, & S. Kempster (Eds.), *The new romantics of responsible leadership* (pp. TBD): London, England: Routledge.

Marks, S. R. (1977). Multiple roles and role strain: Some notes on human energy, time and commitment. *American Sociological Review, 42*(6), 921–936.

Murray, N., Tremaine, M., & Fountaine, S. (2012). Breaking through the glass ceiling in the ivory tower: Using a case study to gain new understandings of old gender issues. *Advances in Developing Human Resources, 14*(2), 221–236.

Neck, C. P., & Milliman, J. F. (1994). Thought self-leadership: Finding spiritual fulfillment in organizational life. *Journal of Managerial Psychology, 9*(6), 9–16.

Parker, P. S. (2001). African American women executives' leadership communication within dominant-culture organizations: (Re)conceptualizing notions of collaboration and instrumentality. *Management Communication Quarterly, 15*(1), 42–82.

Raclin, J. (2011). From leadership-as-practice to leaderful practice. *Leadership, 7*(2), 195–211.

Roccas, S., & Brewer, M. B. (2002). Social identity complexity. *Personality and Social Psychology Review, 6*(2), 88–106.

Scharmer, O. (2009). *Theory U: Learning from the future as it emerges.* San Francisco, CA: Berrett-Koehler.

Schniedewind, N. (1987). Teaching feminist process. *Women's Studies Quarterly, 15*(3/4), 15–31.

Sheridan, E. (2005). *Intercultural leadership competencies for United States business leaders in the new millennium* (Unpublished doctoral dissertation). Phoenix, AZ: University of Phoenix.

Slater, M. D. (2007). Reinforcing spirals: The mutual influence of media selectivity and media effects and their impact on individual behavior and social identity. *Communication Theory, 17*(3), 281–303.

Stets, J. E., & Burke, P. J. (2000). Identity theory and social identity theory. *Social Psychology Quarterly, 63*(3), 224–237.

Suddaby, R., Hardy, C., & Huy, Q. (2011). Where are the new theories of organization? *Academy of Management Review, 36*(2), 236–246.

Tajfel, H. (1972). Social categorization. English manuscript of 'La catégorisation sociale.' In S. Moscovici (Ed.), *Introduction à la psychologie sociale* (Vol. 1, pp. 272–302). Paris, France: Larousse.

Tierney, P., Farmer, S. M., & Graen, G. B. (1999). An examination of leadership and employee creativity: The relevance of traits and relationships. *Personnel Psychology, 52*(3), 591–620.

Trinidad, C., & Normore, A. H. (2005). Leadership and gender: A dangerous liaison? *Leadership & Organization Development Journal, 26*(7), 574–590.

Tudge, J. R., Mokrova, I., Hatfield, B. E., & Karnik, R. B. (2009). Uses and misuses of Bronfenbrenner's bioecological theory of human development. *Journal of Family Theory & Review, 1*(4), 198–210.

Uhl-Bien, M., & Ospina, S. (Eds.). (2012). *Advancing relational leadership research: A dialogue among perspectives.* Charlotte, NC: Information Age.

Uhl-Bien, M., Riggio, R. E., Lowe, K. B., & Carsten, M. K. (2014). Followership theory: A review and research agenda. *The Leadership Quarterly, 25*(1), 83–104.

Von Bertalanffy, L. (1968). *General systems theory: Foundations, development, application.* New York, NY: Braziller.

van Knippenberg, D., van Knippenberg, B., Cremer, D., & Hogg, M. (2004). Leadership, self, and identity: A review and research agenda. *The Leadership Quarterly, 15*(6), 825–856.

Yousafzai, M. (2013). *I am Malala: The girl who stood up for education and was shot by the Taliban.* London, England: Weidenfeld & Nicolson.

CHAPTER 9

THEORIZING WOMEN'S WAYS OF KNOWING AND LEADING FOR INTERNATIONAL DEVELOPMENT PROJECTS

The Adaptive Transformational System Leadership Model

Randal Joy Thompson
Excellence, Equity, and Empowerment, Inc.

International development projects involve the collaboration of differing and often conflicting multicultural organizations in order to initiate transformations in developing country complex systems. During project implementation, the project, donor, and developing country systems couple together to form a temporary and highly complex system designed specifically to introduce change. I argue that leaders of these international development projects can ensure a more successful change effort if they practice a model of leadership that I call *adaptive transformational system leadership*, a variation of complexity leadership theory that combines approaches of

Theorizing Women and Leadership, pages 141–161
Copyright © 2017 by Information Age Publishing

three separately identifiable styles. Such leaders build collective leadership within and between organizations involved in implementing development projects. These leaders help to create the conditions for system adaptation. They empower stakeholders of the change process to take ownership and responsibility for the system as it evolves. Moreover, they help unleash the adaptive processes in the recipient country system. Adaptive transformational system leadership fosters a systems perspective, invites widespread participation, manages the cultural and emotional aspects of change, and opens the change process so all voices are heard and respected.

In this chapter, I argue that adaptive transformational system leadership inherently functions according to qualities associated with women and their ways of knowing and leading. Therefore, achieving successful development outcomes may require a shift from a stereotypic masculine leadership style and approach to a feminine one that more closely reflects women's ways of knowing. There is support in the literature that an overall shift to what has been identified as a feminine leadership style may be more appropriate for a complex globalized world in which relationships between countries are less hierarchical and more balanced (Gerzema & D'Antonio, 2013). Contemporary international development projects function at the intersection between so-called *developed* and *developing* countries, the interactions between which have become more egalitarian and less hierarchical in recent years.

Consequently, I illustrate in this chapter how women's ways of knowing are closely aligned with the connected approach to understanding and the collective approach to implementing international development projects. A new, women-centered leadership model is required for improved management of international development projects. Evidence has accumulated that many projects fail because the organizations involved in implementing these projects are working at cross-purposes rather than collaboratively and that project leadership is directive and, hence, resisted (Easterly, 2013).

I proceed to build this model by first presenting the leadership challenges in international development projects and the weaknesses of the cause–effect change model traditionally employed in these projects. I then develop a systems model of the donor–project–recipient temporary system, illustrating how adaptive transformational system leaders function in this milieu. I demonstrate how this model of leadership addresses the highlighted challenges in international development projects and how the model reflects feminine ways (described below) of knowing and leading. I emphasize the importance of leaders alternately practicing adaptive transformational adaptive leadership and checking to see whether the targeted organizational processes are unleashing creative and adaptive change.

THE LEADERSHIP CHALLENGE IN INTERNATIONAL DEVELOPMENT PROJECTS

International development projects are designed to provide funding, training, and technical assistance to change complex systems in developing nations. These projects are implemented according to a number of models. Bilateral donors often design projects and contract them out to organizations, which then implement them with recipient stakeholder organizations. Private donors may also contract out their projects or implement them directly with the recipient organizations. The projects are generally designed for specific government or civil society sectors. They may be designed, for example, to help upgrade the education system so that school enrollment increases and student drop-out rate decreases, to modernize the health care system and reduce the incidence of certain diseases, to build political parties and establish democratic election processes, to strengthen Parliament or the judicial or the executive systems, to modernize agricultural production, to unleash private enterprise through policy reform and financing, or to implement a host of system-transforming efforts under the umbrella policies of marketization and democratization. The change process requires developing technical knowhow and skills; it also requires radically shifting the way the systems operate. Shifts may occur in the values that drive the systems, the incentives that motivate them, and the social and political structures and processes that support and reinforce them.

Traditional Approach to Development Projects

Historically, donors have designed and implemented projects that mimic their own social, economic, and political systems. Projects reinforce donors' ways of understanding the world and their theories of economic growth (Biccum, 2005; Cassen, 1986; Easterly, 2006, 2013; Riddel, 2007). Donors have conceived of these projects as technical interventions aimed at developing the capacity of recipient country systems to deliver higher valued outputs. Donors have designed and implemented projects according to the donors' values or values that have been established by the international community through policy papers written by the United Nations or the Organization of Economic Cooperation and Development (Biccum, 2005). Easterly (2013) calls this approach authoritarian development, whereby the outside expert introduces a technical solution. This solution is often in support of an authoritarian regime in the aid recipient country, at the expense of the rights of the poor who may not reap any benefits. Biccum (2005) opined whether this donor approach is really a form of new imperialism.

Much critique of this approach has been written over the years, and many project failures have been recorded (Cassen, 1987; Easterly, 2006, 2013; Eyben, 2012, 2014; Foreman, 2012; Moyo & Ferguson, 2010; Riddel, 2007). Donors experience frustration because they do not understand why developing country stakeholders do not sustain but rather resist the donor interventions. Developing country stakeholders complain that donor interventions are not appropriate to their socioeconomic milieu. Often, when interventions are embraced and implemented, the consequences are far different from those envisioned. For example, consequences have included the spawning of the oligarchy in Eastern Europe and the increased povertization of the workers caused by the privatization of state-owned industries in the former Soviet Union, and the eventual ruin of farmers initially helped by the Green Revolution because of the unaffordability of required patented seeds and other inputs (Glaeser, 2011). The development landscape is strewn with projects gone awry (Moyo & Ferguson, 2010).

Antagonism Between Stakeholders

Often, the three parties involved in development projects (i.e., the donors, the contracted project implementers, and the developing country stakeholders) are antagonistic toward each other and even at loggerheads. The frustrations of donors are many. Donors want their vision of the right way of doing things implemented in the recipient country and perceive that the contracted implementer is failing to deliver their vision because this vision inevitably does not materialize as imagined. Donors view the recipient country as being unwilling to change for the better and perceive that aid recipients only want the perks of foreign aid, such as visiting to the donor country and receiving equipment, vehicles, and other tangibles. Finally, donors are frustrated that recipient country stakeholders do not want to change their systems to function more like the donor's system and worry about misuse of the funding because donors are accountable to their constituents, who are generally not supportive of foreign aid.

Contractors are often caught in the middle, frustrated both by donors and recipient country stakeholders. Contractors consider donors to be too demanding that their visions be implemented despite their lacking a clear understanding of the local systems. Contractors consider recipient stakeholders as less committed to change than would be required to implement the donor's vision.

Recipient country stakeholders often feel put-upon by the donors and their project implementers. These stakeholders often feel forced to participate in such projects and may perceive that they are expected to change their way of doing business, especially if they are facing human and financial resource challenges. Recipient country stakeholders desire the influx of financing and technical assistance but want a sense of control over these. As a result, instead of cooperating in the change effort, these three groups of individuals and their organizations are often caught in a tug-of-war.

Shift in Approach to Development

Since the inception of international development from post-World War II until recent years, the *modus operandi* of international development has been driven largely by donors leading the development process and developing country recipients often resisting and feeling disempowered (Sogge, 2002). Donors worked with the attitude that they knew best and that the solutions were technical in nature. Gradually, as developing nations began to collaborate and band together, they negotiated the Paris Declaration on Aid Effectiveness in 2005 and the Accra Agenda for Action in 2008 (OECD, 2005, 2008). These agreements were written so that developing nations could use donor assistance to direct their own development. In order to be compliant with these agreements, donors emphasize capacity development of recipient countries with the goal of enabling these countries to manage their own development. Donors posit various definitions of and approaches to such capacity development.

Aid agencies experience difficulty adjusting to the tenets of this shift toward recipient country management because they have been used to being in the dominant position vis-à-vis aid recipients. Their predominant leadership style has been transactional, more or less enforcing compliance through rewards and punishments. Compliance has traditionally been tied to political conditions associated with assistance (Biccum, 2005; Easterly, 2013). Leadership has been vested in the donors, who expect the recipients to be dutiful followers.

Cause-and-Effect Model of Development Projects

As illustrated in Figure 9.1, donors attempt to transfer knowledge, skills, and abilities, procedures, processes, inputs, and approaches directly through policy dialog and indirectly through their funded projects. These projects infuse the recipient system with donor and/or global standards and values that have been developed by international organizations such as the United Nations. The model is essentially a cause-and-effect model based on a theory of change that is linear. It is founded upon an if–then logic represented by the logical framework such that if the donor encourages the recipient to do such-and-such, then the envisioned results will be achieved (Eyben, 2013; Jensen, 2010).

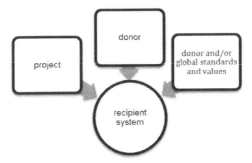

Figure 9.1 Cause-and-effect model of international development projects.

The cause-and-effect model and leadership styles practiced by donors include a number of approaches associated with masculine traits, according to a number of different studies (Gerzema & D'Antonio, 2013; Hofstede, Hofstede, & Minkov, 2010). Masculine traits include assertiveness, control, competition, aggression, directiveness, task orientation, black-and-white thinking, and leader as expert. Masculine traits also include setting goals and expectations unilaterally, employing rewards and punishments to reinforce performance, appealing to individual rather than collective interests and gains, and emphasizing technical rather than social or political solutions. The masculine stance represented by Figure 9.1 manifests "the familiar world of Authority-right-we, as against the alien world of illegitimate-wrong-others" (Perry, 1998, p. 59). The model generated from this masculine perspective ignores the complexity inherent in organizational systems and it denies the resistance in systems that will inevitably arise when recipients feel they are being pushed unilaterally by an external agent.

As I argue below, given the challenges of implementing international development projects, a leadership approach based on women's ways of knowing may improve the chances of successful development projects. Such an approach is collaborative, seeks power sharing and joint responsibility, and attempts to empower people to assume a leadership role collectively rather than individually (Belenky, Chinchy, Goldberger, & Tarule, 1997; Burke & Collins, 2001; Gerzema & D'Antonio, 2013; Helgesen, 1995; Stanford, Oates, & Flores, 1995).

THE NEED TO SHIFT TO A SYSTEMS MODEL AND APPROPRIATE LEADERSHIP STYLE

A systems view of international development projects offers a more realistic perspective from which to practice a leadership style that has a higher chance of helping the developing country recipient system transform in a beneficial direction. In fact, during an international development project, there occurs a temporary coupling of three or more complex organizational systems. These individual systems together form an even more complex yet temporary adaptive system. This temporary system is comprised of individuals "bonded in a cooperative dynamic by common goal, outlook, need, etc." (Uhl-Bien, Marion, & McKelvey, 2007, p. 299). Each of the participating organizational systems has its own objectives, processes, procedures, and values, but suspends these for the common good.

If the participating organizations succeed in forming a truly coupled system, stakeholders within each of the systems develop close synergistic relationships that can generate a positive adaptive change process in the recipient country system. In many ways, this temporary coupling of systems and stakeholders looks like gears working together. In a truly coupled system, the donor does not contract the project to implement a specific predetermined vision in the recipient organization. Rather, stakeholders in the temporary system work together to hone the transformational process such that it makes sense to the recipient organization and will be embraced as a positive adaptation.

Project as a Temporary Coupled System

As seen in Figure 9.2, the project generates a temporary organization designed specifically to introduce transformation and change into the recipient country targeted system. Traditionally, this change has been viewed as technical. In reality, projects represent an *adaptive challenge* (Heifetz, Grashow, & Linsky, 2009; Uhl-Bien et al., 2007) to recipient country systems. Such a challenge requires "new learning, innovation, and new patterns of

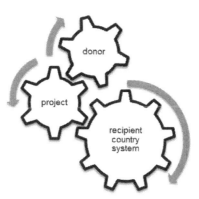

Figure 9.2 Temporary coupling of organizational systems.

behavior . . . exploration, new discoveries, and adjustment" (Uhl-Bien et al, 2007, p. 300).

Traditionally, donors have made two serious mistakes in international development: Donors have assumed that recipient country systems are not functional and that donor-designed projects will make them functional. As Heifetz et al. (2009) pointed out, people set up organizations that they deem to be the most appropriate to accomplish their goals, given the circumstances, values, sociopolitical structures, and economic conditions in their countries. Powerful individuals with vested interests typically maintain organizations and are capable of taking extreme action to prevent the organizations from changing. Further, the reality of the existing organizational system reflects a way of being and relating that is very important to the organization's members. The loss of this reality is painful and threatening (Linsky, 2011), no matter how desirable the change may look to donors.

Need for a Different Style of Leadership

Given the reality of a temporary coupled system as depicted in Figure 9.2, a different style of leadership is required in international development projects. This style is distinguished from the traditional, transactional, directive, masculine, and hierarchical leadership style. Such a leadership approach should facilitate the freeing of the recipient country system to adapt more flexibly to inevitable external forces such as globalization.

Ideally, all individuals in the project system would be involved in leadership. In the best-case scenario, individuals from the donor, project, and recipient country system responsible for the project would initially agree on their collective leadership roles. However, in practice, the leader of the organization contracted by the donor often needs to take the initiative to help build the synergies among the participating organizational systems and stakeholders. This leader directs a project team with skills and experience deemed essential to help further develop the capacity of the recipient system to achieve its redefined goals. The challenge of a leader in this situation is to help build collective leadership among the three organizations (e.g., donor, host country, and project) and to work together to enable adaptive change and system and personal transformation. The additional challenge in the international development milieu is that the leader and leaders who emerge are attempting to influence organizations to which they do not belong. These organizations generally have dramatically contrasting and often conflicting goals, cultures, and values.

ADAPTIVE TRANSFORMATIONAL SYSTEM LEADERSHIP

Adaptive transformational system leadership can facilitate a more positive change process involving external agents coming from different cultures and geopolitical power positions and can help level a playing field that has historically been dominated by donors. The adaptive transformational system leadership style is a variation of complexity leadership theory, which "focuses on identifying and exploring the strategies and behaviors that foster organizational and subunit creativity, learning, and adaptability" (Uhl-Bien et al., 2007, p. 299). This section will provide an overview of adaptive transformational system leadership, highlight its connections to women's ways of knowing, and offer descriptions of the key components of this leadership model (e.g., adaptive leadership, transformational leadership, and system leadership).

Overview of Adaptive Transformational System Leadership

Each component of adaptive transformational system leadership offers critical perspectives on leadership:

- Adaptive leadership involves "improvisational expertise, a kind of process expertise that knows prudently how to experiment with never-been-tried before relationships, means of communication, and ways of interacting that will help people develop solutions" (Heifetz et al., 2009, p. 2–3). Adaptive leadership is "a generative dynamic that underlies emergent change activities" (Uhl-Bien et al., 2007, p. 299).
- Transformational leadership refers to the need to empower stakeholders so that they can help define and subsequently own the transformational change process. This leadership approach allows stakeholders to align the change to their values or, alternatively, to re-align their values to the change.
- System leadership refers to expanding the defining context of the change process to a broad systemic level. At this level, stakeholders can discern the influences initiating the change and those resisting the change and encourage all parties to address each other's issues in order to build a shared understanding among stakeholders. It catalyzes a shift to co-creation of the change trajectory so that the change is owned and sustained by all entities involved.

When combined into one leadership approach, adaptive transformational system leaders are able, through collective leadership, to unleash the adaptive abilities of the system targeted for change. Collective leadership is distributed leadership in which leaders throughout the organization emerge and share in visioning, planning, decision-making, and executing change. At the same time, these leaders inspire, motivate, and empower individuals to embrace the change that they perceive as enhancing their lives. Hence, actions of collective leaders facilitate and respond to leadership as a system property. Uhl-Bien et al. (2007) asserted that leadership should be "a complex interplay from which a collective impetus for action and change emerges when heterogeneous agents interact in networks in ways that produce new patterns of behavior or new modes of operating" (p. 299).

As I argue, adaptive transformational system leadership reflects approaches typically employed by women, including the qualities of collaboration, caring, courage, intuition, and vision. Regan and Brooks (1995) call this *relational leadership*, characterized by displaying empathy, sharing of perspective, responding to recipient needs, being sensitive to culture, and being willing to let go of one's own solution. These approaches are identified as feminine by Gerzema's and D'Antonio's 2013 global survey. They are also labeled as the "web of inclusion" by women leaders (Helgesen, 1995)—an approach that replaces rigid hierarchical thinking and acting. Such leadership approaches are derived from women's ways of knowing, including women's rootedness in a "sense of connection" and inclusion of others, their identification with the "they" rather than with the authorities, their intention to construct knowledge based on a systems view that integrates the views of others, and their focus on care and the empowerment of others (Belenky et al., 1997; Schroeder, 1996).

These feminine traits and women's ways of knowing are evident in adaptive transformational system leadership. Women are less likely to identify with authority (Belenky et al., 1997). Hence, instead of imposing the unilateral will of the donor, women may perceive the recipient country stakeholder "they" as part of a "we" who can work together to understand the system in a holistic, integrated fashion (Belenky et al., 1997). Because women generally do not enter the project setting with set-in-stone ideas, they are more likely to be open to experiment with new relationships and discover the improvisational expertise required by adaptive systems. Additionally, since women are driven by care and the desire to empower others (Belenky et al., 1997; Helgesen, 1995; Regan & Brooks, 1995), they are more apt to listen to the recipient country stakeholders and include them as leaders and as active participants through transformational leading. As connected learners, stakeholders will be open to seeing the system as a whole and to working together to co-create the change process.

The three leadership styles inherent in adaptive transformational system leadership are discussed in more detail below, including the relationship between these styles and women's ways of knowing and feminine traits of leadership. The length of the discussion for each of these leadership styles reflects the roles each plays. Adaptive leadership enables people to thrive on complex and changing challenges. The ability to inspire people to thrive on complex challenges is the most important skill for being an effective leader for international development projects. The four contributions of system leadership also described below are required in order to enhance and support the contribution of adaptive leadership. Finally, transformative leadership fosters a collective identity and empowers stakeholders to make the change their own.

Adaptive Leadership

Adaptive leadership is defined as "the practice of mobilizing people to tackle tough challenges and thrive" (Heifetz et al., 2009, p. 14). Adaptive challenges in organizations are distinguished from technical challenges that can be addressed by authoritative expertise. Heifetz et al. (2009) note that "adaptive challenges can only be addressed through changes in people's priorities, beliefs, habits, and loyalties" (p. 19); these change by mobilizing "discovery, shedding certain entrenched ways, tolerating losses, and generating the new capacity to thrive anew."

An important challenge in international development projects is to ensure that stakeholders not only achieve a particular goal but that they also ensure that adaptive processes are functioning in the system. Adaptive leaders practice change-facilitating skills among stakeholders. At the same time, they periodically review how the recipient country target organization is functioning. These leaders do this to verify that adaptive processes are being generated and functioning within the organization. Such adaptive processes both maintain the change dynamic and open the organization to possible future changes.

Adaptive leadership takes place at many levels, manifesting in the interactions between people; the spaces between people and their actions; relationships that allow for learning, expression of new ideas and dissent; feedback, reflection, and interaction with new technology and new processes; and clashes among ideas (Heifetz et al., 2009; Hogan, 2008; Obolensky, 2010; Torres & Reeves, 2011; Uhl-Bien et al., 2007). Adaptive leaders tap into the collective intelligence of the stakeholders. They help the stakeholders "generate new norms that enable the organization to meet the ongoing stream of adaptive challenges posed by a world ever ready to offer new realities, opportunities, and pressures" (Heifetz et al., 2009, p. 17).

Adaptive leadership requires the ability to let go of a pre-set technical fix for the organization and help stakeholders become collective leaders who collaborate to seek creative solutions by dialoging, challenging the norm, and making transparent the emotions that inevitably accompany giving up the familiar. Women leaders, according to the literature, are more apt than typical male leaders to surrender the authoritative stance of an external expert to a collaborative approach that seeks solutions derived from the experience of all the stakeholders (Belenky et al., 1997; Gerzema & D'Antonio, 2013). Surrendering authority often includes being vulnerable, an emotion more familiar to women than to men (Belenky et al., 1997). Through connected, constructed knowing, women seek information from others and from their subjective selves in order to understand how an organization is functioning. Women do not need to be an expert or rely on an expert for knowledge and can "know" in context through constructing knowledge (Belenky et al., 1997). As a female trait, flexibility opens up an adaptive leader to listen and build consensus (Gerzema & D'Antonio, 2013). Adaptive change can catalyze the grieving process of letting go of the past and embracing an unknown future. Women, with their emphasis on care, are more accustomed to dealing with stakeholder emotions around loss and fear of the unknown. Women are more likely to recognize such emotions, honor them, and facilitate their healing.

Transformational Leadership

Transformational leaders motivate and inspire stakeholders to embrace change and empower them to make the change their own (Burns, 2004; Northouse, 2010). As Burns pointed out, transformational leaders encourage "a sense of collective identity and collective efficacy, which in turn brings stronger feelings of self-worth and self-efficacy...By pursuing transformational change, people can transform themselves" (2004, pp. 25–26). The creation of this collective identity is aligned with the capacity of system leadership to foster a shared understanding and collective *we*.

The collective identity emphasized through transformational leadership is critical for the success of the joint effort required to implement international development projects. In contrast to transactional leadership that appeals to individual gain, transformational leadership appeals to higher social values and mores, motivating stakeholders to see the project as a vehicle through which to operationalize these values and mores (Burns, 2004). Participants move beyond a consideration of their individual gain to a commitment to the whole, collective endeavor. Such a perspective elevates the undertaking to a higher level and provides stakeholders with the possibility of accomplishing something positive for society that they would not normally have the possibility to do. Transformational leadership, associated with "inspiration...empowerment, articulating a vision, promoting group goals, providing intellectual stimulation...and organizational citizenship behavior," enhances stakeholders' sense of achievement (Jha, 2014, p. 22).

Evidence has accumulated that women practice transformational leadership more naturally than men do (Alimo-Metcalfe, 2010; Burke & Collins, 2002; Gartzia & Van Engen, 2012). Gerzema's and D'Antonio's 2013 global survey associated the ability to empower others as a feminine trait. Survey respondents identified empowering others as necessary for desirable leadership, success, morality, and happiness (Gerzema & D'Antonio, 2013). Women leaders typically facilitate communication, involve others in team building, prefer referent power bases, inspire and reward, and foster mutual trust and respect (Stanford, Oates, & Flores, 1995). Care and the desire to empower others have been identified as a fundamental way of knowing for women (Belenky et al., 1997). Engendering trust has also been identified as a feminine trait (Gartzia & Van Engen, 2012). Inspiration is identified as a gender-neutral trait by Gerzema and D'Antonio. When combined with care, the desire to empower, the ability to engender trust, and connected knowing, inspiration becomes a powerful tool for raising the consciousness of stakeholders regarding the importance of their change effort.

System Leadership

Like adaptive leadership, system leadership fosters collective leadership. System leadership makes invisible forces visible. For example, the theory of change undergirding the project is clearly articulated, acted upon, monitored, and modified, if necessary. This leadership style also legitimates the need for transparency and communication. The importance of culture is highlighted through the practice of system leadership, and stakeholders create a shared understanding as well as cognitive and emotional connections. Finally, system leaders build community and networks that support transformative change.

Collective Leadership

System leaders foster collective leadership (Fillingham & Weir, 2014; Senge, Hamilton, & Kania, 2015). Such leadership is virtually a prerequisite for success in international development projects. Stakeholders must become leaders in order to embrace the transformation. They must work together to hone the transformation such that the recipient organization owns it and embraces it. System leaders need to first see the larger system within which the change effort is embedded (Senge et al., 2015). Seeing the larger system includes making transparent the donor system, project system, and recipient country system or systems.

Making the Invisible Visible

Donors generally represent the policies of their governments, and these polices need to be examined to make sure that they do not conflict with the best interests of the recipient country and system. Under previous approaches to development, donors maintained the prerogative of assuming but not disclosing such polices as part of the implementation process. Currently, however, under the tenets of the Paris Declaration, the policies are required to be open for discussion (OECD, 2005).

In addition to donor policies, the project system derives from a donor-created theory of change, which should also be made transparent and discussed. When both the policies and the theory of change undergirding the system are made known, the understanding that results from such an expanded system view "enables collaborating organizations to jointly develop solutions not evident to any of them individually and to work together for the health of the whole system rather than just pursue symptomatic fixes to individual pieces" (Senge et al., 2015, para. 10). Collective leaders also emerge throughout the system because system leadership is an approach that "brokers, resources, supports, challenges and makes connections across the system" (Harris, 2010, p. 9).

The Importance of Culture

Adaptive challenges are human challenges, and seeing the system writ large involves both understanding the cultural and political context of the recipient country and helping stakeholders from that country understand the donor human context. These "challenges are typically grounded in the complexity of values, beliefs, and loyalties rather than technical complexity and stir up intense emotions rather than dispassionate analysis" (Heifetz et al., 2009, p. 70). Hofstede et al. (2010) argue that a cultural expert in the recipient country should hold discussions with donor technical experts in order to blend the two perspectives into a culturally relevant and sensitive intervention.

Community and Networks

System leaders foster community and build networks. Just as systems in nature thrive by creating and nurturing communities, so human systems include interrelationships and communities. System change requires that a critical mass of interrelationships support the change and that stakeholders comprising these relationships are committed to implementing it (Stone & Barlow, 2015).

Contribution of System Leadership to International Development Projects

System leadership involves turning oneself inside out and seeing the world as others see it, deeply examining one's own assumptions and worldview and "appreciating how our mental models may limit us" (Senge et al., 2015, para. 11). Collective leaders in the temporary coupled system ideally form a bond such that they can engage in shared reflection so that they "appreciate emotionally as well as cognitively each other's reality" (Senge et al., 2015, para. 11). Collective knowledge and wisdom emerge from these relationships and provide a view of system reality not available to any individual beforehand. Such knowledge and wisdom come forth over time "through a ripening process that gradually brings about new ways of thinking, acting, and being" (Senge et al., 2015, para. 38). Many approaches have been posited to facilitate this process, including Theory-U (Scharmer & Kaufer, 2013) and the Ladder of Inference (Argyris, 1990; Senge et al., 2015).

After collective leaders have taken a view of the broader system, a *we* identity will form between them based on intense self-examination, combined with true appreciation of the others' perspectives. These leaders and eventually their followers in the coupled system are then able to co-create the system transformation. There is a shift from the negative problem-focused approach to a more positive orientation. The positive orientation is driven by visioning and sorting through the cultural aspects of their past that they want to hold on to (Heifetz, 2009). Senge et al., (2015) note that "The shift involves not just building inspiring visions but facing difficult truths about the present reality and learning how to use the tension between vision and reality to inspire truly new approaches" (para. 12).

The shift also recognizes the fact that "problems 'out there'" are also problems "in here" (Senge et al., 2015, para. 16). Problems are found in our assumptions about the world and our worldviews regarding which paradigms are "the correct ones." Problems also exist in our cultural beliefs and values that influence how we expect ourselves and others to behave.

Connecting System Leadership and Women's Ways of Knowing

System collective leadership includes seeing oneself as part of a system rather than as the director of the system standing outside of it. The ability to see oneself within a system context has been highlighted in the literature on women's management styles and women's ways of knowing (Gilligan, 1993; Helgesen, 1995; Murray, 1997). Women's ways of knowing are characterized by "connectedness, inclusiveness and a desire to overcome opposing dualities...subjectivity and feelings as part of knowing, acceptance of complexity, acceptance of change and a desire for flexibility" (Murray, 1997, p. 127). Female design principles are characterized as more organically ordered, more holistic/complex, more social, more functional, more user oriented, and more slowly growing, (Murray, 1997, p. 128). These qualities are consistent with a leader seeing herself as part of a collaborative system, a stance required of a system leader. The "connected knowing" of women, deriving from experience rather than from authorities, also opens the door to the possibility of learning from others in the temporary project system (Belenky et al., 1997; Schroeder, 1996). Gerzema's and D'Antonio's 2013 global survey identified "community oriented" and "nurturing" as feminine traits. System leadership requires the nurturing of community and strong interrelationships that will support the system transformation (Stone & Barlow, 2015).

How Adaptive Transformational System Leadership Solves Development Challenges

When practiced as a unified leadership approach, adaptive transformational system leadership helps to solve development challenges. These challenges include the resistance of the recipient country to the imposed solution by the donor; the inappropriateness of the donor solution to the sociopolitical, economic, and cultural environment of the recipient country; the suspicion and disharmony between donor, contracted implementer, and recipient country stakeholders caused by lack of communication and mutual planning; and the lack of sustainability of international development projects because of the lack of commitment of the recipient country organization.

Adaptive transformational system leadership ignites a highly participatory and synergistic adaptive change process that levels the playing field between donor and recipient countries. Adaptive transformational system leadership involves these stakeholders in mutually beneficial, higher-level system processes that lead to self-discovery and the strengthening of relationships required to effectively operate in the increasingly complex global order. Adaptive leadership helps create the underlying human and cultural changes that support the transformational change. Adaptive leadership also establishes adaptive processes in the organization. Transformational leadership invites collective identity and the possibility of creating something of social value. System leadership expands the change effort to a higher-level system view, promotes collective leadership, and builds resonance and mutual understanding among stakeholders. Such a leadership practice will lead to mutual agreement and planning between the donor, the implementer, and the host country. The practice of adaptive transformational system leadership will result in international development projects that make sense in their context and to which the recipient organization will be committed and sustain.

As Table 9.1 below illustrates, women's ways of knowing, feminine traits, and women's leadership styles are closely aligned with adaptive transformational system leadership and, hence, are critical to the successful design and implementation of international development projects. Although, as previously stated, studies have shown that women more than men are

TABLE 9.1 Development Challenges and Adaptive Transformational System Leadership		
Challenges in International Development Projects	How Adaptive Transformational System Leadership Addresses These Challenges	How Women's Ways of Knowing and Feminine Traits Align with Adaptive Transformational System Leadership
Inappropriateness of the donor solution to the socio-political, economic, and cultural environment of the recipient country.	Collective leadership designs a solution that is appropriate to the recipient country and will be embraced and sustained.	Women being willing to give up authoritarian role of "external expert" to facilitate a mutual learning and designing process with stakeholders.
Donor attempts to facilitate system transformation through a technical fix rather than recognizing the adaptive challenge.	Recognition of adaptive processes and challenges in the recipient system and understanding how these can be effectively addressed.	Women "know" within a system and construct meaning that includes perspectives of others and, hence, is likely to view adaptive processes and recognize that they go beyond the technical.
Resistance of the recipient country stakeholders to the solution imposed by donor.	Joint planning and collective leadership minimizes resistance and provides stakeholders with a voice and equal role as leaders.	Women willing to accept the "they" as part of a "we" and willing to accept equality of all stakeholders. Women practice connected knowing by definition.
Suspicion and disharmony arise among donors, contracted implementers, and recipient country stakeholders because of a lack of communication and mutual planning.	This leadership approach requires leaders to emerge throughout the temporary system. Collective leadership, combined with community building and strengthening of inter-relationships will strengthen communication and require mutual planning.	Women's desire for community, their connected knowing, and their inclusion of "they" in "we" will work to create harmony between stakeholders and catalyze communication.

(continued)

TABLE 9.1   Development Challenges and Adaptive Transformational System Leadership (continued)

Challenges in International Development Projects	How Adaptive Transformational System Leadership Addresses These Challenges	How Women's Ways of Knowing and Feminine Traits Align with Adaptive Transformational System Leadership
Recipient feels powerless to stand up to donor.	Requirement for collective leadership and inclusion are essential requirements of this leadership approach.	Women's emphasis on care and empowering others helps recipients gain confidence to be equal collective leaders.
Recipients resist adaptive change because it is disruptive and emotionally painful.	Adaptive leadership recognizes that adaptive challenges are emotionally volatile and allows emotions to be part of the change process.	Women are more sensitive and accepting of emotional aspects of change and to feeling vulnerable and can honor recipient's fear and discomfort with change.
Lack of sustainability of international development projects results from the lack of commitment of the recipient country organization.	Stakeholders in recipient country organization become collective leaders and are empowered to design and support the transformation.	Women are community oriented and connected knowers, and, through care, empower stakeholders to adopt and promote the change and sustain it.

likely to practice transformational leadership (Alimo-Metcalfe, 2010; Burke & Collins, 2001; Gartzia & Van Engen, 2012), the literature has not heretofore identified the underlying drivers of transformational leadership as feminine. Nor has the literature argued that feminine traits and women's ways of knowing underlie the successful practice of adaptive leadership and system leadership. In the context of international development projects, I argue that these traits and ways of knowing are definitely critical to the success of adaptive transformational system leadership. I am not arguing that only women can successfully practice adaptive transformational system leadership. However, I am arguing that for people to be successful in practicing this leadership and to facilitate the successful implementation of international development projects in the current milieu, they must practice what has heretofore been considered as a more feminine approach. My assertion is consistent with the findings of Gerzema and D'Antonio (2013) that the world is moving toward a more feminine outlook. Hence, leaders practicing this model of leadership will play an essential role in facilitating this global transformation.

CONCLUSION

I have argued that adaptive transformational system leadership is the most appropriate and effective approach to designing and managing international development projects. These projects are temporarily coupled systems comprised of donor, contractor, and recipient country stakeholder organizations. In order for the projects to address economically, politically, socially, and culturally appropriate transformation in recipient country societies, stakeholders need to emerge as collective leaders who are open to creative, adaptive change; who empower recipient country stakeholders to own and sustain the change; and who view the change at a broad systemic level.

I argued that adaptive transformational system leadership is practiced according to feminine traits and women's ways of knowing. Women are less likely to identify with authority or play the role of outside expert and hence are more open to including the stakeholder "they" as part of a collaborative "we." Women are connected knowers and, hence, tend to assess the project system based on multiple perspectives. They often construct knowledge based on their subjective experience combined with the perceptions of others. Women tend to lead with inclusion, rooted in their sense of connection, care, and intention to empower others. More comfortable than men with emotion, women are equipped to handle the inevitable emotions involved in adaptive changes.

My assertions have been that the three leadership styles included in adaptive transformational system leadership are founded on and best practiced by feminine traits, and that women's ways of knowing provide novel perspectives and new insights to be considered in the discussion of women's leadership models. A shift in the approach to global issues from a masculine perspective to a more feminine one is consistent with the restructuring of the world to more balanced, egalitarian relationships between states.

REFERENCES

Alimo-Metcalfe, B. (2010). An investigation of female and male constructs of leadership and empowerment. *Gender in Management: An International Review, 25*(8), 640–648.

Argyris, C. (1990). *Overcoming organizational defenses: Facilitating organizational learning,* Upper Saddle River, NJ: Prentice-Hall.

Belenky, M. F., Clinchy, B. M., Goldberger, N. R., & Tarule, J. M. (1997). *Women's ways of knowing.* New York, NY: Basic Books.

Biccum, A. R. (2005). Development and the "new" imperialism: A reinvention of colonial discourse in DFID promotional literature. *Third World Quarterly, 26*(6), 1005–1020.

Burke, S., & Collins, K. M., (2001). Gender differences in leadership styles and management skills. *Women in Management Review, 16*(5), 244–257.

Burns, J. M. (2004). *Transforming leadership: A new pursuit of happiness.* New York, NY: Grove Press.

Cassen, R. (1986). *Does aid work?* Oxford, England: Clarendon Press.

Easterly, W. (2006). *The White man's burden: Why the west's efforts to aid the rest have done so much ill and so little good.* New York, NY: Penguin.

Easterly, W. (2013). *The tyranny of experts: Economists, dictators, and the forgotten rights of the poor.* New York, NY: Basic Books.

Eyben, R. (2012). Struggles in Paris: The DAC and the purposes of development aid. *European Journal of Development Research, 25*(1), 78–91.

Eyben, R. (2013, April). The politics of evidence. Framing paper from *The Big Push Forward Conference,* Brighton, England.

Eyben, R. (2014). *International aid and the making of a better world: Reflexive practice.* New York, NY. Routledge. Kindle Edition.

Fillingham, D., & Weir, B. (2014). *System leadership: Lessons and learning from Aqua's integrated care discovery communities.* London, England: The King's Fund.

Foreman, J. (2012). *Aiding and abetting: Foreign aid failures and the .07% deception.* London, England: Civitas.

Gartzia, L., & van Engen, M. (2012). Are (male) leaders feminine enough? Gendered traits of identity as mediators of sex differences in leadership styles. *Gender in Management: An International Journal, 27*(5), 296–314.

Gerzema, J., & D'Antonio, M. (2013). *The Athena doctrine: How women (and the men who think like them) will rule the future.* San Francisco, CA: Jossey-Bass.

Gilligan, C. (1993). *In a different voice: Psychological theory and women's development.* Cambridge, MA: Harvard University.

Glaeser, B. (2011). *The green revolution revisited: Critique and alternatives* (2nd ed.). New York, NY: Routledge.

Harris, A. (2010). Leading system transformation. *School Leadership & Management, 30*(3), 197–207. Retrieved from https://www.researchgate.net/publication/265306472_Leading_System_Transformation

Heifetz, R. A., Grashow, A., & Linsky, M. (2009). *The practice of adaptive leadership: Tools and tactics for changing your organization and the world.* Cambridge, MA: Harvard Business Review.

Helgesen, S. (1995). *The female advantage: Women's ways of leadership.* New York, NY: Doubleday.

Hofstede, G., Hofstede, G. J., & Minkov, M. (2010). *Cultures and organizations: Intercultural cooperation and its importance for survival.* New York, NY: McGraw Hill.

Hogan, T. J. (2008). The adaptive leadership maturity model. *Organization Development Journal, 26*(1), 55–61.

Jensen, G. (2010). *The logical framework approach: How to guide.* Retrieved from http://www.dochas.ie/Shared/Files/4/BOND_logframe_Guide.pdf

Jha, S. (2014). Transformational leadership and psychological empowerment: Determinants of organizational citizenship behavior. *South Asian Journal of Global Business Research. 3*(1), 18–35.

Linsky, M. (2011, April 13). *Adaptive leadership, leading change.* [video file]. Retrieved from https://www.youtube.com/watch?v=af-cSvnEExM

Moyo, D., & Ferguson, N. (2010). *Dead aid: Why aid is not working and how there is a better way for Africa.* New York, NY: Farrar, Straus, and Giroux.

Murray, J. (1997). Can women's ways of knowing lead us to more ecologically responsible design? *Architectural Theory Review, 2*(2), 127–133.

Northouse, P. G. (2010). *Leadership: Theory and practice* (5th ed.). Thousand Oaks, CA: Sage.

Obolensky, N. (2010). *Complex adaptive leadership: Embracing paradox and uncertainty.* London, England: Ashgate.

Organization for Economic Cooperation and Development-OECD. (2005). *The Paris declaration on aid effectiveness: Five principles for smart aid.* Retrieved from http://www.oecd.org/dac/effectiveness/45827300.pdf

Organization for Economic Cooperation and Development-OECD. (2008). *The Paris declaration on aid effectiveness and the Accra agenda for action.* Retrieved from http://www.oecd.org/development/effectiveness/34428351.pdf

Perry, W. G. (1998). *Forms of intellectual and ethical development in the college years: A scheme.* San Francisco, CA: Jossey-Bass.

Regan, H. B., & Brooks, G. H. (1995). *Out of women's experience: Creating relational leadership.* Thousand Oaks, CA: Corwin.

Riddel, R. (2007). *Does foreign aid really work?* Oxford, England: Oxford University.

Scharmer, O., & Kaufer, K. (2013). *Leading from the emerging future: From ego-system to eco-system economics.* San Francisco, CA: Barrett-Koehler Publishers.

Schroeder, C. (1996). From conscientization to connected knowing: The liberatory epistemologies of Paula Freire and "women's ways of knowing." Retrieved from http://eric.ed.gov/?id=ED402596

Senge, P., Hamilton, H., & Kania, J. (2015, Winter). The dawn of system leadership. *Stanford Social Innovation Review, 17.* Retrieved from http://www.ssireview.org/articles/entry/the_dawn_of_system_leadership

Sogge, D. (2002). *Give and take: What's the matter with foreign aid?* Halifax, Nova Scotia: Fernwood.

Stanford, J. H., Oates, B. R., & Flores, D. (1995). Women's leadership styles: A heuristic analysis. *Women in Management Review, 10*(2), 9–16.

Stone, M., & Barlow, Z. (2015). Seven lessons for leaders in systems change. Center for Ecoliteracy. Retrieved from http://www.ecoliteracy.org/article/seven-lessons-leaders-systems-change

Torres, R., & Reeves, M. (2011, July). Adaptive leadership: How many of these practices do you employ? *Leadership Excellence, 28*(7), 8.

Uhl-Bien, M., Marion, R., & McKelvey, B. (2007). Complexity leadership theory: Shifting leadership from the industrial age to the knowledge era. *The Leadership Quarterly, 18*(4), 298–318.

CHAPTER 10

THE LEADERSHIP REPERTOIRE OF SELECT FILIPINA WOMEN IN THE DIASPORA AND IMPLICATIONS FOR THEORIZING LEADERSHIP

Maria Africa Beebe
Portland State University

In this chapter, I posit that every successful Filipina woman in the diaspora has at her disposal a unique leadership repertoire, elements of which have been drawn from a large set of culturally determined understandings of the why and how of leadership. This understanding of leadership is evident in a discourse analysis of their language about leadership. Using discourse analysis as both a theory and a method, I examine mostly written narratives of 35 Filipina women in the diaspora who have demonstrated leadership outside the country of their origin and have been recognized by their peers as influential. Guided by appreciative inquiry, the women wrote about their best selves, skills, competencies, and experiences that influenced their success.

Theorizing Women and Leadership, pages 163–182
Copyright © 2017 by Information Age Publishing
All rights of reproduction in any form reserved.

The goal of this study is to provide a beginning point for theorizing about the leadership of a significant, non-western group of women. The analysis suggests that for these women the *why* of leadership includes a combination of having purpose and meaning, achieving impact, and giving back. The *how* of leadership emphasizes the centrality of relationships, the significance of values, and the importance of the process of self-awareness, self-transformations, and self-transcendence. Themes concerning the how and why of leadership make up the women's leadership repertoires. At the center of their leadership repertoires is the Philippine cultural norm, *kapwa* (shared humanity) that underlies the why and the how of leadership.

FOUNDATIONAL SCHOLARSHIP

Scholarship on the diaspora and leadership, Filipinas in the diaspora, and Filipino leadership provides the rationale and building blocks for the study. The Filipino cultural value of *kapwa*, or shared humanity, is key to understanding the results of the discourse analysis about leadership. The discussion on discourse analysis as a theory and method builds on the work of Allan, Gordon, and Iverson (2006), Fairhurst (2007), and Berkelaar, Williams, and Linvill (2009). The concept of leadership repertoire is based on Goleman, Boyatzis, and McKee's (2013) repertoire of leadership styles and Murthy's (2009) discussion of the ensemble of leadership repertoire.

Diaspora and Leadership

Diaspora "refers to emigrants and their descendants who live outside the country of their birth or ancestry, either on a temporary or permanent basis, yet still maintain affective and material ties to their countries of origin" (Agunias & Newland, 2012, p. 15). Increasingly, the relationship of migration and global development is being recognized, with studies that are starting to show how human mobility and development are intertwined. These studies provide evidence of the impacts of migration on the sending, receiving, and transit countries; the studies also explain diaspora contributions to their homelands in a variety of ways in different policy arenas, including development, democratization, and security (de Haas, 2010; Groves, 2013). Buil and Siegel's (2013) summary of key developmental implications for sending and receiving countries highlighted increases in female empowerment in the sending countries and increases in multicultural diversity in the receiving countries. The International Organization for Migration suggested the achievement of gender equality by eliminating discrimination against women in political, economic, and public life has become part of the development agenda (McGregor, Siegel, Ragab, & Juzwiak, 2014).

Some leadership and diaspora studies focus on the leadership role of women in the sending countries, but few studies examine the leadership role of women in the receiving countries. With about 3.2% of the world's population classified as migrants, and women accounting for 48% of the global migrant population (Groves, 2013), it is important to understand the leadership dynamics in both the sending and receiving countries. This understanding is invaluable for all countries. In particular, the United States, as the country with the largest number of global diaspora members in the world (Groves, 2013), would benefit from knowledge about and advocacy of diaspora leadership.

Filipinas in the Diaspora

The prevailing narrative about Filipina women in the diaspora blurs the distinction between "Filipino" as the name of a national identity and "Filipino/a" as the generic term for designating a subservient class dependent on foreign economies (Rafael, 1997). About 10 million overseas contract workers from the Philippines, mostly women, have been referred to as "servants of globalization" but hailed as the "new heroes and saviors" in the Philippines (Coloma, 2008). Since the mid-1980s Filipinos in the diaspora have contributed up to 10% of GDP, with about $20 billion of official remittances in 2012 (Scalabrini Migration Center, 2013). An additional 5% or about $10 billion may have come from unofficial remittances (Remo, 2012).

A body of academic writing makes extensive use of the language of deficit in describing the Filipina experience in the diaspora. For example, de Jesús (2005) wrote, "Haunted by the ghosts of colonization and imperialism, *Pinay* [another spelling for Filipina] *Power* manifests common themes throughout: alienation, invisibility, trauma, healing, and resistance" (p. 7). De Jesús further explained that Filipino American-centered feminism is the "gendered analysis of imperial trauma—the Philippines' dual colonization by Spain and the United States—and the articulation of Pinay resistance to imperialism's lingering effects: colonial mentality, deracination, and self-alienation" (p. 5). Initial steps are being made to balance this negativity. In response to what can be perceived as blatant marginalization, Filipinas in the diaspora have created their own spaces, organizations, and publications in order to make their feminist voices heard (Castillo, 2007). Aguilar (2002) averred that Filipina migrants are "not passive victims of structures, but [are persons] with human agency and subjectivity who [are] able to navigate through and negotiate with formidable structural forces" (p. 2). After making reference to the power of the *Babaylan*, the term used to describe the powerful priestess in the pre-Spanish Philippines, Strobel (2010) argued there is now a need to return to Filipinas the *Babaylan's* "sense of wholeness and beauty and restore the harmony in the interconnected webs of life in all its forms" (p. 3).

Filipino Leadership

A summary of the key findings from two studies about Filipino leadership in the Philippines situates the leadership stories of these select Filipina women in the diaspora within the broader discourse of leadership and also points to what may constitute their leadership repertoire. Cuyegkeng and Palma-Angeles (2011) defined Filipino leadership as visionary with the ability to engender meaningful change and transform individuals and their institutions through gradual reforms. According to Cuyegkeng and Palma-Angeles (2011), Filipino leadership depends on good judgment in choosing a team to formulate strategy and the ability to negotiate cooperation and build trust and relationships while showing humility. In one of the few studies examining the leadership of Filipina women, Roffey (1999) identified six competencies needed by Filipina women for effective leadership and management of businesses based in Metro Manila. These competencies are: (a) interpersonal, (b) leading by example, (c) initiating, (d) external public relations, (e) market and customer orientation, and (f) integrity and honesty. Roffey noted that in contrast to research on western-based business leadership, Filipina leaders view the organization as an "extended family" (p. 383). In the extended family model leaders have "personal responsibility for the social and psychological well-being of their employees" and employees expect to be "looked after by their managers" (Roffey, 1999, p. 383). Roffey concluded that effective Filipina women leaders in subsidiaries of multinational corporations demonstrated professional skills and transformed strategic vision into operational reality. In examining the role of family kinship, including fictive kinship, Roffey also concluded that effective leaders were able to navigate the "contradictions between contemporary professional and managerial expectations and cultural dynamics" (p. 388). Effective leaders used their networks with integrity and practiced ethical business with their kinship networks.

Filipino Leadership and the Concept of *Kapwa*

Discussion about Filipino values often begins with the fundamental cultural norm of *kapwa*, a Tagalog word that predates the Spanish arrival (Reyes, 2015). Translations for *kapwa* include "shared humanity" (Pe-Pua,

2015), "unity of the self and the others," and "shared inner self" (Enriquez, 1989, p. 33). Contending that the latter two definitions start with a loaded term "self," Reyes's (2015) preferred translation is "together with the person" with the explanation that together is the starting point, and that together "comes first before you break it apart into separate 'selves'" (p. 9). According to Enriquez (1989), *kapwa* helps explain Filipino interpersonal behavior based on differentiating insiders (*hindi ibang tao*) from outsiders (*ibang tao*) and the different levels of interaction associated with differentiating insiders from outsiders. Different levels of interaction include the degree of civility (*pakikitungo*), level of oneness (*pakikiisa*), and degree of sensitivity (*pakikiramdam*). Enriquez posited that *kapwa* is the unity of the "self" and "others," and, unlike the English concept of "others" that is used in opposition to the "self," *kapwa* is a "recognition of shared identity, an inner self shared with others" (p. 34). When the Tagalog prefix *pakikipag*, which means "joining in an intense action of continuing manner" (Panganiban, 1972, p. 745), is added to *kapwa, pakikipagkapwa* denotes a relational value that is an ongoing process. A more nuanced meaning of *pakikipagkapwa* includes the terms "being with others," "shared identity," and "equality" (Guevarra, 2005). "Being-with-others," as explained by Guevarra, comes from the conviction that "Filipinos do not believe that a human individual exists alone," but that Filipinos are "always in relation to the other." To explain "shared identity," Guevarra drew on Buber's notion of the self and the other as having a shared identity "of sharing in the same universal experiences of commitment, love, suffering" but experienced in their own different ways (p. 1). Finally, Guevarra indicated that equality is not about sameness but citing Frankl, "To be equals, to be different." To summarize, *pakikipagkapwa* entails recognition and respect of the other as being different from all others and different from oneself, requiring the ability to be in tune with other people's motives in relation to the self.

This brief overview of some of the relevant scholarship makes clear that leadership in the diaspora is a relevant topic, that Filipinas in the diaspora have often been characterized as marginal and victims, and that studies on Filipino leadership have focused on the role of relationships. Most of the scholarship about Filipino leadership, and especially the leadership of Filipina women, builds upon the central role of the Filipino cultural norm of *kapwa*. The literature provides the context for an analysis of the stories of Filipina leaders using discourse analysis.

DISCOURSE ANALYSIS AS A THEORY AND A METHOD

Discourse analysis is both a theory and a method (Chouliaraki & Fairclough, 1999). Discourse analysis is "not only a description and interpretation of discourses in context but also offers an explanation of why and how discourses work" (Rogers, 2004, p. 2). Discourse scholars refer to "language-in-use" as discourse ("little d") and the historical and cultural forces that lie beyond language as Discourse ("big D") (Fairhurst, 2007; Gee, 2014). The interplay between discourse (as language-in-use) and Discourse (as a system of thought) is sometimes referred to as interpretative repertoire (Gilbert & Mulkay, 1984). An example of discourse analysis is Allan et al.'s (2006) identification of four dominant discourses of leadership in articles published in the *Chronicle of Higher Education*. These discourses were: (a) autonomy, where the image is of a solo leader "who is uniquely qualified, competent, and morally principled" (p. 48); (b) relatedness, where the leader facilitates movement "toward collective action" (p. 55); (c) masculinity, where "masculine traits are taken for granted as desired leader behaviors" (p. 54); and, (d) professionalism, which is "characterized by a focus on individual improvement" (p. 51). Additionally, see Chapter 4 in this volume for further examination of discourse analysis through the lens of gender by Iverson, Allan, and Gordon (2017).

Responding to Fairhurst's (2007) call to examine discourse and leadership, and building on the study by Allan et al. (2006), Berkelaar et al. (2009) used discourse analysis to explore how leaders in leadership development programs talked about leadership. Their analysis revealed five primary discourses that shaped definitions of leadership: (a) autonomy, (b) relatedness, (c) self-awareness, (d) communication as essential to leadership, and (e) visionary leadership. In both the Allan et al. and Berkelaar et al. studies, leadership is about individual autonomy. The notion of autonomy centers on each person's ability to self-govern regardless of context. In these studies, male individuals are often held up as paragons of autonomous leadership, despite the fact that participants were mostly female, particularly in the case of the Berkelaar et al. study. The focus remained on the individual even when *relational process* was added to the definition of leadership and even when "a leader was defined as autonomous qualified individual who engages, develops, and collaborates with others" for either an instrumental or altruistic motive (Berkelaar et al., 2009, p. 17).

METHODOLOGY

Fairhurst (2007) and Berkelaar et al. (2009) called for research that examines leader and leadership d/Discourse in non-Western environments. The statements of the Filipina women in this study, their choice of language, and their discourse provide insights on their leadership repertoires. Gee's (2014) typology of the seven building tasks of language was useful in guiding the analysis. The linguistic features of the text, along with discursive and social practice, were considered in the analysis.

Data Collection

Data for the discourse analysis in this study came from Filipinas who were recognized by the Filipina Women's Network in 2013 as influential in the global arena, outside the Philippine geographic setting. The identification of the Filipina women leaders as "global" is variously based on their organization's global focus, workforce composition, new home base, organizational goals, and corporate services. The Filipina women leaders' strong ties to the Philippines identify them as members of the Filipino/a diaspora. The three sources of data were: (a) the October 2013 issue of the Filipina Women's Network magazine that included written responses to topics such as, most difficult workplace challenge as a Filipina woman, turning points in their professional life, and Filipino custom or tradition they would like to pass on to others; (b) the video-taped responses to a variety of questions about career path, relationships that have affected careers, ideal leadership qualities, and advice to young women; and (c) the chapters written by 35 Filipinas in Beebe and Escudero (2015), where the chapter authors shared their leadership journeys and leadership tips. Refer to Table 10.1 for a summary of the demographics of these women.

TABLE 10.1 Demographics of 35 Filipina Women Authors in Beebe and Escudero (2015)

Characteristics	Details
Latest receiving countries	Afghanistan, Brazil, Canada, Japan, Poland, Singapore, UAE, and USA
Other countries with business or professional interest or work experience as expatriates	China, Hong Kong, Liberia, Russia, South Africa, Sudan, Lithuania, Latvia, and Estonia
Highest educational degree	9 PhD, 3 MD
Migrant status	Immigrated as children to the United States, Immigrated as adults to the United States, Expatriates, and Immigrant + expatriate
Profession	8 academics, 9 CEOS, 3 bankers, 3 medical doctors, 2 military, 1 mayor, 1 judge, 1 racecar driver, 1 chef, 1 journalist, 1 policy maker, 1 ambassador, 1 cabinet level secretary, and 1 regional legal advisor for Asia
Marital status	28 married, 4 widowed, 2 single, and 1 divorced
Age range	30+ to 80+

I was one of the honorees in 2013; I am author of the chapter, "Harmonizing Global Teams in Afghanistan" and co-editor of the book *DISRUPT. Filipina Women: Proud. Loud. Leading without a Doubt* (Beebe & Escudero, 2015). My multiple identities include: Filipina-American, Filipina born and raised in the Philippines, speaker of Pilipino and a couple of other Philippine languages, and someone who has experienced being part of the diaspora as an immigrant to the United States and as an expatriate American living and working in international development in various African, Asian, and European countries.

Data Analysis

The text was divided into thought units that generally were sentences. Codes were applied to thought units, usually based on words identified during the preparation of an index of all words in the text. A decision was then made on which thought units were to be included in the analysis. Thought units were grouped into thematic categories. An analysis of the discourse used by the global Filipina leaders suggested seven general thematic categories. Leadership is (a) rooted in the Filipino cultural value of relationships, (b) based on values, (c) knowing and transforming oneself, (d) exceeding expectations, (e) a response to a call based on a sense of purpose and meaning, (f) purposefully driven to have an impact, and (g) premised on giving back. A review of the thematic categories suggested several focused on motivation for action, while others focused on specific actions linked to leadership. While there were elements of both in many of the themes, there was more focus on one or the other in each category.

As illustrated in Table 10.2, the thematic categories that focused on motivation were labeled "why." Categories that focused more on action were labeled "how." For the *why* of leadership, the most prominent themes concern having purpose and meaning, achieving impact, and giving back. The most prominent themes associated with the *how* of leadership concern the centrality of relationships, the significance of values, and the importance of the process of self-awareness and self-transformations that contributed to self-transcendence. These themes became the findings for the study and are presented in the next section.

FINDINGS

A discourse analysis of the statements of global Filipina women suggests their understanding of leadership includes reference to both the why and how of leadership. The themes concerning the why and how of leadership

TABLE 10.2   Leadership Tips That Highlight the How and Why of Leadership

Examples of Tips	Code Assigned to Tips
The How of Leadership	
• Learn how to talk and relate to everyone equally. • Be a good listener. Living is a team sport. • Recognize that our success also depends on the success of those around us.	Maintain relationships
• Keep true to your core but remain open to other viewpoints and possibilities. • Have courage. Resolve to go forward even when risk is involved. • Keep promises and maintain a good reputation.	Clarify values
• Think positive. Dream big. • Believe in yourself. • Adapt to new challenges; keep excelling in every domain. • Whenever one aims for perfection, one may find it is a moving target.	Transform and transcend self
The Why of Leadership	
• Follow your heart. • You are here for a reason. Live with purpose and passion every day. • Work for something bigger than yourself. • Maintain a good connection to your ancestors and the Divine.	Have purpose and meaning
• Serve the people. • Use your power wisely: for a greater good. • Beyond being a CEO, one should be seen as a management role model, an oracle, as well as an icon for those who wish to ascend to the top.	Achieve impact
• Bring others along; we must pass on the lessons we gained along the way and create pathways for others to work for their own successes. • Give back to society. Civic engagement happens in the present, not when you retire. • Give back to the next generation.	Give back

provide the bases for their leadership repertoires. These repertoires guide, inform, interpret, legitimate, and empower these women leaders as they experience leadership challenges in the diaspora. The discussion below presents the interplay between language use and the historical and cultural forces that lie beyond language. Examples of language used are followed by references to the scholarship on leadership.

The Why of Leadership: Purpose and Meaning, Impact, and Giving Back

The why of leadership consisted of motivations for the women's leadership. The motivations included a combination of having purpose and meaning, achieving impact, and giving back. These motivations are further explained below.

Having Purpose and Meaning for Their Actions

The Filipina women leaders made extensive reference to responding to a "call" and the importance of having meaning and purpose. For some it was their faith, religion, and spirituality that provided their sense of purpose. Illustrative statements are as follows: "I am visionary, passionate about the Lord, and live a principle-centered and purpose-driven life." In God's plan "there is purpose for every person in this world." "We can help shape the future, but only plans that are shaped with the guidance of God will reach perfection." "Everything happens for a reason, and you must be always prepared and thankful for the blessings and challenges that *Bathala/God/Goddess* puts in your path." For others, there was a desire to make the world a better place as evidenced by the following statements: "A very deep commitment to do something in the world—and that is to always do a good deed for others." "Be a voice to the voiceless, be a champion for the most vulnerable, fight with tenacity, forever be humble, forgive when it seems impossible, and love always with never-ending joy."

These statements expressed by the Filipina women are consistent with the concept of calling that according to Hunter, Dik, and Banning (2010) embraces a sense of purpose and meaning, often guided by giftedness, passion, or God. Although some of these leaders recognize a divine call to serve God or a transcendent summon, other leaders depend upon an internal search for meaning and purpose that comes through self-reflection and meditation. This non-transcendent call reflects the concepts and ideas in leadership and management literature of knowing oneself at a deeper level (Astin, Astin, & Lindholm, 2011), living a person's life dream (Levinson, 1986), inspiring a shared vision (Kouzes & Posner, 2007), and realizing a deeper meaning (Murthy, 2009).

Achieving Impact

The Filipina women expressed a deep commitment to having an impact on the world. The numerous areas of impact identified included (a) provision of oversight in the development of policies and programs to benefit overseas Filipinas; (b) empowerment of women by expanding higher educational opportunities for women with special attention to work in Bangladesh and inspiring women in the Middle East to break into male-dominated professions; (c) use of the Internet for teaching and learning in Afghanistan; (d) engagement of Asian Pacific Islanders in the U.S. political process; (e) integration of sustainability into business operations and promotion of operations that mitigate the impacts of climate change; and (f) development of a national model for newborn screening, global model for eliminating Hepatitis B in at-risk populations, and next-generation models for hospice services based on compassionate team care for the dying and their families. Even though some of the Filipina women were leaders in the private for-profit sector, their responses to the question about global impact focused on metrics concerning people and the environment, not just on profits. Metrics beyond profits that focus on people and the planet have been identified as essential to transcendent leadership and were identified as a global imperative of the Global Economic Forum 2007 (Gardiner, 2009).

Giving Back

A significant motivating factor for the Filipina women was the desire to give back not just to the local organization, but to the entire Philippines and the rest of the world. Giving back is consistent with diaspora philanthropy and with transnational philanthropy that links together origin and settlement societies (Opiniano, 2005). Moreover, the choices about which organizations to support are strongly linked to the women's hometown communities and alumni associations or aligned with the women's causes. Giving back demonstrates the principles of servant leadership articulated by Greenleaf in 1970. As servant-leaders, these Filipina women share a commitment to social justice, making a difference, and serving the needs of others.

Having purpose, achieving impact, and giving back are the key elements in the leadership repertoire of these Filipina women leaders. This discourse—published in journals, recorded in videos, and communicated in person—continues to shape the perception of emerging Filipina women leaders and counter the negative stereotype often encountered in the diaspora. The leadership repertoire combines these women's retrospective sensemaking with their vision for themselves and their future and is an important element for understanding leading and leadership for these women.

The How of Leadership: Relationships, Values, and Self-Transcendence

The how of leadership consisted of actions that are relevant to leadership. The actions emphasized the centrality of relationships, the significance of values, and the importance of the process of self-awareness, self-transformation, and self-transcendence. These interrelated actions are further explained below.

Centrality of Relationships

The discourse of the Filipina women provides evidence of relationships as central to their leadership. When asked what family custom or tradition they would like to pass on to others, the answers of the Filipina women were predominantly associated with relationships and included respect, humility, helping, caring, collaboration, generosity, solidarity, hospitality, reciprocity, connecting, and eating together. Tagalog words were often used for concepts that may have been easier to express in Tagalog: *pagmamalasakit sa kapwa* (being solicitous), *kapwa* (shared humanity), *bayanihan* (cooperative undertaking), *malasakitan* (solicitude), and *pakikisama* (fellowship). The women viewed respect as reciprocal. In addition to giving respect, they discussed the desire to gain the respect of peers, students, and others in the workplace; to gain the respect that one rightfully deserves; and to maintain respect while going head-to-head with a diverse set of colleagues.

Significance of Values

The discourse of the global Filipina women suggests the significance of values for Filipina women's leadership. As noted in the methodology section, the 2013 Global awardees were asked to describe their leadership, and their responses were video-recorded. From all the statements they made, 214 words were coded as values. Values are character strengths or virtues that are consistent and that give a person the strength of will to carry out, notwithstanding difficulties or obstacles, her obligation to do what is good and right (Villegas, 2011). These values were then mapped onto the Peterson and Seligman's (2004) positive psychology "values-in-action" categories of humanity, transcendence, wisdom and knowledge, courage, temperance, and justice. Often the desired values are the middle way between two extremes (Crossan, Mazutis, & Siejts, 2013). Thus, courage is the middle way between showing too much courage (being impulsive) or too little courage (avoiding risk). A leadership challenge is to find the balance, the correct proportion that is neither a deficiency nor an excess of the value in question. Finding the balance or middle way associated with values was a topic interwoven in many of the women's stories of leadership, especially in their stories of what it meant to be their very best. Values are inculcated early on by Filipino families, extended kin, and community. Whether they are called good manners and right conduct, values education, or virtue ethics, they are taught as part of the public and private school curriculum in the Philippines. Many of these values-in-action found their way into the leadership tips shared by the Filipina leaders.

Importance of the Self-Transcendence Process

In their narratives, the Filipina women leaders made extensive references to self-awareness, self-examination, self-improvement, self-reliance, self-confidence, self-expression, self-respect, self-trust, and self-esteem that are central to self-transformation and self-transcendence. Consistent with San Juan (2011), the women's statements are examined along the four behaviors that lead to self-transcendence: being attentive, intelligent, fair, and responsible.

All the women conveyed the importance of being attentive to experience. All the women described overcoming one or more barriers related to poverty, social class, or discrimination based on gender, skin color, culture, language, and accent. They made statements like: "I left the Philippines because I was so poor, and I knew my opportunities were elsewhere." "We were all the same until I was told I couldn't audition for *Annie* as a child because I wasn't White." "Boardrooms are (still) not used to having strong Asian women who are well-versed in business, management, and their craft; and are as ballsy as their male counterparts." For some of the women, the sudden death of a loved one was a crucible experience. What characterized these women as leaders was their ability to move on, rise up, and exceed expectations. While resilience is valued, several of the women were explicit in asserting that even more important than being able to bounce back from hardship is the ability to transform oneself and disrupt the status quo by being first and foremost.

Attention to experience is tied to gaining insight about one's experience. Commitment to continuous learning, personal development, and improvement was a recurring theme among the women. Examples included seeking out non-traditional education, specializing in a new field, and learning from failures. Some women recognized that "the strong, the best, and the brightest ruled." For those who may not be the smartest or most qualified person for every position they desire, a leadership tip for success was "to persist in identifying shortcomings and to be passionate in taking action to address them."

Being fair in making judgments is informed by being attentive to experience and being intelligent in understanding one's experience. The first Filipina to be elected a District Court Judge in Nevada observed: "A good judge strives to be fair and impartial even outside the courtroom and in their personal lives." Other Filipina women in Beebe and Escudero's (2015) collection of leadership stories described the role and relevance of fairness to their lives: "Voters knew they could trust me to be fair about competing priorities," "Empower employees by being fair," and "Doing the right thing and being fair." These Filipina women expected fair treatment from others as well: "I did not think it was fair for her to ask me to wait for another year."

Being responsible was learned early on, as depicted in the following statements. "I felt very responsible for what was happening." "Not only was I responsible for helping my mother in her rehabilitation, but suddenly I also found myself, at the age of 21, stepping into my mother's shoes and running her business." "My mother also prepared me early for being financially responsible." Some Filipino families stressed social responsibility: "Their example taught all of us how to become socially responsible. The unspoken but accepted principle in our family was 'for whom much has been given, much is also expected.'" Filipina women in the study reported having significant responsibility in major organizations across sectors. "I am responsible for the strategic direction, implementation, and alignment of the National Guard's integrated global diversity and inclusion initiatives." "I am responsible for the negotiation of multi-million asset financings for Fortune 500 clients." The sense of responsibility on the part of women could be explained by studies that showed more responsibility training being given to daughters than sons in the Philippines (UNICEF, 1999).

By their own accounts, these women worked hard to ensure their leadership reflects their best selves. As suggested by San Juan (2010), being attentive to experience, being intelligent in understanding, being fair in judging, and being responsible in deciding are the building blocks to self-transcendence that lead to authenticity. The connection between self-awareness and authenticity is consistent with Berkelaar and colleagues' (2009) explanation that the prominence of self-awareness discourse is closely tied to authenticity. In transforming themselves, these Filipina women leaders remained authentic, consistent with Taylor's (1991) characterization that authenticity presupposes demands that emanate from beyond the self. The authenticity of the Filipina women leaders in this study is consistent with Taylor's ideal that self-fulfillment demands "our ties with others" (Taylor, 1991, p. 46) as well as Sartre's (1992) notion of engagement by "being-for-others" (p. 301). This brings us back to *kapwa*, which underlies the leadership of the Filipina women.

The Leadership Repertoire of Filipina Women Leaders in the Diaspora

As documented in the previous section, a discourse analysis of Filipina women leaders suggests their understanding of leadership includes reference to the *why* and *how* of leadership. The why of leadership appears to be consistent with Murthy's (2009) discussion of an ensemble of leadership repertoire consisting of sharing fates, exploring deeper meaning, and integrating cognition, conscience, and collective spirit. The how of leadership appears consistent with the leadership styles suggested by Goleman and colleagues (2013), who note that the core task of leaders is to connect emotionally to others in order to inspire action. The themes concerning the why and how of leadership provide the foundation for the study participant's leadership repertoires.

As adopted in this chapter, leadership repertoire builds on Fairhurst's (2007) discussion of Discourse as an interpretative repertoire that merges Foucalt's (1972) view that multiple Discourses are available for appropriation and Wetherell and Potter's (1988) bottom-up approach of understanding Discourse through the little 'd' of text and conversation of life experiences. Thus, a leadership repertoire can be thought of as a toolkit, a set of resources, abilities, or skills that provides options for specific leadership tasks, affords Filipina women leaders the flexibility to mix and match the how's and why's of leadership as they position themselves, encounter different situations, and manage the tension between individual agency and social constraints of leading in the diaspora. Consequently, this chapter suggests that future theorizing about Filipina women leaders should include the concept of leadership repertoire because it is an important influence on how women make sense of their leadership experiences in the world.

The discourse analysis suggests that the leadership challenge for Filipina women in the diaspora is two-fold: (a) the broadening and deepening of their personal leadership repertoires required to succeed in complex diaspora environments; and (b) the decision as to what elements of the leadership repertoire is the best fit for a specific context. Including leadership repertoire into theoretical models and frameworks can contribute to exploring these challenges.

IMPLICATIONS AND CONCLUSIONS FOR THEORIZING FILIPINA WOMEN LEADERS IN THE DIASPORA

In this chapter I analyzed the discourse of selected Filipina women who operate in complex diaspora environments. Honored by the Filipina Women's Network as among the Global 100 most influential Filipina leaders in 2013, their discourse was documented in the October 2013 issue of the Filipina Women's Network magazine, video recording of interviews with some of these women, and their statements in the book *DISRUPT. Filipina Women: Proud. Loud. Leading without a Doubt* (Beebe & Escudero, 2015).

The major conclusions of this analysis are: (a) a leadership repertoire is at the disposal of Filipina women leaders in the study; (b) the elements of the repertoire can be divided into the why and how of leadership; and (c) *kapwa* (shared humanity) underlies both the why and the how of leadership. Both scholars and practitioners can build on these findings to generate new conceptual and theoretical advances in understanding leadership for this population and develop focused and targeted leadership development opportunities for emerging Filipina women leaders. In addition, the chapter suggests that discourse analysis can be one way to achieve a deeper understanding of how leadership is constructed.

Most importantly, in this chapter I illuminated how considering a leadership repertoire can add clarity to theorizing about leadership. As described in this chapter, Filipina women leader's repertoires share significant attributes anchored by *kapwa*, a non-western understanding of the world. *Kapwa* fundamentally shapes the interpretation of experiences and is embedded in the small-d discourse of these women leaders. Future theorizing about the leadership experiences of Filipina women, as well as women anchored by other non-western understandings, can explore the influence of these anchors on women leaders.

This chapter can also inform future practice by including the concept of leadership repertoires in leadership development programs. The ways that recognized women leaders interpret leading and leadership through language offers possibilities for the growth and development of emerging leaders. It also provides legitimacy for countering negative stereotypes, tips for effective leadership, and affirmation for holding on to Filipina identity.

The chapter is consistent with many of the findings from previous scholarship. For example, the findings of the study are consistent with foundational scholarship on diaspora and leadership, Filipinos in the diaspora, and Filipina leadership. Scholarship on migration suggested that migration and being part of the diaspora can significantly impact the receiving nations. That this statement holds true is illuminated in the stories of the women that clarify their impact on a wide range of issues. Moreover, the discussion on giving back provides an indication of the impact of the women on their country of origin, the Philippines. Impact on the sending country appears to be less than their impact in the receiving nations since the immediate sphere of influence for each woman is in her receiving country.

The findings provide evidence that there are Filipina women in the diaspora who do *not* fit the dominant negative stereotypes of being victims or being subservient; in fact, the findings suggest why and how these women lead without a doubt. The work of the Filipina Women's Network can be credited with beginning the process of presenting an alternative image and documenting the enhanced leadership presence of Filipina women. However, the qualitative nature of the study does not allow for examination of the extent to which the women in this study are representative of Filipina women living and working abroad.

The narratives of the Filipina women reported in this study are very consistent with and supportive of the findings of Cuyegkeng and Palma-Angeles (2011) that Filipino leadership is visionary and has the ability to engender meaningful change and to transform individuals and their institutions through gradual reforms. The narratives are generally consistent with Roffey's (1999) six competencies articulated by Filipina women for effective leadership and management of businesses based in Metro Manila. Explicit reference can be found in the discourses that leadership is interpersonal, based on leading by example, and underscores the importance of integrity and honesty. Many of the women view the organization as an extended family. Most importantly, findings on the role of *kapwa* in the leadership of the Filipina women are consistent with existing literature on *kapwa* as a Philippine cultural norm. Many of the Filipina women made explicit reference to *kapwa* in their discussions of important Filipina values. They reported leadership journeys that were based on *kapwa* through their use of words associated with preserving and strengthening human relationships. *Kapwa*, translated as shared humanity, appears to come closest to the way Filipina women used the term. This study's findings on the importance of leadership anchors, like *kapwa*, legitimize the importance of contextualizing leadership theories across different cultures and geographies. Without a deeper understanding of how these key values and principles impact women's leadership development and experiences, we will continue to have only a partial understanding of leading in the 21st century.

REFERENCES

Aguilar, F. J. (2002). Beyond stereotypes: Human subjectivity in the structuring of global migrations. In F. J. Aguilar (Ed.), *Filipinos in global migrations: At home in the world?* (pp. 41–58). Quezon City, Philippines: Philippine Social Science Council.

Agunias, D. R., & Newland, K. (2012). *Developing a road map for engaging diasporas in development: A handbook for policymakers and practitioners in home and host countries.* Geneva, Switzerland: International Office of Migration. Retrieved from http://publications.iom.int/system/files/pdf/diaspora_handbook_en_for_web_28may2013.pdf

Allan, E. J., Gordon, S. P., & Iverson, S. V. (2006). Re/thinking practices of power: The discursive framing of leadership in the *Chronicle of Higher Education*. *The Review of Higher Education, 30*(1), 41–68.

Astin, A. W., Astin, H. S., & Lindholm, J. A. (2011). *Cultivating the spirit: How college can enhance students' inner lives.* San Francisco, CA: Jossey-Bass.

Beebe, M. A., & Escudero, M. O. (Eds.). (2015). *DISRUPT. Filipina women: Proud. Loud. Leading without a doubt.* San Francisco, CA: Filipina Women's Network.

Berkelaar, B., Williams, E. A., & Linvill, J. S. (2009). *Leaders define leadership: Discourses of leadership within an academic leadership development center.* Chicago, IL: International Communication Association.

Buil, C., & Siegel, M. (2013). *A new multilateral framework for labour migration: Options and feasibility. Background paper for the European report on development 2013.* Barcelona, Spain: UNU-MERIT. Retrieved from http://mgsog.merit.unu.edu/ISacademic/docs/multilateral_framework_labour_migration.pdf

Castillo, M. (2007). Flight of the Filipina phoenix: The rise of Pinay feminism. *The Feminist eZine.* Retrieved from http://www.feministezine.com/feminist/international/Rise-of-Pinay-Feminism.html

Chouliaraki, L.., & Fairclough, N. (1999). *Discourse in late modernity: Rethinking critical discourse analysis.* Edinburgh, Scotland: Edinburgh University.

Coloma, R. S. (2008). Border crossing subjectivities and research: Through the prism of feminists of color. *Race Ethnicity and Education, 11*(1), 11–27.

Crossan, M., Mazutis, D., & Seijts, G. (2013). In search of virtue: The role of virtues, values, and character strengths in ethical decision-making. *Journal of Business Ethics, 113*(4), 567–581.

Cuyegkeng, M. A. C., & Palma-Angeles, A. (Eds.). (2011). *Defining Filipino leadership.* Quezon City, Philippines: Ateneo de Manila University.

de Haas, H. (2010). Migration and development: A theoretical perspective. *International Migration* Review, 44, 227–264. doi:10.1111/j.1747-7379.2009.00804.

de Jesús, M. (Ed.). (2005). *Pinay power: Peminist critical theory.* New York, NY: Routledge.

Enriquez, V. G. (1989). *Kapwa theory and indigenous psychology and national consciousness.* Tokyo, Japan: Institute for the Study of Languages and Cultures of Asia and Africa.

Fairhurst, G. T. (2007). *Discursive leadership: In conversation with leadership psychology.* Thousand Oaks, CA: Sage.

Foucault, M. (1972). *The archaeology of knowledge and the discourse on language.* (A. M. Sheridan Smith, Trans.). New York, NY: Pantheon Books.

Gardiner, J. J. Z. (2009, November). *Transcendent leadership: Board metrics for profits, people, and planet.* Paper presented at annual meeting of the International Leadership Association, Prague, Czech Republic. Retrieved from http://bfeild.typepad.com/files/transcendent-leadership-board-metrics-john-gardiner.pdf

Gee, J. P. (2014). *An introduction to discourse analysis: Theory and method* (4th ed.). Hoboken, NJ: Taylor & Francis.

Gilbert, G. N., & Mulkay, M. (1984). *Opening Pandora's box: A sociological analysis of scientists' discourse.* Cambridge, England: Cambridge University.

Goleman, D., Boyatzis, R., & McKee, A. (2013). *Primal leadership: Unleashing the power of emotional intelligence.* Boston, MA: Harvard Business Review.

Greenleaf, R. K. (1970). *The servant as leader.* Indianapolis, IN: Robert K. Greenleaf Center.

Groves, S. (2013). America's largest diaspora populations. *International Diaspora Engagement Alliance.* Retrieved from http://www.diasporaalliance.org/americas-largest-diaspora-populations/

Guevarra, J. P. (2005). Pakikipagkapwa [Sharing/Merging oneself with others]. In R. M. Gripaldo (Ed.), *Filipino cultural traits.* Washington, DC: The Council for Research in Values and Philosophy.

Hunter, I., Dik, B. J., & Banning, J. H. (2010). College students' perceptions of calling in work and life: A qualitative analysis. *Journal of Vocational Behavior, 76*(2) 178–186.

Iverson, S.V., Allan, E.J., & Gordom, S. P. (2017). Constructing the double bind: The discursive framing of gendered images of leadership in The Chronicle of Higher Education. In J. Storberg-Walker & P. Haber-Curran (Eds.), *Theorizing women and leadership: New insights and contributions from multiple perspectives* (pp. 51–68). Charlotte, NC: Information Age.

Kouzes, J. M., & Posner, B. Z. (2007). *The leadership challenge* (4th ed.). San Francisco, CA: Jossey-Bass.

Levinson, D. J. (1986). A conception of adult development. *American Psychologist, 41*(1), 3–13.

McGregor, E., Siegel, M., Ragab, N., & Juzwiak, T. (2014). *A new global partnership for development: Factoring in the contribution of migration.* Geneva, Switzerland: International Organization for Migration. Retrieved from http://publications. iom.int/system/files/pdf/mrs50_20may2014.pdf

Murthy, V. (2009). Managing businesses in uncertain times: Sustainable development and an ensemble leadership repertoire. In M. Hossain, & E. Selvanathan (Eds.), *Climate change and growth in Asia* (pp. 195–213). Cheltenham, England: Edward Elgar.

Opiniano, J. (2005). Filipinos doing diaspora philanthropy: The development potential of transnational migration. *Asian and Pacific Migration Journal, 14*(1–2), 225–241.

Panganiban, J. V. (1972). *Diksyunayo tesauro Pilipino-Ingles.* Manila, Philippines: Manlapaz.

Pe-Pua, R. (2015). Indigenous research: Practice and advocacy. In R. E. Rinehart, E. Emerald, & R. Matanua (Eds.), *Ethnographies in Pan Pacific research: Tensions and positionings* (pp. 87–110). New York, NY: Routledge.

Peterson, C., & Seligman, M. (2004). *Character strengths and virtues: A handbook and classification.* Washington, DC: American Psychological Association/Oxford University.

Rafael, V. L. (1997). Your grief is our gossip: Overseas Filipinos and other spectral presences. *Public Culture, 9*(2), 267–291.

Remo, M. V. (2012, November 14). Stop illegal remittance agents, BSP urged: Informal forex channels a problem in the region. *Philippine Daily Inquirer.* Retrieved from http://business.inquirer.net/93066/stop-illegal-remittance-agents-bsp-urged

Reyes, J. (2015). "*Loób*" and "*kapwa*": An introduction to a Filipino virtue ethics. *Asian Philosophy, 25*(2), 148–171.

Roffey, B. (1999). Filipina managers and entrepreneurs: What leadership models apply? *Asian Studies Review, 23*(3), 375–405.

Rogers, R. (2004). *An introduction to critical discourse analysis in education.* Mahwah, NJ: Lawrence Erlbaum.

San Juan, K. (2011). Leadership, transcendence, and spirituality: Insights from Bernard Lonergan, SJ. In M. A. C. Cuyegkeng, & A. Palma-Angeles (Eds.), *Defining Filipino leadership* (pp. 327–338). Manila, Philippines: Ateneo de Manila University.

Sartre, J. P. (1992). *Being and nothingness: A Phenomenological essay on oncology.* (H. E. Barnes, Trans.). USA: First Washington Square.

Scalabrini Migration Center. (2013). *Country migration report: The Philippines 2013.* Quezon City, Philippines: International Organization for Migration. Retrieved from http://www.iom.int/files/live/sites/iom/files/Country/docs/ CMReport-Philipines-2013.pdf

Strobel, L. M. (Ed.). (2010). *Babaylan: Filipinos and the call of the indigenous.* Davao, Philippines: Ateneo de Davao University.

Taylor, C. (1991). *The ethics of authenticity.* Cambridge, MA: Harvard University.

UNICEF. (1999). *1999 Philippines: How to raise our daughters and sons: Child-Rearing and gender specialization in the Philippines*. [Evaluation Report]. Retrieved from http://www.unicef.org/evaldatabase/index_14239.html

Villegas, B. M. (2011). *The book of virtues & values*. Pasig, Philippines: Center for Research and Communication, University of Asia and the Pacific.

Wetherell, M., & Potter, J. (1988). Discourse analysis and the identification of interpretative repertoires. In C. Antaki (Ed.), *Analysing everyday explanation* (pp. 168–183). London, England: Sage.

CHAPTER 11

THEORIZING LEADERSHIP DEVELOPMENT FOR MARGINALIZED WOMEN STUDENTS

Threading Diverse Experiences Into a Recognized Leadership Identity Development Model

Virginia Byrne
University of Maryland, College Park

Crystal Diaz-Espinoza
Baylor University

Jess Myers
University of Maryland, Baltimore County

From our years working with college women within the higher education context and with a focus on leadership development, we have observed that the typical leadership identity development theories and models do not

Theorizing Women and Leadership, pages 183–202
Copyright © 2017 by Information Age Publishing
All rights of reproduction in any form reserved.

align with the experiences of all college students. These theories and models are not based on the experiences of marginalized groups of women, but instead were developed based on the experiences of traditional-aged college students.

This limitation remains true even with the highly cited and referenced Leadership Identity Development (LID) model. As the authors of LID clearly state, their model has limitations and was developed using a small, targeted sample (Komives, Owen, Longerbeam, Mainella, & Osteen, 2005). Our goal in this chapter is not to recommend discounting LID; rather, our goal is to theorize about leadership identity development in college for a broader spectrum of students by showing how the LID can be amended for two marginalized groups of college students, namely nontraditional-aged college women and women in a masculinized technology program.

Critical to developing relevant theories is to obtain data from practice, and as we are practitioners, our work provides an extensive array of field experiences, stories, and narratives. Our practitioner's voice is grounded by embodied experience as professionals responsible for designing, developing, and deploying leadership development and education programs for college women. The three of us met while facilitating an undergraduate leadership retreat at the University of Maryland, Baltimore County (UMBC). We bonded over our mutual passion for women's leadership education and our shared frustration about the limitations of leadership education theories and models; we each worked, or had worked, with a marginalized population of women students and did not see the current models fitting these populations. We reflected on the ease for one of us to apply leadership identity development theory to the typical-aged college woman student majoring in arts or humanities. However, the two other authors struggled with using those same leadership education theories and models to facilitate leadership development experiences for the women students they served—nontraditional older women students and women students in Information Technology and Engineering (ITE). For the nontraditional older women students, institutional barriers and the lack of adult student peers and role models on campus exposed the limitation of the typical leadership identity model. For the ITE women students, the systematic oppression faced by women in ITE exposed the limitation. Since our meeting and subsequent conversations illuminated our shared concerns, we collaborated to amend the leadership identity development model we use at UMBC to address the unique challenges experienced by women adult learners and women studying ITE.

Although women adult learners and women in ITE seem like unrelated populations, these women student leaders share deep feelings of isolation at the institution. Unlike most American universities, UMBC's student body is majority male. In 2014, students who identified as female made up approximately 45% of the student population. Further, 15% of undergraduates were adult learners over the age of 25 (College Navigator, 2014). Supporting the leadership development and education of such a nontraditional campus requires strategic, inclusive program and curriculum design across the institution.

This chapter describes our practice-based discoveries resulting in two additional concepts enhancing the LID model to better represent the experiences of two marginalized populations of women student leaders: women adult learners and women in ITE. Through vignettes (i.e., narratives we created from the experiences of multiple students), we share how these populations struggle to develop a leadership identity despite engaging in cross-campus leadership education. These narrative experiences serve as portrayals of the stories we hear from women students who struggle to find the unique support they need to develop their leadership identity. These stories are not meant to reflect the experiences of all marginalized students, or even all students from these two populations, but we hope to convey some common experiences based on our extensive work with these populations. These narratives, ultimately, generated new knowledge about these students, which in turn led us to understand how to amend the traditional LID model to serve our students' needs.

We organized the chapter to first describe the leadership identity model typically used in college contexts; next we provide two vignettes of hypothetical women who encapsulate the unique leadership identity development experiences of adult women and women in ITE; finally we summarize how their experiences differ from the LID model and how we have modified the model to support our work with these women. Our modifications are limited to stages one through four of the model because we have not observed enough women in stages five and six.

LEADERSHIP IDENTITY DEVELOPMENT MODEL

Until the development of the LID model, no research had been done to articulate how college students develop a leadership identity. The stage-based LID model was developed by Komives, Longerbeam, Owen, Mainella, and Osteen (2006) based on the results of a grounded theory study. Students who demonstrated relational leadership were interviewed to find language and structure to their shared experience in hopes of deriving a theory describing the process by which students develop a leadership identity (Komives et al., 2005). Informed by student development theory and post-industrial leadership theory, the LID model is helpful for educators designing leadership development curricula and facilitating the development of groups of college students as they practice interdependent leadership. The model assists educators in recognizing the developmental stage of a student and supports the student's transition into higher stages by scaffolding involvement and reflection. Educators routinely use the LID model when working with students individually and with groups of students, helping these groups (e.g., campus organizations, clubs) scaffold the development of many students who are on similar paths and foster an environment of interdependent leadership.

The LID model is made up of six developmental stages depicting how students develop a leadership identity (Komives et al., 2006). In summary, stage one, *Awareness*, occurs when learners begin to identify those who serve as the leaders in their communities. Stage two, *Exploration/Engagement*, is a time when children join groups and begin to practice taking on responsibilities that serve a team. Stage three, *Leader Identified*, is when learners "[perceive] that groups [are] comprised of leaders and followers and [believe] the leaders [do] leadership—that leaders [are] responsible for group outcomes. In this leader-centric stage, one was a leader only if one held a leadership position" (Komives et al., 2005, p. 606). For the students in the grounded theory study, most entered college with this stage three hierarchical approach to leadership (Komives et al., 2006). Stage four, *Leadership Differentiated*, is when learners become aware of their interdependence with other group members. By leaning into this sense of interdependence, learners move to stage five, *Generativity*, whereby "students became actively committed to larger purposes and to the groups and individuals who sustained them" (Komives et al., 2005, p. 607) and began to see themselves as important peer role models in the developmental journeys of other, younger students. Most students in the study had not yet emerged into this stage of development or the final stage, *Integration/Synthesis*, when learners see leadership as a life-long process.

Over the past 10 years, the LID model has become a go-to model among leadership educators and student affairs practitioners who seek to consider how leadership identity development intersects with other social identity development (Komives et al., 2009). The LID model is attractive because as a grounded theory the model is founded in the process of the individual experiences, including quotations and stories that are easy to transfer to the experiences of other students. Implementation strategies and lesson plans have been provided through several sources, making the use of the LID model all the more accessible (Komives et al., 2009; Komives, Dugan, Owen, Slack, & Wagner, 2011; Owen, Komives, Lucas, & McMahon, 2007).

CRITIQUE OF THE LID MODEL

The grounded theory LID research included 13 students who were invited to participate from a pool of nominees identified by educators who work with student leaders (Komives et al., 2005). It is important to note for the context of our work that these students did not identify as adult learners returning to undergraduate studies, and it was not clear if any participants were women in ITE. It is possible that women in ITE were not nominated for the original study. One reason could be because ITE students often focus primarily on academics; many reformers argue that engineering departments foster a competitive philosophy and promote the idea that engineering is academically challenging and only for those who are dedicated (Hill, Corbett, & St. Rose, 2010). Women adult learners and women in ITE often do not have the available time to participate in the campus experiences that would have led to their nomination to participate in the LID study. For instance, women adult learners usually re-enter into higher education as a result of a major life change such as a loss of job, career advancement, financial constraints, or spousal separation, which can equate to juggling multiple responsibilities that impact their ability to invest in experiences outside the classroom (Brown, 2002; Deutsch & Schmertz, 2011; Hardin, 2008).

Little research has been conducted on the extent of transferability of the LID model to the experiences of students outside of the original study participants. A 2005 study by Renn and Bilodeau applied the LID model to a group of LGBT student leaders, finding that much of the LID model translated to the identity development of the sampled LGBT students with one exception—LGBT students were found to articulate an activist identity earlier in their leadership identity development journey than the LID model considers (Renn & Bilodeau, 2005). Renn and Bilodeau echo the call for more research to be done on the transferability of the model.

THROUGH THE EYES OF PRACTITIONERS

In the absence of peer reviewed and published education research, we explore our professional experiences to identify the gaps of how the LID model articulates the leadership identity development experience for two marginalized populations and how the model leaves practitioners with questions regarding how to best support these learners. In the two sections below, we provide vignettes based on our professional experiences. These narratives are influenced by the experiences of students with whom we have worked. These stories are told from our perspective to synthesize the leadership development of students we interact with every day. At each LID model stage we pause our vignette to clarify the gap in the experiences of students and practitioners that the LID model fails to address (see Tables 11.2 and 11.3 later in the chapter). Upon identifying the gaps, we identify how the LID model could be amended to allow practitioners to better serve the leadership development needs of these two marginalized groups.

Vignette 1: Women Adult Learners: A Practitioner's Reflection

I write this vignette as the director of the Women's Center at UMBC, and my name is Jess Myers. Our mission at the Center is to assist women in achieving their full potential through academic and intellectual growth, professional development, and personal empowerment. A subpopulation served by this mission is nontraditional (older) women adult learners working towards their first undergraduate degree. Over the past four years, I have interacted largely with these students through a scholarship program designed for women adult learners. When considering the various complexities of being an adult learner through the lens of campus-based leadership identity development, one of the factors I have observed that can impact a nontraditional woman student the most is her parental status, and research confirms my observations. For example, women with children face cultural and gendered expectations of the "second shift" related to childcare and household responsibilities (Deutsch & Schmertz, 2011). Moreover, these role responsibilities, coupled with the demands of school, are often internalized in women's lives as stress or strain, which consequently impacts their experience related to extracurricular activities on campus (Plageman & Sabina, 2010). With these experiences in mind, I focus the vignette on the intersection of leadership identity and the women adult learner experience on a student who also identifies as a mother.

Michelle is a woman in her mid-30s with two young children. She is in her third year at UMBC and eagerly anticipates graduation at the conclusion of the year. Michelle is pursuing a bachelor's degree in social work. Prior to transferring to UMBC, she obtained her associate's degree at a local community college in general studies.

Identifying Gaps and Modifications in Stages One and Two

Prior to arriving at UMBC Michelle worked for over 10 years in the service industry. She also volunteered in the community and was an active parent at her children's school and childcare center. Despite her leadership skills and identifying as a leader in other areas of her life, Michelle was timid to involve herself in campus activities. Throughout her first year at UMBC she was highly sensitive to the younger students around her and did not want to intrude on their college experiences. She missed her opportunity to attend college when she was younger, and she carried that regret. Consequently, she came to campus for classes each day and left immediately afterwards. Her one and only goal was to get her degree.

The narrative created around who holds undergraduate leadership roles by the university reinforced Michelle's experience. When adult students like Michelle discover how leadership is defined at UMBC, they do not see themselves. Rather, they see younger students with ample time who serve in visible leadership roles, such as orientation advisors and officers in student government, or those who are represented in university marketing. Students with children or older students are not represented. So, while many of these students may come into their college experience feeling like leaders in their jobs or families, they quickly learn and feel their leadership experiences are not equally valued. Much like the *Awareness* stage of the LID Model, Michelle's view of campus leadership was "an external other" in which others were the leaders but never she (Komives et al., 2006, p. 406).

Despite the LID researchers' recognition that stages in the LID model are not necessarily linear and can be re-experienced through a helix model of development, the examples provided assume stages one and two occur only within childhood (Komives et al., 2005). While Michelle recognized leadership on campus was happening "out there somewhere," the developmental influences cited in these stages fail to consider adult learners as students who may be re-experiencing earlier stages of leadership identity when they first return to college (Komives et al., 2006, p. 406). Additionally, adults and older peers are seen as key influences in helping a student in this stage build a self-concept and self-confidence. Although older faculty and staff may serve as helpful mentors, these relationships may not be associated with or enable older students to feel confident in participating in student organizations or activities. Other nontraditional students are also not offered as potential role models or influences. Therefore, we modify the LID model to provide adequate examples of the ways in which adult learners can be identified and influenced as they find peers and role models.

Identifying Gaps and Modifications in Stage Three

Toward the end of her first year, Michelle finally felt motivated by a desire to engage more meaningfully in her college experience. Michelle recognized her desire to attend graduate school one day would set her up to compete with her younger peers for admission, and her resume would fall short in regards to cocurricular experiences and campus leadership. Despite not seeing herself represented in the student leadership on campus, Michelle knew she could and must be a leader. In her second year at UMBC, she ran for student government and became involved in a student organization. She merged her off-campus and on-campus self as much as possible by bringing her children to campus for events and student organization meetings, and encouraging her classmates to attend study groups at her house.

When they first entered college, all the participants in the LID study were identified by the researchers as within the third stage of *Leader-Identified*, which emphasizes leadership as a position and those without a position as followers (Komives et al., 2006). Students in this stage still greatly benefit from older peers who serve as role models and occupy positional student leadership roles (Komives et al., 2005). However, if younger students see age as a marker of leadership, what does this mean for women adult learners like Michelle? Students like Michelle have shared with me their struggles working with others in group assignments or in student organizations because they are seen by their younger classmates as the "mother" of the group. They are labeled by their younger classmates as leaders through age and a marginalized perspective of domesticity, not because of their skills and experiences. It seems as though their identity as adult women overshadows their authentic leadership skills and contributions. Consequently, many of these students will opt out or not engage in traditional student leadership experiences so as to avoid being stereotyped by students of traditional ages. I have found that older adult women students seek student organizations and activities focused specifically on adult women where they feel like they can be more authentic. Without student organizations or activities that are for and/or center on the experiences of adult learners, students like Michelle face this constant struggle to engage with their peers as equal counterparts.

Through the default lens of traditional college students, the LID model continually cites ways in which traditional students' advancement of leadership is facilitated by older peers and adults and through involvement and engagement with peers in a variety of group settings. However, the model does not question what this reliance means for older adult students who often struggle to find other women adult learners to serve as peer role models. The model also does not provide room for younger students with similar interests to be seen as instrumental influences on women adult learners' leadership development, which, when explored, could provide unique opportunities to modify the model. Moreover, the LID model does not articulate how practitioners could support women adult learners who are stereotyped as the elder and/or struggle to find supportive peer role models.

Identifying Gaps and Modifications in Stage Four

In her last year at UMBC, Michelle was not only taking classes but also working at a 20-hour-a-week internship off campus. While she held a student organization leadership position, she had expected some of the newer students to take a lead due to her limited time on campus. She was close to many of the younger students in the group but became weary of spending too much time with them because they expected her to settle organizational conflict and provide counsel. Michelle thrived in providing these skills, but as the year wore on, she simply could not spend the significant time and energy expected of her. Moreover, with multiple responsibilities outside of campus, there was less time and space for Michelle to reflect on and make meaning of her campus-based experiences. The reality of managing home, family, and work with greater pressure to excel in her leadership position became unrealistic. She had burned out.

Throughout the LID model, Komives et al. (2006) emphasized commitment to student organizations and campus-based groups as a central component to leadership development. By exploring only campus-based leadership experiences, other potential experiences and contexts where students, especially adult learners, can develop and refine their leadership identity is missing from the LID model. Although Michelle experienced burnout in her student organization commitment, her leadership development was not halted. She was still navigating the complexities of childcare, volunteering in the community and in her children's schools, and interning with a nonprofit organization. Yet, the LID model depicted students in this fourth stage as progressing in their leadership development when they began to solidify their personal commitment to be an engaged and effective group member by building community within their campus-based organizations (Komives et al., 2006). Moreover, students in stage four (as well as in stage five) are identified as acknowledging they have become elders in the group. This triggers a sense of responsibility to develop and coach younger peers in the leadership development process to support group continuity. Students like Michelle, though, often already acknowledge themselves as the elder and spend time coaching and supporting their younger peers. Again, the LID model's focus on traditional-aged students provides insufficient examples to practitioners using the model for adults in college. Practitioners are left to amend the model in a way that mirrors women adult learners' experiences and supports their leadership development through multiple off-campus responsibilities.

Throughout their time in college, women adult learners often lack adequate peer role models and experience multiple limitations to fully participate in campus life. Although the LID model can serve as a roadmap in aiding their leadership identity, it does not adequately address the barriers women adult learners face in their leadership development as college students. Consequently, as a practitioner, I am left with a gap in the LID model when working with students like Michelle. The existing LID model, which does not include the experiences of women adult learners, leaves me with many questions that, when considered, can create many new opportunities for practitioners working with this population. How can practitioners challenge the notion that, due to their age, women adult learners have already arrived at leadership and do not need further development throughout their college experience? How can practitioners support women adult learners in developing their leadership identity within peer groups? How can practitioners inform women adult learners of the ways that younger peers can also be a source for learning? In what ways can practitioners facilitate a more inclusive culture among the younger students who stereotype older students and equate age with mentorship? What are the long-term implications of women adult learners opting out of traditional campus life to instead only interact with other adult women or in off-campus settings? As seen in Table 11.2, practitioners can modify their responses to build on what the LID teaches us and bridge the gaps that are unique to adult women learners. When considering the gaps and proposed modifications of the LID model for one student population, other marginalized student groups that can benefit from an expanded version of the LID model also come to mind. In the next section we ask similar questions about the LID model when it is applied to women students majoring in ITE.

Vignette 2: Women in ITE: A Practitioner's Reflection

I write as the Assistant Director of the Center for Women in Technology (CWIT) at UMBC, and my name is Crystal Diaz-Espinoza. Our mission is dedicated to increasing the representation of women in the creation of technology in the ITE fields. During the past three years, I have worked primarily with women majoring in ITE by running a four-year, merit-based scholarship program. The program has frequent touch points at which I interact with these students as an advisor and mentor. My observations come from working with these students during their tenure at UMBC.

The following vignette addresses gaps in the LID model experienced by women in ITE because of the intersection of their identities in a community that is often unwelcoming to them. A primary gap that practitioners working with women in ITE must navigate is the LID model's assumption that participation in student organizations and other campus involvement is a key driver for the development of a leadership identity. However, in a masculinized context (like ITE at UMBC), student organization involvement is more challenging for women. Research confirms that women face more distinctive and difficult personal academic challenges than men, particularly within the field of ITE, which is predominantly male (Camecho & Lord, 2011). Involvement in student organizations, especially in ITE, is not gender neutral. It is unsurprising that the majority of students within ITE professional student organizations are men; consequently, the majority of leadership positions are held by men.

Jenny is in her third year at UMBC. She entered as a traditional-aged first-year student and comes from a rural high school. Jenny excelled in Advanced Placement (AP) classes, including calculus and physics. After attending an engineering camp during her junior year of high school, she decided to major in computer engineering despite being consistently told to do otherwise by family, teachers, and friends. As described below, Jenny resisted family pressures to major in her chosen field.

When Jenny arrived at UMBC during summer orientation, she second-guessed her decision to major in computer engineering. She consistently excelled in math and science, but her parents had always told her she should become a doctor. In fact, almost everyone in her family had said she should be a doctor. When she informed her parents she was planning to major in computer engineering, they asked, "Why would you want to be an engineer?" Jenny was not interested in medicine. She did not like her biology or chemistry classes but loved math and physics. When she was younger, she would often get in trouble for sneaking into her younger brother's room to play with his K'Nex, toy helicopters, and Legos. She never understood why she got into trouble because her brother never showed an interest in them.

Fewer girls than boys indicate an interest in science or engineering because of cultural beliefs that science and math are dominated by males (Barnett & Sabattini, 2009). Unlike her brother, Jenny was always fascinated by how things work. She had never considered engineering majors until her junior year of high school, when she overheard a teacher telling one of her male peers about an engineering camp at a local university. She asked her teacher for more information and attended the camp, where she learned about different types of engineering. It was there Jenny decided that she wanted to pursue computer engineering and lead the field in providing access to technology to people with disabilities. Interestingly, the teacher did not initially tell Jenny about the camp; instead, the invitation was extended to one of her male classmates. Only because Jenny overheard the exchange and was passionate about the subject did Jenny create the opportunity for herself to attend the camp.

Identifying Gaps and Modifications in Stages One and Two

In stage one and stage two of the LID model, adults and caretakers play a major role in the development of students' views of leadership and themselves. "The family, particularly parents, was important in this awareness stage and played a crucial role in teaching norms, building confidence, and serving as a building block of support" (Komives et al., 2006, p. 406). The messages sent to Jenny as a child may have aided her confidence to be a leader generally but not when it came to her career interests. Her parents did not serve as affirmers during her time exploring and engaging herself as an emerging engineering leader. While she was involved in clubs that surrounded her with peers, she lacked role models to validate and affirm her interest in engineering.

The LID model does not address what occurs when there is a lack of affirmation or when students are conflicted about the type of affirmation they receive. In this case, Jenny's parents were affirming her as a future leader in the field of medicine, even though Jenny had no interest in that area of study. For women pursuing ITE, these conflicting messages can occur often and early in their lives (Seymour, 1999). In other words, because adult affirmations did not align with her own dreams and interests, she became conflicted about her identity and her personal goals. The LID model assumes that learners were affirmed in their own goals; yet, for Jenny, this was not the case.

It is not just parents or caretakers who perpetuate this message, but teachers, club advisors, and the media (McCarthy, 2009). Family, parents, and teachers should align affirmations and encouragement with the aspirations of the women. While a woman in ITE may move on to the next stages of the LID model, her view of herself as a leader is skewed in a way that has an impact on how she navigates herself in a predominantly male field.

Identifying Gaps and Modifications in Stage Three

Jenny enjoyed being a member of UMBC chapter of the American Society of Mechanical Engineering (ASME). She found the projects meaningful, and the faculty advisor was one of her favorite professors. Early on, Jenny realized she could not join as many student organizations as she initially thought because her coursework was so demanding. Since no other organizations existed specifically for computer engineering, she joined ASME and looked up to the student officers. It was noticeable that all the student officers were men, and she struggled to socialize in ASME because of this male-dominated power dynamic. Jenny began changing her behavior to be "one of the guys" to fit in more. Over time, Jenny eventually considered running for an officer position but hesitated because she had not seen any women in leadership roles.

In stage three, the LID model emphasizes trying on new roles within organizations and modeling older positional leaders. Based on my experience working with women ITE students, these learners understand they need to engage meaningfully in professional student organizations because much of the networking leading to career advancement takes place in that setting. However, because of the demanding academic coursework, there is little flexibility to take on positional or member roles in as many organizations or in non-academic organizations as traditional college students. This means ITE students do not have as much of an opportunity to test out new skills and explore new identities through membership in a diverse selection of student organizations. Thus, women in ITE tend to focus their involvement on their professional organizations.

Jenny expressed a distorted view of leadership in engineering since ASME was predominantly male and she saw no women in leadership roles. Komives et al. (2006) found, "Older peers were increasingly important in this stage and became role models" (p. 408); in Jenny's case she did not have women in leadership positions to look up to within the organization. She even expressed disappointment in feeling more welcomed when she went with a friend to an animal welfare student organization meeting because she saw so many women. Even though Jenny knew she wanted to major in computer engineering, seeing the camaraderie in other student organizations made her struggle with finding her place as a leader because she did not feel qualified to serve as a leader of ASME. Professional organizations can be a key part of students' success, yet for Jenny, they instead made her question her leadership abilities. The LID model fails to address how students navigate their experience in groups in which they are marginalized, assuming that students will only seek out groups in which they feel welcomed.

Identifying Gaps and Modifications in Stage Four
Jenny finally took on a leadership role in ASME during her junior year by taking the lead on a project for a person with a disability. She understood leadership to mean more than having a title and desired to learn more from her peers by leading a meaningful project. However, she struggled with how to lead her peers, who were mostly men. She realized early on that it is important that she act like "one of the guys" to be heard. Though the project was successfully completed, Jenny felt isolated from the process because she never really felt like she was being her true self and could not figure out why. The concept of the imposter syndrome introduces the idea that individuals can feel that they do not belong in an environment, in this case engineering and technology, because they have not earned the right to exist in that environment (Williams, 2012). Jenny confirmed she felt this sense of not belonging and that she had not earned her spot among the group of male leaders in ASME.

In the LID research, a central driver of leadership identity development is commitment to student organizations and campus-based groups. Women in ITE may feel isolated in male-dominated professional organizations, therefore making it harder for them to commit and fully identify as leaders within these student organizations. Stage four of the LID model explains that students "gained confidence in working toward building the feeling of community in the group" (Komives, 2006, p. 410), but if a woman has not felt a part of that community in the first place, it is unlikely she would feel able to build that sense of community for others. Jenny's lack of confidence in her ability to lead her peers prevented her from fully entering stage four, and yet her mindset demonstrated her understanding that leadership was more than simply a title. She wanted to grow as a leader and understood that leadership could come from anywhere on the team, yet she did not fully believe she was considered part of that team.

Women in ITE are in a bind, as they do not feel welcome, yet they know they need to be there. I observe women in ITE feeling the need to be a part of professional student organizations to be successful in their majors and having a continual tension between not feeling a part of community and needing to be there. Camecho and Lord (2011) noted that "because all fields of engineering education are numerically dominated by White men, a certain masculine homogeneity defines its character" (p. 41). The LID model does not address how students should navigate this sense of isolation within their chosen student organizations and how that struggle may have an impact on their ability to interact with the group and develop a leadership identity.

Throughout women's time in ITE majors, the lack of affirmation and role models, as well as the lack of acknowledging barriers between stages within the LID model, manifests repeatedly. While the LID model serves as a roadmap for other students in aiding their leadership identity, it does not address the obstacles women in engineering and technology face in order to move through the stages.

SYNTHESIS OF PRACTITIONER STORIES AND SUGGESTED MODIFICATIONS

The vignettes of Michelle and Jenny depict two examples of how the LID model alone does not reflect or support the leadership identity development of all college students, specifically women who are marginalized on a college campus. These populations of women have shared experiences of isolation from the community and, because of external and internal influences, are not adequately served by the leadership development opportunities provided to the general student population on campus. When faculty and staff see a student who is seeking to collaborate with and lead her peers, it makes sense, based on foundational work on student involvement by Astin (1993), to encourage her to join more student organizations and become meaningfully involved. For students like Michelle and Jenny, however, joining student organizations that do not have the necessary scaffolding by staff can be unhelpful in their leadership development and may not fit their unique needs. The LID model and the traditional approach the authors have previously taken in facilitating student leadership development are not sufficient in supporting isolated and marginalized women because peer and group experiences can hinder their development and create barriers and constraints to their leadership development.

To recognize the experiences of adult women learners and women in ITE, we propose two amendments to the LID model. Table 11.1 is a summary of the original LID model, adapted from Komives et al. (2006).

TABLE 11.1 Summary of the LID Model

Awareness (1)	Exploration/ Engagement (2)	Leader Identified (3)	Leadership Differentiated (4)	Generativity (5)	Integration/ Synthesis (6)
She begins to identify who serves as the leaders in her community.	She joins groups and begins to practice taking on responsibilities that serve a team.	She sees leaders as those with positional authority. All other group members are followers.	She becomes aware of her interdependence with other group members.	She works towards a greater purpose and sees herself as a role model to others.	She sees leadership as a life-long learning process.
She is recognized and encouraged by parents and teachers.	Older peers affirm her group participation and leadership.	Older mentors coach her behavior as she takes on more responsibilities.	She makes meaning of her work with educators and same-aged peers.	She reflects on her learning journey with educators and same-aged peers.	She reflects with others as her leadership context changes.

Source: Adapted from Komives et al., 2006.

Tables 11.2 and 11.3 synthesize the gaps experienced by the women in our vignettes. These gaps are clarified by separately articulating what the woman was thinking and what influenced her thinking, both positively and negatively. We frame these gaps as amendments to the unique stages of the LID model. We hope that future researchers and practitioners will consider our observations when working with or researching women of these marginalized populations. We have limited our amendment only to LID model stages one through four because we have not observed enough students experiencing stages five and six to speak to these stages.

Adapting the LID Model to Accommodate Nontraditional-Aged Students

The vignette describing Michelle's leadership identity development experience as a woman adult learner is analyzed in Table 11.2. Her experiences differed from the LID model's expectation because her college experience did not begin with the recognition that campus leaders shared her identity; she felt isolated as an adult woman when joining traditional student organizations and thus sought out organizations in which she felt accepted. As Michelle emerged as a leadership learner within this foreign environment, her foundational leadership identity built in childhood was called into question, causing her to repeat her development. In other words, we found Michelle re-emerging in stages one and two in the college context in a different way than one might experience in childhood. In college, she felt marginalized by her younger peers who interpret her age as representing a fully-developed leadership identity and/or mother (stage three); and while still enrolled, she shifted her attention to off-campus initiatives run by other adult women leaders and struggled to articulate why these initiatives felt more positive than her on-campus organizations (stage four). Michelle's experiences—and those of the many students across the nation who share her characteristic—differ from the LID model enough for us to warrant clarifying how the informed practitioner might better understand the identity development process of these students. The last row of Table 11.2 contains the perspective of a practitioner as they amend the LID model to better support students like Michelle.

Jenny's Story

The vignette describing Jenny's leadership identity development experience as a woman in ITE is analyzed in Table 11.3. Jenny's experiences

TABLE 11.2 Suggested Modifications to the LID Model With Consideration of Adult Women Learners Based on Michelle's Story

Stages	Awareness (1)	Exploration/ Engagement (2)	Leader Identified (3)	Leadership Identified (4)
Internal Influences (i.e., What is Michelle thinking?)	"Student leaders do not look like me." "I missed my opportunity to be a student leader. I must leave room for traditional students to experience college without my influence."	"I matter." "I want to compete."	"I want to be seen as a leader not only because I am older." "I do not want my role as a mother to determine my leadership role in this group."	"I am being pulled to be a leader in other ways." "My responsibilities are not limited only to my student organization."
Societal & Additional Group Influences from the Perspective of the Practitioner (i.e., Considerations for educators that could help Michelle)	Recognize that in a new environment and with new challenges, LID's early stages can be re-experienced.	Recognition of adult learners needing campus-based experiences to compete with younger peers when applying to graduate school and/or jobs. Provide experiences and groups for adult students to connect with each other.	The influence of younger peers can also be a source of learning for adult students. Age and parental status can inform leadership but are not the only markers of one's leadership position.	Recognize and validate other group memberships and leadership roles off-campus that are experienced by women adult learners.

TABLE 11.3 Suggested Modifications to the LID Model With Consideration of Women in ITE and Other Predominately Male Fields of Study, Based on Jenny's Story

Stages	Awareness (1)	Exploration/Engagement (2)	Leader Identified (3)	Leadership Identified (4)
Internal Influences (i.e., What is Jenny thinking?)	"I like my brother's toys more than my own, but my parents keep buying me girl toys." "My parents keep telling me I should be a doctor. I like math but don't want to be a doctor, and I don't know how to tell my parents. I want to know what else I can do."	"I know there is a robotics club at my high school, but I don't want to be the only girl in it." "I feel like I never see any other girls interested in what I like. Maybe I should just be a doctor."	"Why am I the only girl in my engineering classes? Should I be in this major?" "ASME seems like fun. All the officers are guys, but I can definitely be a member!"	"I tried being a leader, but no one takes me seriously." "I need to be one of the guys to fit in." "I wonder if it will be like this when I get to my job." "I wish someone would tell me I can do this."
Societal & Additional Group Influences from the Perspective of the Practitioner (i.e., Considerations for educators that could help Jenny).	Acknowledge that individual leadership goals are important as a part of validation and recognition. Recognize the importance of exposing women to engineering and computing activities from an early age.	Encourage students to explore clubs or activities that focus on women in ITE, which can help students develop self-confidence. Affirm for the student that professional aspirations are important.	Use professional student organizations as a means of educating men and women about the importance of issues facing underrepresented populations in ITE. Create new organizations; young women benefit from meeting women who are in varying ITE fields.	Establish programs for women to teach them how leadership in professional organizations transfers into internship and full-time employment and can be helpful as they navigate their transition out of college into professional roles.

differed from the LID model's expectation because influential adults' affirmations and encouragement did not align with her leadership and professional goals, which caused Jenny to question her own ability to pick her path (stage one). Jenny avoided clubs and activities focused on ITE because she did not want to be the only woman present, and no one affirmed her interest in those clubs (stage two); she joined ITE-related student organizations in college but did not feel confident taking on leadership roles because she did not see other women as leaders (stage three). Once she achieved a leadership role in an ITE-related organization, she did not become immersed in her role because she still questioned her leadership identity due to a lack of affirming women role models (stage four). The last row of Table 11.3 contains the perspective of a practitioner to amend the LID model to better support a student like Jenny.

IMPLICATIONS FOR FUTURE RESEARCH

In order to encourage leadership development among these isolated and marginalized populations, we offer enhancements to the LID model and challenge other practitioners to use this process when applying the LID model with similarly marginalized students. Future research should focus on the validity of these modifications among the experiences of women adult learners and women in ITE. Other theories and methods need to be threaded into the LID model to support the experiences of learners developing a leadership identity and to acknowledge their other social identities. Future research and practice should highlight the additional student development and psychosocial theories that can to be used in partnership with the LID model to ensure the model's transferability to new populations (Komives et al., 2009). We believe removing the barriers from marginalized women's leadership identity development is an issue of social justice at the core of the mission of higher education; therefore, additional theory building is needed to serve these diverse women more effectively.

REFERENCES

Astin, A. W. (1993). *What matters in college: Four critical years revisited.* San Francisco, CA: Jossey-Bass.

Barnett, R. C., & Sabattini, L. (2009). *A short history of women in science: From stone walls to invisible walls.* Washington DC: The AEI Press. Retrieved from http://www.brandeis.edu/barnett/docs/7654.PDF

Brown, S. M. (2002). Strategies that contribute to nontraditional/adult student development and persistence. *PAACE Journal of Lifelong Learning, 11,* 67–76.

Camecho, M. M., & Lord, S. M. (2011, October). *"Microagressions" in engineering education: Climate for Asian, Latina, and White women.* ASEE/IEEE Frontiers in Education Conference, Rapid City, SD.

College Navigator. (2014). *The University of Maryland, Baltimore County.* Retrieved from http://nces.ed.gov/collegenavigator/

Deutsch, N. L., & Schmertz, B. (2011). "Starting from ground zero": Constraints and experiences of adult women returning to college. *The Review of Higher Education, 34*(3), 477–504.

Hardin, C. J. (2008). Adult students in higher education: A portrait of transitions. In B. O. Barefoot (Ed.) *The first year and beyond: Rethinking the challenge of collegiate transition.* (New Directions for Higher Education, 144, pp. 49–57). San Francisco, CA: Jossey-Bass.

Hill C., Corbett C., & St. Rose, A. (2010). *Why so few? Women in science, technology, engineering, and mathematics.* American Association University of Women, Washington, D.C. Retrieved from http://www.aauw.org/resource/why-so-few-women-in-science-technology-engineering-mathematics/

Komives, S. R., Dugan, J. P., Owen, J. E., Slack, C., & Wagner, W. (Eds.). (2011). *The handbook for student leadership development* (2nd ed.). San Francisco, CA: Jossey-Bass.

Komives, S. R., Owen, J. E., Longerbeam, S. D., Mainella, F. C., & Osteen, L. (2005). Developing a leadership identity: A grounded theory. *Journal of College Student Development, 46*(6), 593–611.

Komives, S. R., Longerbeam, S. D., Mainella, F., Osteen, L., Owen, J. E., & Wagner, W. (2009) Leadership identity development: Challenges in applying a developmental model. *Journal of Leadership Education, 8*(1), 11–47.

Komives, S. R., Longerbeam, S. D., Owen, J. E., Mainella, F. C., & Osteen, L. (2006). A leadership identity development model: Applications from a grounded theory. *Journal of College Student Development, 47*(4), 401–418.

McCarthy, R. (2009). Beyond smash and crash: Gender-friendly tech ed. *Technology Teacher, 69*(2), 16–21.

Owen, J. E., Komives, S. R., Lucas, N., & McMahon, T. R. (2007). *Instructor's guide for exploring leadership: For college students who want to make a difference.* San Francisco, CA: Jossey-Bass. Retrieved from https://nclp.umd.edu/include/pdfs/publications/exploringleadershipguide.pdf

Plageman, P. M., & Sabina, C. (2010). Perceived family influence on undergraduate adult female students. *Journal of Continuing Higher Education, 58*(3), 156–166.

Renn, K. A., & Bilodeau, B. L. (2005). Leadership identity development among lesbian, gay, bisexual, and transgender student leaders. *NASPA Journal, 42*(3), 342–367.

Seymour, E. (1999). The role of socialization in shaping the career-related choices of undergraduate women in science, mathematics, and engineering majors. *Annals of the New York Academy of Sciences, 869*(1), 118–126.

Williams, K. (2012). Helping young women thrive in STEM fields: Karen Purcell's unlocking your brilliance [The Good, the Bad, and the Ugly: Engineering FACTS]. *Women in Engineering Magazine, IEEE, 6*(2), 22–24.

PART III

NEW INSIGHTS AND IDEAS

CHAPTER 12

SOCIAL JUSTICE LEADERSHIP

Theorizing the Relationship Between Leadership and Activism for Latina/Chicana Educators

Marcia Venegas-García
Retired Teacher-Educator and Independent Scholar

Social justice leadership is a complex concept, rooted in meanings associated with awareness and focused on developing consciousness influenced by lived experiences that shape identity and actions (Lyman, Strachan, & Lazaridou, 2012; Marshall & Anderson, 2009). In this chapter I strive to advance a theory of social justice leadership development through a focus on segments from a larger qualitative research project intended to understand the relationship of activism to leadership—a study that brought the voices of Latina/Chicana activist educators situated in working class contexts to the center of analysis (Venegas-García, 2011). For the activist educators in this study, social justice leadership development occurred concurrently with an activist identity over time and in response to injustice and inequity. Making their development visible provides a view of activism as social justice leadership inspired by discrimination and disenfranchisement.

Theorizing Women and Leadership, pages 205–223
Copyright © 2017 by Information Age Publishing
All rights of reproduction in any form reserved.

This chapter is intended to diversify conversations about leadership as female and social justice-centered through the illumination of embedded values and moral purpose of seven Latina/Chicana activist educators. The chapter gives insight into how their life experiences shaped their perspectives and influenced the formation of their social justice consciousness. The research segments included here lay the foundation for an emerging theory generated from narrative data that establishes research participants as initiators and agents of change engaged in social justice leadership. Analysis of the data provides the opportunity for a broader understanding of the meaning of leadership to inform interdisciplinary fields of study concerned with social justice leadership at the intersection of gender, ethnicity/race, and class.

An interdisciplinary approach proves useful in providing opportunities for examining activism within communities where Latinas/Chicanas are often socially and professionally located. This approach provides the opportunity for the contribution of voices often excluded from conversations about leadership. Research into women's/feminist studies and Chicana feminist studies alerts us to the complex and critical role that social contexts, namely, gender, ethnicity/race, and class, play in the formation of leadership perspectives (Cosgrove, 2010; Gutiérrez, Meléndez, & Noyola, 2007; Klenke, 1996; Méndez-Negrete, 1999; Suyemoto & Ballou, 2007).

Literature reviewed for this chapter focuses on the interconnected aspects of culture and context; the literature provides insight into the significance of lived experiences that inspire activism and social justice leadership development. Research is presented that includes relevant women scholars in the field (Gutiérrez et al., 2007; Hurtado, 2003; Klenke, 1996; Lyman et al., 2012; Méndez-Negrete, 1999; Suyemoto & Ballou, 2007). Next, the research design and methodology are described, followed by the research findings with the embedded voices of participants. The chapter concludes with a discussion and conclusion.

CONTEXT AND GENDER, ETHNICITY/RACE, AND CLASS

The way leadership is perceived and manifested depends upon lived experiences within a context and culture and the embedded intersecting social dynamics of gender, ethnicity/race, and class; this provides a framework for thinking about social justice leadership development (Gutiérrez et al., 2007; Klenke, 1996; Méndez-Negrete, 1999; Suyemoto & Ballou, 2007). The pervasive role of gender as a contextual and cultural variable with overlapping interactions and intersections expands the possibilities for greater inclusion of women's voices (Klenke, 1996). Additionally, feminist viewpoints examining systems of privilege and oppression, combined with the impact of multiple sociostructural influences on lived experiences and perspectives, further demonstrate the significance for research in marginalized communities (Suyemoto & Ballou, 2007).

Research and analysis of 13 sociohistorical ethnobiographies suggest connections between Latina/Chicana activism as it relates to social justice leadership, particularly activism motivated by a reflective understanding of social location (Méndez-Negrete, 1999). Women in this study provided manifestations and definitions of leadership grounded in an understanding of community needs, and they acted out a philosophy to create change to benefit the common good over the good of the individual. Taking a stance on issues that negatively impacted others catalyzed their activism. Respondents learned to negotiate the nuances of power from the position of *other*, having internalized messages of race, class, and gender informed by cultural markers. As respondents, they were asked to make sense of their gender identity to determine how it informed their activism and leadership. Four of the women situated themselves within feminist ideologies and claimed feminist values as the foundation for their actions, while others indicated that the intersection of gender, ethnicity/race, class, and cultural experiences shaped their social justice leanings.

Another study identifies the complexities of gender, ethnicity/race, and class within a group of Latinas/Chicanas between the ages of 20 and 30 who were considered to be leaders of the next generation (Hurtado, 2003). Situated in a Chicana feminist framework that places Latinas'/Chicanas' lived experiences at the center of analysis, the study addressed the specificities of the Mexican-descent experience in the United States, acknowledging the *mezcla* (mixing) of different ethnic and racial groups that has always existed within Chicano communities. Knowledge about the influence of the linguistic, historical, and cultural contexts in which they live and work helps to create an understanding how those influences motivate and inspire their actions. The study reinforces the importance of the interconnectedness of social location recognizing working-class origins and the persistence of racism. Women in the study acknowledged how their lives were affected by the fact that they were women, marked by their color, and influenced by their class backgrounds (Hurtado, 2003).

Researchers affirm—and some have long advocated—the inclusion of the intersection of ethnicity and class in gender analyses of leadership. Studies validate the many direct and explicit encounters with discrimination, civil injustices, and human rights abuses, as well as an acute awareness of educational oppression related to social location that inspire activism and leadership (Gutiérrez et al., 2007; Hurtado, 2003; Méndez-Negrete, 1999). In these studies, Latinas/Chicanas reported developing as social justice leaders over time because of real-life encounters that required them to utilize context-specific strategies that largely resulted from lessons in their daily lives. The women participated in political organizations, electoral politics, and church-related activism to bring about social change. With heightened political awareness, women reconnected to their culture, communities, language, and professional passions, but not without the ongoing contradictions in determining whether or when gender or ethnicity was their highest priority. These studies made evident that Latina/Chicana respondents engaged in social justice leadership when their activism was closely connected to their engagement as agents for change in contexts where gender, ethnicity, and class played a significant role.

RESEARCHER POSITIONALITY

My personal motivation for this research project had to do with my longtime interest in women who serve as champions for the poor and powerless, my background and experiences as a teaching professional, and my own dilemmas as a Latina/Chicana in a position of leadership. Questions about the meaning of leadership surfaced when I came to direct the work of a university-based professional development project charged with building leadership capacity for teachers and instructors in the educational environment. My academic motivation had more to do with my desire to broaden academic conversations about leadership toward inclusion, to find perspectives for leadership that were female-centered, and to give those understandings for leadership a scholarly voice. My concerns after several years of study in the interdisciplinary field of leadership studies, in regards to the literature and prior research, were that empirical studies and the experiences of women were few, and the actions and agency of working class Latinas/Chicanas were absent from mainstream conversations. Searching for examples and a vocabulary to legitimize what I experienced and observed working with teachers and administrators in an international border region with Mexico was an arduous journey that led me to design this research project.

RESEARCH DESIGN AND METHODOLOGY

The empirical study presented here brought Latinas/Chicanas to the center of inquiry to examine the roots of their motivation and commitment to social justice activism and to analyze their theories of action relative to their gender, ethnicity/race, and class. The study focused on Latinas'/Chicanas' perceptions of their experiences as agents of change, drawing from their evolution as activists and practice as professionals and the foundational principles that informed their pedagogy and praxis as leaders. This research inquired into their views of leadership and activism and the relationship between leadership and activism in order to shed light on their motivations regarding social justice. In addition, the study sought to understand in what ways Latina/Chicana activism within educational institutions might be viewed as leadership as defined by leadership theorists Burns (1978) and Rost (1993).

Qualitative research methods, which are often used by feminist researchers to examine gender issues because they can explore changes in attitudes and beliefs over time, provided the method to delve more deeply into participants' lived experiences and to offer flexibility and depth for developing understanding (Lather, 2004; Patton, 2002). A grounded theory approach allowed for an examination of lived experiences and perspectives at the level of engagement to expose the phenomenon of activism and leadership and its relationship to gender, ethnicity/race, and class. Constructing and analyzing theories grounded in the data offered opportunities for exploration and discovery through an iterative process of writing, reflecting, and revisiting data (Charmaz, 2006).

Chicana feminist theory and critical inquiry offers a defining lens, providing a philosophical framework and conceptual tools by which to examine the complexities of Latinas/os' positions within society while attending to the means with which individuals engaged to become empowered. Chicana feminist theory recognizes Latinas' diverse ways of knowing, the importance of their experiential knowledge, and how that knowledge informs theory and practice (Elenes & Delgado Bernal, 2010). The theory also recognizes a consciousness coming from the intersection of multiple systems of oppression (i.e., gender, ethnicity/race, and class) and the examination of lived experiences as sites to obtain knowledge (García, 1997; Hurtado, 2003). This epistemology, developed by scholars of color and drawn from intellectual traditions, avoids binary forms of thinking and promotes a theory of agency and praxis committed to social justice (Delgado Bernal, 1998).

Overview of Data Collection and Analysis

After recommendations from their peers, email invitations were sent to Latina/Chicana activist educators; the names of referring peers were included together with general information about the research project. Emails were followed by a phone call and/or a second email that was more personalized with a request for a confirmation of their willingness to participate. Initial and follow-up contacts were important in developing a foundational level of trust. Seven women agreed to participate, signed a consent form, and scheduled a time for a 45-minute interview.

All face-to-face interviews were held in participants' professional space, other campus space, or in their home or mine, wherever participants felt most comfortable, and at times that were convenient for them. Each audio-recorded interview exceeded one hour and was transcribed during the following week. An interview guide was used to focus the conversation but not to impede the natural progression of the narrative. Topics for guiding conversations included descriptions of workplace environments, philosophical underpinnings for actions as educators, and meanings of activism and leadership. Participants were surprisingly forthcoming in their responses, which provided highly descriptive and detailed narratives. They spoke about their beliefs and values, and they shared significant events that inspired their identity formation as activists. Probing for the root of foundational principles and asking how/where/when their ideas and values were formed created opportunities to deepen their reflection and prompted additional narratives.

Transcribed narratives were used as the primary unit of analysis. Patterns and themes were constructed based on data coming from participants' perspectives and my interpretative analysis of the data (Charmaz, 2006; Strauss & Corbin, 1994). The frequency and consistency across transcriptions became apparent and exposed a complexity and transformational meaning assigned to their experiences. Within each narrative, I found that social conditions and circumstances stemming from those conditions interacted with family narratives, significant events, and transformational educational opportunities influencing participants' evolving identities as social justice activists. My critical analysis of the overt and subtle details of participants' transcribed stories exposed a more nuanced understanding of their lives and provided insight into understanding their perspectives of agency, advocacy, and/or activism and the relationship of these concepts to social justice leadership.

RESEARCH FINDINGS

The overarching goal of the study was to begin to construct a grounded theory to understand the relationship between activism and leadership among Latina/Chicana activist educators and the influence of gender, ethnicity/race, and class on this relationship. The participants told rich, detailed stories of courage and perseverance and, in the process, revealed how their lived experiences were tied to their values and actions. Given the objective for this chapter, I present selected findings and quotations structured around themes pertaining to social justice leadership that represent the participants' most significant and meaningful experiences. Themes pertinent to social justice leadership development include the following: family influences, significant life events, developing theories of action, activist educators in professional contexts, and (re)defining leadership. Please note that all names and identifying information were changed for confidentiality.

Family Influences

Participants spoke about their own stories of family migration and activism within their historical family narratives—experiences rooted in the Mexican culture and situating them as part of a group outside of the politically dominant mainstream. Family influence—an influence that aided in the participants' development of a heightened sense of social responsibility for those marginalized or struggling in their communities—was a common theme among all research participants. Some participants spoke about gaining strength from their mothers, who were sometimes heads of household, who became their models of courage. Others spoke of their fathers or remembered narratives of other family members who embraced ideals of social justice and who motivated them to do the same.

Anna provided an impactful example of the importance of family influence to her heightened social consciousness, sense of "other," and Chicana feminist leanings. Anna described her childhood migration experience as one of leaving Mexico and entering a politically hostile environment in the United States. These experiences left an indelible mark on her and shaped her attitudes and dispositions toward migration and the pressures present within the struggling working-class Mexican community of which she was a part. Anna described her courageous mother as a determined "feminist" model and head of their all-female household. She and her six sisters managed to survive, and each graduating from college. She said,

> I am a first generation, working-class [woman]. It is real for me. She [mother] was the first female in that village to come to the United States. She had the self-determination and the work ethic, definitely a feminist. I was never told, no, you can't do that because you are a girl. It was my mom and six of us. We were just the outcast in every sense. So by the time I got to high school I had a good understanding of where I fit in the local community. The politics of my own migration was a source of that awakening, the raising of my political consciousness.

Unlike Anna, who did not talk of the influence of family beyond her mother, Fabiola described being embedded in a large and extended family that promoted an awareness of social issues, the importance of community, and a dedication to service over generations. Fabiola's family celebrated a connection to the issues of the wider Latino community, and her father was involved in the Chicano movement, as the quotation below illustrates. Fabiola told of hearing stories of struggle and resistance as a young girl.

Today she believes these stories, combined with her experience of observing and learning from her parents, were the genesis of her ethic of service and interest in social justice activism. She related,

> My father's family immigrated here in 1914. My father was a union organizer, and I come from a family, cousins and others who have been about service. I grew up on family narratives about the Mexican Revolution, stories about how they were treated when they worked in Kansas on the railroads. My father was always saying, "We have to take care of each other," and my uncle telling his kids, too, that "your role at work is to take care of your co-worker."

Anna's and Fabiola's stories are just two of the multiple examples from the study illustrating the power of family narratives to inform and shape a Latina social justice identity. As depicted in these two stories, family members inspired courage and purpose, and family stories helped to mold an ethnic identity that included a sense of belonging to a historical and/or collective struggle. The findings suggest that family-generated social awareness included an understanding of marginalization that ultimately laid a foundation of empathy for others. This empathy, combined with growing up in poor or working-class communities and being members of a marginalized ethnic group, seemed to foster participants' tendency toward social justice activism.

Significant Life Events

In addition to family influences, participants revealed that significant events led them closer to thinking about themselves as social justice activists and leaders. Participants shared stories of life events they perceived as significant that had a lasting influence on shaping their social justice activist identity. Further, the events seemed to clarify a sense of purpose. These events were pivotal and informed their foundational principles for action. I offer excerpts from four selected stories below. As illustrated, the type of event was different, but the outcome—a stronger commitment to action—was the same.

Fabiola described how she came to embrace participatory democracy not only as a pedagogy for teaching and leading, but also as a way to live based on her experience in Chiapas, Mexico. Fabiola spent two weeks in the jungle with the Zapatista National Liberation Army, and she believed those two weeks substantially changed her life. This experience resonated with her family narratives and historical memory, and it profoundly changed her way of thinking. She described the event,

When I wrote my master's thesis on the revolutionary new technology, which was the Internet and that the Zapatista National Liberation Army were using this, my historical memory and family narratives about Emiliano Zapata and the revolution and that kind of thing, I was immediately drawn. I ended up getting invited to an international conference in the middle of the jungle in Mexico in 1996 after I had graduated. And now I account for my life in two parts, before Chiapas and after Chiapas, because I think that was the thing that changed me profoundly.

Anna told a similar story of deep change resulting from a high school experience. She recalled that she was "baptized early" into a world of collective intolerance and bias, and she spoke of her "meaningful" high school experience as a MEChA President. A politically motivated event, similar to the Lemon Grove Incident of the 1930s, occurred and challenged her to lead as an advocate in a public sphere. The experience is etched in her memory in surprising detail; she says,

The one incident that stands out for me and has always been really meaningful is when I was the MEChA President at our high school...and I got a request from one of the local parents. So, they said, there is a petition right now that is being considered by the school board to bus kids because of overcrowding to a brand new school, in a more middle class neighborhood. Well, this situation...became an extremely controversial issue. So here I am at 15 or 16 years old in this position where I have to speak at the school board meeting, and I remember talking to our advisor and figuring out how to present MEChA's position. So I was baptized early.

Carmen described a similar life-changing experience in graduate school when a Chicano professor inspired her to voice her thoughts and concerns whenever the opportunity presented itself. With heightened awareness about lack of voice for Latinos/Chicanos and empowered to speak out, she committed to engagement as an activist and leader both in the educational setting and in the community. About this she said,

We would do groups and he told me, if you notice, it is always someone else other than a Latino taking the leadership. So we have to be those people. And I noticed he was right. Where's the voice of the Latina? And so I knew I had a lot of work to do.

Carmen pointed to this experience as helping her to clarify her sense of purpose and as a factor that played a significant role in her activism. "So any time I saw some injustices, I would speak up."

Nancee described two events as significant to her political awareness and the shaping of her political activism. The first came from a family narrative about her grandfather and his family who were deported to Mexico for organizing mine workers. "And so, of course, they sent the local sheriff. And what happened was that they unofficially got deported because the company was not happy with him." The second event critical to Nancee occurred when she was 15. She described her community as poor, sometimes treated unjustly, and seemingly powerless to make changes. She said,

> We had potholes. So he [resident] decided to draw up a petition requesting our congressperson address some of our concerns, and basically he recruited me because I was bilingual. He took them to the city council, and they actually started doing things. So I saw the power of the people. Many years later he became a councilman himself. And so he was my first mentor in the social-political arena.

For Nancee this triggered an awareness about how to use the political process to improve people's lives and greatly influenced her decisions to use political activism as a tool to advocate for students.

Developing Theories of Action

Data from the study illustrate the influence of historical events and social responsibility in shaping foundational principles and generating the philosophical underpinnings for theories of action. The excerpts of participants' narratives expressed here offer glimpses into how the research participants described their evolutionary process toward social justice activism. Although experiences were varied for these participants, held in common was their sense of social responsibility as an anchor for their emerging philosophical stance toward social justice leadership.

Esther credited her evolution to becoming a leader and radicalized social thinker to a colleague from the Civil Rights Movement and as a result of her own research. Esther's evolution moved to a deeper, more intentional level—one that influenced her philosophical foundations toward social justice. She explained,

> It was amazing, kind of this transition thing that happened without my even knowing it. Everything that I was reading, it was an evolution for me to get to that place. A woman got hired. She was an African American and came out of the Civil Rights Movement. Being along that struggle with her against some of the institutional racism and other things that were going on. I started studying Paolo Freire, so that was informing me as well.

Laura believed that her understanding of diversity, her realization of the power of inclusiveness, and her experience of coalition building informed her theories of action. She described her sense of her social justice activism and leadership,

> One of the things that I have learned is how Latinas tend to be inclusive in leadership or activist approaches. And that if we are clear about our coalition building and expectations of each other, we are able to make further strides in moving an agenda rather than working in isolation.

When asked about a philosophy that informed her theories of action, Nancee responded with a strong sense of responsibility to the local community. Clearly a courageous activist, she commented on how history seemed to repeat itself and how the struggle for justice never ended. Her work was guided by the philosophy captured in the ten little words she lived by—*If it is to be, it is up to me.* She went on to say,

> I just look at history and I see that things seem to repeat themselves, particularly if nobody says anything or nobody does anything about them. And sometimes you do something about it and it helps for a little while and then starts to go backwards like Proposition 209, 187.

Social Justice Activist Educators in Professional Contexts

Latina/Chicanas in this study engaged theories of action with practical applications as educators. Educational institutions provided the context for leadership in order for them to fulfill their sense of social responsibility and commitment to identify issues that negatively impacted students. Some countered and confronted negative attitudes that continued to exist in educational institutions. Within this context, participants learned to advocate and negotiate for educational equity for marginalized students within their influence. Others advanced educational practices in their courses with students in a more multifaceted and socially critical way.

Having a 30-year history in a large urban school district, Rowena expressed her strong commitment to advocacy for educationally disadvantaged Latinos as well as other marginalized groups. Drawing on her recollection of her early experiences as a struggling Spanish-English bilingual student, she emphasized that she made a commitment to focus service on the student population. A self-identified leader and activist motivated by injustice, Rowena described her position as an educator as a political act focused on countering negative influences against students,

> In the 31 years that I have worked in this district, 28 of those years have been in schools that are predominantly Latino, African American, immigrant, urban, and poor student populations—students I made a commitment to serve.

It really was a political activism kind of motivation that came from that place of seeing an injustice and wanting to be a part of the countering force—countering negative influences and presenting possibilities for a different kind of a future, different kind of a life.

Nancee, a MEChA activist and leader, came to her community college position as counselor, instructor, and Coordinator of the Student Transfer Center. To her position she brought her experiences and knowledge of the political workings of her community and the alliances she had formed as a political activist. She spoke about her connections to the community and the necessity to be an advocate for students.

We get the majority of students from the local community schools in this area for economic reasons. So they are going to stick close to home. I'm in a place where I know all the players from all the other community colleges. It's people from the community that make the job easier for me. It's advocacy, and the students really depend on us.

Helping students gain a voice and advocating for their education was part of her job description, and Nancee enthusiastically engaged in her work with the security of a tenured faculty position, a distinct advantage in helping her negotiate within the system and accomplish her activist goals. At the time of the interview she was concerned about decreasing access for her students at four-year institutions and thinking about rallying the broader community over this issue as she had done before as a political activist. For her, being an advocate for students on campus and political activist in the community were related issues. She said, "I can say what I want as long as I am not disrespectful. I can get things done." Nancee's protocol for accomplishing her social justice goals within the community college always began with informing her dean and other counselors about an educational issue before taking the issue to an advocacy/political community organization. She believed that building coalitions was much more effective than working alone. She explained,

I am really good at accessing information plus all the human resources I have out there, all the networks. Pretty much I can get reports, research that has been done, and then I'll take that research and put it together and present the problem to the board. It works best when you reach out to other groups. If you try to do things on your own, it is not as effective and it takes too long.

Like Nancee, other Latina/Chicana activist educators chose positions in higher educational institutions because of the flexibility provided to navigate and negotiate a social justice and advocacy agenda. Laura, for example, struggled in several institutions before settling into her current university position, realizing the importance of working in a supportive environment and one that understood her commitment to social justice and advocacy for Latinas/os. As Director for Latino Achievement, her job was to recruit, retain, and graduate Latina/o students, which was high on her activist agenda. She said,

> So it's a great place for me because I can still support my diversity goals that I am passionate about. I am able to do civic engagement focused on Latinos and still play an active role with the campus-wide effort whether it's hate crimes or diversity training or engaging staff into the campus culture working with students of color.

As a Latina/Chicana, Laura understood the struggles of obtaining a higher education and, with others in similar circumstances, extended support through the process of developing a group network specifically for Latinas to address school issues, work tensions, and relationships. Such encouragement developed their activism and leadership and hers as well. She explained,

> The university Latina activist group was a place to grow and to be empowered and lifted, to be able to have a voice so that you can create change wherever you go. The organization was built [for Latina students] to develop as change agents. I carry that through everything that I do.

Anna also talked about advocating for the marginalized Latina/o community as Interim Director of a Latina/o Research Center and its development under her leadership. Firmly grounded in the community, she clearly understood the goals of the university and implemented a master vision that moved the university closer to a national conversation. Building networks and partnerships and involving professors across disciplines were key to the growth of the center. She explained,

> It's not common for this type of research entity to be on a state university campus, but we have been able to make the case that it is important to build bridges to local community agencies. We have taken the initiative to sustain ourselves so we do all our own grant development.

(Re)defining Leadership as Social Justice Activism

The participants struggled with the term *leadership*, and responses regarding the term brought about a discussion about patriarchy and hierarchy. Some participants described activism as an integral and interconnected part of leadership and blurred the boundaries between activism and leadership. In other instances, participants gave examples that provided alternative and atypical models of leadership to demonstrate what leadership was, should be, or could be. Important to the study findings was participants' need to (re)define leadership so that it resonated ethically and practically for them. Overall, the participants referred to their experiences as social justice activism through narratives rooted in their community.

For example, Rowena spoke about leadership as an ability to facilitate learning, and she commented about what it meant to be a leader of potential leaders as it pertained to her high school students learning about the meaning of leadership. She explained how important it was to consider ways that leadership could be tied to social justice and to take action in your community, one of her foundational principles for activism. She said,

> To me leadership is the ability to guide and facilitate learning—adult learning and student learning. I'm looking at leadership in the larger context...for preparing leaders for the real serious work that needs to be done. Not that ASB and student leadership is not important for preparing students for leadership positions, but I feel the more serious conversation is about how you translate that into action in your community.

Carmen spoke about leadership as someone having the necessary willingness and "skills to bring about a change" for the good of students, teachers, or whoever else might be involved within the leader's sphere of influence. She explained that "those skills include how to motivate people, how to bring the best from people." She described leadership as an ability to motivate others and a desire to benevolently develop the best in others. She stated, "At the end of the day you feel like you've accomplished the day without humiliating anyone. There is that human aspect or human factor that I'm always conscious of." Carmen talked about leadership and activism as overlapping lines between school and community. She centered her activism in community issues and used that information as a leader in her professional work to bring about positive change as she countered hatred and injustice. She talked about how activism can inspire leadership: "I think activism is what brings about leadership. And I think that's what really drove me to being active in the community and take leadership roles. I became an activist on issues of immigration, issues of education, issues of language, issues of culture."

When asked about her thoughts on the meaning of leadership, Fabiola referred to her experience with the Zapatistas. Her leadership was more fluid than fixed, involving different people at different points in time. She said, "Zapatismo is the notion that everyone is a leader. . . . Women were just as prominent in leadership as men. So I spent two weeks in the jungle being immersed in this notion of a new world order...a philosophy of understanding that there is not one leader." Fabiola elaborated on the difficulties of working against hierarchical models of leadership when engaged as an activist and change agent. She highlighted the difficulties and the need to be specific about the purpose of activism, differentiating it specifically as social justice activism. She explained,

> The challenge for me and maybe for anyone who is honest is the constant interrogation of ego and power. You can be an activist but not moving toward social justice. That's why I say social justice activist. When I talk about social justice, I'm talking about envisioning a world where people's humanity remains intact. It is important to legitimate new waves of activism in the academy.

Summary of Data Analysis

The seven Latina/Chicana activist educators in this study can be characterized as progressive women with a clear sense of purpose, strong affiliations to their communities, and lifelong commitments to social justice. Family narratives and events that they recalled as being significant to their lives heightened an awareness of unjust social conditions in their communities and fostered critique together with an activist identity. The interplay of life events and activism firmly set a foundation for their underlying principles as social justice leaders although they struggled to (re)define their understanding of leadership in order to more accurately express their theories for action. Some described activism as an integral necessity and interconnected part of leadership. Often the boundaries of activism and leadership were blurred or overlapping. Overall, the participants referred back to their early experiences with activism as aiding in their leadership development by providing narratives rooted in their community. While their perspectives of activism and leadership were varied, they accepted activism as a condition of moral responsibility and social justice leadership in practice.

DISCUSSION

The narratives of Latinas/Chicanas in this study advance a theory to frame speculations on activist identity emergence and leadership development shaped by circumstances and encounters from lived experiences in gendered, ethnic/racial, and class positions. Findings and analysis from the study align closely with the belief that leadership is learned through extensive practical engagement and develops over time through a variety of learning experiences in real-life encounters. In that view, varied experiences provide occasions for practice in learning how to lead, and diverse experience offers opportunities to test concepts and theories as well as to learn from failures and successes. Over time, and with reflection and analysis, the ability to solve problems, handle decisions, approach risk-taking, access resources, and network with others develops confidence and the willingness to consider more difficult challenges.

Circumstances and events specific to the social location of these women heightened their consciousness and empathy for oppressed others. Historical family narratives of community organizing, resistance, and activism rooted in the Mexican experience, together with significant life events and ongoing engagement in social issues within their communities, catalyzed and deepened their commitment to counter injustices. Discriminatory life experiences as ethnically marginalized females were offset by the mentoring of mothers who encouraged the pursuit of educational achievement, while other family members shared narratives of perseverance and a work ethic that embraced a sense of service and care for others.

Latinas/Chicanas in this study developed courage, confidence, and a capacity for leadership with each and every engagement in the challenging and politically-charged spaces of community activism. Activism evolved or was created within local communities for the real purpose of improving the necessary conditions of life, and these women developed strategies for collective action and a propensity for leadership. With each new challenge they developed new capabilities and became more competent at creating political and other alliances in various sectors of their communities to achieve a shared goal. These experiences, added to other events they recalled as significant to their lives, influenced their philosophical underpinnings that laid a foundation for social justice leadership.

Educational institutions were sites of struggle as well as sites of opportunity, and these women were informed and transformed by both negative and positive experiences as students. Struggles associated with marginalization, bias, and negative assumptions were noticeably part of their ongoing educational experiences. However, support agencies such as the Migrant Education Program and activist organizations such as MEChA on campus provided intellectual and emotional support as well as spaces for critical dialogue and identity development. Interactions with university professors provided knowledge about an oppressive history and ongoing struggles for equity and justice that deepened their understanding of their social location and further motivated their sense of agency.

This study distinguishes research participants' choices to become activists and educators from other Latinas and other groups of women who do not have similar experiences or make similar choices. The specificity of culture and context for the participants emerged as critically important in shaping their identity and developing their commitment to social change and social action. Their collective identity was shaped by historical influences, namely, the Chicano Civil Rights Movement, that made them part of a larger effort.

CONCLUSION

The purpose of the study was to understand in what ways Latina/Chicana activism within educational institutions might be viewed as leadership as defined by contemporary theorists Burns (1978) and Rost (1993). Although these scholars studied high-profile male leaders, they theorized leadership to be a relational process between leaders and followers intent on actualizing social change that was morally responsible. Their leadership theories about change, transformation, and moral foundations provided a critical beginning point for a more diverse academic conversation about the meaning of leadership. Additionally, Klenke (1996), who examined the role of gender as a contextual and cultural variable using the metaphor of a prism to demonstrate that leadership was seen differently when viewed through different lenses, emphasized context as the critical framework for building leadership models and as important when thinking about marginalized women in working-class communities. Finally, my discovery of the ethnobiographies of Méndez-Negrete (1999) that demonstrated the ways Latinas/Chicanas carried out their activist agendas further fueled my motivation to design a research project that included theories of leadership, context, and activism using a grounded theory approach.

Importantly, the study addresses a void in academic convesations about leadership by giving voice to Latinas/Chicanas engaged as activist educators and leaders, and it adds to the limited empirical research on their everyday actions. The women- and social justice-centered approach presents new possibilities for academic conversations from knowledge acquired from engagement in social issues of the community. An insider's perspective proved important because it offered insights from knowledge acquired from lived experiences and engagement. In addition to the field of leadership studies, the research holds the potential to inform other interdisciplinary fields, such as women's studies, Chicana/o studies, ethnic studies, and others concerned with leadership at the intersection of gender, ethnicity/race, and class.

Additionally, the study can inform the educational community toward more equitable outcomes for Latinas/os and other marginalized groups who are struggling through the educational system. The activist educators held positions where Latinas/os and other marginalized groups were dominant. To these contexts they brought knowledge and insights acquired from their personal experiences as members of a similar marginalized group.

Within their professional roles existed the potential for a greater degree of success because they were able to respond with an ethic of care and goals for empowerment because of an intimate understanding of the social circumstances of the marginalized groups within their sphere of influence.

The study suggests that social justice leadership approaches may be different from other approaches to leadership because they are intimately bound to personal welfare and that of family and extended community. The women in the study chose career paths primarily as a means for effecting social change and were less interested in advancement into leadership positions that might constrain their abilities to engage in advocacy for students and/or agitate for change. While their leadership manifested with thoughtful subtlety, there was little doubt about their capabilities and competence as leaders to take action, create alliances, and build networks of support.

In this chapter I call for a broader interpretation of leadership for a more inclusive conversation, one that challenges researchers to consider the interconnected, lived realities of Latinas/Chicanas in working-class communities. Inquiry into social justice leadership, probing for understanding its complexities, and theorizing about its development offers a relevant and meaningful way forward, enlightening with a diversity of voices and perspectives.

REFERENCES

Burns, J. M. (1978). *Leadership*. New York, NY: Harper and Row.

Charmaz, K. (2006). *Constructing grounded theory: A practical guide through qualitative analysis*. Thousand Oaks, CA: Sage.

Cosgrove, S. (2010). *Leadership from the margins: Women and civil society organizations in Argentina, Chile, and El Salvador*. New Brunswick, Canada: Rutgers University.

Delgado Bernal, D. (1998). Using Chicana feminist epistemology in educational research. *Harvard Educational Review, 68*(4), 555–582.

Elenes, C. A., & Delgado Bernal, D. (2010). Latina/o education and the reciprocal relationship between theory and practice. In E. G. Murillo, S. A. Villenas, R. T. Galván, S. J. Muñoz, C. Martinez, & M. Machado-Casas (Eds.), *Handbook of Latinos in education: Theories, research and practice* (pp. 63–89). New York, NY: Routledge.

García, A. M. (1997). *Chicana feminist thought: The basic historical writings*. New York, NY: Routledge.

Gutiérrez, J. A., Meléndez, M., & Noyola, S. A. (2007). *Chicanas in charge: Texas women in the public arena*. Lanham, MD: AltaMira.

Hurtado, A. (2003). *Voicing Chicana feminisms: Young women speak out on sexuality and identity*. New York, NY: New York University.

Klenke, K. (1996). *Women and leadership: A contextual perspective*. New York, NY: Springer.

Lather, P. (2004). Critical inquiry in qualitative research: Feminist and poststructural perspectives: Science "after truth." In K. deMarrais, & S. D. Lapan (Eds.),

Foundations for research: Methods of inquiry in education and the social sciences (pp. 203–216). Mahwah, NJ: Lawrence Erlbaum Associates.

Lyman, L., Strachan, J., & Lazaridou, A. (2012). *Shaping social justice leadership: Insights of women educators worldwide.* Lanham, MD: Rowman and Littlefield.

Marshall, C., & Anderson, A. (Eds.). (2009). Is it possible to be an activist educator? In C. Marshall, & A. Anderson (Eds.), *Activist educators: Breaking past limits* (pp. 1–30). New York, NY: Routledge.

Méndez-Negrete, J. (1999). Awareness, consciousness, and resistance: Raced, classed, and gendered leadership interactions in Milagro County, California. *Frontiers: A Journal of Women Studies, 20*(1), 25–44.

Patton, M. Q. (2002). *Qualitative research and evaluation methods.* Thousand Oaks, CA: Sage.

Rost, J. C. (1993). *Leadership for the twenty-first century.* Westport, CT: Praeger.

Strauss, A., & Corbin, J. (1994). Grounded theory methodology. In N. K. Denzin, & Y. S. Lincoln (Eds.), *Handbook of qualitative research* (2nd ed., pp. 217–285). Thousand Oaks, CA: Sage.

Suyemoto, K., & Ballou, M. (2007). Conducted monotones to coacted harmonies: A feminist (re)conceptualization of leadership addressing race, class, and gender. In J. Chin, B. Lott, J. Rice, & J. Sanchez-Hucles (Eds.), *Women and leadership: Transforming visions and diverse voices* (pp. 35–54). Malden, MA: Blackwell.

Venegas-García, M. (2011). *Leadership for social change: Learning from Latina/Chicana activist educators.* (Unpublished doctoral dissertation). University of San Diego, San Diego, CA.

CHAPTER 13

TRACING THE DEVELOPMENTAL PRECURSORS OF LEADERSHIP DURING CHILDHOOD AND ADOLESCENCE

A Collaborative Autoethnographic Study of Women's Leader Identity Development

Marlene Janzen Le Ber
Brescia University College

Ann M. Berghout Austin
Utah State University

Judith Babcock LaValley
Kansas State University

Chanda D. Elbert
Texas A&M University

Lynne E. Devnew
University of Phoenix

Lorri L. Sulpizio
University of San Diego

Marianne Tremaine
Massey University

Theorizing Women and Leadership, pages 225–247
Copyright © 2017 by Information Age Publishing
All rights of reproduction in any form reserved.

In response to a call for action, a select group of international, interdisciplinary researchers met in 2014 at the Advancing Theories of Women and Leadership Colloquium in Orem, Utah. One of three small research teams using a leader identity perspective, our team focused on the phenomenon of leader identity development for women and girls, beginning with the internal development of seeing oneself as a leader. Thus, we knew, at a minimum, we would be considering the intersection of gender, leadership, identity, and human development. But, whereas each of these fields independently has a rich, voluminous research history, the areas where they intersect are under-researched. Furthermore, there is a dearth of either theoretical proposals or empirical research regarding the effects of gender on leader identity development.

As Day and Harrison (2006) point out, there is no universal conceptual definition of leadership. There is also disagreement as to the ways in which the terms *leader* and *leadership* should be used. Here, we use the term *leader* to refer to a social role and the term *leadership* to refer to a dynamic process involving leaders, followers, and situations (Day & Harrison, 2006). Furthermore, since leadership development can also refer to a process that happens at a group or organizational level, we use the term leader development at the individual level, that is, the development of individual leaders (Day & Harrison, 2006).

Our research is constructed from the ontological position that individuals are in "continuous interrelationship with their dynamic, temporal, historical, cultural worlds," such that "reality is the whole complex of what is experienced and elaborated in thinking, feeling, and willing," and, therefore, "the researcher is inextricably involved with any phenomenon investigated" (Mitchell & Cody, 1992, p. 56). Collaborative autoethnography (CAE) is epistemologically consistent with this ontology because it respects individuals' co-participation in generating knowledge of lived experiences, and it includes sociocultural context (Chang, Ngunjiri, & Hernandez, 2013). Thus, CAE was selected as an appropriate method for our study of women's leader identity development.

In keeping with autoethnographic practices described by Chang et al. (2013), we studied our own development of leader identities; we recalled significant events and personal narratives and considered how sociocultural contexts shaped our perspectives, behaviors, and decisions and gave meaning to our experiences. Lynham's (2002) general method of theory-building research in applied disciplines provided our guiding methodological framework. Our research moves inductively from practice (our leader experiences) to theorizing and contributes to the conceptual development of women's leader identity development theory. Our research question is, "How do women create, develop, and sustain a leader identity?" Because we all self-identified as leaders, and because we were using the CAE method, we began by asking ourselves two questions: "How did I create, develop, and sustain my leader identity?" and "How did I practice leadership as a child and as an adolescent?"

From our early collective introspection emerged a model describing the factors and processes that shaped our leader identity development. This model suggests that social and personal identities, together with leader role, gender role, and other sectional (e.g., race, socioeconomic status) role schemas embedded in a cultural context, interact to generate a woman's leader identity. These factors are not new and are clearly represented in extant literature (Eagly & Karau, 2002; Ibarra, Wittman, Petriglieri, & Day, 2014), but coupled with them is a new action component of leadership practice, feedback, and personal decision (i.e., "accepting or rejecting feedback"), fueled by personal self-efficacy (Bandura, 1997). We believe our leader identities have their genesis in our actions and behaviors as young girls. Our intended contribution to the women's leader identity development literature is this new action component of leadership practices and feedback embedded in culture, social, and personal identities where gender role schemas, other sectional role schemas, and leader role schemas collide.

We first highlight the extant literature informing our understanding of leader identity development; this is followed by a discussion of our method, our findings, and finally, a discussion of the model and its implications for future research on women's leader identity development.

CULTURAL CONTEXT
OF SCHEMAS AND LEADER IDENTITY

Some sociologists view schema as the basic unit of analysis for the study of culture (DiMaggio, 1997). Schema can be defined as a collection of thought patterns, personal theories, actions, and responses that together form a coherent behavioral system focusing on a particular theme (DiMaggio, 1997). This cognitive structure provides a shortcut to organize, perceive, and react to new situations and information. However, role schemas for leader, gender, race, and social class, as well as other social categorizations, provide conflicting expectations. The resulting intersectionality acknowledges the multiplicative rather than additive impacts of a variety of privileged and unprivileged categories to which an individual might belong (Collins, 2015). Here we address only two schemas: gender and leader.

It is important to explore how leader identity development is affected by gender because gender research "highlights the embeddedness of masculine assumptions in organizational power relations, identities, and practices" (Collinson, 2005, p. 1431). Many jobs remain gender normed or gender segregated, and leadership roles in particular remain gender normed (Koenig, Eagly, Mitchell, & Ristikari, 2011; Schein, 1973; Schein & Davidson, 1993), such that models, styles, languages, cultures, identities, and practices of leadership are shaped by masculinity (Collinson & Hearn, 1996). Thus, women who seek leadership roles encounter role incongruity prejudice (Eagly & Karau, 2002) due to female social role norms or stereotypes conflicting with masculine gendered leader role norms. According to Eagly and Karau (2002), "When a stereotyped group member and an incongruent social role become joined in the mind of the perceiver, this inconsistency lowers the evaluation of the group member as an actual or potential occupant of the role" (p. 574). This has been borne out in research, wherein members of male-gendered organizations rated female leaders lower than male leaders even though the leader profiles were identical except for the leader's gender (LaValley, 2013). Women and girls are thus disadvantaged when seeking to develop leader identities and to hold leadership positions.

SOCIAL IDENTITIES AND LEADER IDENTITY

The assertion that women and girls are disadvantaged as leaders and potential leaders in many societies is supported by social identity theory (Ibarra et al., 2014; Tajfel & Turner, 1979) and Hogg's (2001) social identity theory for leadership, in which leader influence derives from the interdependent roles of leaders and followers within a constructed social system. According to Hogg (2001), "leadership dynamics may be significantly affected by the social cognitive processes associated with group membership" (p. 186). These social cognitive processes go beyond individual cognitive processes, such as implicit leadership theories, by incorporating the effects of the larger social systems of which the individual is a member. Social identity theory posits that an individual's place in society is created and defined by intergroup contexts and social categorizations, with social categorization being defined as a cognitive process that "perceptually segments the social world into in-groups and out-groups that are cognitively represented as prototypes" (Hogg, 2001, p. 187).

In accordance with social categorization, the more closely an individual resembles an ingroup's prototype, the more likely the individual will be thought of as a leader for that group (Ely, Ibarra, & Kolb, 2011). Contrariwise, when individuals deviate from the prototype, they are less likely to be thought of as a leader (Ely et al., 2011). Given all this, what then supports a woman's aspirations and actions as a leader? Is there a particular path that reinforces the notion in a woman that she can, indeed, take on the identity of a leader despite the difficulties of stereotype? In the next section we discuss personal identity development and suggest forces that might contribute to the development of an identity as a leader.

PERSONAL IDENTITIES AND LEADER IDENTITY

Personal identity development is shaped by the cultural forces and personal experiences an individual has encountered throughout their lifespan. Factors that may shape personal identity include, but are not limited to: experiences with family and friends; personal educational opportunities; quality of educational opportunities; and experiences relative to gender, class, and ethnicity. Personal identity influences one's activities, practices, actions, and decisions—perceptions and practices relative to the development of an identity as a leader are of particular importance.

Developing an identity as a leader is essential to the process of exercising successful leadership (Day, 2011; Lord & Hall, 2005). Leadership behaviors may begin in childhood and adolescence although one may not yet acknowledge that she is a leader. Still, this exposure to leader behaviors, either through observation or practice, may serve as an important catalyst to one's development in the future (Lord & Hall, 2005). For girls in particular, practice at leader behaviors not only helps them "try on" a leader identity, but it also allows them to explore the inconsistencies in a gendered stereotype and to practice the ways in which they can challenge the stereotype successfully (Komives, Owen, Longerbeam, Mainella, & Osteen, 2005). In this research, we sought to explore the ways that each of us tried on a leader identity during the formative years of childhood and adolescence. We hoped that this exploration would provide the necessary first step toward understanding the opportunities, activities, and circumstances that ultimately allowed each of us to see ourselves as a leader.

METHOD

Design and Procedure

Since our research question delves deep into internal, relational, and social processes over a lifespan and because theory development in this field of study is still in a nascent state, a qualitative research design is the best methodological fit (Edmondson & McManus, 2007). Grounded theory utilizes an inductive approach to construct theory through the collection and analysis of data (Charmaz, 2006; Corbin & Strauss, 2008). CAE is also inductive, and integrates theory, research, and practice (Chang et al., 2013; Ellis & Bochner, 2000; Hamdan, 2012).

We used CAE as a first step in our research agenda to develop a grounded theory of women's leader identity development. Much as Hernández, Sancho, Creus, and Montané (2010) began their large study of becoming university scholars by conducting a CAE study, we began our theorizing work related to developing leader identity with a similar effort. In each case, we as researchers were studying topics with which we were very familiar because we had experienced them ourselves. Similar to Hernández et al. (2010), we saw a need to understand how we "establish a dialogue, resist, adapt... [ourselves] to or adopt changes in the process of constructing... [our leader] identities" (p. 4) and to prepare ourselves to better adjust our listening. In order to protect the confidentiality of the participants and other individuals who play integral roles in our narratives, we used pseudonyms throughout the process of collecting, storing, analyzing, and reporting the data.

After establishing our research questions, we as participant-researchers reflected upon our own key leader identity development experiences and leader identity development trajectories to construct individual leader identity development narratives. We examined each other's experiential narratives for meaning in order to develop themes and move closer to the development of theory. Each researcher read all of the other narratives and coded two assigned narratives. This resulted in the development of our first themes and an initial descriptive model. As we reviewed existing literature related to our themes, we developed new rounds of questions, which led to new waves of narratives. The narratives were all posted to a common repository, and researchers were encouraged to read each of them and then add to their own narratives if others' narratives prompted additional memories. We then worked collaboratively to modify our themes or develop new ones.

One of the challenges for the research team was geographic separation. The researchers live in five different time zones, with a 21-hour difference between the two farthest time zones. Thus, much of the work took place asynchronously through email and cloud-based data sharing. However, the team also used frequent conference calls, which required intricate schedule juggling across time zones. Additionally, five of the team's members met and furthered the research at subsequent academic conferences.

Participants

Our multidisciplinary, multinational, multicultural, and multigenerational team initially consisted of eight women (one African American/Black, one Hispanic/Latina, one Maori/European New Zealander, and five Caucasian/White; ages ranging from 39–68), but one team member withdrew after the colloquium due to workload constraints (her data are not included). One team member was raised in New Zealand, and one was born in South America but moved to Canada while a toddler. The remaining members are from across the United States. Although all of us are currently in academia, five of us have been in leadership positions outside of academia (agriculture, business, healthcare, military, and sports administration) prior to an academic career. Nonetheless, we recognize that as a group of women with doctoral degrees we are privileged and do not represent the entire spectrum of women leaders.

FINDINGS

To date, we have completed three waves of data collection and analysis, and our findings are reported chronologically in this section. First, we discuss the three major themes (Wave 1) that surfaced as we verbally shared our full life's narratives in May 2014. Next, we present the four themes that emerged through open coding of our written narratives regarding our childhood and adolescence (Wave 2). These four themes guided the third wave of data collection and allowed focused coding. As a result, the four corresponding themes (Figure 13.1) with subthemes emerged during Wave 3 and continue to inform and shape our thinking.

First Wave: Verbal Narratives

Three clear, overarching themes surfaced as we listened to each other's narratives of leader identity development: leadership inclination in childhood, divergence in adolescence, and the twisting trail of adulthood. However, it is important to note several of the subtexts of these themes. Gender roles played a prominent part in childhood and adolescence as some of us adopted traditional patterns associated with appearance, beauty, and caregiving early on, only to eschew traditional roles later. The movement through gender roles in particular and identity formation in general was different for each of us. Notwithstanding, several overriding themes emerged that appear to have moved us toward developing leader identities as outlined below.

Leadership Inclination in Childhood

As would be expected, our families were an important early holding space for our leader identity development. Birth order mattered, as older siblings looked after younger siblings, and for several of us, additional responsibilities were expected due to an absent parent, family difficulties, or special circumstances of conception and birth. We all began to appreciate

First-Order Categories   Second-Order Themes   Aggregate Dimensions

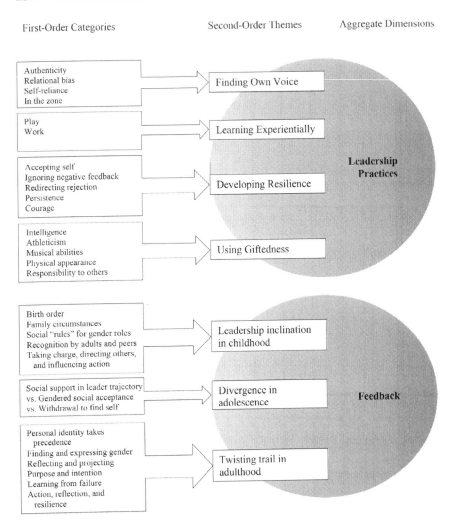

Figure 13.1   Data structure.

societal "rules" regarding gender roles that, significantly, were presented most saliently outside of the home. Although each of our specific childhood stories was unique, we were all "favored" or given special recognition by adults and often other children in our lives. Additionally, we also all had a predilection toward taking charge, directing others, and influencing action. However, the creation or formation of a leader identity during childhood was not intentional. As we approached adolescence, became more conscious of our social context, and continued to face life's challenges, our leadership experiences diverged.

Divergence in Adolescence

Although each of us had leadership experiences in childhood, our experiences of leader identity development diverged in adolescence, with most of us (four) becoming more confident as leaders and finding social support in those roles, but some of us (three) rejecting leadership roles and labels in order to be socially accepted (two) or to withdrawing to find ourselves (one). For those of us who made an explicit move toward leadership, our stories continued in a familiar trajectory from childhood, with leader behaviors reinforced by family, other significant adults, and friends. Both implicitly and explicitly, those of us in this trajectory were told that we were "good at it." We volunteered for and accepted opportunities to develop our leadership abilities. For those of us who made an explicit move away from leadership, the trajectory toward leadership was put on pause; leadership was subverted for popularity (two of us). Leadership was also put on pause for one of us whose sexual orientation identity took precedence over leader identity during adolescence.

What caused these differences, we wondered? Several influences emerged: role models either enhanced or deterred a leader identity (while an absence seemed neutral); significant peer presence and influence selecting the social group to which we belonged; choosing values and what was important to self (regionalization and religious affiliation were influential); and a growing recognition, along with acceptance or rejection, of the social standard for being a female in contrast to the social standard for being a leader. This clear divergence set the stage for the next phase in adulthood.

The Twisting Trail of Adulthood

Each of us actively pursued a leader pathway during our college years or early adulthood. From our verbal narratives, it was evident that leader identity development is not a linear progression, but is experienced more like the childhood game of Chutes & Ladders (i.e., Snakes & Ladders in the Commonwealth), in which one travels a twisting path, doing the work of establishing a leader identity and experiencing sudden advances or discouraging setbacks.

Key to the development of our leader identity was finding one's own authentic self, owning and embracing one's identity. Managing one's self through one's speaking and listening voice and finding gender expression (the feminine and the masculine) became important. Throughout the various ladder opportunities and unexpected chute descents, being grounded in purpose and intention and having a sense of resilience kept our leader identities intact. Similar to childhood experiences, feedback and reinforcement either enhanced or deterred leader identity in adulthood, but learning from "failures" strengthened leader abilities and thus leader identity. With maturity came an appreciation of mentorship and of the reciprocal and collaborative nature of leadership, wherein we could learn from those we led.

Second Wave: Written Narratives Open Coding

Turning to delve deeply into our childhood and adolescence, the second wave of data collection began with written narratives in response to several broad questions (see Appendix A). Line-by-line coding of the data surfaced several gaps in our understanding, which prompted a second round of written narrative (see Appendix B). After each of us completed line-by-line coding of two other researchers' narratives, we held a teleconference call. During our coding-informed discussion, we collectively identified four themes in our childhood and adolescent leader identity development narratives: voice, experiential learning, resilience, and giftedness with its attendant sense of responsibility. Each of the four themes is identified below, with further development of each in the next section, "third wave."

- *Voice.* This theme connected back to our earlier verbal narratives wherein we supposed that the development of an authentic integration of self, values, and voice occurred most commonly in early adulthood. However, when examining our childhood and adolescent experiences in our written narratives, it became clear that "finding of my voice" began in childhood through the tasks and roles we assumed and the challenges that some of us faced and overcame.
- *Experiential learning.* Many of our narratives demonstrated the importance of learning from our experiences practicing leadership and the resultant internal and external feedback; we developed our leader identities through practicing leadership. We divided our learning experiences into two categories, work and play, and we identified workspaces (Ibarra et al., 2014) in each of these categories. Identity workspaces are "social settings that are conducive to the development and maintenance of leaders' identities" (Ibarra et al., p. 293). We identified the workspaces of childhood and youth as home, neighborhood, school, church, and community organizations. Our narratives provide evidence that we learned leadership skills from our childhood and adolescent experiences of play and work.
- *Resilience.* While stories of responses to discrimination based on race, religion, language, gender, sexual orientation, disability, divorced parents, and social economic status were featured in our childhood written narratives, we were particularly interested in the development of resilience in childhood and adolescence whereby

we were able to accept or reject the external feedback regarding our leader identity.

- *Giftedness and associated responsibilities.* Our personal identities, and in turn our leader identities, were shaped by positive reinforcement for specific personal attributes—particularly our intelligence. Most of us also received a message of social responsibility; because we were gifted, we had an obligation not to squander our gifts on ourselves but to use them for the benefit of others.

Third Wave: Written Narratives Focused Coding

Having identified four overarching themes, we then re-coded the written narratives to uncover patterns, multiple layers of meaning, and sub-themes/second-order themes for each of the four broad themes (see Figure 13.1).

Voice

When the written narratives were recoded specifically for voice, four sub-themes were identified. First and foremost was *authenticity*, which we defined as a sense of intricately intertwined voice, mind, and self. Reta most eloquently exemplified authenticity, saying:

> I began to learn with this experience to find a "whisper" within me that would help me learn about good and bad. The inner whisper told me I had just been given a very important secret about human nature and that as I grew I would understand it better. The inner whisper told me that I could learn to have courage like Ruby Bridges. I knew I wasn't a popular leader, but I knew that I wanted to stand up for human rights.

Second, there was a definite *relational bias*, which we defined as strengthening our own voice through others. Lida shared: "I always felt that I needed to protect the other girls by speaking on their behalf when they couldn't, or encouraging them to speak up themselves."

The third sub-theme, *self-reliance*, we defined as personal authority and trust in self. This also related to a growing understanding of when and when not to use one's voice. Susan explains:

> I was quite forceful about the things I was sure of. As an adolescent I was more of a mixture, issuing instructions one minute and bursting into tears the next. I did like to give advice, and I was quite sure of myself. I often corrected my elders or showed surprise at what they didn't know.

The fourth and final sub-theme of voice is what we labeled as *in the zone* and defined as the release of energy in reclaiming self and finding one's voice. Macy explains:

> During the time I was a junior in high school I had a group of girls that wanted to bully me. I suppose that I didn't take too well to the bullying because I showed them that I would fight back and not be a victim to their tactics.

Experiential Learning

For this theme we analyzed the written narratives for our childhood and adolescent leadership experiences in play and work and the responses of others to our leadership. We identified three subthemes describing what we learned from our leadership experiences in play: we were able to *motivate others*; to *encourage others to have faith in themselves*; and to *encourage prosocial behavior*. We also identified seven subthemes describing what we learned from our experiences in work: we were able to *organize activities and people*; we were *responsible*; at times it was important to be *respected versus liked*; our *personal leadership styles* could be honed and polished; our *behavior should be shaped by values*; our leadership behavior was often *reinforced by others*; and the *leadership roles we played were often influenced by our gender*.

We selected two of these sub-themes, one from play and one from work, to illustrate experiential learning: learning we were able to motivate others and learning that our personal leadership could be honed. There were many examples of our ability to motivate others in play, including stories about organizing the neighborhood; for example, Lisa's stories of organizing a backyard circus in the neighborhood and being the ringleader after a similar experience in kindergarten and then in middle school running a camp for a week in the backyard of a different neighborhood, Raquel's story of organizing a rock band, and Susan's stories of lunch time dance parties at her house. Other examples include Lida's stories of organizing play at recess and the activities of her friends while in high school and Poppy's and Reta's stories of sharing opinions that influenced the behavior of others.

Our stories of honing our leadership styles included a variety of positive experiences in which our leadership was accepted and times when we recognized the need to modify our ways. Leadership behaviors that were positively reinforced included Poppy learning that it was appropriate to ignore some negative feedback and Lisa learning that influencing others to want to do what she wanted to do was more effective than ordering others to follow. Examples of strong messages that a leadership style needed changing were Raquel being called "Little Hitler" and responses Susan received when she corrected her elders.

Resilience

Five sub-themes emerged within the theme of resilience in accepting or rejecting responses to our leadership. In no particular order of importance, the first sub-theme was one of *accepting self.* Raquel explains:

I began to recognize that I was different than most other girls. I wasn't as interested in the same stuff they were ... (boys, make-up, clothes). Kept busy—clubs, school governance, sports, academics, read[ing], church youth leader. I couldn't find a social group that seemed to fit me so I did other stuff.

The second sub-theme focused on the helpful strategy of *ignoring negative external feedback.* Poppy exemplified this, stating, "I am, by nature, agentic, independent, extroverted, competitive, and stubborn. Most of the time, I didn't get negative feedback for that, and when I did, I usually ignored it."

Redirecting rejection, the third sub-theme, was evident in several narratives but poignantly described by Reta. She explains:

My interest in social justice leadership was further piqued by unique features of my family. My sister was multiply handicapped, and every time we went out in public her condition drew stares and whispers. She was brutally bullied by the neighbor boys, and my parents were ostracized to a large degree for having had such a child. ... Usually the bullying included only passive-aggressive acts, but sometimes it included physical violence. Thus, my interest in social justice began at an early age and was reinforced by inner spirituality.

The fourth sub-theme, *persistence*, was demonstrated at the very young age of five in Lida's description of her experience:

In Kindergarten ... I wanted to play the big bass drum and lead the class during rhythm time. I knew that I had better rhythm than any of the boys that had played it already and would be a better leader. The kindergarten teacher told me that only boys could play the big bass drum. I persisted and she eventually told me that I could have a turn once all of the boys in the class had had a turn.

Some of us also developed our fifth sub-theme, *courage*, at a very young age. Reta describes this incident:

[On my first day of kindergarten,] my mother was standing in front of the radio and crying. She told me that a little girl who had brand new saddle oxford shoes and white socks like I did was going to her new school for the first time, but bad men threw tomatoes at her to keep her out of school. Fortunately, my mother said, God protected the little girl. She got to school safely and her new shoes, socks, and dress were not spoiled at all. The inner whisper told me that I could learn to have courage like Ruby Bridges.

Giftedness and Associated Responsibilities

Each of us identified as being gifted in one or more spheres (intelligence, athleticism, musical abilities, and physical appearance). At times this exceptionality resonated with traditional gender roles, as in the case of Lisa, for example, who was known as "the cutest little girl ever." At other times, our exceptionality went starkly against traditional roles and helped us think about our own self-definitions. For example, Raquel was an excellent athlete who eschewed any concerns about hair, makeup, clothes, and boys. By reconciling these exceptionalities, she made important progress in thinking through her own identity in the face of social stereotypes.

Many of us experienced the explicit message that with giftedness came the responsibility to use those gifts for the benefit of others. It is possible that there is a strong gendered component in this admonition to use gifts for the welfare of others, but in all cases in our narratives, the admonition created a sense of "mission," wherein we knew we were to seek out and involve ourselves in a larger sphere of influence. For example, Lida stated, "While my mother did speak to me as being special, she also followed this up with, 'God has given you many talents—use them to help other people.'"

While a provisional visual representation of our earliest understanding of women's leader identity development was developed after the first wave of verbal narratives and data analysis, Figure 13.2 emerged after the next two waves of written narratives and data analysis. We next discuss our emerging grounded theory and how it builds on existing scholarship on gender and leader identity development; we also discuss implications for practice and research.

DISCUSSION

We focused on the construction and internalization of a leader identity and believe that identity creation is central to the process of becoming a leader. In particular, the leader identity model created through CAE reflects the competing forces that must be reconciled as a leader identity is acknowledged, allowed to develop (or suppressed), internalized, and enacted (or not). Our model (Figure 13.2) also suggests a mechanism for change and growth or for stagnation and self-suppression.

Our narratives support the extant literature that examines leader identity development through the lenses of cultural role schemas (leader, gender, other sectional), social identities, and personal identities. During childhood, many of us received explicit messages regarding societal rules for gender roles (e.g., Lida leading the marching band), but also less-direct messages regarding race (e.g., Macy and the dance team), religion (e.g., Lida and importance of community), and sexual orientation

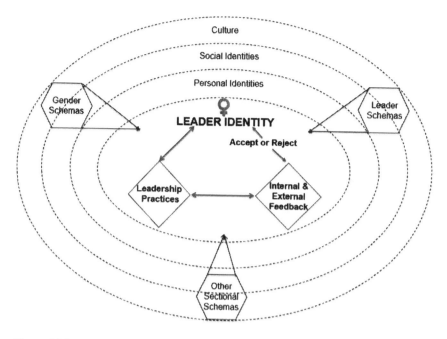

Figure 13.2 Women's leader identity development model.

(e.g., Raquel). Yet, we were also supported and encouraged in leader roles and leadership practice by significant adults. This external feedback served to positively reinforce our leader identity development, and the resulting conflicting schemas created the perfect storm to build resilience. Our research advances the leader resiliency literature by including conflicting schemas as a source of developing resiliency.

Not surprisingly, our narratives describing in-group/out-group dynamics and prototypicality were primarily situated during adolescence rather than during childhood. The divergence in adolescence could be as a result of these dynamics. While this divergence is not necessarily new (see development of voice in adolescent girls in Iglesias & Cormier, 2002), the importance of a baseline identity as a leader in childhood is a contribution to the leader identity literature.

During our childhood and adolescence years, we began to develop our personal identities in terms of the ways we saw ourselves and viewed our relationships with others (Murphy & Johnson, 2011). As was evident in our narratives, we were influenced in this development by the people and experiences in our lives and our responses to them. In the workspaces of work and play we used our voices and "tried on" our leadership skills. As others in our world responded positively to our practice of leadership, our leader identities grew, albeit sometimes following a twisting path. Murphy and Johnson (2011) observe that not all leader identities survive societal challenges. As we all identified ourselves as leaders at the beginning of this CAE, it is apparent that each developed enough resilience to overcome such challenges.

Leadership Practices

At the heart of our model is an action component—a reciprocal loop of personal leadership practices, internal and external feedback in response to these practices, and an acceptance or rejection of the feedback. By leadership practices we mean common patterns of action (Kouzes & Posner, 1995). Examining our childhood and adolescence, we enacted leadership practices of *finding own voice, learning experientially, developing resilience,* and *using giftedness* as central to the development of our leader identities.

Finding Own Voice

The ability to speak up and speak from one's true authentic self is not disputed as a critical leadership skill. The feminist literature similarly gives great import to voice, yet the process of how women leaders develop their voices is not well understood (Bodey & Wood, 2009). In our narratives, voice is critical to the merging of the social identities and personal identities as well as selective appropriations to form a leader identity. Belenky, Clinchy, Goldberger, and Tarule's (1986) conclusion that the development of a sense of voice, mind, and self are intricately intertwined was supported by our narratives.

With some exceptions, we were allowed or even encouraged to express voice, if not at home, then at school, at church, or in our community. For the most part, our mothers (and fathers) allowed some latitude regarding gender stereotypes. At other times our agentic expression was supported by teachers, ministers, friends, and siblings. Not only did we "try out" our voices by defending ourselves during childhood but also by defending others. Given the relational bias in females (Gilligan, 1977) strengthening their own voice through others (Belenky et al., 1986), these results are also not surprising. During our adolescent years, we learned to have personal trust in ourselves and listen to our voices. Iglesias and Cormier (2002) identify confidence in one's personal authority and trust in self during adolescence as an important antecedent of voice. What is most surprising about our narratives, in contrast to the received wisdom, is the development of voice in childhood and not in adolescence or college age (Iglesias & Cormier, 2002).

Learning Experientially

Popper (2004) observed that through real and vicarious experiences in work and play, individuals see and experience the effects of feedback and learn about cause and effect and about the behaviors that merit positive reinforcement from others. Most of the feedback we received from family, teachers, and friends following our leadership practice in our childhood workspaces was positive. The most extreme negative feedback received, consistent with the classic criticism of agentic leadership by females (Eagly & Karau, 2002), was shared by Raquel in her story of being called "Little Hitler." In play and in our work the characteristics of future leaders began to emerge. Our narratives provide evidence that we were learning leadership skills from our childhood and adolescent experiences.

Developing Resiliency

Resiliency, that is, the ability to not only adjust to, adapt to, or bounce back from adverse environmental stressors (Pahuja, 2012) but also to thrive as a result (Luthans, Luthans, & Avey, 2014), is important in leadership (Christman & McClellan, 2012). The narratives of our childhood and adolescence included discrimination based on race, religion, language, gender, sexual orientation, disability, divorced parents, and social economic status. Our narratives are also explicit about a rejection of these messages and a determination to fight against the discrimination. Resilience allows a leader to assess and make meaning of their environments that are filled with dynamic challenges, and then to find solutions (Coutu, 2002).

Girl Scouts of the USA identifies the resilience factor as a key to leadership in girls, particularly for African American and Hispanic girls (Fleshman & Schoenberg, 2011). Similarly, Christman and McLellan (2008) suggest that self-reflection and resiliency together contribute to the creation of identity as a leader. Our childhood narratives are supported by these works. However, the divergence of leadership expression in adolescence might suggest an uneven development of resilience; that is, those of us who were underwhelmed with environmental challenges as girls (i.e., were easily identified as mainstream) or overwhelmed with environmental challenges (i.e., figuring out sexual orientation) had not developed sufficient resilience for our adolescent experience.

Using Giftedness

Our stories reinforced the view that leaders are both made and born (Cawthon, 1996; Conger, 2004). We were fortunate to have been born with enough of the "right stuff" (Kirkpatrick & Locke, 1991, p. 59) to be leaders, and these traits were nourished by our circumstances. We were repeatedly reminded, even as young children, that we were very fortunate and that those to whom much has been given are expected to give much in return. Our leadership behaviors were reinforced by the important people in our lives when we used our gifts to improve the situations around us.

Feedback

The need for feedback in the development of leader identity is intuitive. Yet, as Day, Fleenor, Atwater, Sturn, and McKee's (2014) review of the last 25 years of leader and leadership development literature found, the received wisdom regarding feedback in leadership development is mostly limited to feedback as an adult leader. One exception is Murphy and Johnson (2011), who argue that the sensitivity periods for development during childhood and adolescence, and the self-reinforcing nature of leader development point to a foundation for future leader development being built in childhood and adolescence.

Our work supports this proposed role of feedback to our leadership practices during childhood and adolescence in developing our leader identities. The foundation for our leader identities was clearly laid in childhood; our narratives include generous recognition of our leadership actions of taking charge, directing others, and influencing action, by parents, other adults, siblings and our peers. Our contribution to this nascent literature provides further considerations for developmental feedback to leadership practices during childhood, potential divergence in adolescence, when gender feedback may be privileged over leader feedback, and a twisting trail of positive and negative feedback regarding our leadership practices in adulthood. This developmental approach to leader identity development is very promising.

Implications for Practice

In our early work on leader identity development, which focused on the authors' childhood and adolescent years, it has become apparent that circumstances play important roles. Despite the cultural and societal schemas that discourage the development of a leader identity in young and adolescent girls, those with "the right stuff" can and do develop leader identities when they have the opportunities to lead and receive support as they develop their voices, develop resiliency, and learn from experiences in work and play. Although families are often the first workspace for leader identity development, neighborhood, school, church, and community organizations are also formative workspaces for leader identity development when opportunities to lead are created for girls.

Implications for Future Research

Our work to date is consistent with our intended contribution to the women's leader identity development literature, offering a new action component of leadership practices and feedback embedded in culture, social and personal identities in which gender role schemas, other sectional role schemas, and leader role schemas collide. The results of our CAE support the conviction expressed in Murphy and Johnson (2011) that "early experiences create the foundation for future leadership development to build on" (p. 459). Using the Murphy and Johnson analogy of a snowball, it is apparent we learned from our practice, including both our successful experiences as a leader and the feedback and our resilience when we were not as successful; we were increasingly seen by others and ourselves as leaders. Thus, our leader identities were reinforced throughout childhood and well established before we entered adolescence or adulthood. A similar observation can be made related to our development of voice, which also began in childhood. This is contrary to the current belief that voice begins to develop during adolescence (Iglesias & Cormier, 2002).

Although this point was not as developed because we focused solely on childhood and adolescence only after the first wave, we observed early in our study that our leader identities had been challenged at times, and we compared our paths to the childhood game of *Chutes and Ladders* and to a twisting path. We observed that some of us who had strong leader identities as young girls lost this identity during adolescence and regained it as adults. Our stories begin to provide support for another observation by Murphy and Johnson (2001), who questioned an implicit assumption in previous studies that the development of a leader identity followed a straightforward path or trajectory.

CONCLUSION

The goal of creating a grounded theory of women's leader identity development has proven to be daunting, energizing, frustrating, and revealing. Although we are still in the early stages of developing this theory, we hope that the groundwork we are laying will be instructive to researchers and to mentors and teachers who work with others on leader identity for girls and women. Particularly, we think our model helps to provide some direction for teachers, counselors, coaches, and others who work with young girls during the formative years of middle school and adolescence. Our integrative framework in general and our action—feedback—decision core, in particular, moves the needle in advancing theories of women and leadership.

APPENDIX A
Autoethnographic Reflective Questions—Round One

The scope of each of these questions was restricted to only the life stages of childhood and adolescence prior to college entry.

1. How did you create, maintain, and develop a leader identity?
2. What factors contributed to and what factors deterred from a positive leader identity for you?
3. Describe a time when you felt fully empowered as an effective leader.
4. Describe a time when you felt invisible and silenced in your practice of leadership.
5. How would you describe your gender in terms of being masculine/feminine?
6. How did you feel about expressing your femininity?
7. How did you feel about expressing your masculinity?
8. How did you practice leadership as a child? An adolescent? A young woman?

APPENDIX B
Autoethnographic Reflective Questions—Round Two

As with round one, the scope of each of these questions was restricted to only the life stages of childhood and adolescence prior to college entry.

1. As a child and adolescent, did you demonstrate what are stereotyped as male and/or female leadership styles (please illustrate with examples)?
2. Reta* wrote of social justice motivations for leadership. Lida* noted seeking to break up fights. Are there other examples of societal or group needs that led to leadership responses, perhaps influencing your leader identity?
3. Are you aware of world events influencing your leader identity? If so, please share the story.
4. Please be particularly attuned to turning points in your leader identity process! [Although this does not look like a question, in the context of our collaborative research process, this was socially constructed to mean, "Please describe salient turning points in your leader identity development journey."]

*Pseudonyms

REFERENCES

Bandura, A. (1997). *Self-efficacy: The exercise of control.* New York, NY: W. H. Freeman and Company.

Belenky, M. F., Clinchy, B. M., Goldberger, N. R., & Tarule, J. M. (1986). *Women's ways of knowing: The development of self, voice, and mind.* New York, NY: Basic Books.

Bodey, K. R., & Wood, J. T. (2009). Grrrlpower: What counts as voice and who does the counting? *Southern Communication Journal, 74*(3), 325–337.

Cawthon, D. L. (1996). Leadership: The great man theory revisited. *Business Horizons, 39*(3), 1–5.

Charmaz, K. (2006). *Constructing grounded theory: A practical guide through qualitative analysis.* London, England: Sage.

Chang, H., Ngunjiri, F. W., & Hernandez, K-A. C. (2013). *Collaborative autoethnography.* Walnut Creek, CA: Left Coast.

Christman, D., & McClellan, R. (2008). "Living on barbed wire": Resilient women administrators in educational leadership programs. *Educational Administration Quarterly, 44*(1), 3–29.

Christman, D. E., & McClellan, R. L. (2012). Discovering middle space: Distinctions of sex and gender in resilient leadership. *The Journal of Higher Education, 83*(5), 648–670.

Collins, P. H. (2015). Intersectionality's definitional dilemmas. *Annual Review of Sociology, 41*(1), 1–20. doi:http://dx.doi.org/10.1146/annurev-soc-073014-112142

Collinson, D. (2005). Dialectics of leadership. *Human Relations, 58*(11), 1419–1442.

Collinson, D., & Hearn, J. (Eds.). (1996). *Men as managers, managers as men: Critical perspectives on men, masculinities, and managements.* London, England: Sage.

Conger, J. A. (2004). Developing leadership capability: What's inside the black box? *Academy of Management Executive, 18*(3), 136–139.

Corbin, J., & Strauss, A. (2008). *Basics of qualitative research: Techniques and procedures for developing grounded theory* (3rd ed.). Thousand Oaks, CA: Sage.

Coutu, D. L. (2002). How resilience works. *Harvard Business Review, 80*(5), 46–55.

Day, D. V. (2011). Integrative perspectives on longitudinal investigations of leader development: From childhood through adulthood. *The Leadership Quarterly, 22*(3), 561–571.

Day, D. V., Fleenor, J. W., Atwater, L. E., Sturm, R. E., & McKee, R. A. (2014). Advances in leader and leadership development: A review of 25 years of research and theory. *The Leadership Quarterly, 25*(1), 63–82.

Day, D. V., & Harrison, M. M. (2006). Leadership development. In Greenhaus, J. H., & Callanan, G. A. (Eds.), *Encyclopedia of career development* (pp. 457–461). Thousand Oaks, CA: Sage.

DiMaggio, P. (1997). Culture and cognition. *Annual Review of Sociology, 23*(1), 263–287. doi:10.1146/annurev.soc.23.1.263

Eagly, A. H., & Karau, S. J. (2002). Role congruity theory of prejudice toward female leaders. *Psychological Review, 109*(3), 573–598.

Edmondson, A. C., & McManus, S. E. (2007). Methodological fit in management field research. *Academy of Management Review, 32*(4), 1155–1179.

Ellis, C. & Bochner, A. P. (2000). Autoethnography, personal narrative, reflexivity. In N. K. Denzin, & Y. S. Lincoln (Eds.), *Handbook of qualitative research* (2nd ed., pp. 733–768). Thousand Oaks, CA: Sage.

Ely, R. J., Ibarra, H., & Kolb, D. M. (2011). Taking gender into account: Theory and design for women's leadership development programs. *Academy of Management Learning & Education, 10*(3), 474–493.

Fleshman, P., & Schoenberg, J. (2011). *The resilience factor: A key to leadership in African American and Hispanic girls.* New York, NY: Girls Scouts of the USA.

Gilligan, C. (1977). In a different voice: Women's conceptions of self and of morality. *Harvard Educational Review, 53*(4), 895–910.

Hamdan, A. (2012). Autoethnography as a genre of qualitative research: A journey inside out. *International Journal of Qualitative Methods, 11*(5), 585–606.

Hernández, F., Sancho, J. M., Creus, A., & Montané, A. (2010). Becoming university scholars: Inside professional autoethnographies. *Journal of Research Practice, 6*(1), 1–15.

Hogg, M. A. (2001). A social identity theory of leadership. *Personality and Social Psychology Review, 5*(3), 184–200.

Ibarra, H., Wittman, S., Petriglieri, G., & Day, D. V. (2014). Leadership and identity: An examination of three theories and new research directions. In D. V. Day (Ed.), *The Oxford handbook of leadership and organizations* (pp. 285–304). Oxford, England: Oxford University.

Iglesias, E., & Cormier, S. (2002). The transformation of girls to women: Finding voice and developing strategies for liberation. *Journal of Multicultural Counseling and Development, 30*(4), 259–271.

Kirkpatrick, S. A., & Locke, J. E. (1991). Leadership: Do traits matter? *The Executive, 5*(2), 48–60.

Koenig, A. M., Eagly, A. H., Mitchell, A. A., & Ristikari, T. (2011). Are leader stereotypes masculine? A meta-analysis of three research paradigms. *Psychological Bulletin, 137*(4), 616–642.

Komives, S. R., Owen, J. E., Longerbeam, S. D., Mainella, F. C., & Osteen, L. (2005). Developing a leadership identity: A grounded theory. *Journal of College Student Development, 46*(6), 593–611.

Kouzes, J. M., & Posner, B. Z. (1995). *The leadership challenge.* San Francisco, CA: Jossey-Bass.

LaValley, J. B. (2013). *Leadership schemas: The influence of organizational context on implicit leadership theories* (Master's thesis). Retrieved from The Kansas State University Research Exchange http://hdl.handle.net/2097/16865

Lord, R., & Hall, R. (2005). Identity, deep structure, and the development of leadership skill. *The Leadership Quarterly, 16*(4), 591–615.

Luthans, B. C., Luthans, K. W., & Avey, J. B. (2014). Building the leaders of tomorrow: The development of academic psychological capital. *Journal of Leadership & Organizational Studies, 21*(2), 191–199.

Lynham, S. A. (2002). The general method of theory-building research in applied disciplines. *Advances in Developing Human Resources, 4*(3), 221–241.

Mitchell, G. J., & Cody, W. K. (1992). Nursing knowledge and human science: Ontological and epistemological considerations. *Nursing Science Quarterly, 5*(2), 54–61.

Murphy, S. E., & Johnson, S. K. (2011). The benefits of a long-lens approach to leader development: Understanding the seeds of leadership. *The Leadership Quarterly, 22(3)*, 459–470.

Popper, M. (2004). Leadership as relationship. *Journal for the Theory of Social Behaviour, 34(2)*, 107–125. doi: 10.1111/j.0021-8308.2004.00238.x

Pahuja, Y. (2012). Understanding positive psychology and its relevance to organizations. *Indian Journal of Positive Psychology, 3(2)*, 187–190.

Schein, V. E. (1973). The relationship between sex role characteristics and requisite management characteristics. *Journal of Applied Psychology, 57(2)*, 95–100.

Schein, V. E., & Davidson, M. J. (1993). Think manager, think male. *Management Development Review, 6(3)*, 24–28. doi: 10.1108/EUM0000000000738

Tajfel, H., & Turner, J. C. (1979). An integrative theory of intergroup conflict. In W. G. Austin & S. Worchel (Eds.), *The social psychology of intergroup relations* (pp. 33–47). Monterey, CA: Brooks/Cole.

CHAPTER 14

INTERSECTIONAL LEADERSHIP PRAXIS

Unpacking the Experiences of Women Leaders at the Nexus of Roles and Identities

Faith Wambura Ngunjiri
Concordia College

Jennifer M. Almquist
Oregon State University

Maria Beebe
Portland State University

Chanda D. Elbert
Texas A&M University

Rita A. Gardiner
The University of Western Ontario

Michelle Shockness
Redeemer University College

Theorizing Women and Leadership, pages 249–263
Copyright © 2017 by Information Age Publishing
All rights of reproduction in any form reserved.

As the literature on women and leadership increases, it is necessary to craft new theories that capture the experiences of women at the intersections of gender and other identities. Intersectionality is a theoretical approach that examines how individuals experience social and organizational life at this nexus (Collins, 2000; Crenshaw, 1989). Specifically, intersectionality incorporates different identity characteristics to problematize women's experiences of domination on account of their gender and other identities (Choo & Ferree, 2010; Davis, 2008). Although an intersectional framework has been incorporated into many disciplines, it is rarely utilized in problematizing women's encounters as leaders (Jean-Marie, Williams, & Sherman, 2009; Ospina & Foldy, 2009). This chapter seeks to address this critical oversight and to demonstrate the utility of intersectionality as an interpretive framework.

The chapter begins with an exploration of intersectionality and a discussion of the few leadership studies that employ this interpretive approach, considering its strengths and weaknesses (Calás, Ou, & Smircich, 2013; Holvino, 2010). We briefly introduce collaborative autoethnography (CAE) as the method employed in our study (Chang, Ngunjiri, & Hernandez, 2013), and use our own leadership experiences as data for problematizing and crafting an intersectional leadership praxis. By engaging in individual and collective analysis, we identify places of overlap and divergence, thereby gaining insight into the nuances of gender at the intersections. As a diverse group of women in terms of our salient identities, our stories help to demonstrate intersectional leadership praxis and highlight the crucible experiences that have contributed to our development as leaders and to the ways in which we occupy leadership spaces. We conclude with a discussion of the implications for women's leadership theory development.

INTERSECTIONALITY:
A CRITICAL INTERPRETIVE FRAMEWORK

Existing literature on women and leadership does not sufficiently elaborate and interrogate the impact of women's various identities on their access to leadership and their experiences as leaders (Holvino, 2010; Ospina & Foldy, 2009). This deficit limits the diversity of voices in current theoretical articulations, whereupon the myriad ways in which race, class, geographic origin, and other aspects of identity that complicate women's leadership experiences are ignored.

First employed to explore the multidimensionality of how minority women experience social and organizational life at the nexus of their gender and race (Collins, 2000; Crenshaw, 1989, 1991), the term *intersectionality* refers to the complexity of experiences in social and organizational settings due to the confluence of race, class, and gender, amongst other identity characteristics. As such, intersectionality enables scholars to critically interrogate how identity characteristics have an effect upon individual agency and societal inequity. Furthermore, intersectional analysis can encourage new ways of thinking about structural inequality (Dill & Zambrana, 2009).

Intersectionality proved to be a popular and appropriate concept that feminist scholars from many disciplines and backgrounds could utilize to unpack and consider women's experiences at the nexus of various social identities, with a focus not only on knowledge production, but also on activism, policy, and institutional changes (Collins, 2000; McCall, 2005; Nash, 2008).

By being cognizant of how oppression and privilege operate from an intersectional perspective, we are able to interrogate the various ways in which diverse identities influence leadership in general, and women's leadership in particular. In sum, adopting an intersectional theoretical perspective catalyzes research to problematize women's experiences of leadership along the matrices of sexism, racism, classism, and other "isms" (Choo & Ferree, 2010) and adds conceptual richness to current theory (Holvino, 2010; Ospina & Foldy, 2009).

Through our exploration of the literature and analysis of our own leadership experiences, we identified three critical contributions of intersectionality relating to women and leadership: (a) intersectionality exposes the hierarchical discourse in women's leadership studies; (b) intersectionality foregrounds the complexities of women leaders' identities; and (c) intersectionality explicates the multifariousness of women leaders' experiences.

Intersectionality Exposes Hierarchical Discourse in Leadership Studies

Although scholars in many disciplines have adopted intersectionality as a critical interpretive framework, presently leadership scholars rarely use this theoretical lens (Gardiner, 2015; Ospina & Foldy, 2009). One possible reason is that the dominant paradigm in women's leadership studies is the experience of White middle-class women (Alston, 2005; Holvino, 2010). This narrow focus translates into a "change agenda of equal access" (Holvino, 2010, p. 255) that reproduces social inequality. However, by troubling gender constructions alongside a consideration of the effects of the intersections of identity, scholars can glean important insights about the production and reproduction of hierarchical discourses within leadership scholarship.

Furthermore, an intersectional framework can help leadership scholars develop more nuanced theoretical arguments and allow new, creative thinking to emerge (Davis, 2008). Theorizing from an intersectional perspective enables us to recognize that complex situations cannot be adequately explained through any single identity characteristic (Richardson & Loubier, 2008) and thus to deconstruct the existing canon of leadership literature, opening up the discourse to scrutiny and expansion.

Intersectionality Foregrounds the Complexities of Identity for Women Leaders

An intersectional standpoint reveals that identities are more complex than any one identity category can illuminate (Collins, 2000; Dill & Zambrana, 2009; Von Wahl, 2011). Therefore, we cannot discuss the experiences of any social group as if they are homogeneous—a critique offered by most second-wave feminist theorizing, generally by feminists of color (Collins, 2000). Indeed, theorizing from an intersectional perspective reveals that gender is not always the most salient factor. Moreover, research that considers gender independently from other identity characteristics cannot adequately explain why a small number of women climb the leadership ladder while most do not (Gardiner, 2015). These concerns need to be addressed in leadership theorizing; intersectionality provides a suitable framework from which to do so.

Intersectionality Explicates the Multifariousness of Women Leaders' Experiences

By problematizing the fluidity and global nature of women leaders' experiences, an intersectional perspective offers a different theoretical paradigm through which to understand how global complexities affect women's leadership. For example, identities may change in different locales and cultures (Blackmore, 2009; Calás et al., 2013; Ngunjiri, 2010). Thus, it is more appropriate to think about identity as fluid, rather than static. However, one shortcoming of an intersectional approach is that it may still not be robust enough to address the fluidity of subjecthood in a changing global context (Calás et al., 2013).

INTERSECTIONALITY AND LEADERSHIP THEORIZING

Different situations affect how leaders are perceived, making it necessary to develop a theoretical and methodological framework that is robust enough to explain the myriad ways in which leadership is affected by changing, global contexts. Intersectionality provides a useful theoretical framework for advancing the field of leadership studies. However, as a methodology it can be difficult to operationalize. Feminist collaborative autoethnography offers a strategy for examining our own experiences as leaders by drawing on a collective and interactive methodology to elucidate the complexities of gender at the intersections. Combining intersectional theory with this methodology allows for an in-depth examination of the ways in which women leaders' experiences of privilege and oppression alter in different situations and across diverse cultural milieus (Hernandez, Ngunjiri, & Chang, 2015). Vignettes from our own leadership experiences illustrate that gender, while important, is not always the most salient identity. Consideration of the complexity of identity through an intersectional lens, together with attentiveness to context, opens up new avenues of inquiry for theory building specific to women and leadership.

We suggest that both our findings and our process offer critical contributions to women's leadership studies and point toward new ways in which intersectionality empowers women to engage not only in critical theorizing, but also in agency and action to challenge the status quo.

METHODOLOGY

CAE is a first-person approach to research that utilizes researchers as both instruments of research and sources of data. Drawn from biography, ethnography, and narrative approaches, CAE combines the best of qualitative methods and turns the lens inward to the researchers' own lives. According to Chang et al. (2013), CAE "is a qualitative research method that is simultaneously collaborative, autobiographical, and ethnographic" (p. 17). CAE consists of "a group of researchers pooling their stories to find some commonalities and differences and then wrestling with these stories to discover the meanings of the stories in relation to the socio-cultural contexts" (p. 17).

A summary of the various identities and roles represented across our team is presented in Table 14.1. Each of us chose the identities and roles to include in this table, selecting those most germane to our experiences of leadership at the intersections.

For our purposes, CAE was utilized not only to understand women and leadership from our personal perspectives, but also to inform and begin to craft a new women and leadership theory that is more representative of the intersectional nature of our identities. Our process is illustrated in Figure 14.1.

The CAE work for this chapter began at the Advancing Women and Leadership Theory Colloquium, which took place in 2014 in Utah, where our group was given the concept of intersectionality and a charge to begin to craft a new or adapted leadership theory. We crafted research questions to guide our interrogation using an iterative process (for further explanation

TABLE 14.1   Our Self-Selected Identities

Name	Identities	Roles
Faith	African. Woman. Young-ish. Spiritual. Christian. Immigrant. Black.	Professor. Wife. Daughter. Sister. Aunt. Cousin. Childless. Mother.
Maria	Filipina-American. Global diaspora. Woman. Honored citizen. Spiritual. Green. Expert. Sociolinguist.	Scholar. Wife. Mother. Grandma. Sister. Auntie. Friend. Mentor.
Rita	English/Irish parentage, Canadian immigrant. 50-something. White.	Professor. Wife. Daughter/Daughter-in-Law. Sister. Aunt. Friend.
Michelle	1st Generation Canadian. Black. Woman. Christian/Spiritual. Young-ish. Barbadian, Tobagonian, Grenadian, Nigerian, English, Scottish, Dutch Heritage.	Social Worker. Instructor. Sister. Daughter. Granddaughter. Aunt. Cousin. Friend.
Jennifer	Woman. White. 30-something.	Scholar. Administrator. Wife. Friend.
Chanda	African American/Black Woman. Christian. Youngish.	Professor. Divorced. Single Mother. Daughter. Sister. Aunt. Friend.

Note: As a way of illustrating the fluidity of identity, during the course of writing this chapter, two of us added/changed status. Faith is now a mother through adoption and Chanda got married. These kinds of changes to our identities impact our experiences as leaders and the intersections at which we navigate leadership spaces.

of the process we employed, see Chang et al., 2013). Using a sequential CAE process (Chang et al., 2013), we completed three rounds of data collection. Each round was guided by a research question unique to that round, but subsequent questions often developed collaboratively after discussions of the preceding round. Data was coded and themes uncovered that explained our experiences at the intersections of various identities.

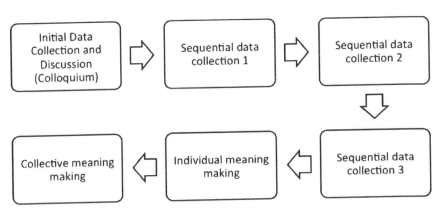

Figure 14.1   Collaborative autoethnography process.

FINDINGS

The results of our collective meaning-making illuminate women's leadership experiences at the intersections, reveal the nexus of gender and other social identities, and elucidate women's approaches to leadership that are both informed and influenced by those intersecting identities. Emerging themes also illustrate the three axes derived from our conceptualization of intersectionality: deconstructing hierarchies, foregrounding complexity, and problematizing identity for women as leaders.

Crucible Experiences: "Tested and Better for It"

Analogous to the crucible as a vessel able to withstand extreme heat to bring forth refined metals, this overarching theme captures experiences that, while negative and rejecting of particular identities of the participant, brought forth "gold" in the form of increasingly developed negotiations of identity. Instead of melting into insignificance, participants extracted strength and wisdom from their most trying experiences across various identities—in the process, problematizing the idea of identity itself. We shared several critical incidents, focusing particularly on impactful early experiences.

While working as an intern at a national agricultural agency, Chanda was part of a leadership-training program. The story highlights her experience at the intersections of age, race, and gender:

> When I needed to speak with [the administrator] about some paperwork, I addressed him using his first name. He stormed out of the room. . . . He was outraged because I called him by his first name. . . . He was usually called by his first name by everyone else in the office, but for some reason he became irate when a 19-year-old Black female called him by his first name. . . . I'm pretty sure I was singled out because of my identities.

Chanda put the situation in perspective: "Everyone else in the office was a White male or female, but . . . others in the office did not support his behavior and treated me respectfully." Chanda considered her time at that office a great training experience that set her on the path to success in agricultural leadership.

Michelle's experience involved a new identity as a Christian and early attempts at leadership intersecting with being a Black female:

> I started a Christian group. . . . I was told that they [a group of male Christians] would not come out because I was female—and that it was wrong for a woman to presume to lead a man. . . . It was one of my earliest memories of feeling I

was doing something wrong—something God wouldn't want—by presuming to lead. . . . Today, this approach to using faith to justify oppression is one that I regularly find space and reason to passionately challenge. It's been a journey to own the fullness of my identity as a Black Christian feminist and leader.

Similarly, Faith shared early critical incidents that had a profound impact on her leadership journey. She was running a meeting in which a board she had helped put together was reporting on their progress in starting a Christian school for the church.

A pastor who had recently joined our board said, "Faith cannot be the inaugural principal because she is young, unmarried, and has no children." . . . When did age, marital status, and motherhood become the qualifications for serving as a principal for a school? Apparently, in this pastor's eyes, I could carry the vision, but I couldn't implement it by running the school I was helping to start.

Collectively, these experiences highlight the role of social location and context at the intersections of identities. For instance, Faith's experiences highlight the intersection of age, marital status, and motherhood as markers of maturity in that community.

Context was a mediating factor across the data in the sense that gender is not always the singular or most salient aspect of identity to inform our experiences as leaders—this fact foregrounds complexity in talking about identity for women as leaders, or what Patricia Hill Collins (2000) named *the matrix of domination* highlighting the intersections of identities. We found that some aspects of identity may be foregrounded, depending on the contextual significance and that the expression or experience of a particular aspect of identity may vary across contexts.

As Rita notes, "Depending upon where I am, the perception of who I am changes." In Canada, where she now lives, Rita was in the middle of running a meeting when she overheard someone whisper to her neighbor, "I bet she was born with a silver spoon in her mouth." Rita is from a working-class community, hardly known for its gentility. She explains that "class functions in such a powerful way in England that it is common to pinpoint one's social location from the color of their vowels." Thus, location influences how a person's social class is perceived.

Despite the challenge of navigating differing contexts, we were able to extract strength from the crucible moments to continue to develop as leaders and to deepen our understanding of the intersection of identities. The next theme connects crucible experiences and the issue of context by looking specifically at women occupying leadership spaces, and at the challenges and opportunities that arise at the intersections of our various identities.

Occupying Leadership Spaces

She showed me the air and taught me how to fill it.
—Janis Joplin, describing Bessie Smith (cited in Echols, 1999)

People use space to communicate ownership/occupancy of areas and possessions. According to Wood (2007), people with power tend to enter the spaces of those with less power, and "men go into women's spaces more than women enter men's spaces" (p. 145). The subthemes discussed in this section unpack women's experiences with occupying leadership positions or spaces, particularly the ways that they are silenced through "mansplaining" and confrontation, or the ways that they articulate their voice as leaders and deconstruct normative hierarchies of leadership praxis.

"Mansplaining" as a Filtering Function

Mansplain, a portmanteau of *man* and *explain*, originated from Solnit's (2008) essay *Men Explain Things to Me*. Solnit wrote about men who wrongly assume they generally know more than women and therefore continuously seek to explain things to them. Jennifer illustrated the phenomenon, explaining that it extends beyond "men explain things to me" to "men explain me to others":

> An older, male, tenured faculty member took it upon himself to restate nearly everything I was saying.... I would make a point then the male faculty member would lend his authority and credibility to my statement. "I just said that," I muttered under my breath. "Why is no one picking up on this?" I thought to myself.... He is not talking over them [other men]; instead, he is taking up my space. Not my physical space, but my air space, my place at this meeting, my contributions to this conversation.

Michelle elaborates this theme further:

> I'm with you on that experience of being "restated" and my voice being "mediated" in a meeting. The clear message I have felt at those times is of being corrected—that how I said it the first time was not good enough to have been left "uncorrected." Sometimes... I have reasserted after the mansplainer with hopes of having the last word or have tried to correct the restatement (to regain ownership of my words).

As part of her reflection, Michelle acknowledges how we "work in the shadow of powerful stereotypes." These stereotypes about the way women talk stem from "nonlinguistic, societal assigned sex role traits and the linguistic correlates of those traits" (Edelsky, 1978, p. 1). Edelsky (1978) concluded that, even if a woman "exactly duplicates man's language use, she will not be evaluated nor responded to with a similar degree of positiveness" (p. 10) because language use is a reflection of the broader gender role stereotype. Deconstructing such hierarchical discourses within leadership studies is necessary if women are to deal with the resistance to their authority as leaders and educate others about the sources of such resistance.

Resistance to Women's Leadership

Women experience resistance to their authority as leaders and decision-makers as a matter of course within organizations. Michelle describes a critical incident at a small organization that demonstrates attempts at domestication:

> One of my coworkers responded by saying, "You women really dropped the ball on this one." ... He proceeded to share that baby showers fell within the domain of women's planning. ... I was so angry. ... In the meantime, the other men in the room made statements like they knew better than to say something like what my co-worker said as they would face the upset of their wives, as though "getting caught" was the problem with what was said! I finally stated that I was their co-worker, co-equal, and not their communal wife.

Whether it is the expectation that women will serve everyone else coffee or some other attempt at domestication, such acts disempower women, situating them as "less than" the men in the room and confining them to stereotypical associations with the home/hearth. Resistance to such attempts takes many forms, including, as Maria notes, overt confrontation:

> A young male Afghan college student reacted to my suggestion that he deal with the equally young female computer instructor. He stormed into my office and exclaimed, "My instructor is a girl!" In the Afghan context, *girl* is used to describe any female who is not yet married. ... My response was, "She is the most qualified even if she is a girl." His response: "Why should I listen to you? You're a woman." After taking a deep breath, I pulled out the status response, "I am in charge here. I hired the best qualified persons; most of them happen to be girls. And if you don't like to be taught by a girl and to listen to a woman, you can sign up for computer classes somewhere else."

The excerpt further raises the specter of the implicit credentials of a leader that women scholars must deconstruct and problematize across the globe. Though varying given contextual/cultural expectations around a leader's race, class, gender, and age, they still result in a similar conclusion: "You are [just] a woman." Maria's response was to assert her authority, but many women feel marginalized and silenced by such encounters.

Silence and Voice

Gender stereotypes dictate ways of thinking about who gets to have a voice in leadership spaces, a situation that appears to be fairly universal. Experiences with remaining silent and harnessing our voice indicate that our leadership was predicated on the effective use of both. As Rita explains, voice can be utilized to engage and demarcate one's space, presence, and position:

> In a management meeting, I was the only one voicing this contrary position. However, as soon as the meeting was over, colleagues came up to me to say they agreed. "Then why didn't you say anything?" The problem is that power works to silence opposition.

For Jennifer, the experience of age intersecting with gender led to feelings of being silenced and invisible:

> "Oh, is this your daughter?" The hostess of the gathering of faculty women looked from my colleague to me as she asked the question. I stared, stunned and unable to speak.... In that moment I was invisible, small, less-than. And yet, I was there with my colleague as a new leader of a commission reporting to the university president on the status of women.

This experience raised doubts about ever being "taken seriously as a leader" and prompted Jennifer to wonder, "How will I find my voice?" As she further explained:

> The intersection of age with gender can be particularly powerful for women developing identities as leaders. We struggle to find our voice, to be taken seriously. Already discounted by the fact that we are women, being youthful—or the perception of youth—can be an additional barrier as we step into an array of leadership roles.

The theme of silence was described in the data as an outcome of both "silencing" by powerful others as well self-silencing in response to contextual pressures. As Faith notes:

> In many situations for me, it's not someone else necessarily silencing me; sometimes I choose to be silent. I sometimes feel overwhelmed by the power in the room.... I have to tell myself, "Woman, speak up—otherwise they will think you have nothing worthwhile to say!"

Jennifer also reflects on silence as complicity versus silence as strategic choice:

> I don't use that term [complicity] to relieve patriarchy and sexism and those who participate of their responsibility, but I do often wonder why I sometimes

remain silent.... I find my sense of agency to be greatly context-dependent, and I am most reserved when interacting with older White male full professors or senior-level administrators.

These two broad themes of crucible experiences and occupying leadership spaces, further elaborated through the stated subthemes, enabled us to look at our experience of leadership at the intersections of race, gender, class, age, geographic location, and national origins. The two themes, and the subthemes of mansplaining, resistance, and voice versus silence help to demonstrate how employing a critical intersectional analytical framework helps us to uncover how we experience being women and leaders in various contexts. An intersectional lens helps us to deconstruct hierarchies that exist in leadership scholarship and our everyday experiences of leadership, to foreground the complexities in our identities, and to problematize gender. We find that for us as women leaders, our experiences are located at the nexus of gender, cultural and institutional context, race/ethnicity, social class, age, and location. Next, we suggest a preliminary model of intersectional leadership.

DISCUSSION

What becomes clear through the sharing and discussion of our vignettes is that gender is not experienced as homogeneous, nor can it be separated from other, sometimes more salient, aspects of identity. We cannot fully understand such experiences as feeling silenced or occupying space as a leader without troubling the (mis)perception that these phenomena can be adequately understood solely through the lens of gender—it is simply not enough to use a single axis of analysis (Collins, 2000; Dill & Zambrana, 2009). In our studies on women as leaders, we must demonstrate the complexity of women's identities across different locations and illuminate the global nature of women's experiences without essentializing them.

According to Creed (2003), voice and silence are ambiguous, intertwined phenomena enacted within the context of "the progressive loss of the self [and to] exercise some power over our lives and stories" (p. 1,504). Indeed, in our experience, we are compelled to articulate voice by the need to empower ourselves and own our stories. We shared examples in which speaking up sometimes involves starting with, "In my experience," or "Speaking as a woman," or some other signifier suggesting that we are voicing a perspective based on our experiences with various identities. This is particularly relevant in leadership spaces where women are in the minority.

However, the incorporation of intersectionality is not intended to suggest an additive approach where gender plus age plus race, for example, leads to a particular outcome. Rather, we begin to see the myriad of ways in

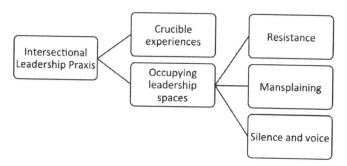

Figure 14.2 Intersectional leadership praxis.

which we experience social and organizational life at the nexus of our multiple identities (Collins, 2000; Hernandez et al., 2015). Thus, it is necessary to develop a robust framework able to account for the ways in which leadership is affected by changing contexts. Our emerging model incorporates the themes and subthemes of our research to articulate an *intersectional leadership praxis*, as shown in Figure 14.2.

We suggest that intersectional leadership praxis arises out of the interplay of crucible experiences in our early emergence as leaders and out of our everyday experiences of occupying leadership spaces at the intersections of our various identities. Both of these themes are informed by an intersectional lens that enables us to foreground the complexity of our various identities, deconstruct the hierarchies of leadership, and problematize the global nature of our experiences as women leaders. The three themes of resistance to women's leadership, mansplaining, and silence and voice reflect our experiences in attempting to occupy leadership spaces, not only as women (gender), but more so as women who are of a particular age or social class, who come from specific national and cultural origins, and so forth. All these statuses occur within specific organizational, social, and cultural contexts.

CONCLUSION AND IMPLICATIONS

Introducing intersectionality as a theory relevant to present and future conversations about women's leadership is intended to expand our understanding of the complexities of women's lived experiences. Rather than explore each possible intersection, our aim has been to elucidate the need for added nuance to theorizing about women and leadership. This emerging model of intersectional leadership praxis serves as a starting point for further theory-building work. Thus, we commend an intersectional framework to other researchers as they continue crafting leadership theories that are relevant to women's various identities and experiences, are sensitive to context, and can contribute to both knowledge and practice. Recognizing that what is relevant to six women may not be true for all women, we particularly see the need for more theories that will subject our model of intersectional leadership praxis to further testing, including the development of quantitative measures that would enable large-scale studies. Our goal in this study was not to generalize, but rather to begin the work of culturally and experientially relevant theory building.

Additionally, we commend a collaborative autoethnographic approach, as we found it an appropriate, empowering feminist approach to voice our identities, interrogate our experiences, and build community among us as researchers and leaders. The approach has helped us recognize the commonality in our experiences in spite of our differences, unpack the role of context in our leadership identities, and develop strategies for theorizing about our organizational lives at the nexus of our multiple identities.

REFERENCES

Alston, J. A. (2005). Tempered radicals and servant Leaders: Black females persevering in the superintendency. *Educational Administration Quarterly, 41*(4), 675-688.

Blackmore, J. (2009). Leadership for social justice: A transnational dialogue. *Journal of Research on Leadership Education, 4*(1), 1–11. Retrieved from http://files. eric.ed.gov/fulltext/EJ875405.pdf

Calás, M. B., Ou, H., & Smircich, L. (2013). Woman on the move: Mobile subjectivities after intersectionality. *Equality, Diversity and Inclusion, 32*(8), 708–731. doi:10.1108/edi-05-2012-0037

Chang, H., Ngunjiri, F. W., & Hernandez, K. C. (2013). *Collaborative autoethnography.* Walnut Creek, CA: LeftCoast.

Choo, H., & Ferree, M. (2010). Practicing intersectionality in sociological research: A critical analysis of inclusions, interactions, and institutions in the study of inequalities. *Sociological Theory, 28*(2), 129–149. doi:10.1111/j.1467 -9558.2010.01370.x

Collins, P. H. (2000). *Black feminist thought: Knowledge, consciousness, and the politics of empowerment* (2nd ed.). New York, NY: Routledge.

Creed, W. E. D. (2003). Voice lessons: Tempered radicalism and the use of voice and silence. *Journal of Management Studies, 40*(6), 1503–1536. doi:10.1111/ 1467-6486.00389

Crenshaw, K. (1989). Demarginalizing the intersection of race and sex: A Black feminist critique of antidiscrimination doctrine, feminist theory, and antiracist politics. *University of Chicago Legal Forum,* 139–167. http://chicagounbound. uchicago.edu/uclf/vol1989/iss1/8

Crenshaw, K. (1991). Mapping the margins: Intersectionality, identity politics, and violence against women of color. *Stanford Law Review, 43*(6), 1241–1299.

Davis, K. (2008). Intersectionality as buzzword. *Feminist Theory, 9*(1), 67–85. doi:10.1177/1464700108086364

Dill, B. T., & Zambrana, R. E. (Eds.). (2009). *Emerging intersections: Race, class, and gender in theory, policy and practice.* New Brunswick, NJ: Rutgers University.

Echols, A. (1999). *Scars of sweet paradise: The life and times of Janis Joplin.* New York, NY: Holts Paperback.

Edelsky, C. (1978, November). *Genderlects: A brief review of the literature.* Paper presented at the 68th Annual Meeting of the National Council of Teachers of English, Kansas City, MO.

Gardiner, R. (2015). *Gender, authenticity and leadership: Thinking with Arendt.* London, England: Palgrave Macmillan.

Hernandez, K. C., Ngunjiri, F. W., & Chang, H. (2015). Exploiting the margins in higher education: A collaborative autoethnography of three foreign-born female faculty of color. *International Journal of Qualitative Studies in Education, 28*(5), 533–551. doi: 10.1080/09518398.2014.933910

Holvino, E. (2010). Intersections: The simultaneity of race, gender and class in organization studies. *Gender, Work and Organization, 17*(3), 248–274. doi:10.1111/j.1468-0432.2008.00400.x

Jean-Marie, G., Williams, V.A., & Sherman, S. L. (2009). Black women's leadership experiences: Examining the intersectionality of race and gender. *Advances in Developing Human Resources, 11*(5), 562–581. doi:10.1177/1523422309351836

McCall, L. (2005). The complexity of intersectionality. *Signs, 30*(3), 1771–1800. Retrieved from http://www.jstor.org/stable/10.1086/426800

Nash, J. C. (2008). Re-thinking intersectionality. *Feminist Review, 89,* 1–15. doi:10.1057/fr.2008.4

Ngunjiri, F. W. (2010).Lessons in spiritual leadership from Kenyan women. *Journal of Educational Administration, 48*(6), 755–768.

Ospina, S., & Foldy, E. (2009). A critical review of race and ethnicity in the leadership literature: Surfacing context, power and the collective dimensions of leadership. *Leadership Quarterly, 20*(6), 876–896. doi:10.1016/j.leaqua.2009.09.005

Richardson, A., & Loubier, C. (2008).Leadership and intersectionality. *International Journal of Leadership Studies, 3*(2), 142–161. Retrieved from http://www.regent.edu/acad/global/publications/ijls/new/vol3iss2/IJLS_V3Is2_Richardson_Loubier.pdf

Solnit, R. (2008). *Men explain things to me.* Chicago, IL: Haymarket Books.

Von Wahl, A. (2011). A woman's revolution from above? Female leadership, intersectionality, and public policy under the Merkel government. *German Politics, 20*(3), 392–409. doi:10.1080/09644008.2011.606569

Wood, J. (2007). *Gendered lives: Communication, gender and culture.* Belmont, CA: Thompson/Wadsworth.

CHAPTER 15

THEORIZING LEADERSHIP IDENTITY DEVELOPMENT IN GIRLHOOD THROUGH COLLABORATIVE AUTOETHNOGRAPHY AND WOMEN'S WAYS OF KNOWING

Heather I. Ricks-Scott
Kennesaw State University

Katherine L. Yeager
Yeager Consulting

Julia Storberg-Walker
George Washington University

Lisa M. Gick
Antioch University; [c u r i o u s]®

Paige Haber-Curran
Texas State University

Denise Bauer
The Culinary Institute of America

Theorizing Women and Leadership, pages 265–289
Copyright © 2017 by Information Age Publishing
All rights of reproduction in any form reserved.

265

The focus on leadership experiences of women has gained prominence in the scholarly and practitioner literature over the last several decades (Eagly & Carli, 2007; Kellerman & Rhode, 2007). However, it is clear that gaps exist, particularly in theoretical knowledge, models, and frameworks generated from a women-centered point of view (Gross, 2014). In addition, the need for woman-centered theory mirrors that found in the world of practice where new opportunities and challenges for women leaders arise across all organizations and disciplines (Fletcher, 2001; Kellerman & Rhode, 2007). The complex, recursive, and dynamic nature of change in societies and organizational life has created new contexts, relational expectations, and opportunities to develop a deeper understanding of woman-centered leadership. We believe this shift in the general modality of leadership requires the advancement of new theoretical constructs of leadership through new forms of inquiry or knowledge generation (Gherardi, 1995; Storberg-Walker & Haber-Curran, 2017). Specifically, the study of leadership needs new theories that can imagine, conceptualize, and catalyze new women-centered theories to explain leadership development experiences of women (e.g., the Asilomar Declaration, 2015).

This chapter represents a milestone in a research journey that we (the six authors) began in January of 2014. The research question guiding our inquiry was "How do early experiences influence adult leadership identity of women?" We represent different generations, races, ethnicities, religions, and sexual orientations. Despite our differences, we share a collective belief in women-centered knowing and the perspective it adds to the field of research. While this type of knowing has been marginalized over the ages (Lerner, 1993), a sizable feminist scholarly response to its marginalization has mushroomed across a range of disciplines since the American Second Wave Women's Movement of the 1960s. Our work situates itself in this broad critique that seeks to identify and affirm women's points of view. The collaborative autoethnography qualitative research method used in this study is closely aligned with the principles undergirding feminist research methodology.

The purpose of this study was to explore new theories of women's leadership identity development, answering the call to close the gap in the literature related to theories generated by women (Gross, 2014). Building women-centered theory in this context meant moving beyond the bounds of traditional methods of research to understand the emergence of leadership identity in women. Specifically, the research team examined the literature and collected data based on our leadership experiences as girls and young women to contribute to the understanding of how leadership identity develops in women leaders.

FITTING ROUND PEGS INTO SQUARE HOLES: THE RESEARCH PROCESS

Our collective research work began by following traditional research practices (Gioia & Pitre, 1990; Lynham, 2002; Torraco, 2005), including conducting a literature review to categorize existing scholarship on leadership identity in women, with particular interest in new knowledge developed through women-centered voice and methods. Following the standard practices of scholarship, we classified, analyzed, and labeled (Byron & Thatcher, 2016). We worked together to dissect the research on women leadership identity into its pieces so that we could discover the internal mechanisms of leadership identity (Van de Ven & Poole, 2004). We used a recognized theory building process (Lynham, 2002) and tried to make all of the empirical and conceptual research evidence on women's leadership identity fit into some type of representational framework or model that would make sense and be representative of our collective leadership development experiences.

No matter how hard we tried, the existing theory mechanisms and scholarly pieces would not fit our specific leadership development experiences. In other words, the dissecting, categorizing, and organizing did not resonate with our personal leadership identity development experiences. Each time we discussed our emerging research, the conversation always wandered into how disconnected we "felt" from the research findings we were analyzing and organizing. We struggled to reconcile existing theories with the knowledge about leadership we were finding from our personal experiences as leaders. Simply stated, we found that we could not privilege our knowledge of the research process over our personal knowledge of leadership.

The tension we felt pushed us beyond the scientific method to break through and include our own knowing as women leaders as evidence. To help us understand our own experience, we needed a new, emergent way to think about how to conduct rigorous social scientific inquiry. We ultimately decided to privilege our own knowing about leadership and utilize a method, collaborative autoethnography (CAE) (Chang, Ngunjiri, & Hernandez, 2013), which legitimized adding our knowing into the research process. Once we let go of our attempts to stay removed from the object of study and be the objective scientists we were trained to be, patterns and themes of our leadership experiences emerged from the data. The remaining sections of this chapter describe the research foundations relevant to our work which include research on women's ways of knowing (Belenky, Clinchy, Goldberger, & Tarule, 1997) and ground-breaking research on leadership identity development (Komives, Owen, Longerbeam, Mainella, & Osteen, 2005), a description of the method used for this collaborative autoethnographic study, the findings of the study, and a summary of implications for future theorizing.

GUIDING FOUNDATIONAL RESEARCH

The two streams of research that significantly inform our research agenda are women's ways of knowing (WWK) (Belenky et al., 1997) and leadership identity development (LID) (Komives et al., 2005). We believe WWK can inform theorizing in general, particularly theorizing women's leadership identity development. Further, our findings suggest that while WWK generated findings that were aligned to some elements of contemporary leadership identity models such as Komives et al. (2005), these models only partially represented the breadth of our findings.

Women's Ways of Knowing

From a WWK perspective, our work can be situated in the body of work initiated by Gilligan (1982) in her highly influential feminist text, *In a Different Voice: Psychological Theory and Women's Development*, which first mapped out a different moral development for girls and women. Building on Gilligan's work was *Women's Ways of Knowing: The Development of Self, Voice, and Mind*, collectively written by Belenky et al. (1997). This pivotal feminist text sought to outline women's cognitive development by identifying five perspectives through which women view themselves and their relationship to knowledge.

At the beginning of our work together, WWK was not being considered. In fact, it was only after experiencing the "round peg in a square hole" episode that we found deeper meaning in this foundational work. The struggle we experienced and the "truth" that emerged for us mirrored the *constructed knowledge* phase of WWK (Belenky et al., 1997). We knew that we could not deny our personal understanding of our own leadership identity development, but the emergent meaning did not resonate with the literature supporting traditional methods of research. Only later, after re-reading Belenky et al.'s (1997) book, did we realize how deeply our experiences aligned with the *constructed knowledge* phase of WWK.

WWK involves an empathetic connecting process that generates knowledge quite differently from a male-normed point of view (Belenky et al., 1997). The collaborative and constructed knowledge involve deep listening and self-reflection that generate a contextual knowledge connecting the knower, the known, and the context. "*All knowledge is constructed, and the knower is an intimate part of the known*" (Belenky et al., 1997, p. 137, authors' emphasis). In contrast, the male-normed, post-positivist traditional social scientific epistemology with which we initially began the study separates knower from known, has been the keystone of knowledge generation, and has guided scientific "progress" over time.

Because constructed knowledge is a holistic combination of passion (self) and intellect (research), we realized we had to use our own selves as "instrument[s] of understanding" (Belenky et al., 1997, p. 141). The qualitative research method of CAE (Chang et al., 2013) emerged as the research tool that would enable us to examine personal experiences with research rigor. CAE provided an empowering feminist approach to discover and uncover our authentic leadership identity development experiences as girls and young women.

Building on Belenky et al. (1997), our work now stands intentionally opposed to the typical gendered knowledge system, and it provides an example of how women-centered leadership identity development theories can be generated by women theorists. We define women-centered leadership theories as theories generated through women's ways of knowing that place gender at the center of analysis. This view does not minimize other intersectional identities, such as race, religion, sexual orientation, or ethnicity; rather, these components of identity are critically important to leadership identity development as they emerge and recede at different times and in different contexts (for examples see chapters 8, 11, 13, and 14 in this volume). Our research team represents differences in many of these intersecting identities, but for this first contribution we are narrowing the scope to focus specifically on gender. Future work is planned that will expand theory development beyond this limitation.

Leadership Identity Model

Komives et al.'s (2005) LID research made an instrumental contribution to our understanding of the process by which young people develop a leadership identity. The model provides a useful and approachable framework for leadership educators to understand this process and to help guide students in their leadership identity development. It is a well-known model within the college student leadership educator population. Some limited research has been conducted using LID as a framework. For example, Renn and Bilodeau (2005) used the model to examine the leadership identity development of lesbian, gay, bisexual, and transgender students. Additionally, Wagner (2011) conducted a validation study of the LID model to further understand and confirm the six stages of the model.

Komives et al. (2005) were motivated to study leadership identity development because they found that "most leadership development focuses on skill-building...rather than on the process of how leadership capacity or leadership identity is created or changes over time" (p. 594). The LID model draws from the experiences and perceptions of a group of diverse college students who were observed to demonstrate relational leadership (Komives, Lucas, & McMahon, 2007). The researchers used grounded theory methods and incorporated interviewing and narrative analysis to identify categories for the process of leadership identity development in a college student population. The analysis revealed a shift from a leader-centric view of leadership to one that embraces leadership as a collaborative, relational process. These findings add important insights into the early influences and experiences contributing to one's leadership identity development.

This study expands the research by further examining early influences on leadership identity development for girls and women leaders. Although the LID research did not focus on gender specifically, the researchers noted that gender emerged as an important consideration in one's leadership identity development (Komives et al., 2005). Specifically, we focus on early girlhood experiences that influence leadership identity development, building from the themes identified in the LID research on *developing self* (i.e., deepening self-awareness and self-confidence), *developmental influences* (i.e., adult influences, peer influences, and meaningful involvement), and *group influences* (i.e., involvement in groups).

To further examine these themes, we take an alternative methodological approach to that of the original LID research. While the LID researchers used grounded theory, we instead use CAE, described further below. Supported by our understanding of WWK, the CAE epistemological approach explicitly connects ourselves to the research and knowledge being generated. This study specifically extends the work of Komives et al. (2005) by interjecting a component of gender and early childhood experiences. Further, we add to the literature by developing a framework for women's leadership identity development based on these early leadership experiences.

RESEARCH METHOD

CAE (Chang et al., 2013) combines collaborative, autobiographical, and ethnographic elements as researchers work in community to collect their autobiographical materials and analyze and interpret their data collectively to gain meaningful understanding of sociocultural phenomena reflected in it (Chang, Longman, & Franco, 2014; Walker & Taylor, 2015). Refer to Chapter 7 in this volume for additional information about CAE as a research method. The benefits of engaging this research methodology include

1. Collective exploration of researcher subjectivity
2. Power-sharing among researcher participants
3. Efficiency and enrichment in the research process
4. Deeper learning about self and other
5. Community building (Chang et al., 2013)

Appealing to us was the notion that research generating new knowledge could be achieved through integrating the researcher, the research process, and the research content. This shift in perspective facilitated our movement away from the more fixed notion that the separateness of the researcher and research process (and theorist and theory-building process) is an exclusive requirement of rigorous research and data integrity. Our process catalyzed us into becoming what Belenky et al. (1997) describe as *passionate knowers*, where we came to understand that "connected knowing is not simply an 'objective' procedure but a way of weaving [our] passions and intellectual life into some recognizable whole" (p. 141). Constructing knowledge utilizing CAE legitimized our individual knowing through our personal reflection and collaboratively generated stories. This epistemological perspective and choice of method challenges the more dispassionate and objective approaches of building theory and conducting research. The collaborative aspects of CAE were particularly appealing and fitting for our team as we constructed and deconstructed our experiences through the iterative sharing of our stories in a way that was purposefully informed by our common and uncommon experiences as girls and young women. Our research adopts a lifespan perspective of leadership development (Murphy & Johnson, 2011), beginning with our earliest girlhood memories of meaningful leader-shaping experiences.

Our Process: Collaborative, Rigorous, and Generative

To uphold the scholarly rigor of our work, we followed standard research protocols, including seeking required approval for human subjects research, developing research protocols, identifying data collection and analysis strategies, and implementing member checking and triangulation (Creswell, 2014). To enhance the relevance of our work, we turned to our personal journeys of leadership identity development. We studied individually and collectively about CAE methods, read or re-read Belenky et al.'s (1997) book, committed to reflection and review, and created a foundation of trust and loyalty in the group. We knew on two levels—gut and brain— that trust was key for us to successfully honor each of our individual leadership identity experiences. Our brains knew it was important because of the way Belenky et al. (1997) described this state of knowing (pp. 134–135).

Our guts knew it was important because we deeply felt the responsibility of care and empathy to each other, another signal of Belenky et al.'s (1997) constructed knowledge.

Emergence of the Domain Model of Leadership Identity Development

Adopting the focus of leadership identity development in women, we reflected on personal leadership experiences that shaped our leader selves. Through storytelling and considering the deep dive we took earlier into the leadership literature, we noticed three domains of leadership identity development experiences: self, relationships, and context. These three domains kept repeating during our discussions and reflections, and they resonated with all of us. Ultimately, we decided that we had enough evidence—both personal and scholarly—to affirm that this model sufficiently represented our leader development experiences.

The three domains of this framework share some commonality with Komives et al.'s (2005) model; however, our exploration of the data interjects new understanding in light of the integrative nature of these themes and a more granular analysis of how early childhood experiences matter in one's leadership identity development. As we examined the data, it became clear that these three themes were enjoined and overlapping as they were each present in our individual experiences and served as containers for the memorable and meaningful sound bytes present in the shaping of our leader selves. We recognized a recursive movement about our experiences within the themes that suggested an open and fluid model, which we call the Domain Model. Figure 15.1 provides a visual representation of this model. Additional support for this model appears in the Research Findings section of this chapter.

Using the Domain Model to Analyze Data

Using the aforementioned CAE method for our research, we were guided in our analysis by the Domain Model, which shaped the data collection and analysis procedures used for the study. Our format included inviting the research team to respond to prompts designed to draw data from our experiences. We then shared our responses to the prompts with the team for collaborative discussion, analysis, and knowledge construction within the framework we established. The first prompt, "Describe an early event or experience that contributed to identifying yourself as a leader," focused on a simple reflective exercise to tell the story of an early girlhood memory

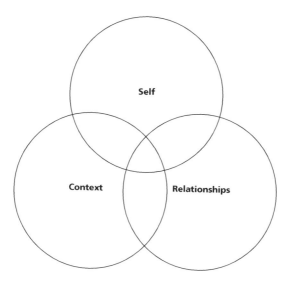

Figure 15.1 Domain model of leadership identity development for women.

that was recognizable and formative in the shaping of our leadership identity. We shared the written narrative documents, which ranged from 399 to 1188 words, with each other and participated in a conference call to discuss our stories, offer questions to clarify, and understand the core data relevant to our purpose. As a team we agreed on the sense making around the data (Weick, Sutcliffe, & Obstfeld, 2005) and extracted meaningful elements and themes pertaining to our conceptual framework (Boyatzis, 1998).

This recursive process involved responding to further prompts as we fully vetted our girlhood experiences related to leadership identity development. In addition to reflective methods, we also split into pairs to interview each other in order to more deeply examine our experiences. Further, we modified a data collection tool offered by Chang et al. (2013) that involved identifying and mapping key girlhood experiences and influences to our leadership identity development; we named this tool *Leadergram*. After each of us created our own Leadergram, we shared them with each other as further data.

During the data collection process we checked in as a team to continually examine the data collaboratively for discussion and meaning making. Throughout the data collection, our framework sustained its viability as a clear and relevant model. The process of CAE generated rich data, highlighting key experiences, influences, and other themes from girlhood to emerging young adulthood that contributed to our leadership identity development.

The research was conducted over a period of approximately eight months. When we felt new information was needed, we developed new prompts for reflective journaling, and the interactive, recursive methods repeated. We created a secure shared Dropbox for our data. We communicated via Skype, conference calls, and emails. If one of us missed a session, a recording was available to listen to after the fact. We met at research conferences at various locations in the United States and abroad. We created workshops to share with other women our process of combining CAE with WWK to examine leadership identity development, and we presented emerging findings at conferences. Our collective experiences have had a profound impact on each of us.

FINDINGS

Not surprisingly, the data analysis provided affirmation that each of the domain findings (i.e., self, relationships, and context) mattered to our leadership identity development. This was not surprising because the model was generated by combining our personal experiences with our knowledge of leadership literature. However, what is important is the specific concepts that emerged within each domain—this we see as a key contribution to the literature. See Figure 15.2 below. Our findings section is arranged to tell the supporting story of each domain and contains a descriptive narrative of

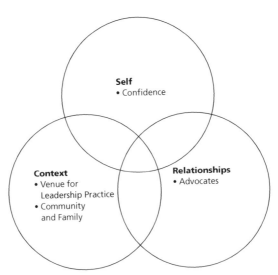

Figure 15.2 Domain model of leadership identity development for women with key concepts.

each concept as well as a discussion of how each concept aligns with prior research or makes a new contribution to the women-centered leadership identity development literature.

Interestingly, through the CAE process, we learned that stories we told ourselves at the time of the event were different from the stories we tell ourselves now about that time in our lives. This could be an example of retrospective sense making (Weick et al., 2005), the idea that the greater understanding of experiences can be gained through backward reflection (Schutz, 1967). Note also that pseudonyms are used to identify direct quotations attributed to researchers so as to honor the confidentiality of the researchers, who were also the participants.

Each of our narratives contributed to the constructed knowledge of the concepts. For the domain of self, we each experienced *confidence*, which increased our willingness to assume the role of leader. We identified influential *advocates* who were central to our leadership identity development, reflecting the domain of relationships. Last, the *venue where leadership was practiced* was salient and helped shape how we each viewed ourselves as a leader, reflecting the domain of context.

Some supporting data may appear to cross domain boundaries. In other words, a data example used to support the presence of confidence in the domain of self might also fit within the domain of context. This phenomenon merely confirms the intersecting nature of the model's domains.

The Domain of Self, the Concept of Confidence

Descriptive Narrative

A significant construct of self that we identified from the data was that of confidence in ourselves during this period of our lives. We found that stepping into leadership challenges that built leader capacity was a product of our self-confidence that also furthered our confidence building. We each had different catalysts for our respective sources of confidence, but each found that confidence played a significant role in our leadership identity.

Some of the data suggests that a personal growth spiral influenced the development of confidence. For example, conquering a challenge provided more confidence in our ability to meet the next challenge. To Samantha this meant facing the challenge of umpiring in a boy's baseball league. Samantha's confidence spiral centered on selecting and meeting challenges in what were traditionally "non-girl" activities, and this in turn fostered her nascent leadership identity.

The spiral was different for Michelle, who was voted to be the "mayor for a day" in middle school. She led a meeting in her local town hall and put forth an agenda for the "town council" to discuss. This role positioned her as a perceived leader, created a core of confidence, and allowed her to ease into other leader experiences, including several years as class president. Michelle's confidence spiral centered on selecting and meeting challenges relating to leading others, which in turn developed her leadership abilities. Her eighth grade teacher's suggestion that she run for mayor for a day "was a real boost to [her] confidence and sense of self."

Nicole's leadership journey began by being elected to office, which initiated her confidence spiral. She was elected to the office of 4-H Reporter in the fourth grade, which gave her unquestionable confidence that showed its greatest strength early in girlhood as she remembers:

> Holding this office was more than a passing notion for me and, I knew that my role was important and that my skills and talents were valued and appreciated. I distinctly had a confidence that resounded in me. I felt with unapologetic pride that no one could fulfill this role in a greater capacity than I and what I brought to the table was sheer brilliance!

In contrast, Linda's journey to building confidence that supported her leadership development began while attending a two-week summer camp for gifted and talented children each summer, beginning in fifth grade:

> I got to be with a group of kids and in an environment where I could really just be myself. It was cool being smart and everyone had a passion for learning—people weren't afraid to share their talents. This was such an important experience for my own sense of self-esteem, self-worth, and identity. The camp was what I looked forward to every year.

Linda's camp experiences helped her "develop that stronger sense of self," which gave her the confidence to step up into taking on more leadership experiences and getting involved more in middle and high school.

The interrelatedness of the self and context through our lived experiences emerged as we made sense of our early girlhood experiences that developed our leadership identities. Through our continued and subsequent analysis of confidence, we also determined that confidence was an evolving part of our leadership identities across our lifespans. While some indicated that confidence was linked to certain time frames of life, others felt confidence was linked to external life factors and interactions with others. For Abigail, her early leadership experiences "meant showing up, standing in front of people, leading meetings, participating in events, and doing the work. Those early experiences gave me confidence and a knowledge base to take in to future roles." As Nicole further reflected on her days as a 4-H Reporter, she recounted:

Moments of unabashed brilliance and confidence were perhaps some of the most authentic of my life; long before the tainted years of teenage and early adulthood, long before I understood the concept of self-doubt and weighed others' opinions of my talents and skills as more valuable than my own. These vestiges of my early identity as a leader have been enough to sustain me over the years, but now as I raise my own fierce and precious daughters I contemplate how to instill in them an unwavering confidence—confidence that is not shaken when a teacher questions their intelligence or a beloved friend betrays their trust.

Although Zoe had a long list of early leadership experiences with various organizations, including grade school flag patrol, National Honor Society, and YMCA counselor, confidence was not a word that she used in describing her leadership experiences. She reflected on the early years as feeling like she only "acted the part of leader;...most of the time, I just wanted to be liked. Just wanted to be noticed, and taken account of. Just wanted to be important and meaningful." Other life events, such as a change in family dynamic with the death of her mother early in life and a lack of parental support when she headed off to college, presented challenges to her claiming the identity of a leader. She had early validation from church and Girl Scout activities but explained "that it's taken me until only recently to begin to wear the label 'leader' comfortably. I'm 55, and I'm sad it's taken so long."

In making sense of our girlhood experiences, personal confidence to claim the identity of a leader was shaped by internal drive, strength, resistance to the status quo, brilliance, eagerness, self-esteem, and positive self-worth. Our findings suggest that taking on more and more leader-like behavior-building activities that appealed to us as girls reinforced our leadership identity development. Our early leadership experiences produced varying levels of confidence, which shaped our fledgling identities as leaders in both positive and negative ways. Only through the use of CAE and WWK were we able to construct knowledge as mature women to understand the impact these experiences had on our leadership identity development (Belenky et al., 1997; Chang et al., 2013).

Advancing Theory

Examining our research through the lens of Komives, Longerbeam, Owen, Mainella, and Osteen's (2006) LID model, we identified parallels that substantiated our findings and differences that create a deeper understanding of the role of confidence in leadership identity development for women. First, as previously mentioned, the work of Komives et al. (2006) references confidence as an integral aspect of leadership identity in their work with college students of all genders. Reflecting their work, our findings supported confidence as integral to developing young girls' identity as a leader. As a point of differentiation between the two models, our research revealed a narrative of specific leadership experiences and opportunities in early childhood that contributed to confidence building, which proved foundational in leadership identity development. This expands the perspective of the LID model, which emphasized early development of viewing leadership as something external to oneself and demonstrated by prominent adults in their lives, reflecting dependence (Komives et al., 2006). Our research suggested that pivotal early childhood experiences helped some of us more readily begin to see ourselves as leaders, rather than solely seeing leadership as external to oneself.

The LID model describes stages through which individuals pass as they come to recognize themselves as leaders, particularly for a college student population, which included participants' reflections on their college experiences as well as some focus on their earlier childhood experiences. Our research does this similarly, though we narrowed the focus of our reflections for the purpose of our study to solely focus on our early childhood experiences; further, we engaged in this reflection at a later point in our life; it is possible that our reflections on our leadership identity would have been different while in college. Through this reflection, our data suggests that confidence building can and does begin at an earlier age than college for girls who experience leadership opportunities. Further, some girls who have exposure to leadership experiences in adolescence may progress through these stages earlier in the lifecycle than suggested by the LID model (Komives et al., 2006). As previously mentioned, our findings included leader experiences occurring as early as fourth grade.

The Domain of Relationships, the Concept of Advocate

Descriptive Narrative

In the domain of relationships, advocates emerged as a top influence in leadership identity development, and our findings suggest these could include parents, siblings and extended relatives, and teachers. We recognized early in our experiences the value of those who uplifted us, and as adults the memories and stories continue to resonate within us as powerful affirmations of value, competence, and self worth. Familial relationships as well as those outside of the family were significant in our willingness and ability to take on challenges that would further develop us as leaders. These relationships brought added value to our ability to navigate the daunting path that we traversed as we developed our leadership identity.

Examples of parental role models were present as Samantha offered a vivid account of her mother, one of her first leadership role models, scaling a big oak tree at a family picnic to retrieve a valuable, motorized toy plane from its heights:

> Of all the strong men watching in the field that day, none of them made a move to retrieve it. It was my mom who took action—without hesitation—to reclaim the toy. That day, she showed me that as a woman, you can do whatever you put your mind to—it didn't take a man to do the difficult, or the physical, or the risky. Nope, women can do all that—and more. It was about being a problem solver, being assertive, leading with strength and capacity; . . . it was about being courageous. . . . My mom was a bit of a rock star in this way. She was (is) scrappy, an adventurer, a woman not to be sat down. She taught me the power of curiosity through what I observed about how she lived her life.

Similarly, Abigail recalled being involved in multiple organizations during her early years and being "supported by my parents but specifically by my mom as she was an assistant adult leader in both organizations. . . . She believed in the value of the experience and the role participation played in the development of children."

Findings indicate that family relationships were not always positively supportive of the young girls. Sometimes change in family dynamics placed great responsibility on young family members. Sometimes the responsibility came from a change in the family dynamic due to divorce or death of a parent. For instance, as previously mentioned, Zoe experienced the death of her mother at five years of age. Even though Zoe came to identify herself as an authentic leader later in life, she recalled feelings around her leadership identity and how others perceived her were pivotal to developing her internal dialogue about her role as a leader:

> From an early age, . . . I had the identity given to me by my family as the fixer and the problem solver. So in a way, I was a leader in my family unit. . . . Certainly [parent figure] and my siblings always would turn to me with problems and I was the fixer. . . . I really relished that role and I was good at it. It's probably not appropriate today for a [parent figure] to turn to her teenage daughter or junior high daughter with problems. But that was the only time that I would feel like I was there. If someone had a problem, they would come to me. I would always listen and help them through it.

Having relationships with supportive individuals outside of the family and with those who served in the advocate role were also meaningful in girlhood. Samantha reported, "An elementary school teacher approached me and said, 'I've selected you to be one of the directors of our school's Olympic Day.' She talked about qualities she recognized in me that would help me do a strong job for the school and students." Similarly, Michelle shared that her social studies teacher reached out to her with words of encouragement and "often initiated conversations with me and showed an interest in me as a person.... I was thrilled to be recognized by him."

Even though Michelle had generally strong support from her peers, family, and community, a lack of support from her father her senior year in high school changed her leadership identity development trajectory:

> I ran unopposed for high school class president in the following three years and won "most likely to succeed" as a high school senior. This is the happy part of my leadership story. The ambivalence and self-doubt began at the end of my high school experience. It was prompted by my father questioning why I was running again to be class president and making note of the fact that a girl had never been a class president before.

In making sense of the role of relationships in leadership identity development of women, we discovered that advocates played an importantly supportive role in the lives of the women in this study. Embedded relationships with trusted advocates such as family members and teachers were central to our leadership experiences. Family relationships also provided us with the opportunity to practice leadership with siblings, as being the eldest provided us with a sense of responsibility and duty for their care and development. Elders uplifted us by inviting and offering engaging opportunities and living in ways that curiously caught our attention. In the absence of the support, the findings show that leadership identity development trajectories can change or be delayed, as in the case of Michelle.

Advancing Theory

In the relationships domain, parallels again are present with the LID model, further validating that model. Adults in our lives made us feel special, sponsored us in challenges and opportunities, and served as role models, which parallels findings from Komives et al.'s (2006) research. Reflecting on those early experiences as examples of received knowledge (Belenky et al., 1997), we were able to make the connections from positive experiences with advocates, which gave further definition to the development of our leadership identity. The negative experiences we encountered sometimes derailed or postponed our development as leaders. The CAE (Chang et al., 2013) process provided opportunity to examine the relationships and understand their influence on how we came to see ourselves as leaders.

The LID research states that recognition and endorsement by others is significant in progressing to the leadership identity stage of Awareness (Komives et al., 2006). Our findings reflect this aspect of the LID model; positive advocates played significant roles in encouraging the development of our leadership identities. Our work extends the LID model by suggesting that young girls also adopt what they observe in the lived experiences of others as they develop their leadership identities. Some of the researchers (i.e., Linda and Nicole) actually took action based on observation and implemented the actions of others, demonstrating social learning (Bandura, 1977) combined with two forms of WWK: received knowledge and the early part of subjective knowledge. Findings suggest that received knowledge catalyzed the development of the *inner voice* (Belenky et. al., 1997), an early manifestation of subjective knowledge as the quest for self. Samantha's experience with her mom, for example, seemed to initiate a self-definition of herself—an inner voice she started to listen to as she matured. Implications of these connections will be detailed further in the conclusion of this chapter. These experiences illustrate a deeper understanding of how advocates influence leadership identity development. Our research suggests advocates not only open doors, but they can help girls start to decide which doors they want to open. We believe this finding can enhance the conceptual clarity of related LID model concept(s).

The Domain of Context, the Concept of Venue for Leadership Practice

Descriptive Narrative

Throughout the research process, it became evident that the larger environment and context in which we found ourselves, or the venue, had an impact on our leadership identity development. Context played a role in how we navigated our environments and about how the perceptions that existed about us in these environments affected how we saw ourselves as leaders. The contexts on which we found our most significant influencers of identity development centered were the contexts of *family* and *community*.

Within the two realms, we took on varied and differentiated roles over time that contributed to our leadership identity development. Some of these roles seemed to be put on us, while others were self-created. The influence of context on our individual roles illustrates the complexity of the data, and it posed one of our analytical challenges. While self, relationships, and context emerged as our three domains, the three domains sometimes interacted and influenced each other as we constructed our knowledge (Belenky et al., 1997). Context is one of the domains that seems to matter all the time. However, for this analysis, we are artificially separating context from the self and relationship domains to more deeply explore how each contributed to our leadership identity development.

An example of the salience and power of context is Michelle's experience of being mayor for the day:

> We got to sit in the town hall and conduct a meeting and put forward our agenda.... This was fun, and I felt confident and had a good time. I don't

remember feeling scared or self-conscious at all sitting in the town court in the center chair running this town hall meeting before all these adults and our local newspaper reporter. It is amazing for me to remember that. This was my younger, freer self.

The environment provided a safe, supportive, and inviting context for Michelle to practice leadership. The relationship domain was also activated for this encounter as her mother supported the junior high civic project and taught her a sense of service for the great good; consequently, family emerged as key to our emergent leadership identity within the domain of context.

The context of family also was significant for many of us in regard to the roles we played in our family units and how those roles contributed to leadership identity development. Those of us who were firstborn children in our families assumed roles of responsibility to serve as mentors for younger siblings. Linda created her role as a leader in her family. When she reflected on how she interacted with and led her brother, she stated, "[I would] sit my brother down every day after I got home from school and teach him everything I learned in class that day—and he wasn't allowed to get up until he had learned it all!" Linda relished this role and drew strength and a sense of responsibility from it, feeling that she played an important role in her family by helping her brother. Likewise, the role of teacher/leader was reflected in Nicole's story, who also shared "vivid memories of my patient little brother sitting amongst the stuffed animals that I lined up in front of the 40-inch chalkboard that was a treasured Christmas gift from my parents as I gave my latest lecture."

Zoe likewise described leadership at quite a young age but in a less than supportive family context: "I felt I needed to protect my younger sisters from what I had experienced [sexual abuse], and I remember always being around to ensure they weren't alone with [name removed], especially when he was babysitting. I was fierce in my determination on the inside, but I acted 'normal' on the outside." Later, she recalled being the "fixer" in the family and in her thirties finally and officially announced her resignation from that role. Zoe drew strength and seemed to develop an internal pillar of righteousness from her early experiences that carries forward through today.

The context of community also contributed to our leadership identity development. Abigail noted her engagement in the community that helped her grow as a leader; she identified that 4-H "provided structure and the opportunity to practice public speaking, develop organizational skills and establish relationships with others outside my immediate circle of influence." Similarly, Nicole recalls her membership in 4-H leading to an elected leadership role as a reporter:

It was in those moments that I came to identify myself as a leader. I thrived on the responsibility of crafting my articles for the monthly newsletter. I found it energizing to interview and speak with others, recounting their stories from my reporter's perspective. The exhilaration of having an article written, edited and ready for publication thrilled me to the core.

The context domain provided us with the ability to practice leadership in different venues. These contexts provided a leadership laboratory of sorts where access to experiences and leader-like skill building occurred. Even though we made a distinction between the contexts of family and community, we developed a sense of responsibility and found pride and excitement in our roles and experiences across contexts. This analysis demonstrated the intersection of domains of our model.

Advancing Theory

Our research expands the notion of context present in Komives et al.'s (2006) model. The LID research suggests context as an important consideration in one's leadership identity development, with a particular emphasis on group experiences and learning from consistent membership in groups (Komives et al., 2006). The focus of these group experiences in the LID research were more traditional student leadership contexts, such as student organizations.

Our research expands the concept of context to include earlier childhood contexts that played a role in leadership identity development; further, the context in our research expanded beyond the setting of student groups or organizations. The contexts of family and community as well as engaging in leadership behaviors that had both positive and negative contexts in "everyday life" emerged as salient in our research. The connections and experiences we had in these contexts enriched our leadership identity development. More about the importance of this finding, and others, is offered below.

CONCLUSIONS AND IMPLICATIONS

It is clear that who we become as leaders is substantially and continually shaped by our impressions and experiences in girlhood and by our reflections on these experiences as adults. Our research builds on the Komives et al. (2005, 2006) LID model by examining more deeply and differently an earlier part of the life cycle through CAE methods and WWK epistemology. Our study supports as well as suggests modifications to elements of the LID model.

Before expanding on the implications in detail, it is important to note that our study differs from the LID study in three ways: First, our study focused on adult professional women who examined their early childhood, whereas the LID study focused on college-aged students who reflected on their experiences up until college, which in some cases included their early childhood experiences. Second, our study focused on girls/women, whereas the LID study included women and men and did not specifically focus on gender. Third and finally, the LID study participants were selected because they were recognized as relational leaders. Our study did not have selection criteria based on how they demonstrated leadership; indeed, one of our study participants shared, "I wouldn't have been in the LID sample because no one recognized me as a leader at that time in my life, including myself." Because of these important differences, our findings should be framed as supplemental to the LID and as avenues for future exploration.

Through examining early girlhood experiences and influences to one's leadership identity development, the findings of our current study offer implications for future research on leadership identity development and the LID model on two fronts. First, the findings suggest new considerations to the stages and sequencing as presented in the LID. Second, the findings both confirm and dis-confirm some of the key concepts, experiences, relationships, and contexts present within the LID stages.

Our current study has implications for the *stages* of leadership identity development as represented in the LID model. The LID model includes a focus on early childhood experiences within the early two stages of the model conceptually titled *Awareness* and *Exploration/ Engagement*. These stages are characterized by viewing leadership as involving dependence on others, and some of our data clearly reflects these stages. However, we found that in addition to these two stages, some of us were also experiencing aspects of the third stage, conceptually titled *Leader Identified* in the LID model. This stage of the model is characterized both by dependence and independence in terms of relationships with others. Interestingly, though, our research suggests that although some of our perceptions of leadership focused specifically on our leadership positions and roles (which many of us relished), in early childhood our views of these roles were focused on relationships with others as opposed to top-down and hierarchical perspectives. The LID findings suggested that "all students believed in leader-centric, positional, and often hierarchical views of leadership" (Komives et al., 2006, p. 408) at the beginning of stage three. Our research suggests that leadership was experienced as embedded within a relational network rather than a hierarchical network, emphasizing relationships with others moreso than authority. Further, the leadership experienced was more about the other or the group or one's growth and opportunity with the role rather than on power.

Our findings in relation to the different LID stages suggest that a more developed sense of leadership identity can be experienced earlier on in girlhood than the LID model may suggest, particularly when individuals are exposed to leadership opportunities. Our data suggest that individuals can move in and out of these three stages of the model in early childhood and that various relationships and contexts played a role in the stages in which we may have been operating.

These findings suggest that the stages may not be as linear as the LID model might suggest, while at the same time our study affirms the predicted cyclical nature of leadership identity development. Komives et al. (2006) clearly highlighted the recursive nature of the stages in their model:

> The LID model is stage-based and entails students progressing through one stage before beginning the next.... Stages are linear, but they are also cyclical. Even as development through the stages occurs, development proceeds in a circular model. A helix model of development allows for stages to be repeatedly experienced, and each return is experienced with a deeper and more complex understanding and performing of the stage. (pp. 404–405)

Future research could explore the early stages of the LID to generate a more comprehensive understanding of the leadership experiences in childhood; this could be explored among both women and men. In addition, the ways that we (researchers) are making meaning about the stages may be different from those of the researchers who created the LID, which may be an interesting avenue for future exploration. We suggest that future research should be conducted from multiple paradigms. For example, complexity methods could possibly be used to tease out the cyclical, dynamic, and seemingly chaotic patterns of leadership identity development. Alternatively, extensive research using narrative or CAE methods could probe more deeply into the connections between seemingly disparate leadership identity development moments.

In addition to the stages/sequencing finding, our study affirms some of the key concepts present within the LID stages, and it suggests modifications to these concepts. Our study affirms the importance of key concepts, relationships, and contexts to one's leadership development that was suggested by the LID research, including: confidence (self), adults to encourage and advocate (relationships), and group experiences (relationships, context). New insights for modification to the LID model also emerged in our research with particular focus on context.

The LID research, perhaps because it focused on college-aged students, resulted in the salient role that high school and college contexts played as vehicles to leadership identity development; there were fewer examples of contexts outside of school and college settings. Our study suggests that context is extremely important when examining early childhood experiences, and there were a range of different contexts present in each of our childhoods. The presence of affirming and supportive contexts was very important and was present within families, schools, school groups, community organizations, and camps. Additionally, the data suggested that although positional roles were important, as was also suggested by LID, early opportunities for leadership identity development existed outside of formal leadership roles and organized groups; opportunities were present very early on and were all around "in everyday life," such as with family or in environments that supported growth, development, and confidence (i.e., camp, church, and 4-H).

Our study also generated findings unrelated to the LID. Our experience as co-researchers suggests that we can continue to learn and re-learn from our childhood experiences into adulthood through critical reflection, genuine dialogue, and deep listening. These findings are in alignment with those in Chapter 3 of this book, where both study teams found interesting connections between collaborative autoethnography and leadership development. Specifically, the remembering and re-telling of earlier experiences compelled us to reconsider the meaning driving our earlier interpretations. We found that experiences of the past continued to inform us even today of new ways to understand historical influences on our evolving leadership identity.

The scholarly literature supports these experiential findings. Retrospective sense-making (Weick et al., 2005) and reflection have been suggested as powerful leadership learning opportunities (Boyce, Zaccaro, & Wisecarver, 2010) that are needed for the ambiguous and constantly changing world of work. However, there remain opportunities for continued research to understand how reflection supports leadership identity development (Nesbit, 2012). For example, our team consists of women in different life stages, from mid to late adulthood. Some of us are reflecting on experiences that happened 20 years ago; for others the span is 50 years. We believe there may be a difference in how the past is understood based on the accumulation of experience. Future research could explore how early childhood leadership identity development experiences are interpreted at different stages of adulthood. Findings from this type of research could possibly contribute to a more focused and targeted leadership identity development intervention because the ways we make sense of past experiences seem to vary across time.

Finally, applying the WWK perspective throughout the methodology offered a new way to combine intellect and body, mind and experience. Holding ourselves as *passionate knowers* as well as researchers enriched the research process to produce deeper emergence in learning, reflecting, and understanding. Through our reflections and dialogue, we remembered times when we felt silenced and when we felt a connected knowing. The ways of knowing (Belenky et al. 1997) we found in our data included being told by others (e.g., *received knowledge* in WWK), listening to our inner voice (e.g., *subjective knowledge*), and using reason (e.g., *procedural knowledge*).

As co-researchers, we experienced *constructed knowledge* in this journey first when we realized the limits of traditional theory building methods and made the decision to honor our own experiences as women as much as the scholarly literature. While we did not know it at the time, when we took this step we initiated an important journey. Constructed knowledge assumes that knowing is intimately connected to being; there is no separation between the knower (e.g., researcher) and the known (e.g., leadership identity development). When we threw out the traditional theory building method, we started a process suggested by Belenky et al. (1997), "to learn to speak in a unique and authentic voice, women must 'jump outside' the frames and systems authorities provide and create their own frame" (p. 134). We took the jump outside of normal science to produce this work, which has had profound impact on each member of our team.

As this study continues beyond this writing, we plan to continue working together and aspire to contribute an experientially generated theory across the lifespan that can inform and give rise to enriched, mindful women's leadership identity construction. Ibarra (2003) suggests that identity changes in practice as we do new things, engage with new people, and reinterpret our stories through emerging possibilities. By engaging in reflective practices, we continue to explore the value and relevance of these new actions and practices and give space and place to them as our new leadership identity emerges. The CAE method and WWK epistemology honors the diverse experiences of the authors, allowing for mindful, self-other learning (Chang et al., 2013). We will continue to understand how these experiences and practices contribute to our leadership identity formation over time and how together they can inform and illuminate the construction of women's leadership identity.

AUTHOR NOTE

All authors contributed equally to this chapter.

REFERENCES

Asilomar Declaration and Call to Action on Women and Leadership. (2015). *Report on the International Leadership Association Women and Leadership Affinity Group.* http://www.ila-net.org/Communities/AG/Asilomar_Declaration2015.pdf

Bandura, A. (1977). *Social learning theory.* Englewood, NJ: Prentice Hall.

Belenky, M. F., Clinchy, B. M., Goldberger, N. R., & Tarule, J. M. (1997). *Women's ways of knowing: The development of self, voice, and mind* (10th anniversary ed.). New York, NY: Basic Books.

Boyatzis, R. E. (1998). *Transforming qualitative information: Thematic analysis and code development.* Thousand Oaks, CA: Sage.

Boyce, L. A., Zaccaro, S. J., & Wisecarver, M. Z. (2010). Propensity for self-development of leadership attributes: Understanding, predicting, and supporting performance of leader self-development. *The Leadership Quarterly, 21*(1), 159–178.

Byron, K., & Thatcher, S. M. (2016). Editors' comments: "What I know now that I wish I knew then"—Teaching theory and theory building. *Academy of Management Review, 41*(1), 1–8. doi:10.5465/amr.2015.0094

Chang, H., Longman, K. A., & Franco, M. A. (2014). Leadership development through mentoring in higher education: A collaborative autoethnography of leaders of color. *Mentoring & Tutoring: Partnership in Learning, 22*(4), 373–389. doi:1080/13611267.2014.945734.

Chang, H., Ngunjiri, F. W., & Hernandez, K. C. (2013). *Collaborative autoethnography.* Walnut Creek, CA: Left Coast.

Creswell, J. W. (2014). *Research design: Qualitative, quantitative, and mixed methods approaches* (4th ed.). Thousand Oaks, CA: Sage.

Eagly, A. H., & Carli, L. L. (2007). *Through the labyrinth: The truth about how women become leaders.* Boston, MA: Harvard Business School.

Fletcher, J. K. (2001). *Disappearing acts: Gender, power and relational practice at work.* Cambridge, MA: MIT.

Gherardi, S. (1995). *Gender, symbolism and organizational cultures.* Thousand Oaks, CA: Sage.

Gilligan, C. (1982). *In a different voice: Psychological theory and women's development.* Cambridge, MA: Harvard University.

Gioia, D. A. & Pitre, E. (1990). Multiparadigm perspectives on theory building. *Academy of Management Review, 15*(4), 584–602. doi: 10.5465/AMR.1990.4310758

Gross, N. (2014). Afterward. In R. Swedberg (Ed.), *Theorizing in social science: The context of discovery* (pp. 205–215). Stanford, CA: Stanford University.

Ibarra, H. (2003). *Working identity: Unconventional strategies for reinventing your career.* Boston, MA: Harvard Business School.

Kellerman, B., & Rhode, D. L. (Eds.). (2007). *Women and leadership: The state of play and strategies for change.* San Francisco, CA: Jossey-Bass.

Komives, S. R., Longerbeam, S. D., Owen, J. E., Mainella, F. C., & Osteen, L. (2006). A leadership identity development model: Applications from grounded theory. *Journal of College Student Development, 47*(4), 401–418.

Komives, S. R., Lucas, N., & McMahon, T. R. (2007). *Exploring leadership: For college students who want to make a difference* (2nd ed.). San Francisco, CA: Jossey-Bass

Komives, S. R., Owen, J. E., Longerbeam, S. D., Mainella, F. C., & Osteen, L. (2005). Developing a leadership identity: A grounded theory. *Journal of College Student Development, 46*(6), 593–611.

Lerner, G. (1993). *The creation of feminist consciousness: From the Middle Ages to eighteen-seventy.* Oxford, England: Oxford University.

Lynham, S. A. (2002). The general method of theory-building research in applied disciplines. *Advances in Developing Human Resources, 4*(3), 221–241.

Murphy, S. E., & Johnson, S. K. (2011). The benefits of a long-lens approach to leader development: Understanding the seeds of leadership. *The Leadership Quarterly, 22*(3), 459–470. doi:10.1016/j.leaqua.2011.04.004

Nesbit, P.L. (2012). The role of self-reflection, emotional management of feedback, and self-regulation processes in self-directed leadership development. *Human Resource Development Review, 11*(2), 203–226,

Renn, K. A., & Bilodeau, B. L. (2005). Leadership identity development among lesbian, gay, bisexual, and transgender student leaders. *NASPA Journal, 42*(3), 342–367.

Schutz, W. C. (1967). *Joy: Expanding human awareness.* New York, NY: Grove.

Storberg-Walker, J., & Haber-Curran, P. (2017). Theorizing women's leadership as praxis: Creating new knowledge for social change. In J. Storberg-Walker & P. Haber-Curran (Eds.), *Theorizing women and leadership: New insights and contributions from multiple perspectives* (pp. 1–16). Charlotte, NC: Information Age.

Torraco, R. J. (2005). Writing integrative literature reviews: Guidelines and examples. *Human Resource Development Review, 4*(3), 356–367. doi:10.1177/1534484305278283

Van de Ven, A. H., & Poole, M. S. (2004). *Handbook of organizational change and innovation.* Oxford, England: Oxford University.

Wagner, W. (2011). *Examining developmental stages of leadership for college students: A validation study of the leadership identity development model.* (Unpublished doctoral dissertation). University of Maryland, College Park, MD.

Walker, T. L., & Taylor, C. M. (2015). Collaborative autoethnography: The method is the message. In C. White, (Ed.), *Critical qualitative research in social education* (pp. 53–69). Charlotte, NC: Information Age.

Weick, K. E., Sutcliffe, K. M., & Obstfeld, D. (2005). Organizing and the process of sensemaking. *Organization science, 16*(4), 409–421.

CHAPTER 16

AFRICAN-AMERICAN WOMEN ADMINISTRATORS IN HIGHER EDUCATION

Adapting the Centered Leadership Model to Reflect African-American Leadership Experiences

Marcelle C. Holmes
University of California, Irvine

Denise Hayes
Claremont University Consortium

The issue of leadership development for African-American women administrators in higher education is worthy of examination (Miles, 2012; Nealy, 2008). African-American women are currently underrepresented at the top echelons of the academy (Miles, 2012), therefore, educating and motivating women with leadership potential to strive for senior positions remains a high priority. When it comes to identifying a leadership model for

Theorizing Women and Leadership, pages 291–311
Copyright © 2017 by Information Age Publishing
All rights of reproduction in any form reserved.

African-American women administrators, we believe one model has potential: The Centered Leadership Model (CLM). As African-American women administrators ourselves, many aspects of this model resonated with our personal experiences, and we wanted to explore how well, or to what degree, this leadership model would resonate with others.

The CLM was developed over six years at McKinsey and Company with Joanna Barsh as the principal researcher. The evolution of this model is documented from 2008 through 2014 in a variety of publications (Barsh, Cranston, & Craske, 2008; Barsh, Cranston, & Lewis, 2011; Barsh & Lavoie, 2014). In this chapter we explore, through an empirical study, how the CLM may be useful for developing and unleashing the leadership potential of African-American women administrators. Our study found that certain elements of the model did not represent specific experiences relating to race, and we offer suggestions for modifying the model to better represent African-American women's experiences.

The CLM includes five dimensions relevant to leadership development that, when mastered, allow leaders to "extend [the] range of choices and actions" (Barsh & Lavoie, 2014, p. 7) for their leadership experiences. The model contains the concepts of *meaning, framing, engaging, connecting,* and *energizing.* Part of what makes the model interesting to us as African-American senior administrators is the way in which it highlights the importance of having broad social networks, the role of professional risk taking, and the important role of self-promotion. Some of these concepts are often not associated with the behaviors of women professionals (Barsh & Lavoie, 2014). However, because we have few role models, many other aspects of this theoretical leadership model resonated with our personal experiences and philosophies. We were curious to explore whether the components of this model could likewise be meaningful to other African-American women administrators in higher education and, by extension, help us develop more significant leadership development opportunities for others.

The creation of the CLM, as described by Barsh et al. (2008), was triggered by an exploration of remarkable leaders. Barsh's understanding of positivity, energy, and success eventually led to a research- and evidence-based leadership model consisting of five dimensions, a survey testing the model taken by approximately 2,000 global business leaders, and results of the survey clearly indicating a positive correlation between the five dimensions and leaders who "reported a high level of effectiveness, a high level of satisfaction at work and at home, and a high level of preparedness for the current challenging environment" (Barsh & Lavoie, 2014, p. 4). We believed the model could be helpful to our exploratory qualitative research, in part because we were challenged to find a significant amount of leadership research in the scholarly press focused on African-American women administrators in higher education.

In this chapter, we review existing literature, provide readers with a short explanation of our motivation for conducting this exploratory study, describe the CLM and explain its relevance to the issues, describe our exploratory study, and share the findings of our study based on the model. We discuss the findings in terms of how the CLM allows for exploration of key issues specific to African-American women. The chapter concludes with recommendations for the CLM to expand and integrate cultural aspects of leadership expressed and experienced by the African-American women in our study.

CONTEXT AND REVIEW OF LITERATURE

Federal legislation in the 1960s attempted to address racial and gender inequality across professional occupations and educational opportunities. Laws—such as Title VII, The Equal Pay Act, Title IX, and The Equal Opportunities Amendment—and policies related to Affirmative Action were enacted to ensure women and minorities were fairly considered for employment and educational opportunities. Although laws have sought to level the playing field, research findings and statistics described below reflect ongoing inequities for African-American women administrators in higher education.

Research demonstrates that African-American women are underrepresented in leadership positions, earn less than peers in comparable positions, and face unique barriers (Miles, 2012). Miles (2012) found that African-American women were often in the lower administrative ranks, earned significantly less, and were less likely to hold senior level student affairs positions despite being similarly qualified compared to people of other genders and races. In terms of barriers, Harvard (1986) conducted qualitative research on successful African-American women administrators and found three major barriers to women seeking administrative positions: sex-role stereotypes, organizational barriers, and women internalizing traditional female behaviors.

Nealy (2008) references an American Council on Education (ACE) report indicating that although the number of women college presidents has increased in the last 14 years, the growth in the share of minority presidents has been slower. Additionally, between 1986 and 2012, the percentage of women college presidents more than doubled from 9.5% to 26%, respectively (http://www.acenet.edu/the-presidency/columns-and-features/Pages/The-American-College-President-Study.aspx), the percentage of minority presidents increased from 8.1% to 12.6% during the same time, and the percentage of African-American women presidents increased from 5% to

5.9% (Nealy, 2008). Although the overall increases are noteworthy, clearly African-American female presidents remain behind in advancement.

Beyond the numbers, however, there is a sustained body of research demonstrating that the quality of the experience for African-American women working in higher education is of concern. Singh, Robinson, and Williams-Green (1995) noted that African-American women working at predominately White institutions experienced lower satisfaction with their professional lives, a greater sense of isolation on campus, and more negative treatment by colleagues compared to male participants. Some researchers identify racism, sexism, isolation, loneliness, and lack of trust as barriers that interfere with African-American women's full participation in higher education institutions (Edwards & Camblin, 1998; Moses, 1989; Sandler & Hall, 1991). Further, in a case study by Lloyd-Jones (2009) highlighting an African-American woman in a senior administrative role in higher education, the participant reported that despite believing she had achieved her level of professional success because of her education and hard work, she did "not see herself being afforded the luxury of making an error" (p. 612) due to the increased scrutiny she received because of her gender and race. Further, she noted that she felt underprepared for the level of negative attention attributed to her Blackness. She also noted that some subordinates implied they could never accept a Black person as their supervisor. Lloyd-Jones (2009) suggested that educating women about the dilemmas posed by their intersectionality as African Americans and as women is important for their career advancement.

This brief overview of research suggests that African-American women have intersecting identities that appear to affect their job satisfaction and experiences. We believe that this research, combined with our experiences of organizational barriers and the lack of representation in upper levels of administration, makes this population worthy of study. We are driven to understand how to better prepare African-American women for the rigors of these high-status positions. We want to identify what wisdom and skills African-American women administrators could share with each other as institutions strive to increase diversity in administrative ranks. And, we want to contribute to the theoretical development of the CLM. Our motives and goals are important to this research and are described in some detail in the next section.

OUR POSITIONALITY
AND PERSONAL CONNECTION TO THE CLM

To align with accepted research practice, it is important to share our experiences and positions in addition to why we were interested in the CLM. As African-American senior administrators in higher education, we noted both the lack of representation of African-American women in the senior ranks and the influence of our intersecting identities (female and African American) on our own experiences of professional triumphs and struggles. The CLM was of interest to us because of its elegance and applicability to women in leadership roles. We were drawn to the model's emphasis on self-care, risk taking, and making meaningful networking connections. In our roles we have worked hard to find the kind of work–life balance that would allow us to thrive. This model spoke to us as an approachable way to integrate self-care into our leadership styles and as a way to increase professional and personal satisfaction as leaders. Due to our experiences, we were curious to determine whether Barsh et al.'s (2011) findings were also transferable to African-American women and to the higher education context.

We had a variety of thoughts about the applicability of the CLM to women such as ourselves. We wondered if female African-American higher education leaders would connect with these concepts. Would they talk about connecting and mention cross-cultural difficulties with communication, a phenomenon that we did not find sufficiently covered in the CLM literature? How might they discuss their coping styles, and might there be any ways of energizing that resonated more with African-American women? Additionally, might there be any perceived cultural impediments to achieving in their career fields, particularly if they worked at predominately White institutions? What would they say about race and gender and how those dual, intersecting identities have affected their careers? We sought to introduce the model to African-American female administrators in higher education and get their thoughts about their connection to the model.

This chapter presents our efforts at this work, and our hope is that the findings offer new ways to understand African-American women leaders in higher education and the ideas in the CLM. We also hope that the chapter provides a new way to understand how to adapt a leadership model from one context to another. We believe context is critically important in understanding leadership, and we seek to discover new ways to successfully translate models or frameworks for improving the leadership landscape of African-American women.

DESCRIPTION OF THE CENTERED LEADERSHIP MODEL

The CLM is based on the research of Joanna Barsh and colleagues (2008, 2011, 2014), who have published their observations on the qualities that seem to coalesce to produce exceptional women leaders. The research suggested exceptional women leaders exuded positive energy, were eager to connect, and bounced back from failures (Barsh & Lavoie, 2014). The studies generating the model collected data through qualitative (interviewing) and quantitative (surveying) methods. The research participants were successful business leaders (a large majority of whom were women), and the key themes that emerged led to the creation of the CLM. Survey findings suggest that the five dimensions appear to work more effectively together and, while practicing one dimension may produce small leadership improvements, that practicing all five produces outstanding leadership success (Barsh & Lavoie, 2014). The five dimensions "build on and reinforce one another, bringing... the inspiration, motivation, and energy to continue" (Barsh & Lavoie, 2014, p. 5) for women leaders. We provide a brief description of the five dimensions below; readers who are interested in more detail are referred to the original texts by Barsh and colleagues (2008, 2011, 2014). Following these brief descriptions, the next section connects each dimension to the research evidence supporting their inclusion in the model.

- *Meaning:* This dimension is the anchor of the model, and it suggests that the core of women's leadership is to know what really matters and to know one's own purpose, mission, and vision. Meaning inspires leaders, guides careers, sustains optimism, and generates gains in previously unidentified skills.
- *Framing:* This dimension highlights the importance of self-awareness and self-reflection to help women leaders notice their emotional and psychological reactions to interactions, environments, and circumstances. Women leaders must "avoid downward spirals, in order to move ahead, adapt, and implement solutions" (p. 10). Framing and reframing are perspectives that allow individuals to choose how to react, process, and respond to others.
- *Connecting:* This dimension describes the value of connections at work and in the service of one's career. Connecting enables leaders to derive meaningful community from their networks. For women leaders, being linked with strong professional networks, sponsors, and supportive mentors often results in better opportunities, more promotions, and higher pay.
- *Engaging:* This dimension addresses women who take ownership of situations, set goals and systems for self-improvement, and choose to take risks. Engaging "enables our pursuit of purpose, helps us see more opportunity, draws others to us, and... releases positive energy" (p. 7).
- *Energizing:* This dimension is both about managing energy reserves and incorporating self-care into daily work and home routines. Energized women leaders "build on strengths, pause and reframe in challenging moments, attract and mobilize others, accept risks, and take action" (p. 7).

The CLM has been refined slightly since the original publication of *How Remarkable Women Lead: The Breakthrough Model for Work and Life* (Barsh et al., 2011). There are three preconditions or assumptions underlying the model: desire to lead, sufficient talent and knowledge, and capacity for change.

Enacting the five dimensions of Centered Leadership can lead to impactful leadership, fulfillment, and a sense of resilience (Barsh & Lavoie, 2014). While the focus of this chapter is on women, enacting the five dimensions can be powerful for both men and women, and it works "across cultures, across industries, across pretty much everything" (Barsh & Lavoie, 2014, p. 7). Barsh, et al. (2008) reported correlations between Centered Leadership and self-reported performance, satisfaction, and success in their own survey data. Further, Barsh et al. (2008) appropriately give credit to the empirical data from other research scholars that inspired some of the key theoretical dimensions. Some of the empirical underpinnings of the theory are included in the descriptions of the five dimensions below.

Meaning

Meaning is "the anchor of Centered Leadership" (Barsh & Lavoie, 2014, p. 6). Meaningful engagement gives us energy and inspires us. Positive psychologists have defined a progression of happiness that leads from pleasure to engagement to meaning (Barsh et al., 2008). Identifying what gives us a sense of personal fulfillment can be useful in finding meaningful work; using the CLM as a development tool, the model encourages leaders to reflect on their peak experiences at work to establish the work environments that would give them the most enduring pleasure. Barsh et al. (2008) note that determining what makes one happy and what gives one meaning and purpose can lead to becoming an inspiring leader; further, a leader who is deriving meaning from work can connect with others and exude positive energy.

The Centered Leadership dimension of *meaning* is supported by and aligned with the empirical work of Sonja Lyubomirsky (2007), who found that about 50% of happiness is determined by a genetic set point, 10% is determined by circumstances, and 40% is determined by the intentional activities in which one can engage. The notion that about half of the happiness equation is not subject to genetics or our life circumstances can be an empowering and freeing proposition to many. The happiness literature is critical to understanding the dimension of *meaning*, as it suggests that a sense of purpose, satisfaction, and fulfillment can be cultivated. Therefore, creating a life and career with meaning that provides satisfaction is an achievable goal.

Framing

The Centered Leadership notion of *framing* refers to one's mindset. *Framing* encourages optimism to avoid a downward pessimistic spiral that can accompany the receipt of bad news and contribute to depression. Like the concept of meaning above, framing is also tied to the research literature on positive psychology. Describing optimism as an explanatory style, referring to how one explains the causes of bad events, Buchanan and Seligman (1995) explained that individuals who describe bad events with external, unstable, and specific causes are described as optimistic, whereas those who prefer internal, stable, and global causes are described as pessimistic. Peterson (2000) found that people high in optimism tend to have better moods, be more successful, and enjoy academic, athletic, military, occupational, and political success. He also reported that optimists tend to experience better physical health. Using the CLM as part of a leadership development program can encourage tapping into strengths, shifting negative mindsets, and reframing negative events.

In a review article, Nolen-Hoeksema, Wisco, and Lyubomirsky (2008) discussed rumination, a response style characterized by focusing on distress, its causes, and its consequences. Ruminators fixate on a problem rather than take action. Focusing on the antecedents and consequences of symptoms does not lead to active problem solving. Instead, ruminators remain fixated on the problem and their feelings about the problem (Nolen-Hoeksema et al., 2008). The ruminative coping style leads to depressive symptoms and impairs thinking, problem solving, and social relationships. It is also a style of coping more frequently experienced by women, potentially negatively affecting how women cope with negative events. Studies with adults suggest women are more likely to ruminate than men, and that this difference in rumination accounts, at least partially, for the gender differences in depressive symptoms (Nolen-Hoeksema, Larson, & Grayson, 1999). The concept of framing takes from diverse empirical findings and emphasizes the benefits of shifting one's mindset.

Connecting

Connecting, the third element in the CLM, refers to the relationships we create with others in our social and work circles. Those who are able to successfully connect with others, the model suggests, are able to build a meaningful community that can result in successful leadership. In Barsh et al.'s (2011) work, the authors note that women and men have different approaches to developing professional networks. Women are more likely to build deep relationships with a narrow band of colleagues, whereas men are often inclined to build shallow but large networks, which are typically many times the size of a typical woman's at the same occupational level (Barsh et al., 2011). Barsh et al. (2011) found that sponsors—senior-level leaders—are beneficial to women's advancement through creating opportunities for the protégé, and that reciprocity is important. The CLM encourages women and men to broaden their social networks, see mentoring relationships as reciprocal, and look for allies and sponsors who can open up opportunities.

Engaging

Engaging allows us to embrace opportunities, take ownership of our own careers, and take risks. Confronted with the reality that hard work sometimes does not actually pay off unless we draw attention to the work we are doing, the concept of *engaging* reminds us to showcase our efforts, seize leadership opportunities, face fears, and get noticed. The notion that bringing attention to one's professional presence and *engaging* can be useful was supported by interview data collected by Barsh et al. (2011). A prominent component of engaging involves stepping beyond one's comfort zone and taking risks. Risk taking is frequently associated with fear of failure (Barsh et al., 2011). Gilbert (2007) asks the fearful to consider the catastrophic outcome and then move forward with a plan to accommodate the worst outcome.

Taking ownership for one's career relates to the psychological concept of locus of control (Barsh et al., 2011). Internal locus of control refers to the belief that an individual can influence their destiny. Individuals who ascribe to internal locus of control, "can be more confident and self-motivated, less afraid to take risks" (Barsh et al., 2011, p. 210). Conversely, individuals with an external locus of control tend to rely on reinforcement and praise from the others in order to feel a sense of worth. The CLM urges women to take ownership of their career and develop the ability to proactively influence their professional development and advancement.

Energizing

Finally, *energizing* refers to the realization that work-life balance might be a myth (Barsh et al., 2008). In any given day or week it may be impossible to feel balanced. Managing relationships, families, and work seamlessly in the course of a day or week is not necessarily the goal. Instead, the authors argue that demanding work lives can be complemented by drawing energy from engaging and sustaining self-care practices and hobbies. These authors challenge the traditional notion of work–life balance:

> We found that work-life balance is a myth—so the only hope women have is to balance their energy flows. This means basing your priorities on the activities that energize you, both at work and at home, and actively managing your resources to avoid dipping into reserves. (Barsh et al., 2008, p. 40)

The concept of *energizing* connects to the positive psychology work mentioned earlier and refers to the literature on what makes people feel content and energetic. Barsh et al. (2011) draw from their own interview data and the science of sport and performance psychology to recommend *energizing* practices, such as practicing yoga, nurturing one's creative impulses, and especially getting proper sleep in order to feel connected and energized.

DESCRIPTION OF THE QUALITATIVE STUDY

Based on our literature review, we were convinced that the underpinnings of the CLM were sound. The CLM gave us a framework to conceptualize the leadership styles of our participants, allowed participants to discuss how they navigated their careers, and allowed participants to name personal issues that contributed to their campus leadership. The research question guiding this study was "How well does the CLM reflect African-American Senior Administrators leadership experiences?"

Using a qualitative theoretical approach, we wanted to know if the CLM model would resonate, in full or part, with our participants. We were aware that as researchers we served as a non-objective instrument (Staller, 2010). We were closely aligned with the participants in professional roles, personal relationships, ethnicity, gender, and, in some cases, religion and spirituality. Staller (2010) refers to our roles as participant-observers, or, in other words, as collaborators.

We developed interview questions based on Barsh et al.'s (2008) CLM dimensions. We believed that our transparency as researchers resulted in candid responses by the participants. Our participants shared openly, revealed personal and confidential information, and served as referrals for other African-American women administrators in higher education to participate in our study. Because of the information the participants provided, our research questions evolved through the interview process. It is common in qualitative inquiry for emerging information to impact the ongoing study, and, as Staller (2010) affirms, "the research question evolves during the process" (p. 1,160).

Participants

During 2013 and 2014, we interviewed 15 African-American women senior administrators in higher education. Some interviews were face to face and others were via telephone. Our participants worked in Florida, Tennessee, Indiana, Pennsylvania, California, and Texas. We used our professional networks of African-American female senior administrators who worked in higher education to recruit our sample, and some of these participants referred their colleagues to the study. Three participants worked in Historically Black College/Universities (HBCUs), and the remainder worked at Predominately White Institutions (PWIs). Participants ranged in age from 43 to 63. Seven participants worked at public institutions, and eight worked at private colleges or universities. One participant worked at a community college; the remaining worked at four-year institutions. Forty-six percent of participants were divorced or never married/partnered, and 54% were married. The participants came from a variety of sub-specialty areas in higher education. Examples included a former college president, a counseling center director, and a vice president for enrollment services.

Data Collection

Using a semi-structured interview protocol, we asked the women a variety of questions about their career trajectory and their thoughts on the five key dimensions of the CLM. First, we asked the participants to read an article explaining the core dimensions of the CLM (Barsh et al., 2008). We then asked for examples of whether and how meaning was found in their work; how they connected with others for the benefit of their careers; and how they engaged at work, coped with and framed setbacks, and energized themselves. We also asked the participants to describe their leadership style and share career struggles and successes.

Data Analysis

Thematic analysis (Staller, 2010) was utilized by reviewing transcripts of interviews and identifying CLM dimensions that were endorsed or rejected by participants. Additionally, we borrowed from Bower and Wolverton's (2009) qualitative analysis approach in that we categorized data by emerging themes and patterns. Based on a grounded theory framework (Corbin & Strauss, 2014), themes that emerged from the interview data were compared across participants as we looked for commonalities. To ensure confidentiality, participant names and characteristics that would reveal their identities were changed or disguised. Participants' responses were clustered on each dimension. This process enabled us to examine emerging and recurring themes.

OUR FINDINGS: RELEVANCE OF CLM
FOR AFRICAN-AMERICAN WOMEN

Our findings revealed some unanticipated themes. Our initial exploration was to examine to what extent, if any, our participants would endorse or reject the CLM. We discovered that the dimensions posited by Barsh et al. (2008) were, for the most part, endorsed by our participants. However, important socio-cultural factors appeared to interfere with their ability to implement skills and strategies recommended by the CLM.

Meaning

The participants overwhelmingly identified the dimension of meaning as important to them in their professional careers. Nine of the 15 felt their current jobs had meaning in the deep sense conveyed by the CLM. Winona, a former college president, said she desired to be "a wave to cause other waves or ripples; a force to help others to propel forward." Catherine, a vice president for enrollment at a private university, quoted Robert Frost to exemplify her connection between the personal and the professional: "My avocation and my vocation as my two eyes make one in sight." These comments suggest both participants had connected to some inner source of meaning or personal mission.

Gabrielle, a participant working in career services, described her inner source of meaning a bit differently when she noted that the meaning she finds in her work is rooted in her own experience of not knowing what to do with a liberal arts degree. This motivation kept her focused and gave her a sense of happiness. She said, "I want to give what I missed to others." Likewise, Whitney, a senior administrator at a large private institution, discussed her lack of mentorship when she was an undergraduate as a motivation and source of energy for her work. She said, "I see every student as me," and strived to mentor students in ways that she felt she was never mentored. By reflecting on their experiences as students, these women were inspired to continue their work and were driven by their personal mission to serve others.

Some participants found meaning closely connected to their African-American identity. Melanie, an administrator in the arts, spoke about the importance of advocating for students of color, particularly in her institution, which has virtually no diversity in its administration. Likewise, Peggy, a dean of faculty, wanted to "promote the next generation... [and wanted] to serve her community."

The diversity among the participants regarding meaning was interesting, and we discovered two distinct themes: (a) personal mission related to helping African-American students who had similar backgrounds (e.g., first generation), and (b) personal mission related to supporting future generations' success, including African-American students.

Not all women found meaning in their work, however. Renee did not feel that her current position was in alignment with her degree or passion for social justice. Helen, dean of students at a community college, stated, "I'm a racquetball enthusiast and I am excited about going to play and feel equally as excited while playing.... I'd like to feel that way about my job but I don't." Helen found the open enrollment of her community college challenging. She explained that the issues she must address are related to students not being prepared for college and are often disconnected from academic issues altogether. To make up for this lack of meaning, she and her family created a foundation to provide scholarships for students to attend college. She described a great deal of satisfaction from this endeavor.

Framing

Participant statements confirmed the importance of optimism as described in the CLM. Ten participants commented that they consciously practiced reframing challenging situations with optimism. For example, faculty administrator and assistant professor Tanya said the following:

> Setbacks pave the way for comebacks. Just because something doesn't happen in the timeframe I've allotted, it doesn't mean I won't consistently work at it. I don't believe in accepting "no" as a final answer. I might accept it as an intermediate response.... I have a lot of positive energy.

Similarly, Brenda, a counseling center director, said, "If I stay faithful, I will win, even if I don't like the outcome." Gabrielle counts herself as a positive individual; she shared, "All things are possible; I try to remember that." However, she acknowledged having some fears about getting to the next logical step in her career. She stated that she wanted to manage her fears without being paralyzed by them. "Growth happens if you push beyond your comfort zones. My fears have kept me from doing things. But I have to go back to 'you have a good head.' When push comes to shove, I will figure something out."

Some of the participants commented that they found it challenging to be optimistic when it came to their careers. Renee described herself as one who leaned towards pessimism and tried to be more positive. Perhaps not coincidentally, she also did not find any meaning in her current work. She reported low energy, professional isolation, and loneliness. Renee's unfortunate circumstance seemed to confirm the inter-relatedness of the five dimensions of the model and the physical, social, and emotional consequences of a job lacking in meaning. When meaning is lacking, the ability to positively frame work may also suffer.

Connecting

We found that discussing connecting with participants brought out the unique African-American experiences not captured in the current form of the CLM. Although some aspects of connecting did align with the model (i.e., being proactive, developing meaningful relationships, and the importance of trust), other aspects were unique to the African-American experience.

Participants commented that it was important to connect socially at work, and they found sponsors, colleagues, and senior staff to mentor them. Participants noted that it was important to find people who would be willing to extend their professional reputation for them. They found it was important to find mentors who would be critical colleagues and would be able to provide direct feedback when one was about to make a bad decision, or as Grace, an attorney at a large institution, put it, "step in the poop."

Catherine noted she arranged meetings where there would be positive associations with her, such as meetings involving food. She believed this helped her social relations at work. Other participants advised it was important to establish a range of networks to gain various perspectives and acknowledged that career-beneficial networks could come from friends, church, and other non-work-related social organizations. Peggy, dean of faculty at a private college, did not consciously think about her networks. She saw herself as a good "connector." Many of her connections came through graduate school, her academic discipline, and common interests, especially diversity. Participants also noted the importance of finding role models who, if possible, were also African American. They found that it made the unknown more achievable.

Participants revealed that making connections can be challenging, and the challenges expand beyond one's personality or social skills. Barbara, a director of financial aid at an elite institution, was very clear that it was important for her to know the power players in her institution. She joined committees and introduced herself directly to those she wished to meet. She met colleagues at conferences and had mentors. However, she had to overcome some important issues, which were rooted in her childhood. She shared,

I had to let go of some of my racism. I grew up in the South in the 1970s being told, "You'll never be anything." There was a lot of anger there.... Talking to people who are not African American does not come naturally to me.

This sentiment struck us as particularly interesting, given that the CLM is not explicit about how to overcome barriers to cross-cultural communication. The essential skill of connection may come with more difficulty for some. Similarly, Gabrielle noted,

There's a fine line that African-American women have to toe. There's a stereotype of the angry African-American woman. If you speak up about something, there's a question of how are you going to be perceived. That might be something that is overlooked. How do we balance the perception?

Renee, in a moment of candidness, also shared some comments about race by stating that her fair skin color likely gave her an advantage over other darker-skinned African-American women. This moment of sincerity and self-disclosure was powerful and has implications for how she connected with Caucasian individuals on the job and with other African-American women.

Engaging

The African-American experience also emerged as relevant for this dimension; we found both race and religion impacted engagement. Participants were supportive of the notion that hard work alone does not automatically lead to recognition. Many had experiences giving themselves fully to their jobs, only to be passed over for opportunities, not properly credited, or even significantly underpaid. Tanya noted that, although one may have many leadership qualities, if the institution does not support the advancement of African-American women, there would be no opportunity to demonstrate these qualities.

The participants also had to overcome many internal psychological obstacles to engage fully in the workplace; some of these obstacles were influenced by gender, race, and culture. Whitney noted that she felt "pressure not to mess it up because then they won't hire anyone who looks like us." Noting that there are not very many of "us" [African Americans] on campus, she felt very conscious of her performance. Wendy, a faculty administrator and professor offered, "Every time I start something new I have fears, nightmares. I still feel like an imposter." To cope, she stated:

My fears are not going to keep me down.... When [I am] faced with setbacks, there's a little voice that pushes me to continue. I've learned I don't have to be strong all the time; I allow myself time to process disappointments because I know I'll get back up.

We found that the dimension of engaging was also influenced, in part, by religiosity. Gabrielle noted that engaging and risk taking in the workplace were difficult for her because of her cultural upbringing. As an African-American child growing up in the South, she was raised to be seen and not heard. She found that this child-rearing style resulted in some impediments in her ability to engage fully at work. Further, she found that her Christian values might play a role. Believing that "the first shall be last," she noted that the Biblical assertion to be humble might be a drawback in the workplace for her.

Peggy described taking risks when faced with personal values over professional consequences. She shared a story of a student of color who had been accused of a serious crime, but Peggy had felt that racial factors were involved. She attended public meetings in spite of being admonished not to attend. She attended because she felt she "had to."

Melanie was encouraged by her supervisor to take risks, but she found risks and setbacks challenging because she was concerned about how she would be perceived if she failed.

Brenda faced a difficult situation with a supervisor who had unrealistic expectations for her, including working extensive hours, setting last-minute deadlines, and a disregard for her life outside of work. Brenda explained that the work environment began to take a negative toll on her family, and she needed to confront her supervisor. Her risk to confront her supervisor resulted in negative consequences. Her relationship with her supervisor became strained; she lost a formerly collaborative partnership, and her supervisor decided not to provide a letter of support for her promotion.

In the face of professional setbacks, participants coped by acknowledging that their personal lives were still intact. One respondent indicated that an apology is a good remedy for taking a stand or risk that was disappointing. The impediments to and consequences of risk taking in the context of engaging were compelling.

Energizing

The work–life challenge impacted our participants undoubtedly in ways similar to Barsh et al.'s (2011) participants. Our participants had a wide range of re-energizing strategies, and some women seemed more attuned to the need to manage stress and recharge than others. The women also had varying levels of success in managing their energy reserves. Barbara commented that she has difficulty managing her energy:

I literally was working myself into an early grave as an African-American female in a heavily male-dominated field. I had to be twice as good just to be on the same playing field.... I was burning out. When a doctor tells you, "either quit your job, find balance, or plan for an early grave," you have to make some decisions.

Creating better networks for herself so that people knew how hard she was working, which also touches on the engaging theme, was helpful to Barbara. She also tried to walk 30 minutes a day and took short trips for relaxation.

Participants used many coping mechanisms to deal with stress and rebuild their energy reserves, including yoga, meditation, counseling, exercise, and going out in nature. Participants used singing to recharge, rediscovered old passions like playing the piano, and others watched television and played video games. Additionally, many said they spend time with good friends and family to recharge, and occasionally they said "no" or left work early. One participant talked about the relaxing effect of ironing. Another, Grace, spoke of cooking and how relaxing it is to chop and stir. Last, another participant mentioned taking naps in her office and setting aside time to literally recharge physically during what she knew would be a draining week.

DISCUSSION

Our exploratory study found the CLM informative and helpful in understanding participants' experiences. Most participants experienced or desired to engage in work that is personally meaningful (*meaning*), strived to approach their work with an optimistic outlook (*framing*), understood that it was necessary to acknowledge their efforts to receive recognition (*engaging*), and intentionally developed strategies for positively managing their energy (*energizing*). Most of the women agreed that taking risks was vital to professional success. The experiences of our participants also suggest that the dimensions of *engaging* and *connecting* are limited as described in the CLM; our research suggested racial identity, culture, and religion often interfered with the participants' ability to fully embody these aspects of the model.

Limits to the Dimension of Engaging

The experience of risk taking, an aspect of engaging, was a key finding that identified a limitation of the model as it is currently described. Many of our respondents questioned how they would be perceived if they failed because of taking risks. Most concerns were associated with the intersecting identities of being an African-American woman. One participant felt that speaking up may be interpreted as fulfilling the stereotype of the "angry

Black woman." Several others expressed concerns that if they took risks and failed, they would be seen in a negative light by their supervisor, and/or they would be responsible for eliminating future opportunities for other African Americans. This finding is reflective of previous research. Consideration of cultural differences related to risk was addressed in the League of African-American Women (LAAW) survey findings (2011) that debunked the notion that African-American women are risk averse; results suggested that African-American women lack sponsorship for risk taking at work and for career advancement even though 78% felt that risk taking for personal and professional fulfillment is valuable. The LAAW respondents felt they lacked powerful and trusted advisers who could provide strategic and informed counsel on how to evaluate risk opportunities, and 61% reported seeking support from their friends rather than from family members and co-workers. Many attributed aversion to risk taking to a lack of encouragement from managers, genuine diversity, or inclusion efforts, and to the "concrete wall." Risk taking is considered a hallmark of leadership (McGowan, 2007), so exploring the barriers preventing risk taking for African-American women is crucial. Our study confirms this is an important area for future research.

Limits to the Dimension of Connecting

According to the CLM, the establishment of strong professional networks and mentoring relationships is critical to professional success. The CLM describes having mentors who expend their professional capital to advance their mentees (Barsh et al., 2011). While our study participants were intentional in their efforts to create strong networks, most mentioned a desire to have African-American mentors to increase trust. They also described needing a role model who knew how to navigate the higher education system. Similar to the LAAW study findings described above, our participants also described seeking advice from friends and family.

Connecting is also addressed in research focused on educational leadership among African-American female doctoral students preparing for faculty careers (Grant, 2012). Grant's (2012) study found that participants believed that a White male or female mentor could not relate to the experience of being an African-American woman in predominately White settings. Our study findings are aligned with these previous findings. Our participants expressed a preference for African-American mentors because they believed same-race mentors would have a better chance to understand their professional experiences and challenges. Further, they felt that same-race mentors could provide advice on processing personal experiences of discrimination, prejudice, and negative stereotypes. Although many people are willing to serve as mentors, it is important to recognize that race and culture may impact the authenticity needed for a meaningful mentoring relationship.

Stereotype Threat as Possible Cause of the Limits to CLM

It is interesting to note that Harvard (1986) described the typical African-American female administrator in higher education as possessing the following characteristics: committed, independent, dominant, active, adventurous, sensitive, secure, and self-confident. The contrast between the characteristics of these successful women and, to some extent, their challenges in certain areas, such as risk taking or connecting/communicating assertively, seems to align with the definition of Steele and Aronson's (1995) theory of stereotype threat, which "means that in situations where the stereotype is applicable, one is at risk of confirming it as a self-characterization, both to one's self and to others who know the stereotype" (Steele & Aronson, 1995, p. 808). The women mentioned several aspects of performance that they steered away from, not because they were not capable, or aware of its potential positive impact, but because for African-American women the costs of potentially confirming a negative stereotype associated with their race outweighed the benefits.

Steele (2011) proposed that to offset the sociocultural impediment of stereotype threat, supervisors (and, we would add, mentors) must attend to building "identity safety." Identity safety creates an environment or situation that reinforces one's skills as a capable professional, thereby diminishing the impact of stereotype threat. In other words, to mitigate the impact of this threat, mentors and supervisors should consider explicitly acknowledging the skills, talents, and professional identity of the individual.

A revised model of CLM based on the experience of African-American women leaders might take into account these cultural implications, which, of course, extend beyond race. Identities such as gender and sexual orientation have also been shown to be impacted by stereotype threat (Steele, 2011; Steele & Aronson, 1995). Incorporation of cultural competency for mentors and organizational audits to encourage professional risk taking, reduce stereotype threat, and create an environment that strengthens identity safety could be useful for African-American women who aspire to administrative leadership (Davies, Spencer, & Steele, 2005).

RECOMMENDATIONS AND FUTURE RESEARCH

We recommend cultural integration into the CLM model with the introduction of two added assumptions. The first is recognition of potential stereotype threat, and the second is acknowledgement of the value of creating identity safe contingencies. Ongoing exploration into stereotype threat and ways to ameliorate impact on performance is critical. We believe that what is good for African-American women administrators will likely enhance the higher education environment for all.

Future research for this unique population could explore relationship status to determine whether there are differences for African-American women as compared to other women professionals. It was interesting to observe that slightly over half of our participants indicated they were not married or partnered, and some had never been married or partnered. The authors question whether career choices may divert energy and impact relational choices.

The CLM provides substantive information for all women administrators, and yet attention is needed to better incorporate cultural and racial implications. We were deeply gratified by the courage these women exhibited by sharing their narratives. We believe their perspectives can help us refine the CLM, which we believe to be an excellent tool for supporting the growth and development of African-American women leaders.

AUTHOR NOTE

We want to acknowledge that one of our participants, Renee, unexpectedly died in May 2015.

REFERENCES

Barsh, J., Cranston, S., & Craske, R. A. (2008). Centered leadership: How talented women thrive. *McKinsey Quarterly, 4*, 35–48.

Barsh, J., Cranston, S., & Lewis, G. (2011). *How remarkable women lead: The breakthrough model for work and life.* New York, NY: Crown Business.

Barsh, J., & Lavoie, J. (2014). *Centered leadership: Leading with purpose, clarity, and impact.* New York, NY: Crown Business.

Bower, B. L., & Wolverton, M. (2009). *Answering the call: African American women in higher education leadership.* Sterling, VA: Stylus.

Buchanan, G. M., & Seligman, M. E. P. (Eds.). (1995). *Explanatory style.* Hillsdale, NJ: Lawrence Erlbaum Associates.

Corbin, J. M., & Strauss, A. (2014). *Basics of qualitative research: Techniques and procedures for developing grounded theory* (4th ed.). Thousand Oaks, CA: Sage.

Davies, P. G., Spencer, S. J., & Steele, C. (2005). Clearing the air: Identity safety moderates the effects of stereotype threat on women's leadership aspirations. *Journal of Personality and Social Psychology, 88*(2), 276–287.

Edwards, J., & Camblin, L. (1998). Assorted adaptations by African American administrators. *Women in Higher Education, 7*(11), 33–34.

Gilbert, D. (2007). *Stumbling on happiness.* New York, NY: Random House.

Grant, C. M. (2012). Advancing our legacy: An African American feminist perspective on the significance of mentoring for African-American women in educational leadership. *International Journal of Qualitative Studies in Education, 25*(1), 101–117.

Harvard, P. A. (1986, April). *Successful behaviors of African American women administrators in higher education: Implications for leadership.* Paper presented at the Annual Meeting of the American Educational Research Association, San Francisco, CA.

League of African American Women. (2011). *Risk and reward: Black women leading out on a limb.* Chicago, IL.: League of African American Women.

Lloyd-Jones, B. (2009). Implications of race and gender in higher education administration: An African American woman's perspective. *Advances in Developing Human Resources, 11*(5), 606–618.

Lyubomirsky, S. (2007). *The how of happiness: A new approach to getting the life you want.* New York, NY: Penguin Books.

McGowan, J. (2007). Swimming with the sharks: Perspectives on professional risk taking. *Journal of Medical Library Association, 95*(1), 104–113.

Miles, S. (2012). *Left behind: the status of Black women in higher education administration.* (Doctoral dissertation). Florida State University, Tallahassee, FL..

Moses, Y. (1989). *African American women in academe: Issues and strategies.* Washington, DC: Association of American Colleges.

Nealy, M. J. (2008, February). ACE: Significant efforts needed to improve diversity in college presidency ranks. *Diverse: Issues in Higher Education.* Retrieved from http://diverseeducation.com/article/10621

Nolen-Hoeksema, S., Wisco, B. E., & Lyubomirsky, S. (2008). Rethinking rumination. *Perspectives on Psychological Science, 3*(5), 400–424.

Nolen-Hoeksema, S., Larson, J., & Grayson, C. (1999). Explaining the gender difference in depressive symptoms. *Journal of Personality and Social Psychology, 77*(5), 1061–1072.

Peterson, C. (2000). The future of optimism. *American Psychologist, 55*(1), 44–55.

Sandler, B., & Hall, R. (1991). The campus climate revisited: Chilly for women, faculty, administrators, and graduate students. Project on the Status and Education of Women. Washington, DC: Association of American Colleges and Universities.

Singh, K., Robinson, A., & Williams-Green, V. (1995). Differences in perceptions of African American women and men faculty and administrators. *Journal of Negro Education, 64*(4), 401–408.

Staller, K. M. (2010). Qualitative research. In N. J. Salkind (Ed.), *Encyclopedia of research design.* Thousand Oaks, CA: Sage.

Steele, C. M. (2011). *Whistling Vivaldi: How stereotypes affect us and what we can do.* McKeesport, PA: Norton & Co.

Steele, C. M., & Aronson, J. (1995). Stereotyped threat and the intellectual test-performance of African-Americans. *Journal of Personality and Social Psychology, 69*(5), 797–811.

ABOUT THE EDITORS

Julia Storberg-Walker is Associate Professor and Co-Director of the Executive Leadership Program at George Washington University and an Affiliate Faculty at George Washington University's Global Women's Institute. Julia serves as Editor-in-Chief of the SSCI-rated journal *Human Resource Development Review*, a theory and conceptual journal. She is also an Associate at the Taos Institute, "a community of scholars and practitioners concerned with the social processes essential for the construction of reason, knowledge, and human value." In 2015, Julia was recognized for her contributions to women and leadership theory when she received the International Leadership Association's Women and Leadership Affinity Group's Outstanding Scholar Award. She has published and presented globally on theoretical and conceptual development for applied disciplines, and she incorporates a variety of critically informed research strategies in her theorizing projects. She is currently focused on feminist theorizing as a catalyst for leading social change. Holistically, the purpose of her work is to de-center male-normed processes for generating new knowledge and to legitimate other forms of knowing in and about the world.

Paige Haber-Curran is Assistant Professor and Program Coordinator for the Student Affairs in Higher Education master's program at Texas State University. Paige earned her PhD in Leadership Studies from the University of San Diego and her MA in College Student Personnel from the University of Maryland. Paige has more than 12 years of experience working with student leadership programs—both co-curricular and curricular. Paige's research

Theorizing Women and Leadership, pages 313–314

interests include college student leadership development, women's leadership, and college student learning. Paige is author of the book *Emotionally Intelligent Leadership: A Guide for Students* (Jossey-Bass, 2015) and the accompanying facilitation guide and student workbook. In 2013 Paige was recognized as an Emerging Scholar by the American College Personnel Association, and in 2014 she received the Presidential Award for Excellence in Teaching at Texas State University. Paige serves on the Executive Leadership Team of the International Leadership Association's Women and Leadership Affinity Group and as a Co-Lead Facilitator for the LeaderShape Institute. She consults and speaks around the world on topics of leadership.

ABOUT THE CONTRIBUTORS

Elizabeth J. Allan is Professor of Higher Education at the University of Maine. She is the author of *Women's Status in Higher Education: Equity Matters* (Jossey-Bass 2011), and *Policy, Gender, and Education: Constructing Women's Status* (Routledge, 2008). Elizabeth has authored articles and book chapters related to gender, diversity, and campus climates in higher education. Her work has been published by the *Harvard Educational Review*, *The Journal of Higher Education*, *The Review of Higher Education*, and *Innovative Higher Education*.

Jennifer M. Almquist is the Project Manager for OREGON STATE ADVANCE at Oregon State University. Previously, Jennifer served as the Associate Director of the Office of Equity and Inclusion at Oregon State University. Jennifer is also program faculty in the School of Language, Culture, and Society, where she teaches courses in Women, Gender, and Sexuality Studies. Jennifer earned her PhD in Applied Anthropology from Oregon State University. Her scholarship and professional experience are grounded in the application of anthropological and feminist theories and methods to address persistent questions about experiences of gender, the nature of work, and the structure of organizations.

Denise Bauer is Dean of the School of Liberal Arts and Food Studies at The Culinary Institute of America, where she leads a department of 16 full-time and 15 adjunct faculty in a range of disciplines including history, foreign languages, writing, social sciences, math, and science. She is also responsible for a bachelor's major in Applied Food Studies and a Global

Theorizing Women and Leadership, pages 315–326
Copyright © 2017 by Information Age Publishing

Cuisines and Cultures study abroad program. Denise earned her PhD from New York University in Arts and Humanities Education with a certificate in Women's Studies.

Maria Beebe is an applied sociolinguist whose research interests include critical discourse analysis, women's leadership, and information communication technologies (ICT) for development. She has a Master of Arts in Anthropology and PhD in Education from Stanford University. Her 25 years of global development work led her to launch Global Networks, a not-for-profit that works at the intersection of technology, content, and pedagogy. Maria recently co-edited *DISRUPT. Filipina Women: Loud. Proud. Leading without a Doubt*, based on the leadership journeys of 35 Filipinas who shared their stories.

Ann M. Berghout Austin received her PhD in Child Developmental Psychology from Iowa State University. She is Professor of Child Development and the founding director of the Center for Women and Gender (CWG) at Utah State University. In 2013 CWG was recognized as the "Emerging Center" by the National Council for Research on Women (NCRW). Ann received the "Trailblazer 2013 Making a Difference for Women and Girls" award from NCRW. She has served as major professor and research advisor for more than 50 masters and doctoral degrees and has received more than $10 million in external grants.

Belinda Blevins-Knabe is Professor of Psychology at the University of Arkansas at Little Rock. Belinda has an active interest in the role of women in leadership positions and has held several leadership positions on her campus. She has a special interest in the leadership of women in academia and played a key role in establishing the university's Gender Studies program. Her research interests include the developmental origins of leadership skills in women, the contributions that developmental theories can make, and the influence of the early home environment on young children's mathematical skills. Belinda has a PhD in Developmental Psychology.

Carol Burbank is an independent scholar, coach, and educator. She currently teaches at Pacifica Graduate Institute and serves as lead advisor in the University of New England's Educational Leadership PhD program. Her research explores different approaches to the formation of negotiated authentic identities in the intersection of leadership and social change. Recent publications include a leadership workbook, *Answer the Call to Adventure*, and articles in *Integral Leadership Review*, *Transformational Thinking for the 21st Century*, *Women in Global Leadership*, and *Business Leadership Review*.

Virginia Byrne is currently pursuing her PhD in Teaching and Learning, Policy and Leadership from the University of Maryland, College Park. Previously she served as the Student Life Coordinator for Leadership Development at the University of Maryland, Baltimore County (UMBC). She earned her master's degree in Higher Education from Florida State University and a bachelor's degree in Business Administration and Marketing from the University of Illinois, Urbana–Champaign. Her research focuses on adult learning and leadership development, specifically in an online learning environment.

Constance Campbell is the W. E. Carter Distinguished Professor of Business Leadership in the College of Business at Georgia Southern University, where she teaches MBA courses in Leadership, Organizational Behavior, and International Management and provides leadership development training for rising organizational leaders. Her current research focuses on managing high-potential, but morale-destroying, employees; causes of high-potential leader derailment; and leadership identities construction, particularly among women leaders in STEM professions. She holds a PhD in Organizational Behavior from Florida State University.

Emily Chan is an Organizational Behavior (Psychology) doctoral student at Claremont Graduate University. She is currently a Research Intern at the Leader Evaluation Assessment and Development Labs, an evidence-based (leadership assessment and development) consultancy that builds leadership capacity in businesses. Emily's research focuses on developing women leaders, mitigating gender biases in the workplace, gender stereotypes, and issues regarding work-life balance. She has also examined factors that influence women's interest in STEM fields. Emily graduated with honors and received her BA in Psychology from UCLA and earned her MA in Organizational Behavior (Psychology) from Claremont Graduate University.

Heewon Chang is Professor of Organizational Leadership and Education in the PhD in Organizational Leadership program at Eastern University. Trained as an educational anthropologist at the University of Oregon, her dissertation was published as a book, *Adolescent Life and Ethos* (1992). Since then, Heewon has published articles and three books focusing on autoethnography, including a methodology book, *Autoethnography as Method*. Her research interests also include leaders of color, leadership-followership in health research, multicultural and diversity education, educational equity and justice, and online graduate leadership education. Heewon founded two open-access scholarly journals and currently functions as the Editor-in-Chief of the internationally ranked *International Journal of Multicultural Education*.

Amber S. Cotton is a doctoral student in the Industrial-Organizational Psychology program at DePaul University. Her research interests include negotiation behaviors and outcomes, particularly as related to backlash, and the specific challenges that women face at the bargaining table. She is currently an Organizational Development and Assessment Intern in the food business industry. She was a Minority Access to Research Careers (MARC) scholar while studying her bachelor's degree at Jackson State University, where she focused on examining the correlates of stress and its prevalence among African American college students.

Lynne E. Devnew teaches leadership as an associate faculty member in the practitioner-doctorate programs of the University of Phoenix and is a senior research fellow responsible for the Women and Leadership Research Group in their Center for Leadership Studies and Educational Research. She is a former senior level manager at IBM, where she was among the first women to manage professionals. She serves as a church development coach. Lynne has degrees from Simmons College and Columbia University's Executive Masters Degree Program in Change Leadership and earned her DBA in Strategy from Boston University. She has redefined her leadership identity multiple times as she assumed greater responsibilities and changed industries and professions.

Crystal R. Diaz-Espinoza earned her PhD in Higher Education Administration from the University of Tennessee. Her dissertation examined the lived experiences of undergraduate women engineering majors through the lens of gender microaggressions. She earned an MS degree in Higher Education & Student Affairs from Baylor University in Waco, Texas. Crystal is currently the Director of Enrollment and Alumni Services for the Garland School of Social Work at Baylor University. She is also continuing research efforts to explore the experiences of women in engineering.

Chrys Egan is Associate Professor at Salisbury University in Communication Arts and in Gender and Sexuality, examining the intersections of relationships, culture, and media. Her community-based research promotes civic engagement, gender/sexuality support, family and children's programs, and wellness campaigns. She has published journal articles, book chapters, textbook ancillaries, reviews, and magazine articles, plus serves as co-chair for two conferences. She holds an MA in Speech Communication and Rhetoric from the University of North Carolina at Greensboro and a PhD in Communication and Media Studies from Florida State University.

Chanda D. Elbert is Associate Professor in the Department of Agricultural Leadership, Education, and Communications at Texas A&M University. She has developed and taught courses in Multicultural Leadership, Women's Leadership, and Leadership Theory. Her research interests include multicultural/diversity education, identity development, and leadership development. She earned a BS degree in Agribusiness Management from Southern University, an MS degree from University of Nebraska in Agricultural Leadership, and a PhD in Agricultural and Extension Education from The Pennsylvania State University.

Carole Elliott is Professor of Human Resource Development at University of Roehampton Business School in the U.K. Her research interests include media representations of gender and leadership, second generation gender bias, and the development of critical hermeneutic and visual methods in management and organization research. Carole has authored several book chapters and has published articles in journals such as *Advances in Developing Human Resources, Journal of Management Education, Leadership,* and *Management Learning.* Her recent books include *Critical Thinking in Human Resource Development* (Routledge) and *Women's Leadership* (Palgrave). She is Editor-in-Chief for the Routledge journal *Human Resource Development International.*

Kelly Fisher is Assistant Professor in Management at Westchester University. She received her PhD in Management with a focus on leadership at Monash University. She has published in top journals such as *Military Psychology* and *Journal of Organizational Behavior,* and presented at conferences sponsored by the Academy of Management, International Leadership Association, and Inter-University on Armed Forces and Society, among others. Her research interests are in leadership, culture, and gender differences as influenced by context. Her prior career to academia was in the United States Navy.

Rita A. Gardiner is an Assistant Professor in the Faculty of Education at The University of Western Ontario in London, Ontario, where she teaches leadership and ethics. Rita is author of *Gender, Authenticity and Leadership: Thinking with Arendt* (Palgrave MacMillan, 2015). Other publications include journal articles and book chapters on women's leadership, Hannah Arendt, and Simone de Beauvoir. In 2014, Rita received the Paul Begley Award for her outstanding contribution to postgraduate research in the study of values and educational leadership by the CLSEE, an international consortium of leadership educators. She received her PhD in Women's Studies from The University of Western Ontario.

Lisa M. Gick brings 25 years of retail industry experience to her current role as Founder and CEO of [c u r i o u s]®, a research-grounded, creative agency focused on shifting leader mindsets to center on humanness for growth in the contemporary workplace. Lisa's corporate experience includes a successful 25-year career with the Macy's Inc. enterprise, most recently as Vice President of Employee Engagement. She is current a PhD student in Leadership and Change at Antioch University, with her research focusing on reframing leader engagement to support organizational agility in growth-focused, complex companies.

Suzanne P. Gordon is a Professor and Director of the School of Physical Therapy at Husson University in Bangor, Maine. Her research interests focus on higher education leadership, and on multicultural and social justice education of healthcare professionals. Suzanne has written about these topics in several book chapters and articles published in *The Review of Higher Education* and the *Journal of Physical Therapy Education.*

Kathleen S. Grove has been consulting, advising, and counseling in a professional capacity throughout a career that has encompassed the fields of law, business, mental health counseling, and higher education. In her current position as the Director of the Office for Women at Indiana University–Purdue University, Indianapolis, she focuses on women's leadership development and mentoring and helping the university recognize, utilize, and advance women's talent. She holds a BS in Speech from Northwestern University, an MA in Marriage and Family Therapy from Christian Theological Seminary, and a JD from the Indiana University McKinney School of Law.

Maylon Hanold teaches in the Sport Administration and Leadership master's program at Seattle University. Her courses include sport leadership, human resources, and organizational behavior. Her research focuses on the physicality of leadership as related to embodied biases and leadership development. Concurrently, she studies endurance lifestyle sports, such as ultrarunning, and their connection to identity development. Maylon's research also encompasses second generation gender bias and women in sport leadership. Maylon received her EdD in Leadership from Seattle University and an EdM in Education from Harvard University.

Denise Hayes, formerly President of the Association for University and College Counseling Center Directors (AUCCCD), holds a PhD in Counseling Psychology from Indiana University and has served as an administrator in Student Affairs for 15 years. Denise is the Vice President of Student Affairs for the Claremont University Consortium, which services The Claremont Colleges. Her work has been published in a variety of outlets including *Journal of College Student Psychotherapy, Journal of Counseling and Development, The Wall Street Journal,* and *Ebony* magazine. Her research interests include self-esteem, management, leadership, cultural competency, and organizational change.

Kathy-Ann C. Hernandez is Professor of Educational Psychology and Research Methods and Director of Research for the Loeb School of Education at Eastern University. She is also CEO of Nexe Consulting and regularly consults with school districts, churches, schools, government offices, and colleges and universities nationally and internationally. She is an author/presenter on several autoethnographic-related scholarship projects. Her research is focused on the Black Diaspora and the salience of race/ethnicity, gender, and social context in identity formation, leadership development, and social and academic outcomes. She is co-author *of Collaborative Autoethnography* (2013). She earned a PhD in Educational Psychology from Temple University.

Marcelle C. Holmes is Associate Vice Chancellor of Wellness, Health, & Counseling at the University of California, Irvine. She is a licensed Clinical Psychologist in California. She has authored articles on African American mental health and college mental health and has presented on a variety of topics, including African American women's mental health, campus threat assessment and threat mitigation, and yoga for depression. Marcelle received her PhD in Clinical Psychology from the University of Michigan and her BA in Psychology and French from Vassar College, where she graduated Phi Beta Kappa.

Herminia Ibarra is the Cora Chaired Professor of Leadership and Learning, and Professor of Organizational Behavior at INSEAD. Prior to INSEAD, she taught in the Harvard Business School faculty for 13 years. She is an expert on professional and leadership development, having been ranked #8 among the most influential business experts in the world. Her most recent book, *Act Like a Leader, Think Like a Leader* (Harvard Business School Press, 2015), explains how to step up to a bigger leadership role. She received her MA and PhD from Yale University.

Susan V. Iverson is Professor of Higher Education Leadership at Manhattanville College. Susan's research interests focus on equity and diversity, the status of women in higher education, and feminist pedagogy. She co-edited *Reconstructing Policy Analysis in Higher Education: Feminist Poststructural Perspectives* (Routledge 2010) and *Feminist Community Engagement: Achieving Praxis* (Palgrave, 2014). Susan earned her doctorate in Higher Educational Leadership with a concentration in Women's Studies from the University of Maine.

Mary M. Keegin is a doctoral student in the Industrial-Organizational Psychology program at DePaul University. She researches gender issues in conjunction with other social and organizational roles, attitudes, and attributions on the enactment and perception of conflict and aggression in the workplace. Her dissertation examines a goal-setting intervention aimed at equalizing negotiation outcomes between men and women. Her master's degree focused on the relationship between the experience of power and gender-related beliefs on the enactment of relational aggression within organizations.

Wendy Fox Kirk is Assistant Professor and Management scholar in the Goddard School of Business & Economics at Weber State University. She teaches a range of courses focused on leadership, training, development, and staffing. After working as a management consultant for a number of years, she moved back into academia to engage in research addressing issues of disadvantage in the workplace, with a particular focus on women's careers and the gendered organization. Her current research examines women's leadership journeys in higher education. She received her PhD in Business from the University of Birmingham, U.K.

Judith Babcock LaValley is a doctoral candidate at Kansas State University and holds graduate degrees in Organizational Behavior, Security Studies, and Industrial/Organizational Psychology. Her research examines constructs at the intersection of culture and leadership, including leader development, leader identity, and gender and leadership. Judith has conducted research at the RAND Corporation, the U.S. Army Research Institute for the Behavioral and Social Sciences (ARI), and the United States Air Force Academy. A former U.S. Air Force pilot and master parachutist, Judith has conducted leader development training in the military and nonprofit sectors.

Marlene Janzen Le Ber is Assistant Professor, Dimensions of Leadership, at Canada's only women's university, Brescia University College, where she teaches Women in Leadership. Her current research is in leader character and leader identity development in women. Prior to her doctoral studies, Marlene was a health care executive within academic health sciences centers; she was known as a strategic leader who spearheaded numerous health system innovations. Marlene has a PhD (Strategy) from Ivey Business School and an MScN (Admin) and BScN from Western University.

Karen A. Longman serves as Program Director and Professor of Higher Education at Azusa Pacific University. Her primary teaching responsibilities include Higher Education Administration, Critical Issues in Higher Education, and Ethical Issues in Higher Education. She also serves as a Senior

Fellow of the Council for Christian Colleges & Universities (CCCU), where she worked for 19 years as Vice President for Professional Development and Research. Karen co-edits the journal *Christian Higher Education: An International Journal of Research, Theory, and Practice* and the book series *Women and Leadership*. She holds a PhD in Higher Education from The University of Michigan.

Jess Myers is Director of the Women's Center at the University of Maryland, Baltimore County (UMBC); she has worked with college student leaders for nine years. She received her master's degree in Student Affairs and Higher Education with a certificate in Women's Studies from Colorado State University in 2010. Since working in the Women's Center at UMBC, Jess has worked closely with women adult learners at UMBC and has taken great strides in developing programmatic support and resources for this student population.

Brionne G. Neilson is a doctoral student at Utah State University studying human development and family studies. Her research focuses on investigating leadership development in providers of early childhood care and education in relation to classroom quality and child outcomes. She is also interested in exploring perceptions regarding a lack of support for women's leadership in her state. She received her MEd in Elementary Education and a BS in Early Childhood and Elementary Education from Utah State University.

Faith Wambura Ngunjiri is Director of the Lorentzsen Center for Faith and Work and Associate Professor of Ethics and Leadership at Concordia College in Minnesota. Her research interests include women and leadership, particularly at the intersections of identities and locations; spirituality in the workplace; and culturally appropriate qualitative methods. Faith authored *Women's Spiritual Leadership in Africa* (SUNY, 2010) and co-authored *Collaborative Autoethnography* with Heewon Chang and Kathy-Ann Hernandez (Left Coast Press, 2013). Faith serves as co-editor for this *Woman and Leadership* book series (ILA/IAP) and *Palgrave Studies in African Leadership* (Palgrave McMillan).

Jennifer L. Petriglieri is Assistant Professor of Organizational Behavior at INSEAD. Her research explores identity dynamics in organizations in crisis and contemporary careers, the social function of business schools, and the dynamics of identity development in management education. Her research has appeared in the *Administrative Science Quarterly, Academy of Management Review, Academy of Management Learning & Education*, and the *Journal of Organizational Change Management, in addition to* the online editions of *Business*

Week and the Harvard Business Review. She received her PhD in Organizational Behavior from INSEAD.

Heather I. Ricks-Scott is Assistant Professor of Leadership Studies at Kennesaw State University. She holds a bachelor's degree in Theatre, a master's of education in College Student Affairs Administration, and a PhD in Educational Leadership with a Higher Education specialization. Heather has published and presented in the areas of women and leadership and adult learners with a particular focuses on ascension patterns and experiences of women leaders. Heather is a member of The Association of Junior Leagues International Incorporated (Douglas County), Delta Sigma Theta Sorority Incorporated (Douglas Carroll Paulding Alumnae Chapter), and the International Leadership Association.

Michelle Shockness is Assistant Professor in the Department of Sociology/ Social Work at Redeemer University College. She is a PhD candidate in Organizational Leadership at Eastern University, an alumna of the University of Toronto's School of Social Work, and a registered social worker. Her 25 years of experience as a practitioner in the non-profit, private, and grassroots sectors include direct practice, consultation, and supervisory work in economically disenfranchised communities, primarily in Canada. Michelle's interests and research focus on the experiences of marginalized groups in negotiating power, leadership, and identity, with particular focus on women.

S. Lynn Shollen is Associate Professor in the Department of Leadership and American Studies at Christopher Newport University, where she teaches courses in Leadership Studies. Her current research focuses on the effects on identity of the transition from faculty to academic administrator; identity and leadership, including gender and perceptions of leadership; and teaching and learning about women and leadership. Her early research focused on faculty mentoring—particularly for women and racial minority faculty, including those interested in pursuing administrative leadership roles. She holds a PhD in Higher Education Policy and Administration from the University of Minnesota.

Amy E. Smith is Associate Professor in the McCormack Graduate School of Policy and Global Studies at the University of Massachusetts (Boston). Her research draws upon concepts from public administration and organizational behavior and theory to examine gender diversity in leadership in public organizations, informal structures, and teaching and mentoring in graduate education. Amy is active in the Public & Nonprofit Division of the Academy of Management and serves on the editorial board for the journal

Public Performance & Management Review. Amy holds a PhD and MPA in Public Administration and Policy from the State University of New York–Albany.

Valerie Stead is Senior Lecturer in the Department of Leadership and Management at Lancaster University Management School. Valerie's research interests include women's leadership, gender and leadership learning, gender and media representations, and critical leadership methodology. Her current research projects include an ESRC-funded seminar series with Roehampton and Bradford Universities, "Challenging Gendered Media Mis(s)representations of Women Professionals and Leaders." Valerie's publications include *Women's Leadership* (Palgrave), and several book chapters and articles in journals including *Management Learning, Leadership, Human Resource Development International,* and the *International Small Business Journal.* Valerie is an Associate Editor for the *International Journal of Management Reviews.*

Alice F. Stuhlmacher is Department Chair and Professor of Psychology at DePaul University. Her research interests include negotiation and conflict in organizations, particularly related to gender, occupational health, performance appraisal, and computer-mediated communication. She has been active in applying meta-analyses to summarize existing research and has also published research relating to personality, labor mediators, motivation, and attachment styles in the workplace. She holds a PhD and MS in Industrial-Organizational Psychology from Purdue University.

Lorri L. Sulpizio is the director of the Leadership Institute and an adjunct professor at the University of San Diego (USD). She is the founder of the Center for Women's Leadership at USD, and co-founder and principal consultant for Lotus Leadership Institute, a leadership and business consulting company. Her research and prior publications focus on women, authority, and leadership, specifically women's use of voice when exercising leadership. Lorri is a speaker and author on leadership topics and has a PhD in Leadership Studies from the University of San Diego.

Randal Joy Thompson is an international development professional with more than three decades of experience in the field. As a U.S. Foreign Service Officer for 28 years, Randal has advised senior government officials on key policy changes, assisted local non-governmental organizations in establishing themselves, organized interest group coalitions, and worked in small rural villages and large urban centers in Southeast Asia, Central and South America, Eastern Europe, and Africa. Randal now consults and publishes in the areas of monitoring and evaluation, organization capacity development, appreciative inquiry, the Commons, and gender equality.

Marianne Tremaine is Senior Lecturer and Associate Head of School in Massey University's Department of Communication, Journalism and Marketing (Palmerston North, New Zealand). She teaches Gender and Communication in Organizations and researches gender and leadership in organizations and political settings. She was a founding member (and co-director) of the New Zealand Centre for Women and Leadership, which had the mission of Advancing Women as Leaders. Her most recent research is on academic women and the factors that are likely to help or hinder their promotions to senior positions in the university hierarchy.

Marcia Venegas-García is a retired teacher educator and independent scholar with a PhD in Leadership Studies from the University of San Diego. Her dissertation received the 2011 American Education Research Association (AERA) Leadership for Social Justice Award. Segments of her research have been published in the *Journal of School Leadership* (2013) and presented at the *Hispanic Association of Colleges and Universities (HACU) Preconference Leadership Institute*. Marcia's academic experiences include teaching women's leadership at California State University, San Marcos and serving as Academic Coordinator and Director, San Diego Area Writing Project, University of California, San Diego.

Katherine L. Yeager received her PhD from Texas A&M University in Human Resource Development; she has taught in the Human Resource Development programs at Texas A&M and the University of Houston. Her research interests include leader identity development, women and leadership, team development, and team performance. Her dissertation work on leader identity development was recognized as second runner-up for dissertation of the year at the 2014 AHRD Conference in the Americas. The first article based on her dissertation is pending publication in the August 2016 issue of *Advances in Developing Human Resources*.

92956524R00188

Made in the USA
San Bernardino, CA
06 November 2018